XML in Theory and Practice

Chris Bates

Sheffield Hallam University

Email (for orders and customer service enquiries): cs-books@wiley.co.uk
Visit our Home Page on www.wileyeurope.com or www.wiley.com

Other Wiley Editorial Offices

John Wiley & Sons Inc., 111 River Street, Hoboken, NJ 07030, USA

Jossey-Bass, 989 Market Street, San Francisco, CA 94103-1741, USA

Wiley-VCH Verlag GmbH, Boschstr. 12, D-69469 Weinheim, Germany

John Wiley & Sons Australia Ltd, 33 Park Road, Milton, Queensland 4064, Australia

John Wiley & Sons (Asia) Pte Ltd, 2 Clementi Loop #02-01, Jin Xing Distripark, Singapore 129809

John Wiley & Sons Canada Ltd, 22 Worcester Road, Etobicoke, Ontario, Canada M9W 1L1

Wiley also publishes its books in a variety of electronic formats. Some content that appears in print may not be available in electronic books.

British Library Cataloguing in Publication Data

A catalogue record for this book is available from the British Library

ISBN 0-470-84344-6

Typeset from author-supplied PDF files.
Printed and bound in Great Britain by Biddles Ltd, Guildford and King's Lynn.
This book is printed on acid-free paper responsibly manufactured from sustainable forestry in which at least two trees are planted for each one used for paper production.

Contents

Preface

If you are an outsider to the computer industry, it might seem like a sober suited, straight-laced sort of place. If you work in the industry or deal with it on a regular basis then you will know that IT, perhaps more than any other industry, is driven by fashion. Computer technology is in a state of perpetual revolution, with old technologies, often simply last year's model, being swept away and replaced with the latest thing. The new technology isn't always better but it does have the benefit of being newer. You might think that since the development and implementation of software and systems is a logical and ordered activity, those who use IT would act based on cold facts and hard evidence but too often they don't.

There are massive pressures on corporate IT departments from the rest of the organization. IT is expected to bring *competitive advantage*, to create instant results and to maximize profitability. Yet when IT goes wrong, it often does so spectacularly. If a store gets broken into, physical goods are stolen; if an e-commerce Web site is broken into then financial details of all the company's customers may be stolen. Business managers often fail to understand the pressures that they put on IT departments; all too often they assume that implementing a new system is just like buying a new car. Simply choose the one you want, put your things in it and off you go. Because of this lack of understanding, there is a tendency to look at what competitors are doing and try to do the same. Basing a business around the Web has been just such a fashion. Many businesses created e-commerce offshoots because *everyone else was doing it* – with predictable consequences.

In the *dotcom* boom of the late 1990s many self-styled business experts were predicting that everything would soon be done on the Web. Customers would place orders through Web sites, then track the progress of their orders online. Businesses would exchange data exclusively using Web protocols. The companies that make the infrastructure of the Web became phenomena beyond imagining. Hardware manufacturers who were selling large volumes of routers, switches or cables were treated by investors as of they were IBM or General Electric. The software houses whose products would process all the data that pundits were expecting received huge levels of financial investment. Many of these companies would never have been able to pay off all of their borrowings, or satisfy investors with a decent return. The problem was that the customers simply weren't there. Since the turn of the millennium a harsh wind of reality has replaced that earlier optimism. Investors, manufacturers and customers are starting to examine the intrinsic worth of Web businesses and the technologies that support them. Many will disappear but a few will survive and succeed.

Many useful technologies have been created to assuage the continual desire for something new or revolutionary. As more people tried to run online organizations, the limitations of HTML became apparent. Also apparent was the ease of use of the HTML tag system. Why not, therefore, combine simple and readable tags with a set of rules which let document authors target meaning rather than presentation? That is exactly what XML does. You can use XML to describe almost any data; that description is platform independent, as is the data. Hey presto, the limitations of the Web start to disappear, to be replaced with a raft of new applications.

This book is an introductory guide to the world of XML. Not just what it is and how to write XML documents, but also an overview of many of the technologies that surround XML and are required to make it usable. It's also based on practical examples and, in Part Four, demonstrates how XML is really used.

Acknowledgments

Although this book is my baby, it didn't appear without help from numerous other people. I'd like to thank Gaynor Redvers-Mutton, my editor for suggesting I write this book in the first place and then for making it happen. I must also mention her assistant Jonathan Shipley, Robert Hambrook who has supervised the production of the book at John Wiley and Sons, and copy editor Annette Abel. I'd also like to thank the technical reviewers, especially Bruce Donald Campbell whose comments and suggestions made the book far better than it might otherwise have been.

Most importantly I'd like to thank my family: my parents for giving me self-belief and for their love; my wife Julie and our daughters Sophie and Faye. Living with an author isn't easy and they do an admirable job of it. It's now time to devote some time to them.

Contacting the Author

I would be delighted to hear from readers of this book. There are bound to be mistakes and those can only be rectified if readers point them out, and I'm sure there are things that I can improve in the future. Anyone who teaches will tell you that education is a dialog in which teacher can learn from pupil just as pupil learns from teacher. Not everything in this book will make sense; you may have problems with exercises or with changing technologies and standards. I'd be happy to discuss those things with you. I have a Web site which contains material related to this book at:

`http://homepages.shu.ac.uk/~cmscrb`

More information, exercises and errata will appear there. If you want to send me e-mail I'll try to respond as quickly and accurately as I can. My email address is `c.d.bates@shu.ac.uk`

CHRIS BATES

Sheffield, UK

Chapter 1

Introduction

Data. Probably the most important thing about any piece of software or computer system is the data that it manipulates. Whether playing games, using Internet chat rooms or performing financial transactions, everything that we use computers for has data somewhere near its heart. Data can be pretty complicated. You might think that your name and address are quite simple things, but try developing a computer storage format for them that is simple to use, efficient, that allows you to manipulate the data exactly as you want to, and that you will still understand in 20 years. Suddenly that simple data becomes more complex and interesting. Now scale the problem so that instead of data for one person you are storing and manipulating many millions of data records. If the data format is too complex, the system may struggle to work through the data when it is asked to make changes to it. If the format is too simple, important information may be difficult to extract.

Anyone who has used computers for a few years will have faced one particular problem. It doesn't matter how much you know about IT or how much experience you have, you are almost guaranteed to face this problem at some point. The data that most PC users create is stored in proprietary formats. The software developers who create typical PC applications all invent their own data structures, and when a user saves data to a file it is stored in that unique format. Often data, even plain text, is saved in a binary format such that when looking at the contents of the file, finding the actual data within a mess of control codes is impossible. While the application that created it still exists, the data remains usable. But over time users upgrade operating systems, delete applications that they are unable to reinstall or change the type of computer they use. Eventually users have important data stored on disk but are unable to use it. Sometimes they are even unable to access the physical medium – who, these days, has a $5\frac{1}{4}$ inch floppy disk drive available?

Some applications can import data that was created in another piece of software. For instance, the open-source word processor OpenOffice.org can import data created using various versions of Microsoft Word. However, there is no guarantee that a particular format will be supported by any other application. The solution *might* be to reverse engineer the data format. Reverse engineering is the process of looking at the data and trying to figure out how the data and formatting are encoded within the file so that the data itself can be extracted. The only problem here is that doing so may be illegal. The Digital Copyright Millennium Act, DCMA, passed by the United States Congress makes the reverse engineering of copyrighted material illegal in the USA. As I write this, the European Union is seeking to impose similar legislation on its member states. The result may be that the possession of data remains legal but using it at some arbitrary point in the future may require illegal actions.

If the data had been saved in a format that was both freely available and readable none of this would matter. A cynic might suggest that the reason for proprietary binary data formats is that the software manufacturer is then able to sell updated versions of their programs to users on a regular cyclical basis. If users could use any word processor to read and write their letters, they would choose the ones that were easiest to use and available at a price they liked.

Big business has an even more pressing problem. Large organizations often have gigabytes of data which they have created over time and which is stored on systems that have reached the end of their working lives. Moving that data to new systems cannot be achieved simply by loading the tapes onto a different piece of hardware. Imagine the same problems that PC users have multiplied a thousand fold. Then imagine that the data is mission critical – without it there is no business. That's the exact position in which banks, government agencies and retailers all over the world find themselves. Many continue to run mainframe systems which are decades old simply because the cost and difficulty of moving old data to new systems are prohibitive.

One way of solving these problems is to structure data using a simple grammar. XML is a universally available language which provides just such a grammar. If all data were in XML, structuring problems would still exist but solving them using the technologies described in this book would be a relatively simple task.

How the Web Changed Everything

The problems presented by data formats are important but would have remained the preserve of a small minority of computer scientists if the World Wide Web had not been invented. The Web really changed everything in computing. If anyone can connect to any piece of data, that data had better be available in a format that they can all use. At the very least, that format needs to be well publicized; ideally it should be open source. The common data formats on the Web are HTML and PDF. HTML is open, anyone can read the specification, no one owns HTML and no individual or corporation controls how it will develop in the future. PDF is owned by Adobe, but they publish the specification so that anyone who has sufficient skill and knowledge can write software that manipulates it.

Both HTML and PDF are presentational formats: they describe how data should look either on screen or on a printed page. They have nothing to say about what the data actually means. When search engines such as Google build indexes of Web pages, they attempt to do so based upon the meaning of the data contained within the page. If that data is identified only as headings, cells in tables or paragraphs, finding what it means is almost impossible to do using software. You might be thinking that HTML tags which defines headings are adding meaning to data. Intuitively a level one heading, `<h1>`, identifies a major section of a document, whilst level two, `<h2>`, identifies a subsection. That might be intuitive but it isn't necessarily correct. HTML tags specify the formatting of content, so that an `<h2>` element can be used to highlight or emphasize text rather than to carry the meaning *subsection*. What is needed is a way of formatting data based upon meaning, and some method of converting that formatted data into other forms which are suitable for presentation to humans rather than to software.

XML provides a solution to the first problem since it structures data based upon meaning, not appearance. Indexing can, therefore, be done more easily, with results which are more useful. If a document is structured using XML, viewing it in a Web browser is likely to be near impossible, too. What's needed is a way to convert meaningful data structures into presentational structures. In the XML field that is done using the Extensible Stylesheet Language, XSL.

There's one more way in which the Web changes things. If data has meaning and can be accessed using URIs, then why can't applications access that data directly? Why do they need to be controlled by humans? This is a problem which has attracted interest from researchers in AI and distributed systems for years. XML seems to provide at least part of the solution here too.

SGML, The Origins of XML

XML didn't magically appear from nowhere. It grew out of dissatisfaction with HTML which simply lacks the expressive power that many applications developers require. Both HTML and XML are simplified subsets of SGML, the Standardized General Markup Language. SGML grew from a number of pieces of work, notably that of Charles Goldfarb, Edward Mosher and Raymond Lorie at IBM who created a General Markup Language in the late 1960s. In 1978 The American National Standards Institute (ANSI) set up a committee to investigate text processing languages. Charles Goldfarb joined that committee and led a project to extend GML. In 1980 the first draft of SGML was released and after a series of reviews and revisions became a standard in 1985.

The use of SGML was given impetus by the US Department of Defense. By the early 1970s the DOD was already being swamped by electronic documentation. Their problem arose not from the volume of data, but from the variety of mutually incompatible data formats. SGML was a suitable solution for their problem – and for many others over the years.

The development of XML and related technologies is undertaken by the World Wide Web Consortium, W3C. This a cooperative organization of interested parties, usually industrial and academic experts, who produce *Recommendation* documents which are *de facto* standards for the Web. W3C Recommendations are produced by working groups in areas such as data structuring, protocol definition and data transformation.

The design goals for XML, as set out in its Recommendation document, were:

- XML shall be straightforwardly usable over the Internet.
- XML shall support a wide variety of applications.
- XML shall be compatible with SGML.
- It shall be easy to write programs that process XML documents.
- The number of optional features in XML is to be kept to the absolute minimum, ideally zero.
- XML documents should be human-legible and reasonably clear.
- The XML design should be prepared quickly.
- The design of XML shall be formal and concise.
- XML documents shall be easy to create.
- Terseness in XML markup is of minimal importance.

I'm not going to provide a critical commentary on the XML Recommendation, or any of the others that I discuss. Once you've worked through the book, you can look back at that list and see for yourself how close XML is to its original design goals. You may also like to ponder on whether those goals were appropriate in the first place.

Target Audience

The world is awash with books about XML. Not just XML, though, that's just the beginning. If you want to develop an XML application you are likely also to need to be able to define a document structure and convert XML into other forms. You may also need to handle XML in programs you write in Java or C++. Every XML technology, and there are many of them, seems to be described in its own 1,000-page book. Every technical publisher has its own set of XML books available. Where does the XML novice begin?

Many novices try to use the Web for research and tuition, where they meet two types of Web page. Firstly, there are dozens of Web developer reference sites that include a few words about XML and some small snippets of code. Generally that code is relevant only to a particular application and is not explained in detail. Learning XML, XSLT or XML Schema from Web sites like these is impossible. The second type of Web document is the W3C Recommendations. These are comprehensive but not necessarily comprehensible. Generally written for people who understand XML, these are more likely to confuse beginners than help them.

This book is an attempt to fill some of these gaps. It's not a comprehensive reference guide but it does include some reference information. Instead, I've tried to introduce the key XML technologies and demonstrate how they relate to each other. There is also lots of code which is used both to help the explanations, and to give you a starting point in your own development work.

I imagine that the typical readers of this book will already have plenty of technical savvy. They may be students, probably in the final year of an undergraduate degree or doing postgraduate study. They will be using XML but it's not their primary focus. These readers want complete answers quickly and from a single source. The second type of reader is likely to be a programmer or software designer who has to get up to speed on all of the XML technologies quickly. These readers will not want to read a lot of large reference books until they understand just what it is that thy need to know.

Preparing the Book

Writing about a technology implies that the author has faith in that technology. Going to all the trouble of producing a textbook while simultaneously thinking that the technology is useless or has no future would be perverse to say the least. I have great faith in XML. I firmly believe that it helps simplify some pretty intransigent problems in distributed computing. Interoperability has long been a dream and some XML technologies are helping to make that dream into a reality – at relatively low cost. Having said which, I haven't used XML to produce this book.

Ideally I would have created the text of this book using my favorite XML editor, written a stylesheet and converted directly from XML to PDF. When I started writing that was actually the path I tried to take. Two obstacles lay before me.

First, I needed to find a suitable DTD or schema to provide a definition of the structure of a textbook. That was easily solved since this is a technical book. DocBook met my needs. Secondly, there was the process of transforming to PDF. There are two choices here: DSSSL and XSL Formatting Object, XSL-FO. DSSSL is a well-established technology which has been used with SGML documents for a number of years now. DSSSL is not an XML technology and the output it produces, while generally of decent quality, is not acceptable for a textbook. XSL-FO is an immature technology although it is defined by a W3C Recommendation. No processor exists which supports the full Recommendation and the output of those processors that do exist is, frankly, rather ugly. I have no doubt that in the near future XSL-FO processors that can do an excellent job will appear, but that won't be any help to me in producing this particular book.

Some textbooks have been written in XML. Their authors, or more usually their publishers, import the XML into an application such as FrameMaker and use that to typeset the book. Some of the applications that publishers use can import, and export, XML. Some even have some ability to understand complex DTDs like DocBook. However, the conversion between the author's XML source and the completed book leads to many potential problems. To avoid all of these difficulties I have written the book using the tried and tested LaTeX typesetting language. This gives excellent, high quality results. Because I've used it for a number of years now for most of my document preparation I know what it will do and can bend it to my will. In writing a textbook, pragmatism sometimes has to overcome idealism, unfortunately.

Structure of the Book

This is a book in four parts. Each can be read in isolation, although later parts require a lot of the knowledge from the earlier ones.

Part One is concerned with the basic technologies of XML. These include a description of what XML is and how to write it, and how to navigate through documents using XPath and XLink. I also look at how to formally define XML documents using Document Type Definitions which are increasingly obsolete but widely supported and how to use XML Schema which is one of the replacements for DTDs.

Part Two describes how XML documents can be converted into formats that can be displayed on screen or printed as hard copy. This part starts with Cascading Stylesheets, CSS, which should be familiar to you if you've done any HTML development. CSS is a way of providing information about how HTML elements should be displayed on screen: the font to be used, their color and placing etc. CSS stylesheets can be used with small XML documents so that some Web browsers, notably Internet Explorer and Mozilla, are able to display them. CSS is not an XML-based technology and is rather limited. For serious applications and power users they have been supplemented with Extensible Stylesheet Language, XSL. This has two variants: XSL Transforms, XSLT, which is used to transform XML for on-screen display; and XSL Formatting Object, XSL-FO, which is used to provide high quality printed documents. I'll look at both of these, showing how XPath expressions can be used to extract and process subsets of complex documents.

Part Three looks at using XML in your own applications. How do you develop applications that can read and write XML documents? I give plenty of code that does both. There are two programmatic interfaces to XML: the Document Object Model, DOM; and the Simple API for XML Processing, SAX. In Part Three both get a thorough airing. The code here is all written in Java. DOM and SAX libraries are available for just about any programming language that you care to name. I have used Java because it's powerful yet syntactically relatively simple, many programmers and students know the language, and it's widely used for server-side applications. The stuff that you learn here should, though, give you a leg-up if you're coding in Visual Basic, Perl or even C++.

In Part Four, I look at real uses of XML. I have chosen four different types of application. DocBook is used to format technical documentation. Although it has been around for a few years, interest in DocBook has been sparked since its adoption by the Linux Documentation Project as their standard data format. If you are a programmer or an IT student, chances are that you will need to write technical documents at some point and DocBook is an excellent starting point. Web Services are widely seen as the *coming thing* of the Web. E-commerce and business-to-business transactions will be important in driving the development of next-generation Web applications. I look at the technologies that underpin these developments: Resource Description Framework, RDF, Web Services Description Language, WSDL, and Universal Description, Discovery and Integration language, UDDI. Then I examine how applications can be plumbed together across the Web using a networking technology called SOAP. Finally, I examine something slightly different. The Mozilla browser can be used as the basis of other applications. It contains a language called XUL which is used to describe application interfaces. Although XUL is slightly off-the-wall and definitely not the normal type of XML application, I've included it because it shows that the possible uses of XML are limited only by the imaginations of users.

Throughout the book two applications are used to demonstrate how the technologies can be used. One is a simple business letter which is structured using XML, transformed into HTML and PDF and manipulated with Java programs. The other is a small file of recipes which acts as a simple XML database. As well as transformations and Schema development, the database can be searched with just some recipes retrieved. Taking the code from these applications won't give you a complete, functional suite of programs but it should show how the same set of data can be used in many different ways.

Typography

I have used a number of different fonts throughout this book. Each has a particular meaning. I've also structured some parts of the book, especially definitions of code, to clarify the meaning of the content. It's important that you understand what I've done, otherwise you may end up writing code that doesn't work.

First, all code is written in a `monospaced Courier` font. This is done to distinguish it from the descriptive text within the book. Here's a simple example:

```
<?xml version="1.0"?>

<greeting style="informal">
  <from>Chris Bates</from>
  <to>Mr. M. Mouse</to>
  <message>Hi, how're ya doin'?</message>
  <signature />
</greeting>
```

Notice that the XML tags are highlighted. Throughout the book I highlight those tags that are part of the particular language or grammar under discussion. Code samples like this can usually be used directly in functional programs, although longer listings are interspersed with descriptive text.

Definitions of terms appear as **`bold monospaced Courier`**. Again, these stand out from the text but the use of **`bold`** text indicates that they are *not* functional code. You cannot type the definitions straight into a program and expect them to work. Here's a definition of a typical XSLT element followed by part of its explanation:

```
<output
method="xml" | "html" | "text"
version="nmtoken"
encoding="string"
omit-xml-declaration="yes" | "no"
standalone="yes" | "no"
doctype-public="string"
doctype-system="string"
indent="yes" | "no"
media-type="string" />
```

The XSLT processor has no way of knowing what output format it should use for a transformation. Processors default...

- XML tags are all surrounded by angled brackets (< and >). Where you see these brackets used in HTML they are part of the code and must be reproduced in your programs.
- Tags that close XML elements always include a slash (/).
- Many elements in XML, XSLT and the other programming languages used here have optional attributes. Because these are optional you can *choose* to use one of them if you so desire. Throughout this book these optional attributes are listed inside square brackets (`[ ]`). The square brackets are not part of the HTML code and *must* be omitted from your pages.
- Optional items in lists are always separated by short vertical lines (|). These lines are not part of the code and *must* be omitted from your programs.
- The values given to attributes of XML elements are always placed in inverted commas.
- Many of the element definitions include an ellipsis (...). These are used to indicate places where you should add your own text. For instance `<h1>...</h1>` might become `<h1>A HEADING</h1>` in your document.
- The letter `n` is used to indicate a place where you must enter a numerical value, usually in the definitions of XSL expressions and programming functions that require parameters.

Part One

Extensible Markup Language

Chapter 2

Writing XML

Before diving into the process of learning XML, one common misconception needs to be cleared up. XML is *not* a programming language. In the early chapters of this book you will not be learning to program. XML is a grammar which is used to define and describe data structures. All that we are interested in at the moment is the structure of data and how it is used. We're not thinking about the development of applications that can process data. That sort of development is introduced in Part Three when I examine how the Java programming language can be used to manipulate XML structured data.

Although the XML Recommendation from W3C, the World Wide Web Consortium, is moderately long and complex, the language itself can be very simple. XML documents must follow a number of rules; fortunately, though, understanding and applying those rules are not difficult tasks. In this chapter I'll show you how to write simple XML structures and explain the rules of the language. Once you've read through, and understood, this material, you will be able to write your own XML and, just as importantly, read other people's. This chapter won't turn you into an XML expert; before that can happen you will need to digest the more complex material in later chapters, but it will give you enough information to start using XML in your own applications.

The first thing you need to know before you can start to understand XML is just what the language is like. If you come from a programming background you'll be used to the idea that computer languages are limited vocabularies used to describe the operation of a program. Computer programs usually consist of a set of instructions and some data. The instructions tell the computer how it must manipulate the data, although the selection of individual parts of the program is often controlled by a user. Computer scientists call such languages *declarative* since variables and instructions are explicitly declared by the programmer. Declarative languages include, among others, C++, Java and Visual Basic.

Most of the software that you'll use today was written using a declarative language, but not all of it. There's an alternative[1] called *functional programming*. In programs written in functional languages, the developers state what they want from the program rather than how to achieve it. In a functional language the programmer has no control over the order in which the instructions in a program are executed and is unable to use techniques such as assignment to dynamic variables. Languages that operate in this way include Scheme, ML, Haskell, and, of course, Lisp which has been used since the 1950s. You'll see in Chapter 8 that functional programming is important for XML developers since some of our core technologies are based on it.

Broadly speaking, XML is functional in intent. It describes the structures of data sets but has no consideration of how those structures are to be created or manipulated. In fact, XML isn't a programming language. XML is used to define data structures, yet developers and users often refer to XML *programs* rather than the more correct *structures*. The difference is important because we can write programs that manipulate XML structured data sets using standard programming techniques, as described in Chapters 13 and 12, or functional languages as in Chapter 8.

This gets us no nearer to understanding what XML actually looks like. If you've ever written a Web page, or looked at the source code of one, you'll have seen something that is almost XML. In fact, to the untutored eye, spotting the differences between HTML and XML can be very difficult. XML has two components: tags which are used to mark the structure of the data; and the data itself. This will make most sense when you've seen an example.

2.1 A FIRST EXAMPLE

Throughout the book I'm going to present a couple of different XML applications. The applications are a business letter, which could be easily adapted to provide a simple memo structure, and a recipe book. Each of the technologies that I introduce in the book is going to be used on these two applications. You'll see many of the different ways one can use XML being applied to these two data structures. Both are fairly complex so I'm not going

[1] Actually there are many alternatives but the others aren't important right now.

to introduce them until you know a bit more about XML. Instead I'll begin with a much simpler structure.

Whilst Listing 2.1 is definitely not the most complex piece of XML code you'll ever see, it does show some of the major features of the language. Take a moment to read through the code and try to spot its key features before you read on.

Listing 2.1 A Sample XML Structure

```
<?xml version="1.0"?>

<greeting style="informal">
  <from>Chris Bates</from>
  <to>Mr. M. Mouse</to>
  <message>Hi, how're ya doin'?</message>
  <signature />
</greeting>
```

You should have noticed that XML tags tend to occur in pairs, that they are surrounded by angle brackets and that tags are used to describe the structure of the data. I'll describe the exact rules for the structure of XML files in detail in Section 2.3.

2.2 WHY NOT USE HTML?

If you've done any Web development using HTML, you may be wondering why it can't be used instead of XML. HTML tags are just like XML tags; they contain content and have attributes,[2] and plenty of applications understand HTML. The latter point is really important. As I write this, relatively few pieces of software can display XML, and not many more can be used to edit it. HTML viewers, usually Web browsers, are widely available, in fact most PCs and handheld devices such as PDAs have one installed. HTML editors are now commonplace, there are dedicated pieces of professional software such as Macromedia Dreamweaver, and even common applications like Microsoft Word can save files in HTML format.

What about XML tools? Some Web browsers such as Mozilla and Netscape 6 can display raw XML, but only Internet Explorer[3] does a good job of it. User-friendly XML editors are rare and tend to be expensive. If you want to parse XML files, that is, run them through pieces of software that can understand their structure, or transform them into other structures using XSL, you need to install additional software. Often these require

[2]Don't worry if you are confused by some of the terminology. It will soon become clear.
[3]You may need to install additional pieces of software before this works for you.

a Java environment on your machine, which may mean downloading a large file from the Internet. Installing such an environment may also require skills and knowledge that many users may not have.

The effect of opening the sample XML file from Listing 2.1 in Internet Explorer and in Mozilla 1.0 is shown in Table 2.1. Notice that, although both of them can clearly parse XML and separate content and tags, only Internet Explorer presents it in a meaningful way.

Table 2.1 XML in Internet Explorer and Mozilla

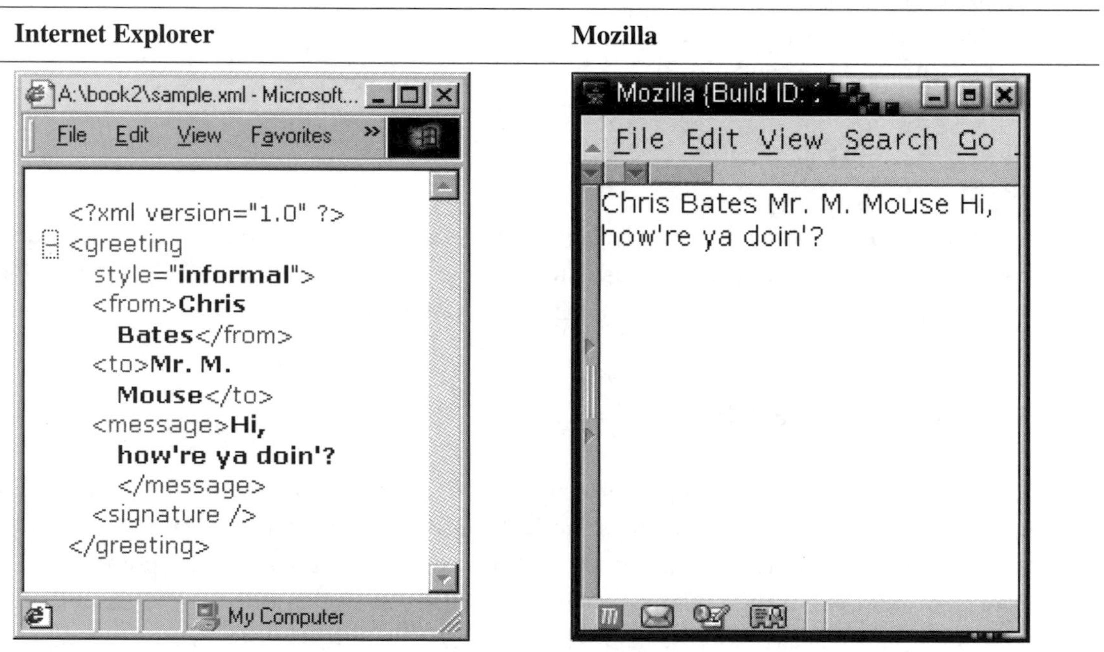

This seems like a no-brainer, doesn't it? HTML holds all of the aces when it comes to availability and quality of software, yet XML is clearly the better technology. Let's try formatting the sample XML file in Listing 2.1 as HTML. The result is shown in Listing 2.2.

Listing 2.2 The XML Sample Written in HTML

```
<html>
  <head>
    <title>The XML Sample Written in HTML</title>
  </head>
  <body>
    <h2>Chris Bates</h2>
```

```
    <h2>Mr. M. Mouse</h2>
    <p>Hi, how're ya doin'?</p>
  </body>
</html>
```

Although the HTML version can be displayed neatly formatted in a Web browser, much useful information from the XML version has been lost. Sure, it still contains the same data, but the meaning of that data has totally disappeared. For instance it is clear that this code indicates where the greeting originates:

```
<from>Chris Bates</from>
```

whereas

```
<h2>Chris Bates</h2>
```

conveys nothing about the role of the content within the greeting. Remember, HTML elements such as `<h2>` don't even carry simple meaning such as *heading level two*. They're just a set of instructions about font, color, typeface and spacing which must be applied to their content. It is this ability to convey the meaning of data that makes XML so important. Sure, using HTML you can present your data in Web pages, but only through XML can you turn that data into *information*. The difference between data and information is simple: information is data presented within a particular context. The string `Chris Bates` is data, but what does it mean? The XML element:

```
<from>Chris Bates</from>
```

is information because we now know the meaning of the string.

Which is, of course, all very well. But surely no one expects users to look at raw XML. The modern computer user rightly expects that the things they view on screen will look good. XML has a number of solutions. Firstly, Web browsers are becoming XML browsers too. Internet Explorer leads the way here. It can display raw XML in tree structures, whereas browsers like Mozilla simply display the content of an XML file without any structure. Soon, though, all Web browsers will be able to handle XML. Secondly, all modern browsers can use Cascading Stylesheets, CSS, to format XML. Finally, XML can be converted into HTML for display purposes using XSLT. I'll examine CSS and XSLT in Chapters 5 and 8.

> **Note:**
> XML only has meaning if you understand the language in which the tags are written. I can't read Italian, so XML marked up in that language would be meaningless to me. Meaning also requires context. If the context of the tag is clear, there's more chance that it will make sense to a reader.

2.3 THE XML RULES

Computer languages need to be formally defined in some way. Developers need to know what facilities are available in a language and that those facilities will work in the same way in all implementations. Languages are usually standardized by an international body such as the International Standards Organization, ISO, or the Institute of Electrical and Electronic Engineers, IEEE. For those languages that have defined standards, all compilers or interpreters must adhere to the standard: if a C++ compiler doesn't work according to the ANSI/ISO C++ standard then it really isn't a C++ compiler. Often these standards are minimum requirements which will be available in all products and on all platforms. Manufacturers of compilers are free to extend the language by adding their own proprietary features, although this does mean that the extended version will no longer be *standard*. Often large or powerful companies try to force their extensions into the standards. This can be extremely beneficial when it leads to improvements – too often standardized languages are developed by committees and become lowest common denominator languages. New extensions may only be available on one platform. If developers wish to write code on a Linux box but later compile and execute it on an Apple Macintosh, they can only do this if no extensions have been used. Problems like this tend to force people either to adhere rigidly to the standard or to work exclusively for a subset of all available platforms. When developing for heterogeneous systems such as the Web, adherence to the standard is clearly the preferred option.

XML requires a common set of rules. In fact, since any Web technology must work on every platform in a plethora of software applications, standardization is even more important than for programming languages. Perhaps surprisingly, XML, like HTML, isn't actually an international standard. It's a *Recommendation* of the World Wide Web Consortium (W3C). W3C Recommendations have much of the force of international standards but the process of creating them is far more flexible and far faster than standardization.

The current XML Recommendation is Version 1.0 (second edition). It can be viewed online at `http://www.w3.org/TR/2000/REC-xml-20001006` or downloaded in a variety of formats. The second edition makes no major changes to the first edition of the Recommendation but does incorporate all of its errata. Most standards documents are necessarily complex. They don't make for an easy read, and the XML Recommendation is no exception. If you want to know just how much thought went into the design of XML, download a copy of the Recommendation and spend a few minutes leafing through it.

2.3.1 XML Tags

XML documents are composed of elements. An element has three parts: a start tag, an end tag and, usually, some content. Elements are arranged in a hierarchical structure, similar to a tree, which reflects both the logical structure of the data and its storage structure. A tag is a pair of angled brackets, <... >, containing the name of the element, and pairs of attributes and values. An end tag is denoted by a slash, /, placed before the text. Here are some XML elements:

```
<book>The Lord Of The Rings</book>
<chapter>Helm's Deep</chapter>
<name>Professor J. R. R. Tolkien</name>
```

XML elements must obey some simple rules:

- An element must have both a start tag and an end tag unless it is an empty element.
- Start tags and end tags must form a matched pair.
- XML is case-sensitive so that `name` does not match `nAme`. You can, though, use both upper and lower-case letters inside your XML markup.
- Tag names cannot include whitespace.

Here are those same elements with introduced errors:

```
<book>The Lord Of The Rings</Book>
<cha pter>Helm's Deep</chapter>
<name>Professor J. R. R. Tolkien</n>
```

2.3.1.1 Nesting Tags Even very simple documents have some elements nested inside others. In fact, if your document is going to be XML it *has* to have a root element which contains the rest of the document. Tags must pair up inside XML so that they are closed in the reverse order to that in which they were opened.

The code in the left column of Table 2.2 is not valid XML since the ordering of the start and end tags has become confused. The correct version is shown on the right side of the same table.

2.3.1.2 Empty Tags Sometimes an element that *could* contain text happens not to. There may be many reasons for this – the attributes of the element may contain all the necessary information, or the element may be required if the document is to be *valid*. These empty elements can be represented in two ways:

```
<book>The Lord Of The Rings</book>
<book></book>
<book />
```

The empty element can be included by placing an end tag immediately after the start tag. More simply, a tag containing the name of the element *followed by a slash* can be used.

Table 2.2 Nesting Elements

Incorrect

```
<?xml version="1.0"?>

<greeting style="informal">
  <from>Chris Bates
  <to>Mr. M. Mouse</to>
  </from>
  <message>
    Hi, how're ya doin'?
  </greeting>
</message>
```

Correct

```
<?xml version="1.0"?>

<greeting style="informal">
  <from>Chris Bates</from>
  <to>Mr. M. Mouse</to>
  <message>
    Hi, how're ya doin'?
  </message>
</greeting>
```

2.3.1.3 Characters in XML When the XML Recommendation talks about *characters*, it means characters from the Unicode and ISO 10646 character sets. Until relatively recently most computing applications used a relatively small set of characters, typically the 128 letters of the ASCII character set which could be represented using seven bits. The ASCII character set, defined in ISO/IEC 646, only allowed users to enter those letters typically found in the English language.

In a multilingual world this is clearly an impractical limitation which led to the development of many alternative character sets. Web applications typically use ISO 8859 which uses 8 bits for each character and which defines a number of alphabets. These include the standard Latin alphabet used as default by most Web browsers. Unicode goes further and uses two bytes to represent each character. This means that Unicode includes 65,536 different characters, insufficient for Chinese but suitable for most uses. ISO 20646 extends the Unicode idea by using *four* bytes for each character, giving approximately 2 billion possible characters. Unicode is implemented as the default encoding in Microsoft Windows and the Java programming language, among others. But it clearly needs extending to access those extra characters, and has been. Version 2.1 of Unicode includes some facilities that give access to the ISO 10646 character set.

Using ISO 10646 to represent ASCII data is highly inefficient – effectively three bytes of memory are wasted. Even though computer memory and storage are extremely cheap today, such inefficiency is expensive if an application is handling gigabytes of data. Therefore applications use encoding schemes to store data more efficiently. Applications that process XML *must* support two of these: UTF-8 and UTF-16. UTF-8, for instance, uses a single byte for ASCII data and two to six bytes for extended characters.

> **Note:**
> XML applications support extended character sets. These allow up to 2 billion different characters. When you develop using XML you can use any language and character set that you need to in your applications. You are not restricted to the English language or to the set of languages supported on a particular operating system.

It's worth noting that everything in an XML document that is not *markup* is considered to be character data. Markup[4] consists of:

- start tag,
- end tag,
- empty tag,
- entity reference,
- character reference,
- comments,
- delimiters for CDATA sections,
- document type declarations,
- processing instructions,
- XML declarations,
- text declarations.

The final, important thing about characters is that some of them have special meaning or cannot be easily represented in your source text using a conventional keyboard. Most of the characters in ISO 10646 clearly fall into this category. Some mechanism is therefore required to permit the full range of characters to be included in documents. This is done through *character references*. To demonstrate the use of character references, I'll look at those characters that can have special meaning inside markup. Characters such as <,>,' ," are used as part of the markup of the document. If they're encountered by the parser

[4] You'll meet each of these components as you read through this book.

inside an XML file, it assumes that they are control characters which have special meaning to it, and it then acts accordingly. The obvious example of this behavior is found in handling attributes. The following two examples would be illegal in XML:

```
<message src="here is the "source" of the message" />
<message src='here is the 'source' of the message' />
```

In each case, the parser will assume that the content of the `src` attribute starts at the first apostrophe or set of quotation marks, and stops at the second. Attribute content following this point cannot be parsed since it is not valid XML.

Table 2.3 Character References

Character	Sequence
<	<
>	>
’	'
&	&
"	"

What happens when the file should legitimately contain < as part of its character data? The appropriate character reference is entered instead.[5] Table 2.3 shows the references which must be entered in an XML document if you want a particular character. Here’s the previous example reworked to be valid XML:

```
<message src="here is the &quot;source&quot; of the message" />
<message src='here is the &apos;source&apos; of the message' />
```

Listing the complete set of character entities is beyond the scope of this book. If you want to see them all, look on the Web where there are comprehensive listings. If you are using a fully featured commercial editor the list may be available in its help system.

2.3.2 Attributes

Associating information with an element without making that information into a separate element is sometimes important. This can be seen on the HTML `<img>` tag:

```
<img src="../images/uncle_fred.png"
```

[5] CDATA sections may also be used.

```
    height="120"
    width="34"
    alt="Uncle Fred at the beach" />
```

Each piece of information is an attribute of the element. Making those attributes into elements doesn't add clarity, rather it adds a little complexity, as Listing 2.3 demonstrates. The choice of using attributes or creating additional elements is left up to you. It may be that some technologies or particular parsers work better with extra elements. If you are presenting your XML in raw form for human readers, attributes might be easier. Some elements need to be empty. One example of that is the HTML <img> which is a reference to another file and has no content. There are, as so often, no hard and fast rules to help you.

Listing 2.3 Separating HTML Attributes into Elements

```
<img>
  <src>../images/uncle_fred.png</src>
  <height>120</height>
  <width>34</width>
  <alt>Uncle Fred at the beach</alt>
</img>
```

2.3.3 Comments

Here is a firm rule: all program files should contain comments. Comments are pieces of descriptive text placed inside the source code of programs as annotations. They describe the structure and functionality of the code. If you have relatively little programming experience, you may wonder why the code itself can't provide this information. After all, code is supposed to be written and read by humans, isn't it? Unfortunately, the answer to that is both *yes* and, at the same time, *no*. Programming languages and programs are now so complex that they are rarely *self-documenting*. XML files, in particular, have a tendency to be both large and verbose. The structure may not be clear, and the meaning certainly isn't likely to be. It's important to place comments inside your markup so that you, or whoever has the job of maintaining your code in the future, can understand its intent.

XML comments are nice and straightforward. Here's an example:

```
<greeting>
  <from>Chris Bates</from>
  <!-- The &lt;from&gt; element denotes the
  sender of the message
  -->
```

```
</greeting>
```

Comments start with the character sequence `<!--` and end with `-->`. They may be just one line long or may span a number of lines. You don't need to place any sort of continuation character at the start of multi-line comments.

2.3.4 Entities

The XML Recommendation lets an author separate an XML document into a number of components. Each of these components is called an *entity*, each of which is identified by a unique name. Entities are used for a number of reasons, including:

- The document is large and must be split apart for practical reasons.
- Some content needs to be used in a number of places within the document. Duplication of the section would be difficult, time-consuming or lead to transcription errors.
- Different systems may render the same content in different ways.

An entity may be *internal*, in which case it is defined alongside the source of the main document, or *external*. External entities are, not surprisingly, defined in separate files.

2.3.4.1 Character Entities Perhaps the commonest use of entities is to include in a document characters that cannot be entered from a normal input device. Using a keyboard only a limited set of characters can be typed; however, the ISO 10646 standard allows for approximately two billion different characters. All of those characters can be entered in an XML document through the use of character entities. References to character entities take the form `&#;` or `&#n;`. In the former case a decimal representation of the character's value is given, in the latter the representation is in hexadecimal format. All character references start with ampersand, `&`, and end with a semi-colon, `;`. The sequences in Table2.3 are typical of character entities.

Those letters and symbols that are not available in ASCII all have standard ISO values. If you want to use one of these characters, it will have to be defined on your system and available to your XML parser. You can define character entities at the top of your XML files. For instance to define the character È, you would use:

```
<!ENTITY Egrave "&#200;">
```

If you need to use more than a few characters, defining all of them for yourself is a very tedious task. Much better to get hold of the standard definitions from elsewhere. Sets of ISO character definitions are widely available for download from around the Web.[6]

[6] Perform a Web search using the term `ISO entity set` to find lots of examples.

You'll need to make those entity sets that you are planning to use available to your XML parser. Each parser works in a different way so be sure to spend some time reading the documentation with yours. Parsers that have an SGML heritage will generally be happy if you create a *catalog* file. This file simply relates the name of each entity set to a particular file on your system. The parser will use these relationships when handling your XML.

XML parsers treat whitespace differently depending upon its context and how they are being used. There is a discussion of this in Section 2.4.3. All you need to know for now is that if you want to make sure you get a single whitespace character output by the parser you must put the character reference inside your XML source. I mention this now, because, while your parser may understand ` `, there is no guarantee that it will. If your parser has problems, you will need to get hold of entity set ISOnum.

I shall discuss how to configure your system, set up catalogs and handle entity sets in Chapter 17.

2.3.4.2 External Entities An entity may be stored outside of the current document. The document then needs to be able to refer to these entities. This is done by creating a *reference* to the file that contains the entity. The following example points to an image file:

```
<!ENTITY logo SYSTEM "./images/logo.png" NDATA png>
```

The creates an entity called `logo` which is actually a pointer to a file. In this case the entity is a binary file. The location of the external file is given using a URI. An application that processes the XML needs to know where the entity is and how to process it. Typically, processing of binary data such as images will be performed by other applications. That's how Web browsers work. They get so-called helper applications to handle complex formats such as streamed radio broadcasts. The `NDATA` attribute will be examined in the discussion of Document Type Definitions in Chapter 3. It refers to a `NOTATION` which is used to identify an application that can process this particular data type.

The keyword `SYSTEM` indicates that the entity is defined within a particular organization or by an individual. The definition of the entity is usually stored locally and may not be available outside the organization that created it. If an entity is defined by a standards body or is widely needed, the word `SYSTEM` is replaced with `PUBLIC`:

```
<!ENTITY logo PUBLIC "-//Smiggins Inc//Images//EN"
     "http://www.smiggins.com/images/logo.png" NDATA png>
```

Although the URI remains, an additional item has been added to the entity definition. The string `"-//Smiggins Inc//Images//EN"` is a system-independent way of identifying an entity. It points to a *catalog* entry which some applications are able to use to help them resolve and locate the entity.

2.3.4.3 Defining Entities An entity definition consists of the name of the entity and a value associated with it. The value may be a numerical value which represents a character, a piece of text or the name of a file. Whenever the parser encounters the name of the entity, it substitutes the content for the name. In Listing 2.4, an entity called `signature` is defined and used.

Listing 2.4 Defining Internal Entities

```
<?xml version="1.0"?>

<!ENTITY signature "Yours Sincerely, Chris Bates">

<greeting style="informal">
  <from>Chris Bates</from>
  <to>Mr. M. Mouse</to>
  <message>Hi, how're ya doin'?</message>
  &signature;
</greeting>
```

Entities are defined using a special type of tag. Many of the control tags you need to use in XML break the XML rules. This one is no exception. The `ENTITY` element doesn't have an end tag, and it doesn't require a closing slash. Always use it like this:

```
<!ENTITY signature "Yours Sincerely, Chris Bates">
```

You'll see more declarations of this form when I discuss Document Type Definitions (DTDs) in Chapter 3. Notice that the `signature` entity is referenced using the same construction that I showed you for character entities. The name is preceded by `&` and followed by `;` which gives constructs such as `&signature;`.

2.3.5 Processing Instructions

You may have noticed the line

```
<?xml version="1.0" ?>
```

at the start of Listing 2.1, which is a *Processing Instruction*. Processing instructions contain information which must be passed to applications that are processing the XML source. Processing instructions are not really part of the markup; to differentiate them they are delimited by `<?` and `?>`.

The content of a PI depends upon the application that will be processing it. Generally it starts with a keyword which may be used to identify the application, this is followed by content which has meaning to that application and which is formatted for it. The following example would include an XSL stylesheet with the XML document. A parser capable of performing XML transformations would then be able to transform the XML document according to the rules in the stylesheet.

```
<?xml-stylesheet type="text/xsl" href="./styles.xsl"?>
```

The XML Declaration What about the first example:

```
<?xml version="1.0" ?>
```

That is an *XML Declaration*. This should be included at the start of all of your XML.[7] It has three parts, two of which are optional:

```
<?xml version="1.0" encoding="UTF-8" standalone="no"?>
```

If you include an XML declaration, you must state what version of XML it corresponds to. Current applications understand only version 1.0, so always use this version. The encoding parameter indicates which encoding scheme was used to create the document. If it is absent, UTF-8 is assumed. Finally, the standalone parameter indicates if an external file contains declarations that may affect this document. If you use external entities this should be set to `no`.

2.3.6 Formally Defining XML Structures

Adhering to the rules about elements and content and ensuring that you use valid ISO 10646 entities throughout your documents will mean that you are creating good XML. It won't give your files any *meaning*. The structure of your document depends upon the hierarchy of elements inside it, the content of those elements and their relationships to each other. The structure of your particular XML application is usually defined in an external file that the parser can access if it is validating your document. These external files take one of two forms: Document Type Definitions, more commonly called DTDs, or schemas, which will usually be XML Schema.

I'll describe the contents of both types of file in Chapters 3 and 4. At the moment I'll just show you how to include these elements in your XML files. It's unlikely that you'll need to include them before you know what they are, but in reading XML code written by other people you'll certainly come across examples of their usage.

[7]The XML Declaration is optional in Version 1.0, but is not guaranteed to remain so.

> **Note:**
> Study as many XML documents as you can. Examining other developers' XML is sure to help you improve your own. Much of the code you'll come across is likely to be poor quality or relatively simple, but it can still teach you things if it makes you ask questions. When reading other people's code always refer to formal definitions of their documents, if available, and the relevant W3C Recommendations.

2.3.6.1 Document Type Declarations The Document Type Definition file is really a return to the SGML roots of XML. DTDs have their own syntax which allows for limited expressiveness. Although many XML developers and gurus recommend replacing DTDs with XML Schemas, this is happening very gradually. It's likely that for the foreseeable future, XML developers will need to understand how to use DTDs.

Listing 2.5 Using a Document Type Declaration

```
<?xml version="1.0"?>

<!DOCTYPE greeting SYSTEM "greets.dtd">

<greeting style="informal">
  <from>Chris Bates</from>
  <to>Mr. M. Mouse</to>
  <message>Hi, how're ya doin'?</message>
  &signature;
</greeting>
```

Including a DTD is really simple. Listing 2.5 shows how it is done. The code that includes a DTD is called a Document Type *Declaration*. Beware the terminology here: the *declaration* includes the *definition*. Let's examine the declaration statement:

```
<!DOCTYPE greeting SYSTEM "greets.dtd">
```

This is another element that doesn't follow the rules of XML. The tag starts with `<!` and ends with `>`. The content of the tag has four components. The first is the keyword `DOCTYPE` which is an instruction to the parser. The second word is the name of the root node of the document. The third word is either `SYSTEM` or `PUBLIC`. `SYSTEM` is used when the DTD is local to a specific individual or organization, `PUBLIC` when it is published by a standardizing body or is available to the public. The final piece of content, a system identifier, is the URI, address, of the DTD file.

2.3.6.2 XML Schema Using XML Schema, the definition of an XML structure is done using another, valid, XML document. The definition and use of schemas are complex topics which are covered in detail in Chapter 4. At this stage I'll just show you an example of a reference to a schema from within an XML document. Schemas define *namespaces* as well as XML structures. The use of namespaces is covered in Section 4.1; all that you need to know right now is that a namespace is a way of ensuring the uniqueness of variable names. This is vitally important in complex documents that are made available across networks.

Some possible names for XML elements, such as `user`, may occur in hundreds of XML documents, and have different meanings in many of them. It's really important that processing software separates `user` in document `A` from `user` in document `B`.

Schemas are included using normal XML tags to associate a document with a namespace, and the namespace with a schema definition:

```
<my_namespace
      xmlns='urn:my-schema'
      xmlns:xsi='http://www.w3.org/1999/XMLSchema-instance'
      xsi:schemaLocation='urn:my-schema
      http://myserver.org/my-schema.xsd' />
```

Don't worry about the meaning of that code. There's a lot more to understand before it will start to make much sense. The `xsi:schemaLocation` attribute indicates the location of a schema document and defines a namespace prefix for it. The schema can be loaded automatically by schema-aware parsers when they handle the XML source.

2.4 PARSING XML FILES

Applications that manipulate XML need to be able to move through the data structure, finding elements, tags and content. Processing data to extract meaning from it is called *parsing* in computing. The same term is used to describe the processing of sentences in human languages to extract their meaning. The idea, in both cases, is the same. Few developers choose to write their own XML parsers. Although the rules of the grammar are relatively simple, writing fast and accurate parsers is a difficult task. Most people use a parser written by someone else. Many XML parsers are freely available; the choice of which you use tends to depend upon your system and the language that you are developing in. Two popular choices are MSXML from Microsoft, which can be programmed using C++ or Visual Basic, and Xerces from the Apache Foundation. Xerces comes in Java, C++ and Perl versions and can be used on many different operating systems. Both these parsers can be used directly from the command line or called from within applications.

Once you have installed MSXML on your system, it is automatically available within Internet Explorer. This means that you can, for instance, open XML files in Explorer and view them as tree structures.

As you read through this book, you'll find that XML parsers can do lots of interesting things with your XML. One of the most useful is to check if the XML you have written is correct, and if it adheres to the rules set out in the DTD or schema for that particular document.

2.4.1 Valid or well-formed?

XML documents may be either valid or well-formed. The two terms relate to differing levels of conformance with the XML Recommendation, the DTD, or schema, and the basic structure of the XML. All XML documents must be well-formed. Tags should be paired, elements should be properly nested, the document should have an XML declaration. Entities should be properly formed. Any application which can handle XML will be able to cope with a well-formed document. A valid document takes conformance rather further. To be valid, a DTD or schema should be identified for the XML data. The data must meet the rules set out in that document.

All XML parsers are able to check that a document is well-formed. For some such as MSXML, this is where their capabilities end. Other parsers such as Xerces are able to validate an XML document against a DTD. At the time of writing, Schema support in Xerces is in the alpha stage of development. That means it's far from ready for the big time – but it is being implemented. XML is a new technology, it's evolving rapidly and tool support does tend to lag slightly behind. In the near future, though, the tools will be available to use XML Schema as well as DTDs. It's at that stage that we'll start to see DTDs becoming less popular with developers.

Figure 2.1 shows what happens when some invalid XML is loaded into the Mozilla Web browser.

2.4.2 Unparsed Character Data

Most of the content in an XML file will be handled by the parser. Generally elements and entities contain text that has some meaning. The content will not include characters such as < which have special meaning to the parser, and when it does contain them, those characters are usually entered as character entities. Sometimes a document will include large numbers of these characters. In such cases using entities may be impractical. The XML standard allows for this. Your document can include sections of `CDATA`, unparsed character data. All characters inside a `CDATA` section are assumed to be content, rather than

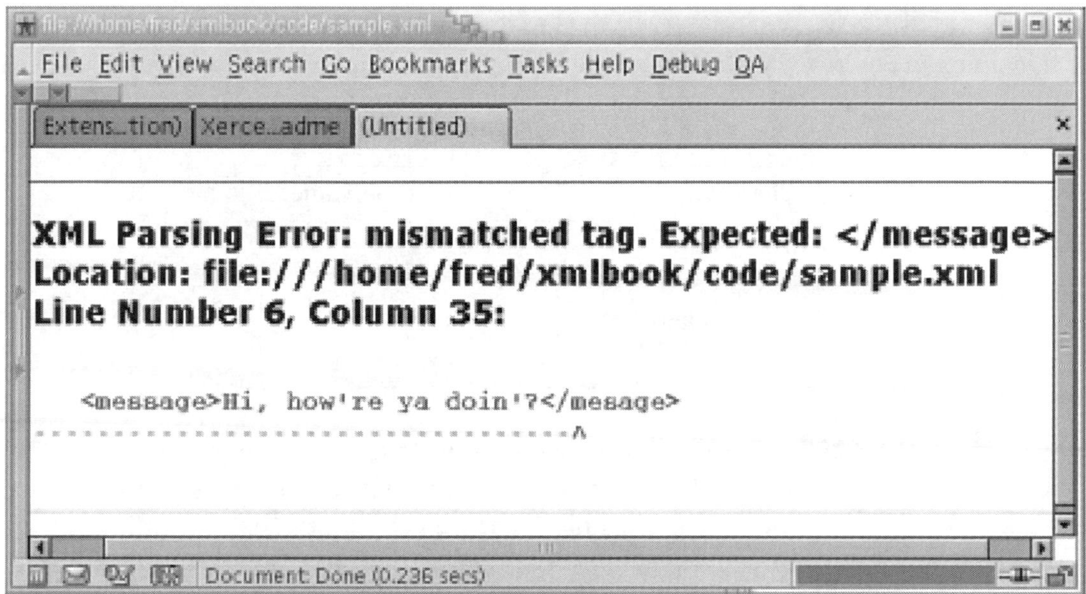

Figure 2.1 Invalid XML in Mozilla

markup. A section of CDATA is started with the string <![CDATA] and ended with]]> as shown in Listing 2.6. You'll meet CDATA again in the discussion of DTDs in Chapter 3.

Listing 2.6 CDATA Sections

```
<?xml version="1.0"?>

<greeting style="informal">
  <from>Chris Bates</from>
  <to>Mr. M. Mouse</to>
  <message>Hi, how're ya doin'?</message>
  <![CDATA[ The text in << here can contain & markup >
  characters until the end of the section is reached
  ]]>
</greeting>
```

2.4.3 Whitespace

When the parser moves through content it *normalizes* it. Normalization is the process of removing excess whitespace from the data. The rules for the removal of whitespace characters by XML parsers are clearly defined in the XML Recommendation. In this section I'm going to describe those rules and the effect they have upon your documents.

Table 2.4 XML Whitespace Characters

Character	Unicode Value
tab	`#x9`
newline	`#xA`
carriage return	`#xD`
space	`#x20`

Whitespace is defined in XML as being one of the four characters shown in Table 2.4. Combinations of linefeed and new line are used by operating systems to position the cursor at the start of the next line. Apple's Mac OS uses `carriage return`, `CR`, Unix systems use `linefeed`, `LF`, and Microsoft Windows uses `carriage return` followed by `linefeed`, `CR LF`.

When creating XML that is intended for human readers, for instance the sample code in this book, most authors indent elements to represent the structure of the data. This indentation is created using either tabs or spaces. Each new element tends to appear on a new line and content may span several lines. None of this formatting means anything to the parser. Indeed, XML created for the use of computers by software on other computers won't usually be formatted. When XML is parsed, all the whitespace, which humans like, is removed and the document treated as if it were created by a machine.

The problem that whitespace causes for application developers is that the parser must know which whitespace characters are significant. These characters should be made available to stylesheets and other publishing applications. Whitespace that the application *must* receive from the parser is called *significant* or *preservable* whitespace. Whitespace that the parser can strip out and not pass to the application is called *ignorable* whitespace.

2.4.3.1 Preserving Whitespace Sometimes data has to be formatted in a particular way. The formatting conveys meaning as well as aiding legibility. An example of this might be the inclusion of a program listing inside an XML document. Listing 2.7 shows code being included within XML.

Listing 2.7 Including Source Code

```
<?xml version="1.0"?>

<program language="Java">
  <metadata>
```

```
    <author>Chris Bates</author>
    <date>16/01/02</date>
    <version>1.0</version>
  </metadata>

  <code xml:space="preserve">
    import java.io.*;

    class Hello {
      public static void main(String[] args) {
        System.out.println("Hello everybody!");
        System.exit(0);
      }
    }
  </code>
</program>
```

The default behavior in XML is for whitespace to be *normalized*. When runs of more than one whitespace character occur, these are converted to a single space character. This is said to *collapse* the space. As a rule this behavior is desirable. If you load the previous example into a browser such as Mozilla, the text is collapsed onto a single line. This seems at odds with the idea that the parser should preserve whitespace. In fact, though, it may do so but when it passes the result to the HTML rendering engine for display *it* will collapse the whitespace. Two different and contradictory behaviors are being exhibited by the same application, yet both are correct.

The easiest way of making the parser preserve whitespace is to use the `xml:space` attribute. This can be applied to any element and given one of two values. The value of the attribute may be `default` or `preserve`. When set to `preserve`, the parser will leave all whitespace characters inside the element. When set to `default`, in most situations, the whitespace inside the element is normalized. You'll see throughout the book that developers can control the presentation of whitespace in the output of XSLT transformations. For straightforward XML applications, the whitespace is either there or it isn't. To use `xml:space` easily, it should be declared in a DTD. Without introducing any of the complexity of DTDs, here's a simple example:

```
<!ELEMENT code (#PCDATA)>
   <!ATTRIBUTE code xml:space #FIXED "preserve">
```

When this DTD document is available alongside the XML document, all whitespace is left inside `code` elements. It would also be preserved in subelements of `code`, if that element had any. Because the attribute has been explicitly declared in the DTD and assigned a default value, it does not have to be used in the XML document. Thus the code below is equivalent output to Listing 2.7.

```
<?xml version="1.0"?>

<program language="Java">
  <metadata>
    <author>Chris Bates</author>
    <date>16/01/02</date>
    <version>1.0</version>
  </metadata>

  <code>
    import java.io.*;

    class Hello {
      public static void main(String[] args) {
        System.out.println("Hello everybody!");
        System.exit(0);
      }
    }
  </code>
</program>
```

I'll discuss how to add whitespace to an output document using XSLT in Chapter 8.

2.5 THE RECIPE BOOK

XML can be used in many different ways. These could be demonstrated using a series of trivial examples. Unfortunately, unless small examples are very well defined, they often fail to include all of the key points that need discussing. Throughout this book I'm going to take an alternative approach and use two substantial, and realistic, XML applications. Each has a different style and approach. Using the two examples will demonstrate many of the practical aspects of XML and related technologies.

The first XML application is a simple recipe book. XML is often used to create structured, hierarchical data sets. A recipe book is one common example of this type of data. Recipes are organized into categories, although these may sometimes be quite arbitrary. For instance a beef chilli may be placed into categories such as Meat Recipes, Beef, Chilli,

Mexican Food, Spicy Food or Main Meals. A vegetarian chilli would fit into a different, but overlapping, set of categories, as shown in Figure 2.2.

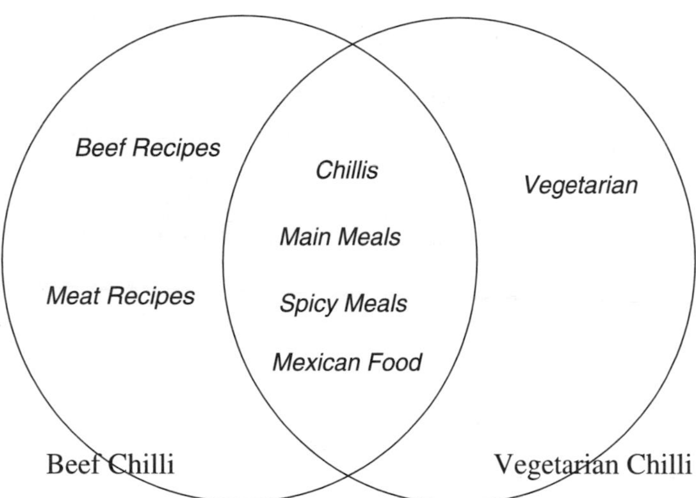

Figure 2.2 Sets Containing Types of Chilli

This demonstrates one of the great things about XML: flexibility. Each developer is free to choose their own approach. Even if two developers are working from the same document structure, each of their applications can be created to work in its own way. This flexibility is also one of the worst things about XML. When applications are exchanging data no assumptions can be made about the meaning or content of that data. In the Recipe Book example in Listing 2.8, categories of recipe are found below the document root. Each category has at least one title and a set of recipes. There's no restriction on what categories are available. When applications are developed to handle this XML, they must assume that all categories are equally valid. Provided documents follow the rules of XML and of the DTD for this application, the content they hold will be processed. There are ways of restricting the set of values that attributes can hold. These will be demonstrated in Chapter 3 but they are not really suitable for situations where hundreds of possible values may be permitted.

In some situations, the flexible rules can lead to confusion. For instance in a Recipe Book, a vegetarian recipe might also be found in a category such as meat-free. Being meat-free doesn't make a meal vegetarian. Vegetarian meals are a particular subset of both meat-free and fish-free meals. Applications creating or handling this data must allow for all of the cultural and linguistic nuances which are carried with it.

> **Note:**
> XML documents are sometimes called self-documenting. As we can see when discussing recipes, they are not. You must comment your XML so that it is properly documented.

Listing 2.8 A Recipe Book

```
<?xml version="1.0"?>

<cookbook>
<category>
    <title>bread</title>
    <recipe>
      <name>The Basic Loaf</name>
      <ingredient>
        <quantity amount="825" unit="ml" />
        <name>Warm water</name>
      </ingredient>
      <ingredient>
        <quantity amount="20" unit="g" />
        <name>Granulated Dried Yeast</name>
      </ingredient>
      <ingredient>
        <quantity amount="20" />
        <name>Sugar</name>
      </ingredient>
      <ingredient>
        <quantity amount="450" />
        <name>Stoneground wholemeal flour</name>
      </ingredient>
      <ingredient>
        <quantity amount="900" />
        <name>Strong white bread flour</name>
      </ingredient>
      <ingredient>
        <quantity amount="20" />
        <name>Salt</name>
      </ingredient>
      <ingredient>
```

```
        <quantity amount="55" />
        <name>Fresh Lard</name>
      </ingredient>
      <cooking>
        <note>Bake at gas number 8 for 15 minutes</note>
        <note>Bake at 230c for 15 minutes</note>
      </cooking>
      <method>
        <instruction>Add the yeast and sugar to the warm water
           and leave to activate</instruction>
        <instruction>Sieve the flour and salt into a large bowl
           </instruction>
        <instruction>Crumble the lard into the flour until it
           has a &quot;breadcrumb&quot; texture</instruction>
        <instruction>Mix all of the liquid into the flour</
           instruction>
        <instruction>Turn onto floured surface and knead for
            300 strokes</instruction>
        <instruction>Form into a ball, place in a warm place
           until doubled in size</instruction>
        <instruction>Knead the dough once more. This time for
            100 strokes</instruction>
        <instruction>Form into a ball, place in a warm place
           until doubled in size</instruction>
        <instruction>Form into five loaves and leave to rise for
            30 minutes</instruction>
        <instruction>Bake!</instruction>
      </method>
    </recipe>
  </category>
</cookbook>
```

The code for the Recipe Book is, on the whole, straightforward.[8] Notice that the `quantity` element is always empty. I could have made it into a container, then made `amount` and `unit` into subelements of it. In my opinion they work better as attributes; certainly the structure of this XML is simpler because they are used that way.

I spent some time thinking about how to design the following section:

[8] I haven't commented it simply because that takes too much space for inclusion in a textbook.

```
<cooking>
  <note>Bake at gas number 8 for 15 minutes</note>
  <note>Bake at 230c for 15 minutes</note>
</cooking>
```

Most recipes have some information about cooking times, temperatures and so on. These differ between oven types and are not always complete. Indeed, they may differ between countries. When using this example structure in the past, I have built complex element trees to try to encapsulate cooking instructions. These efforts have not really been successful which is why I'm including the `<note></note>` element here. This is meant to be a free format text field in which any type of information can be entered. The main limitation of this approach is that this part of the document can no longer be searched. That's not a great problem, as few cooks will ever hunt through their recipes looking for meals which can be baked at 230 Celsius. The notes field also has the advantage that it can be used to provide more complex information. For instance, a `<note>` can be used in a recipe for Tarte Tatin where the food is cooked in a pan on the hob and the whole thing, including the pan, transferred to the oven.

When the Recipe Book is turned into a full database with large numbers of recipes in many different categories, it can easily be made into a fully searchable, Web-enabled application. By the end of this book, much of the necessary work will have been outlined for you.

2.6 THE BUSINESS LETTER

The Recipe Book is a good example of the use of XML to structure hierarchical data. XML can also be used for much simpler data structures. One use for markup is to identify the component parts of a document. This may be done so that the document can be typeset and printed, as in the LaTeX typesetting system, or so that the document can be archived, indexed and later retrieved. The latter type of markup is increasingly required on corporate intranet systems where memos and reports are created, transmitted and stored electronically.

XML has a role to play whether the finished document will be typeset or indexed. The origins of XML within the SGML community fit exactly into these applications, and make XML a good solution to both problems. You may wonder why documents which will eventually be printed can't be prepared in a common application such as a word processor. The standard SGML/XML answer is that they can but doing so may lead to difficulties in the future. The largest problem in the field is the obsolescence of software. Large organizations around the world have gigabytes of document data which was created using software packages that are no longer available. Often these packages run on systems which have, themselves, been consigned to history. Yet the content of the documents, which in truth is why they were created, may remain important today – even if it cannot be accessed. XML offers a solution to these problems. Because XML is a plain text format, based on open standards, data structured using it will be available for the foreseeable future.

The Business Letter is a typical application of XML. The following code gives an example of just such a letter.

Listing 2.9 A Business Letter in XML

```
<?xml version="1.0"?>

<letter title="Your complaint of 03/03/00">
    <header>
      <metadata>
        <keyword value="complaint" />
        <keyword value="trouser press" />
        <keyword value="waffle maker" />
      </metadata>
      <sender>
        <name>
          <title>Mr.</title>
          <firstname>William</firstname>
          <firstname>James</firstname>
          <surname>Smiggins</surname>
        </name>
        <address>
          <line1>Bill Smiggins Incorporated</line1>
          <line2>Unit 5</line2>
          <line3>Tax Havens Industrial Park</line3>
          <city>Enterprise City</city>
          <state>California</state>
          <code>CA 11223</code>
        </address>
      </sender>
      <recipient>
        <name>
          <firstname>Bill</firstname>
          <surname>Gates</surname>
```

```
    </name>
    <address>
      <line1>Microsoft Inc.</line1>
      <city>Seattle</city>
      <country>United States</country>
    </address>
  </recipient>
  <date>
    <dayname>Thursday</dayname>
    <day>27</day>
    <month>December</month>
    <year>2001</year>
  </date>
  <signature>
    <greeting type="formal"/>
    <name>
      <firstname>Bill</firstname>
    </name>
  </signature>
</header>

<content>
  <para>Here at Bill Smiggins Inc. we're really proud of our
      ten-year reputation for the development of quality
     products. We're sorry to hear that you were unhappy
     with the Combined Trouser Press and Waffle Maker that
     you recently purchased from us. I can only restate that
      it was in full working order when we shipped, and the
     presence of fluff in your breakfast waffles was as much
      of a shock to us, as we're sure it was to you.</para>

  <para>If you return the Combined Trouser Press and Waffle
     Maker in its original packaging, we'll arrange a full
     refund<footnote><para>Please note, we will not pay the
     cost of shipping goods back to us.</para></footnote>.</
     para>
```

```
    <para>Bill Smiggins Inc. Giving you the <emphasis>quality
       </emphasis> of service you deserve.</para>
  </content>

</letter>
```

The business letter has two sections. The `header` holds information about the letter such as who wrote it, and to whom it was sent. The `content` section of the letter holds the actual data intended for the recipient. These are placed inside `para` elements. Conventionally each of these would hold a paragraph of text, some of which can be modified by placing it inside `emphasis` elements. When rendered for printing, the content of the `emphasis` elements would probably be formatted in an italic or bold font. Since this Business Letter is only an example, it has few refinements, although it does allow for the presence of footnotes within the letter. We'll see in Chapter 9, that not only can these be presented at the bottom of the letter, they can also be numbered. Including tables, lists or images in the `content` section would be useful additions. The sender's address would be required in many different letters, therefore it could profitably be an external entity. Using external entities for common content will lead to fewer transcription errors and make for a more robust set of documents.

The structure of the Business Letter is designed with two goals in mind. Firstly, it needs to include all of the data that is necessary for indexing and retrieval. Years after writing a series of letters, you may need to find all of those that relate to a particular product or event. To allow for this eventuality, I have included a `metadata` section which holds `keyword` elements. Each letter would be stored in a separate file so this XML structure is not suitable for use as a database. With many XML applications, developers can create database-style facilities without a significant overhead. This is no exception. Faced with many letters spread around an intranet, retrieving those that are relevant is straightforward.

Exercises

1. Write an XML document which contains your name and address. Open the file in as many Web browsers as you can. Which ones provide meaningful or usable output? Which do nothing useful?

2. Why does XML require adherence to such a rigorous set of rules to control the structure and form of documents?

3. XML and HTML share a common ancestor in SGML. HTML documents work in Web browsers even if badly, or incorrectly, formatted. Why don't Web browsers require compliance with the language?

4. List some of the differences between programming languages such as Pascal, and markup languages such as XML.

5. XML is a Recommendation of the W3C not an internationally agreed standard. What advantages are there to the W3C approach?

6. Why must XML tags be properly nested?

7. XML supports Unicode data. Why is Unicode more suitable for Web applications than ASCII or EBCDIC? How does Unicode solve one of the problems that you might have identified with ASCII?

8. What are character entities? Try to find a comprehensive list of those which can be used in XML documents.

9. Enter the XML code for the business letter application. Try loading it into a modern Web browser, does it display properly?

10. Can you find any ways in which the structure of the business letter might be improved? Make those changes then view you new document in a browser.

Chapter 3

Document Type Definitions

Deciding on an XML structure is only part of the process of developing an XML application. Developers and users need to be able to create documents that conform to a fixed structure. XML documents need to be written against a formal set of rules which can be used to guarantee their structure. Validating parsers can check that the XML conforms to these rules. If the rules are made available whenever, and wherever, the document is used, any processing performed by any application on that document is likely to be more accurate. Two technologies exist for defining XML grammars: Document Type Definitions (DTDs) and XML Schema. XML Schema is the newer technology, one that is often called a *pure XML solution*. It's certainly both fully featured and complex. I'll be examining XML Schema in detail in Chapter 4. It's worth noting that when you need to validate a document, you will currently need to supply a DTD since few tools have support for XML Schema. This is starting to change, more tools are being developed, but DTDs will have a place and a purpose for the foreseeable structure.

Document type definitions, DTDs, have been in use for as long as SGML has. In fact, DTDs are probably the most important aspect of SGML left in XML. A DTD describes the formal rules of the structure of the document. It lists those elements, attributes and entities that can be used in a document and shows how they may be used in relation to each other. The structure of an XML document is, logically, a tree. The DTD outlines that tree structure, although it is not, itself, a tree. Within the document, each element may be compulsory, optional, occur just once or be repeated a number of times. Elements can also be reused and may occur throughout a document in a variety of contexts.

A DTD is primarily a hierarchy of elements. It defines their relationships to each other, their attributes and their contents. DTDs are not XML applications, and do not use the XML syntax. They have their own structure and syntax which are easily mastered. That's not to say that writing DTDs is easy. Once you have created a suitable document structure; putting it into DTD syntax is not hard, but developing the structure in the first place can be a challenging task. A good document structure can only be created following detailed analysis of requirements and of existing structures and best practice. DTDs exist for many different applications and the best solution for a particular problem may be to use one of these. The DTD that you are basing your work on may need to be extended or modified. Why not always build a DTD from the ground up? If you get a system into production and the DTD has to be changed, you may find parts of the system simply stop working. You need to be sure in advance that the DTD you are using is solid and accurate. When I discuss the DTDs I wrote for the Business Letter and Recipe Book, you'll see some of the design decisions, and compromises, that have to be made. Remember those are just trivial examples. Unlike a Web business, I don't have millions of dollars, euros or yen worth of business riding on them.

I'm going to show you how to structure a DTD and demonstrate each of the components that you might use in one. I'll then show you the DTDs for the Business Letter and Recipe Book applications and describe their structure. I'll also look at some of the decisions I took when designing them.

3.1 STRUCTURE

The DTD is a series of declarations. Each declaration takes the form:

```
<!        >
```

and contains one of four keywords. These are:

- `ELEMENT` which defines a tag,
- `ATTRIBUTE` which defines an attribute of an `ELEMENT`,
- `ENTITY` which is used to define an `ENTITY`,
- `NOTATION` which defines a data type.

The easiest way to understand the structure of a DTD is to look at a simplified one. Rather than create a novel structure, I'm going to use part of the DTD for the Business Letter. This is shown in Listing 3.1.

Listing 3.1 Partial DTD for the Business Letter

```
<!DOCTYPE letter [
  <!ELEMENT letter (address)>
  <!ELEMENT address (line1, line2?, line3*, city, (county|state)
     ?, country?, code?)>
  <!ELEMENT line1 (#PCDATA)>
  <!ELEMENT line2 (#PCDATA)>
  <!ELEMENT line3 (#PCDATA)>
  <!ELEMENT city (#PCDATA)>
  <!ELEMENT county (#PCDATA)>
  <!ELEMENT state (#PCDATA)>
  <!ELEMENT country (#PCDATA)>
  <!ELEMENT code (#PCDATA)>
]>
```

The DTD describes the structure of the XML document, starting with the *root node*. All XML documents must have a single root node which holds all their content and which has the same name as the top-level name in the Doctype element of the DTD. In this case, the root node is `letter`. Look back at Listing 2.9 if you need to confirm this structure.

3.2 ELEMENTS

Each tag in the XML structure is declared as an `ELEMENT`. Each element may contain either data or further elements, and may also have attributes. Starting at the beginning of the document, although the root node has already been used, its structure must be declared as the first element:

```
<!ELEMENT letter (address)>
```

I've changed this declaration slightly. The full DTD for the Business Letter is rather more complex than this example, as you'll see if you skip ahead to Section 3.8. The content of the `ELEMENT` follows its name and is placed into parentheses as shown above. The content forms a set of items separated using either commas or the pipe character, |. In the previous example that set contained just one item, `address`. Items within the set may include: elements, sets of other elements from which only one item may be present in the document, and content. This set is called a *content model*.

In the example, the `letter` element, the root node, has another element as its content:

```
<!ELEMENT letter (address)>
```

3.2.1 Sequence and Selection

In turn, the address element contains all of the components that we would expect to find there.[1] The symbols in the following example are described in Table 3.1.

```
<!ELEMENT address (line1, line2?, line3*, city, (county|state)?,
   country?, code?)>
```

Inside the parentheses is an unordered list of element names. Each is separated by a comma. The comma means that all of these items may be present in the XML document. Their presence, or absence, is controlled by the symbol that appears after the element name. Elements can appear in any order in the XML itself, provided that they follow the <address> tag, appear before </address> and are properly nested within the element. From a maintenance point of view, putting the elements in their logical order is probably a good idea, though.

The nesting of elements within the XML document is important since it provides structure. Element ordering is not important since it has no structural implications. To a human reader, having city appear before line1 in an address might seem peculiar, but that does not mean that those elements cannot be stored in either possible order. It just means that applications that process the XML need to be written to take account of the needs of the user. If line1 *has* to appear before city, the application extracting the data needs to make that happen. The application that created the data probably doesn't need to care.

In the middle of the content of the address element, you should have noticed:

```
(county|state)?
```

The vertical bar, the pipe character, means *OR*. It is used to separate items in groups where only one of those items can appear in the XML document. The parentheses are used in this case because the set of optional items occurs inside another set. They are used for grouping, if those parentheses were absent then the meaning of the code would alter. In fact, in this case, it wouldn't make sense. If all of the content of the element forms a set of options only one pair of parentheses is needed:

```
<!ELEMENT address (line1 | line2 | line3 | city)>
```

[1]Remember about context and meaning? In this context *address* means a location, not a public oration.

3.2.2 Text Content

So far I've looked at elements that contain other elements. There comes a point, though, at which elements must contain data. The data inside an element will be *parsed character data*. This is data comprised of characters which *will* be passed through XML parsers. Because the data is being parsed it cannot contain characters such as < which form part of XML markup. Such characters must be replaced with character entities. Parsed character data is shown in this example:

```
<!ELEMENT line1 (#PCDATA)>
```

Some elements may contain either character data or other elements. This is known as a *mixed content* model. Here is an example in which the element may contain character data, or a `house_number` element or a `street_name` element.

```
<!ELEMENT line1 (#PCDATA | house_number | street_name)*>
```

Mixed content always takes the same form. The first item in the list must be `#PCDATA`. The content must be a list of options, separated by a pipe and followed with an asterisk indicating that zero or more instances of the element may be present. This is part of the XML standard, so if you don't obey this rule your parser will complain. Loudly.

3.2.3 Repetition

Some elements occur just once, others occur more often. Some may not appear at all. The DTD author needs to be able to specify how often each element will appear in the document. Since the exact content of the XML document is not known when the DTD is written, specifying that an element appears, for instance, four times is not possible. Instead, authors just state that an element repeats. Repetition can happen in two cases. In the first, an element may appear *at least* once. In the second case elements may appear multiple times or not at all. Notice that the latter also lets the item appear just once. In DTDs there are often several ways of writing the same thing. Just because your DTD is different to one someone else may write for the same application doesn't mean that one is right and the other wrong. Table 3.1 shows the symbols that you can use in your DTD – and what they mean. You can see these being used in Section 3.7.

3.3 ATTRIBUTES

Some XML elements have attributes. Attributes give additional information about the element or its content, which is not, itself, part of the element. Each attribute must be declared separately and associated with an element. The attribute declaration is identified by the keyword `ATTLIST`.

Table 3.1 Symbols Used in DTDs

Symbol	Example	Meaning
Asterisk	`item*`	The item appears zero or more times.
Comma	`(item1, item2, item3)`	Separates items in a sequence in the order in which they appear.
None	`item`	Item appears exactly once.
Parentheses	`(item1, item2)`	Encloses a group of items.
Pipe	`(item1 | item2)`	Separates a set of alternatives. Only one may appear.
Plus	`item+`	Item appears at least once.
Question Mark	`item?`	The item appears once or not at all.

`<!ATTLIST element attribute type default>`

The `element` is the name of the element to which the attribute applies. This is followed by the attribute name. The `type` is an XML data type taken from the attribute being declared. Attribute types are listed in Table 3.2. Finally the default value for the attribute is given. Possible defaults are listed in Table 3.3.

The fragment of DTD given in Listing 3.1 doesn't have any attributes. The following code modifies the `country` element to include some attributes:

```
<!ELEMENT country (#PCDATA)>
  <!ATTLIST country
      continent (Europe | Asia | Africa | North America) "Asia"
      language CDATA #IMPLIED>
```

Two attributes have been added to the element. The `continent` attribute has an enumerated list of possible values. A default value, `Asia`, is given. If the `continent` attribute is omitted, this default value is assumed to apply. The second new attribute is `language`. This takes text, `CDATA`, as its value. The `language` attribute has the default value `IMPLIED`. This means that it is optional and may be left out of the XML.

3.4 ENTITIES

In Section 2.3.4 I discussed the role of entities within XML documents. Entities have to be defined in the DTD before they can be used in an XML document. Once an entity has been defined it can be referenced as the value of an attribute. The attribute becomes, in effect,

Table 3.2 XML Attribute Types

Type	Usage
CDATA	The attribute can only accept character data. This data will *not* be parsed.
ENTITY	The value of the attribute is a reference to an entity. The entity must be declared elsewhere in the DTD.
ENTITIES	Multiple entities can be referenced. They must be separated, within the list, by whitespace.
ID	The attribute uniquely identifies a location within the document.
IDREF	The attribute references an ID which is declared elsewhere in the DTD. IDs may be used for hyperlinking within an XML document.
IDREFS	Works like `IDREF` but a list of IDs can be linked to. Items in the list must be separated by whitespace.
NMTOKEN	The attribute value can be any word or token. The value may contain any combination of numbers, letters, periods, dashes, colons or underscores.
NMTOKENS	A list of space-separated `NMTOKEN` values.
NOTATION	The value of the attribute is a `NOTATION` which is declared elsewhere in the DTD.
Enumeration	A list of possible values is given. The list must be in parentheses with its items separated by pipes. The value of the attribute must be one of the items in the list.

Table 3.3 XML Attribute Defaults

Default	Usage
#REQUIRED	A value *must* be given for each element that has this attribute.
#IMPLIED	The attribute is optional; no value has to be given.
`#FIXED` value	The attribute has to have the value given. If the attribute is omitted from the element, it is assumed to be equal to the value.
Default	A default value is given for the attribute. Other values may be given in the XML document, but if the attribute is omitted it is assumed to have the default value.

an entity reference. When manipulating the XML, the attribute is replaced with the value of the entity. Entities do not have to be specified as part of an attribute. XML documents can contain both internal and external entities as described in Section 2.3.4. Before an entity can be used, it has to be declared in the DTD. An *ENTITY* may be declared in a number of different ways:

```
<!ENTITY name definition>
<!ENTITY name SYSTEM system_identifier [NOTATION]>
<!ENTITY name PUBLIC [public_identifier] system_identifier
[NOTATION]>
```

The simplest definition is for an *internal entity*. Both the entity and its content are declared in the DTD. Wherever the entity is referenced in the XML document, the content specified in the DTD will be substituted for the reference. In defining an internal entity reference, the keyword `ENTITY` is followed by the name of the entity and then its content.

An entity may also be an *external reference*. Here the entity refers to content held outside of both the DTD and the XML file. External entities may be held on the same system as the XML file or on a remote system. Dealing with the easier case first, where the entity was developed by an individual or organization such as a company: following the keyword `ENTITY` and the name of the entity, the keyword `SYSTEM` is given. The location of the entity is then specified using a Uniform Resource Identifier, URI. The URI is an address for the file that holds the entity; it may be local or remote. When you surf the Web or if you've worked with HTML you will be familiar with URLs. A URI is effectively the same thing. A `NOTATION` may follow the URI. Notations are described in Section 3.5.

If the DTD was developed using an established standard, for instance from ISO or W3C, the keyword `PUBLIC` should be used instead of `SYSTEM`. A public identifier may then be given.[2] The public identifier may be used by applications that understand SGML catalogs to help them resolve the public identifier. If a library of standards is available, the processor will use this to identify the entity. Next a URI for the entity is given. If the public identifier could not be used to identify the entity, the URI will be used. Finally, an optional notation may be given.

Again, a simple modification to the sample DTD demonstrates the use of an `ENTITY`.

```
<!ENTITY locationmap SYSTEM "./images/home.png" NDATA PNG>
<!ELEMENT country (#PCDATA)>
  <!ATTLIST country
```

[2]The use of square brackets, `[...]`, indicates optional content.

```
        continent (Europe | Asia | Africa | North America) "Asia
            "
        language CDATA #IMPLIED
        location ENTITY &locationmap; >
```

In this example, the external entity references an image file. The entity is used as an attribute of the `country` element. When entities are used within XML documents or referenced in DTDs, they follow the same standard syntax: the name of the entity is preceded by an ampersand and followed by a semi-colon.

3.4.1 Parameter Entities

If a complex part of a DTD is repeated in a number of places, it may be replaced with a parameter entity. Once declared, the parameter entity can be referenced throughout the DTD. Using parameter entities can make DTDs easier to read, and easier to author.

```
<!ENTITY locationmap SYSTEM "./images/home.png" NDATA PNG>
<!ENTITY % continent "(Europe | Asia | Africa | North America)">

<!ELEMENT country (#PCDATA)>
  <!ATTLIST country
        continent %continent; "Asia"
        language CDATA #IMPLIED
        location ENTITY &locationmap; >
```

The parameter entity introduces a new symbol into the DTD. In the declaration, a percentage sign, `%`, is placed between the keyword `ENTITY` and the entity name. When the entity is referenced `%` is used instead of the normal reference symbol of ampersand, `&`. The semi-colon remains after the entity name.

3.5 NOTATIONS

When an entity contains non-XML data, the processor needs to know the object type and how to embed it in a document or otherwise deal with it. While a `NOTATION` declaration usually specifies an application to process the data, this is not required by the XML recommendation. Even if an application is specified, there is no requirement that it is actually able to handle the data. Here's a simple example of a `NOTATION` which identifies an application that can handle the image file in the last example:

```
<!NOTATION PNG SYSTEM "/usr/bin/display">
```

3.6 USING DTDS

A DTD may be declared in the same file as the XML. This isn't very convenient since you will usually want to use the same DTD for many documents, but is useful during development or if the DTD would otherwise be inaccessible. A DTD used like this is called an internal DTD. When they are located within the XML file, all Document Type Definitions begin in the same way. The content of the DTD is placed inside a declaration so it is surrounded by `<!    >`. The DTD starts with the keyword `DOCTYPE`, then the name of the *root* element of the document. Following the root node, the elements that make up the document are placed within `[ ]`. All internal DTDs, therefore, are enclosed inside:

```
<!DOCTYPE rootnode [

]>
```

3.6.1 External DTDs

When a DTD is to be reused, it should be placed in its own file which is placed on a system somewhere so that it will be accessible from many XML files. The structure of the DTD changes slightly as shown in Listing 3.2. By convention, Document Type Definitions are stored in files that have the extension `dtd`.

Listing 3.2 An External DTD

```
<?xml version="1.0" ?>

<!ELEMENT letter (address)>
<!ELEMENT address (line1, line2?, line3*, city, (county|state)?,
   country?, code?)>
<!ELEMENT line1 (#PCDATA)>
<!ELEMENT line2 (#PCDATA)>
<!ELEMENT line3 (#PCDATA)>
<!ELEMENT city (#PCDATA)>
<!ELEMENT county (#PCDATA)>
<!ELEMENT state (#PCDATA)>
<!ELEMENT country (#PCDATA)>
<!ELEMENT code (#PCDATA)>
```

`<!DOCTYPE rootnode SYSTEM|PUBLIC [public_identifier] URI>`

The external DTD needs to be referenced from the XML file. This is done using the Document Type *Declaration*. The declaration is placed inside `<!    >` and starts with the keyword DOCTYPE. This is followed by the name of the root node of the document. If the DTD is local to an individual or an organization, the keyword SYSTEM should appear next. If it is a standard, the keyword PUBLIC is used instead. Finally the URI of the DTD is given.

```
<?xml version="1.0" standalone="no" ?>

<!DOCTYPE letter SYSTEM "letter.dtd">
<!-- Rest of XML file here -->
```

If a validating parser, or an application capable of validating XML, is used, the parser may not be required to check the document against the DTD. If the XML document can stand on its own, the XML declaration should be modified to reflect this. The XML declaration has a standalone parameter which can be set to either yes or no.

3.6.2 Customizing DTDs

Sometimes you will want to use an existing DTD suitably modified to meet your needs. This is done through *inheritance*. Your DTD can reuse another one, called a *base DTD*, and adapt it. This has many advantages. If you are working within a business, for instance, you can create a global DTD for the whole company. This can be altered, ideally by adding elements, so that it meets the specific needs of individual departments or projects. The base DTD can thus be kept relatively simple. Listing 3.3 shows how the partial DTD from Listing 3.1 might be altered to add entities and attributes to the country element.

Listing 3.3 Modifying a Base DTD

```
<?xml version="1.0" ?>

<!DOCTYPE letter SYSTEM "letter.dtd" [
  <!ENTITY locationmap SYSTEM "./images/home.png" NDATA PNG>
  <!ENTITY % continent "(Europe | Asia | Africa | North America)
     ">

  <!ELEMENT country (#PCDATA)>
    <!ATTLIST country
         continent %continent; "Asia"
         language CDATA #IMPLIED
         location ENTITY &locationmap; >
]>
```

```
<letter>
  <!-- The XML goes here -->
</letter>
```

3.7 THE RECIPE BOOK

Designing a DTD is a non-trivial exercise, with a number of factors affecting the finished structure. These may include the amount of complexity that designers and users are willing to deal with, the tool support available and the nature of the problem domain. Let's consider each of those in turn. Firstly, complexity. XML is not just a grammar for defining languages that only machines ever encounter. The historical roots of XML, and some of its most common applications, lie in human-edited documents. The DocBook specification, discussed in Chapter 17, is used throughout the world to create technical documentation. It's possible that because of the adoption of DocBook by many Open Source projects, it is one of the most widely encountered XML applications currently in use. Generally, when working with an application such as DocBook, or when using XML in editors such as Framemaker, the user will need to select tags from lists and menus. The editor will make only those tags available which the DTD says are valid at a given point in the XML document. Figure 3.1 shows a composite image of how this works in Xemacs.[3]

If your XML documents are going to be edited by hand, you'll want to keep the DTD relatively simple. The reference for DocBook DTD, for instance, is over 400 pages long. Few users will ever be able to understand such complex documents. If your users are going to edit by hand, such long DTDs are completely impractical.

Increasingly, good tool support will be provided for XML development. Many companies that develop desktop applications are moving to XML for their storage format. Applications such as Microsoft Office are moving to XML as their standard format. With programs like those found in office suites, the user will never see the XML. Often, they won't even be aware that the application they are using is based on XML. Therefore, the DTD can be far more complex.

Finally, there is the application domain. Again, a more complex domain will require more complex data structures.

The Recipe Book has a straightforward structure. A recipe contains basically two types of information: a list of ingredients and a list of instructions. The Recipe Book extends this structure slightly. Recipes can be organized into categories as shown in Figure 2.2. This presents the first challenge to a document designer. The recipe appears at first sight to be

[3]For Emacs/Xemacs users, I'm using PSGML mode.

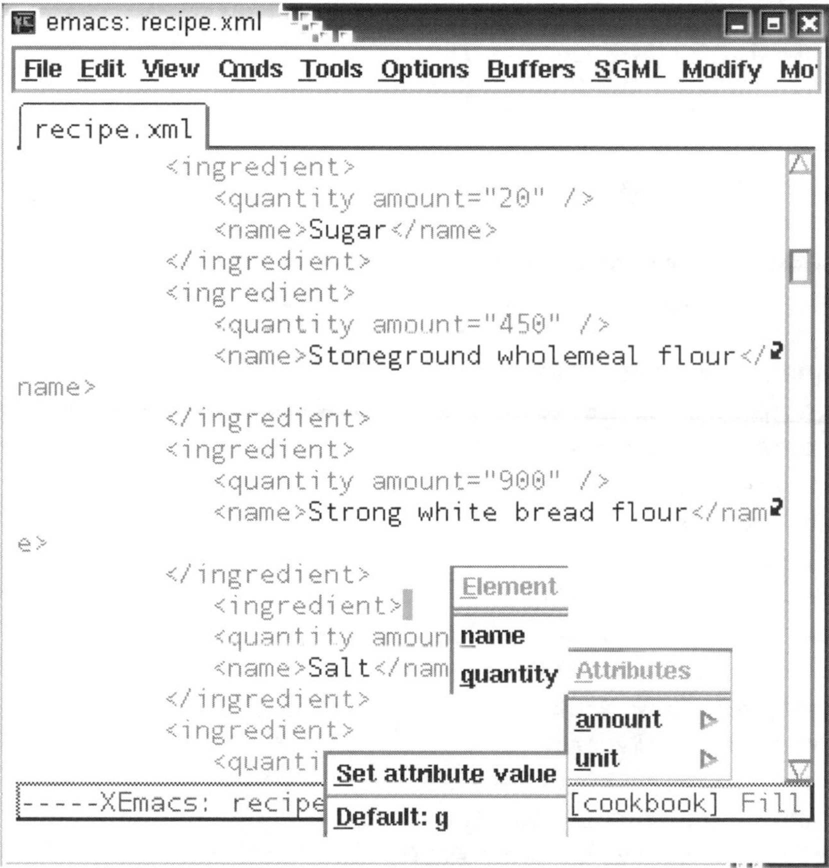

Figure 3.1 Editing XML in Xemacs

an element of category. A recipe for Vegetable Broth would clearly belong in the category *soup* but not all choices are so clear cut. Consider a recipe for Chicken Korma. This may fit into several categories, including: Curry, Poultry, Spicy, Main Meals, Indian Food. If recipe is an element of category, Chicken Korma can only go into one of those categories.

Is there an alternative? Of course there is. Why not make category an *attribute* or subelement of recipe? If that is done, all recipes stand alone; they are not organized into any form of hierarchy. If the category subelement is allowed to repeat, the recipe can be linked to many different categories. This is immediately appealing, but the hierarchical structure maps onto traditional cookbooks. It also means that each category *could* be kept in a separate file. The Recipe Book would be built by assembling these individual files into a single document. In the DTD in Listing 3.4 I have used the hierarchical approach both because I prefer its structure, and because it maps on to the way cookery books tend to be ordered.

Listing 3.4 The Document Type Definition For The Recipe Book

```
<!DOCTYPE cookbook [
  <!ELEMENT cookbook (category+)>
  <!ELEMENT category (title+, recipe+)>
  <!ELEMENT title (#PCDATA)>
  <!ELEMENT recipe (name, ingredient+, cooking*, serves?, method)
     >
  <!ELEMENT name (#PCDATA)>
  <!ELEMENT ingredient (quantity*, name)>
  <!ELEMENT quantity (#PCDATA)>
  <!ATTLIST quantity
    amount CDATA #REQUIRED
    unit CDATA "g">
  <!ELEMENT unit (#PCDATA)>
  <!ELEMENT amount (#PCDATA)>
  <!ELEMENT name (#PCDATA)>
  <!ELEMENT cooking (note+)>
  <!ELEMENT note (#PCDATA)>
  <!ELEMENT serves (#PCDATA)>
  <!ELEMENT method (instruction+)>
  <!ELEMENT instruction (#PCDATA)>
]>
```

In this DTD, a cookbook is made from multiple categories. The category element has to appear at least once, as indicated by the + sign. This places a restriction on the way that the DTD can be used. I am forcing users to put all recipes inside a category. This might be regarded as an unreasonable assumption; after all, I've just said that the category *could* be an attribute of the recipe. Here the DTD designer is faced with another facet of DTD development. By creating a set of rules to define the structure of the document, restrictions are being imposed upon the developers who will use these structures.

A category comprises at least one title and at least one recipe. The number if inclusions of the recipe element could have been indicated with an asterisk. That symbol means that the element can be present as often as needed, including zero. There's no point having a category that doesn't hold any recipes, therefore I force each category to have at least one. Again, here's a restriction which dictates how applications must process the document. If I allowed zero or more recipes in a category, a template application could be set up in which all potential categories were already present. Recipes could be added as required.

In my version, when an application tries to add a recipe to a non-existent category, a new one must be created.

Moving along, each ingredient has zero or more quantity elements and exactly one name. Multiple quantities are allowed since weights and measures *might* be specified using Imperial, Metric or some other system. In the UK, weights are often specified in pounds and ounces. Throughout most of the world, grams and kilograms are used. In North America, recipes often specify cups rather than weights. Ideally, any recipe would specify each of the different systems for weights and measures. Each user could then be shown the one most appropriate to their locale. The quantity has two attributes: one for the unit being used, and one for the amount. These could be subelements but, since they are really properties of the quantity, they work better as attributes.

3.8 BUSINESS LETTER

The Business Letter is a much simpler proposition than the Recipe Book. Each letter stands alone. I'm not imposing any database-style features here. I don't feel that there is much sense in storing all letters under a single structure since they tend to be independent items. This could be questioned; surely all letters sent to, or received from, one person could profitably be stored in a single file. Of course this structure would be useful in some circumstances. Generally, though, I don't think it would be very useful.

Why might letters be stored? Retrieving and reviewing letters after they are written, often years later, is important to many people but this doesn't, necessarily, need a database. When a system has to manipulate large numbers of text documents, one effective technique is to store each document in its original file and to create an index which points to those files. Consider an archive of letters. Indexes could be created based upon keywords, sender, recipient or the date that the letter was written. Using XML to structure the letters makes building indexes relatively trivial.[4]

The Document Type Definition for the Business Letter application is shown in Listing 3.5. A letter has two components. Firstly, there's a header which holds information such as the addresses of the sender and recipient. The header includes a date element which is broken down into optional subelements. The date is broken down because it can then be stored and manipulated in different ways.

Listing 3.5 The Document Type Definition for the Business Letter

```
<!DOCTYPE letter[
  <!ELEMENT letter (header, content)>
```

[4]Large systems, such as corporate intranets, require the additional facilities a database provides.

```
    <!ATTLIST letter title CDATA #IMPLIED>
  <!ELEMENT sender (name, address?)>
  <!ELEMENT recipient (name, address?)>
  <!ELEMENT name (title?, firstname*, surname)>
  <!ELEMENT address (line1, line2?, line3*, city, (county|state)
     ?, country?, code?)>
  <!ELEMENT date (dayname?, day?, month?, year?)>
  <!ELEMENT signature (greeting, (name | firstname))>
  <!ELEMENT header (metadata*, sender, recipient, date, signature
     )>
  <!ELEMENT content (para+, footnote*)>
  <!ELEMENT para (#PCDATA | emphasis)*>
  <!ELEMENT footnote (para+)>
  <!ELEMENT title (#PCDATA)>
  <!ELEMENT firstname (#PCDATA)>
  <!ELEMENT surname (#PCDATA)>
  <!ELEMENT line1 (#PCDATA)>
  <!ELEMENT line2 (#PCDATA)>
  <!ELEMENT line3 (#PCDATA)>
  <!ELEMENT city (#PCDATA)>
  <!ELEMENT county (#PCDATA)>
  <!ELEMENT state (#PCDATA)>
  <!ELEMENT country (#PCDATA)>
  <!ELEMENT code (#PCDATA)>
  <!ELEMENT dayname (#PCDATA)>
  <!ELEMENT day (#PCDATA)>
  <!ELEMENT month (#PCDATA)>
  <!ELEMENT year (#PCDATA)>
  <!ELEMENT emphasis (#PCDATA)>
  <!ELEMENT greeting (#PCDATA)>
  <!ATTLIST greeting
    type (formal | informal | other) "formal">
  <!ELEMENT metadata (keyword+)>
  <!ELEMENT keyword (#PCDATA)>
    <!ATTLIST keyword value CDATA #REQUIRED>
]>
```

The header section of the letter includes a signature element. All letters have to end with a salutation. In English this might be *Yours Sincerely* or *Yours Faithfully*. We don't want to include this in the text of every letter. A much easier solution is to make this information part of the header and let the processing application place the information correctly. The header also includes optional metadata, which is made from keywords and associated values. Metadata simplifies the process of indexing and archiving the letters.

Letter content is made from paragraphs and footnotes. While few personal letters actually use footnotes, they can be useful in business. This is a very simplistic structure for the content of a letter. Useful extensions to it might include provision for lists, tables or images within the content. I've omitted these for the sake of clarity. If you wanted to extend this structure, I would recommend looking at the way that DocBook, as described in Chapter 17, handles them. A further refinement would be to make the addresses, greeting and salutation into external entities. These could then be used in any number of documents without the need to enter the same information repeatedly in each.

Exercises

1. Write a DTD for the name and address structure which you created at the end of Chapter 2. If you are unable to make your DTD match the structure of your document, modify the document so that it is simpler.
2. Why is it necessary to create a formal definition for the structure of XML documents.
3. Describe three advantages and three disadvantages which DTDs have when compared to alternatives such as XML Schema.
4. Research the structures used for addresses in the US, Japan and Brazil. Can you modify your DTD so that it supports all of those forms?
5. Why do DTD files use their own syntax and structure rather than being written as XML documents?
6. What is the difference between `PCDATA` and `CDATA`?
7. Why are entities used in DTDs?
8. Try to find software which can be used to validate XML documents against their DTDs. Is you name and address structure valid?
9. If you modified the business letter at the end of Chapter 2, modify the DTD to match the new structure.

Chapter 4

Specifying XML Structures Using Schema

We've already seen that XML documents can be described using Document Type Definitions, DTDs. DTDs originated with SGML and show those origins all too visibly. XML documents are far more complex and varied than their SGML cousins because XML is used in far more ways than SGML. This creates a problem. While DTDs are perfectly suitable for SGML, where they have been used successfully for many years, they are inappropriate for the newer technology of XML. DTDs cannot be processed by XML-only applications. Developers need to learn two relatively complex languages to use DTDs and they cannot be validated using XML validators. XML has more data types than can be expressed in DTDs, and is generally far richer. Basically DTDs cannot be used to express XML documents.

To remedy this situation, W3C has created a language called XML Schema which can be used to define XML structures. A number of different schema languages exist. In this chapter I will be writing specifically about XML Schema because it is a Recommendation of W3C. I'll be using the terms XML Schema and schema interchangeably – my choice being based purely upon which reads better in a given context. If I wanted to be precise all of the time I would use XML Schema when referring to the language and Recommendation, and schema when referring to a particular document that uses the language.

As I write this, far more tools exist to handle DTDs than XML Schema. This situation is changing rapidly since everyone sees the advantages of using schemas. DTDs are really a technical dead-end, although understanding them will remain important since so many exist. It's likely that when you are using older documents, they'll continue to be described using DTDs. New documents should *always* be described using XML Schema.[1]

The most important omission in the DTD is the idea of a data type. SGML documents tend to contain mostly plain text. Almost all data in an SGML application can be treated as strings of characters in definitions and applications. XML documents require a far richer set of data types, including strings of characters, numbers, both whole and decimal, and complex types such as dates and times. XML Schema introduces data types which, in turn, leads to more tightly defined XML structures which can be used with current database technologies or in conventional applications written in general-purpose programming languages. Other new, and useful, features in the XML Schema Recommendation include:

- a simple pattern matching grammar which might be used, for example, to define the structure of an order code,
- defined ordering of subelements so that document structure can be tightly controlled,
- selection between different elements so that documents can share a schema without having identical structure.

DTDs are described using their own, unique, syntax. Using them means having to learn, and apply, two sets of syntactic rules in one application. While DTDs are not the most complex documents imaginable, it is vital that developers define them correctly. Equally as important, parsing and manipulating DTDs within applications requires special libraries. XML Schema documents can be handled much more easily because they are fully compliant XML documents in their own right. What does this mean in practice? The tools that you use to develop, parse and manipulate your XML can also be used for your schemas. Developers need learn only one set of rules for schema and document, and both could be created using the same pieces of editing software.

[1] Although pragmatic realities such as organizational politics, historical preferences or the tools you have available may force you to use DTDs.

Using XML Schema requires an understanding of namespaces. Schema definitions always use namespaces, so much so that namespaces are one of the cornerstones of schema technology. I've mentioned namespaces before; now is the time to examine them in detail and learn how to use them.

4.1 NAMESPACES

Many situations arise during XML development in which different elements or attributes have the same name. In any reasonably complex document all obvious names soon get used. Resorting to cryptic names or names that are overly long and complex is unsatisfactory since it makes the document harder to read and to parse. Many programs, especially those in the Web applications domain, pull together data from a multitude of sources and combine it into a single global whole. One key question in all of these areas is how the unique names from each document can be preserved. Let us consider an illustrative example.

Bill Smiggins Inc. is a leading supplier of custom-made *widgets*. They have started to trade electronically with their suppliers and customers. Since each company has their own systems and structures, Smiggins have decided that they will accept and provide all data in XML format. Two of their suppliers, MegaCorps Industries, a multinational conglomerate, and Ray Jones, a typical *mom and pop* business, are among the first to start using XML. Each supplier provides details of parts, unit costs, order sizes and so on. The part details typically include a part number and a textual description. MegaCorps uses complex part numbers such as `12-07-abcd-3`, while Ray Jones uses simple integers such as `235` to identify his products. When these numbers are being processed at Smiggins Inc. the systems need to be able to identify each type of part number and use the appropriate ones on order forms. A number of possible XML structures can be envisaged:

```
<part_number>
  <supplier>MegaCorps</supplier>
  <number>12-07-abcd-3</number>
</part_number>
```

uses elements to denote each part of the data. The same thing could be achieved using attributes:

```
<part_number supplier="MegaCorps">12-07-abcd-3</part_number>
```

Both of these schemes suffer from the same problems. The XML becomes somewhat messy and difficult to manage. If each element that refers to MegaCorps has to specifically state its origin either through an attribute or a subelement, the document will soon grow out of control. There is also a danger that if Smiggins start to deal with another supplier called MegaCorps, they must somehow identify two identically named organizations.

Being able to relate each element uniquely back to its origin is vital. The W3C recognized this and developed a Recommendation for *Namespaces*. A namespace is a unique identifier for a set of names within an XML document. The Recommendation document states that they were developed to avoid the problem of *collisions* among element and attribute names where more than one markup *vocabulary* is used in a document. Essentially this is exactly the problem outlined above.

Here is an XML fragment in which element names are qualified by the use of namespaces.

```
<smiggins:part_number>
  <smiggins:supplier>MegaCorps</smiggins:supplier>
  <smiggins:number>12-07-abcd-3</smiggins:number>
</smiggins:part_number>
```

4.1.1 Declaring Namespaces

An XML namespace is identified by a URI. The URI is associated with a *prefix*. The prefix is attached to the front of element and attribute names in the XML document so as to associate them with the namespace. Where more than one namespace is used in a document they may be unique. If two namespace have exactly the same combination of characters in their URIs they are considered identical, that is, they are the same namespace. It is worth noting that two namespace URIs may be different, yet may identify the same thing and, hence, be functionally the same.

The association between prefix and URI is created using an attribute, `xmlns`, which is specially reserved for this purpose. Here's an example:

```
<recipe xmlns="http://www.foodlinks.org">
```

This code creates a default namespace for the recipe document. A default namespace applies to all elements in the document but doesn't have to be expressly stated. The `recipe` element and all of its subelements are associated with the default namespace. Actually, that's not quite true. Any elements that appear as subelements of recipe *and* which have a namespace prefix are part of the namespace associated with their prefix. Here's an example in which a namespace is declared and given a prefix:

```
<recipe xmlns:food="http://www.foodlinks.org">
```

To associate elements and attributes with the namespace, its prefix, `food`, must be concatenated to the front of their name with a colon separating the two parts:

```
<food:ingredient />
```

The three parts of the name become the namespace, the prefix and the local name of the element or attribute. The local name is, fairly obviously, the name that the element or attribute has in the current document.

Although the namespace is identified by a URI, the Recommendation does not specify that the URI point to an actual document or location. If that statement is simply taken at face value, it seems most peculiar. Surely a URI *ought* to identify a document; there must be *something* that gives meaning to the URI. Actually, the answer is no. In this case the URI is really identifying a domain which is globally unique and hence creates a set of unique names. When a URI is specified for a namespace there can only ever be one instance of that domain so that elements can be uniquely identified. This identification is unique across all XML documents that exist, not just those being used by the current application. Clearly, guaranteeing this is not the easiest thing. To make sure that the process works as intended, wherever possible the domain that you use for your namespaces should be one to which you actually own the rights to.

> **Note:**
> When creating a prefix, you cannot use any combination of the three letters **x, m** and **l**.

4.1.2 Applying Namespaces

If creating, or defining, namespaces is not difficult, using them is even more straightforward. Any element, or attribute, that belongs to a particular namespace is renamed so that the prefix and local name become one identifier:

```
<food:ingredient />
```

The namespace is then in use throughout a particular instance of the element. The rules that define when a particular namespace is being used are called *scoping* rules. The basic principle is that when a namespace is applied to an element, all subelements of it belong to the same namespace. If, for a particular element, no prefix is used, that element belongs to the default namespace. Elements can each belong to their own namespaces provided that the namespace has been declared and the appropriate prefix is used in the element name. Listing 4.1 shows how namespaces can be used in XML documents.

Listing 4.1 Using Namespaces

```
<?xml version="1.0"?>

<letter title="Your complaint of 03/03/00">
    <header xmlns:from="http://www.smiggins.com"
          xmlns:to="http://www.microsoft.com">
```

```
        <from:sender>
          <from:name>
            <from:title>Mr.</from:title>
            <from:firstname>William</from:firstname>
            <from:firstname>James</from:firstname>
            <from:surname>Smiggins</from:surname>
          </from:name>
        </from:sender>
        <from:recipient>
          <to:name>
            <to:firstname>Bill</to:firstname>
            <to:surname>Gates</to:surname>
          </to:name>
        </from:recipient>
        <from:signature>
          <from:greeting type="formal"/>
            <from:name>
              <from:firstname>Bill</from:firstname>
            </from:name>
        </from:signature>
    </header>
</letter>
```

Two separate namespaces are declared. Notice that more than one namespace can be declared at the same point in the document. Both will remain *in scope* for the same portion of the document, which in the example is the `header` element. The namespaces can be applied to appropriate elements. In the example, the `sender` and `recipient` elements have identically named subelements. Since these might contain different data or have different meanings, a different namespace is applied to each. The `recipient` element is part of the document created by Smiggins Inc. and so belongs in their namespace. Its content comes from the actual recipient and so belongs in *their* namespace.

4.2 USING SCHEMAS

Two documents are required to actually use XML Schema. One contains the schema definition, the other is an XML *instance* document. While at least one schema is *required* if a document is going to be validated, an XML document can use elements from more than one. When a compound document is built from a number of XML documents, as might happen during transformation, or a document uses elements from multiple sources, a number of different schemas will usually be needed. Schema documents must use the schema namespace `http://www.w3.org/2001/XMLSchema` which is normally associated with the prefix `xsd`. The following code shows how to use the namespace declaration:

```
<?xml version="1.0"?>
<xsd:schema xmlns:xsd="http://www.w3.org/2001/XMLSchema">
  <xsd:element name="letter">
  </xsd:element>
</xsd:schema>
```

Mostly the content of a schema consists of element definitions. Elements may contain other elements, so-called subelements, data content which might be strings or numbers, or a mixture of both. Those elements that contain only data are called simple types, the others are called complex types. Rather than begin an abstract discussion of schemas, let's look at a more concrete example. Listing 4.2 is a schema for the address component of the Business Letter.

Listing 4.2 Simplified Letter Schema

```
<?xml version="1.0"?>
<xsd:schema xmlns:xsd="http://www.w3.org/2001/XMLSchema">
  <xsd:element name="header">
    <xsd:complexType>
      <xsd:sequence>
        <xsd:element name="name">
          <xsd:complexType>
            <xsd:sequence>
              <xsd:element name="title" type="xsd:string"
                 maxOccurs="1"/>
              <xsd:element name="firstname" type="xsd:string
                 " />
              <xsd:element name="surname" type="xsd:string" />
            </xsd:sequence>
          </xsd:complexType>
        </xsd:element>
        <xsd:element name="address">
          <xsd:complexType>
            <xsd:sequence>
              <xsd:element name="line1" type="xsd:string" />
```

```
                <xsd:element name="line2" type="xsd:string" />
                <xsd:element name="line3" type="xsd:string" />
                <xsd:element name="city" type="xsd:string" />
                <xsd:choice>
                  <xsd:element name="state" type="xsd:string" />
                  <xsd:element name="county" type="xsd:string" />
                </xsd:choice>
                <xsd:element name="line1" type="xsd:string" />
                <xsd:element name="line2" type="xsd:string" />
                <xsd:element name="country" type="xsd:string" />
                <xsd:element name="code" type="xsd:string"
                   minOccurs="1" maxOccurs="1"/>
              </xsd:sequence>
            </xsd:complexType>
          </xsd:element>
        </xsd:sequence>
      <xsd:/complexType>
    </xsd:element>
</xsd:schema>
```

Schemas can be developed in a number of ways. Intellectually, the simplest approach is to mimic the structure of the original XML document. That's what I've done in Listing 4.2. Elements and subelements occur in the same order and with the same nesting that they do in the original document. A slightly more complicated approach is to define the elements and attributes first and to reference them from the structure of the document. This approach is demonstrated in Section 4.3.4. The third common approach is to define *data types* based upon the contents of both complex and simple elements, and then to use those types to define the elements and attributes in the document. This approach is demonstrated in Section 4.3.1.

Seeing a piece of code is one thing, understanding what it means is a totally different matter. Let me explain the structure shown in Listing 4.2. Following the usual XML processing instruction, the namespace is declared and bound to the prefix `xsd`. The XML document starts with the `letter` element but that makes for a far longer example.[2] Instead I'll concentrate on the `sender` section which must be defined first. It's a complex type which is composed from a set of elements. DTDs allow you to specify nesting but not to impose order on subelements. Not so schemas. The `sender` element contains ordered

[2] See Section 4.6 for the whole thing.

data. In XML Schema ordered sets of elements are created inside a sequence element. In this example, the sender contains two complex types, the name and address.

The name is another complex type which contains a sequence of elements. Each of the elements inside the sequence is simple. Since these are simple elements, they hold content which can be given a particular data type. The data type is declared using the type attribute. Notice that because the data types are part of the XML Schema Recommendation, the namespace prefix is used as part of the attribute value. The data types that are automatically available in XML Schema are described in Section 4.4. Defining your own data types is possible in XML Schema. This is also covered in Section 4.4. All of the simple elements in the Business Letter accept character strings, but the Recipe Book schema in Section 4.6 uses some other data types.

Elements in schemas can have a number of different attributes. The title element shows the use of one of these. The maxOccurs element specifies the maximum number of times that a particular element can appear at a given point in the XML document. And, yes, if you were wondering, there is a minOccurs attribute which controls the minimum number of times that the element must appear. It's used in the code element of the address.

Finally, notice the <xsd:choice> element. Depending where you are in the world, a city may belong to a state or a county.[3] It would be convenient if all of the possible options could be specified in the schema and just one used in the finished document. This is the role of the choice element. Any number of elements can be defined as subelements of a choice but only one may be used in the instance document.

4.2.1 Validating Schemas

XML is still a relatively new concept. Sure, SGML has been around for twenty years or so, but its user base was always relatively small. XML is in a period of explosive growth at the moment. New applications for XML are being developed all the time and it's moving into a diversity of domains, from graphics, through networking and on to artificial intelligence. Wherever software is used, someone is trying to replace[4] existing data structures with XML.

New schemas and applications are pouring out of the developer community, but what about software to handle it? Plenty of XML parsers are now available as libraries in programming languages such as Java, and embedded in applications such as Internet Explorer. That wasn't the situation even two or three years ago, and it isn't the situation right now for XML Schema. The Recommendations and applications need to be in place before

[3]Or a province or region or I'm trying to keep this simple, though, which is why I've not included them all.
[4]Or supplement.

the processing software is developed. That might seem paradoxical, but consider XML Schema. Developers were using DTDs with all their attendant limitations. Until W3C had produced a stable Recommendation and a body of support had coalesced around it, no one would undertake the long process of writing the software. That situation is going to change. Limited XML Schema support is starting to appear in some applications.

Once you've created a schema, it needs to be validated. The rules of XML Schema are pretty complicated. There's little point in writing a schema if it breaks the rules since doing so will automatically invalidate your XML documents. Software support is essential. A quick search of the Web reveals the existence of a few XML Schema validators. In preparing this chapter, I chose to use IBM's Schema Quality Checker version 2.0 (SQC2). This is a pure Java product, bundled with which are all the necessary libraries.

Installing Java applications *can* be something of a pain. If you have a recent[5] Java runtime environment or software development kit installed on your machine, you should be able to configure it to run SQC2. Typically, Java installations set a number of environment variables which must be modified when products such as SQC2 are added to the system. Modifying the environment for every Java application that you need is, frankly, not advisable. If you make an error you're likely to break your existing configuration. A much better solution is to use batch files to initiate all of your Java applications.

SQC2 comes with two batch files which can be used to run it. `SQC.bat` is for Microsoft Windows systems, `SQC.sh` for Unix-type systems. My approach to working with batch files like these is the same under both Windows 2000 and GNU/Linux. I have a directory called `bin` in my GNU/Linux home directory and on my Windows `c:` drive. Both these directories are added to the `PATH` environment variable. I edit `SQC.sh` or `SQC.bat` to suit my system, then add a batch file to `bin` which fires off the SQC file. In the following examples there are long lines of code which will wrap strangely on the page. If you can't make sense of them as printed here, use the examples supplied with SQC2 to help you format yours properly. Here are the changes under Windows:

In `c:\bin` I create `SQC.bat`:

```
c:\SQC2.0\SQC.bat
```

with the `SQC.bat` that came with the product, changed to:

```
java -classpath c:\SQC2.0\xmlParserAPIs.jar;c:\SQC2.0\xercesImpl.
    jar;c:\SQC2.0\xschemaREC.jar;c:\SQC2.0\xml4j.jar;c:\SQC2.0\
    mofrt.jar;c:\SQC2.0\regx4j.jar;c:\SQC2.0\mail.jar;c:\jdk1.3\
    jre\lib;.
com.ibm.sketch.util.SchemaQualityChecker %1 %2 %3 %4 %5
```

Under GNU/Linux, it's the same thing. I create a batch file called `SQC`, which contains:

[5] At least Java version 2, release 1.2.

```
#!/bin/sh

/opt/SQC/SQC.sh $*
```

The batch file needs to be made executable using:

```
chmod 700 ~/bin/SQC
```

The SQC.sh file supplied with the product is changed to:

```
java -classpath /opt/SQC/xmlParserAPIs.jar:/opt/SQC/xercesImpl.
    jar:/opt/SQC/xschemaREC.jar:/opt/SQC/xml4j.jar:/opt/SQC/mofrt.
    jar:/opt/SQC/regx4j.jar:/opt/SQC/mail.jar:/opt/jbuilder5/jdk1
    .3/jre/lib com.ibm.sketch.util.SchemaQualityChecker $*
```

Of course, the paths are specific to my system. They'll need to be changed to suit your installations.

4.3 DEFINING TYPES

I've already mentioned that elements may be simple or complex. The distinction is clear: complex elements may contain other elements, may contain content and may have attributes. Simple types may only contain content, cannot contain other elements and cannot have attributes.

Although building a schema that follows the structure of the intended instance document is straightforward, it's not necessarily efficient. A much easier approach is to define a series of data types that express the pieces of the document. The actual definition can then be based upon these. An example of this is shown in Section 4.3.1. The following discussion assumes the use of user-defined data types but can also be applied to simpler structures such as the one in Listing 4.2.

4.3.1 Simple Types

The simplest form of XML element is assigned one of the default data types which are listed in Section 4.4. These include such standard programming data types as strings, integer numbers and decimal numbers. These provide much of the functionality that is required in schemas but not all of it. Remember that a simple type is used for an element that contains only document content. This content may be something straightforward such as a character string, but it may be more complicated. The content of the element may be an integer value within a particular range, a string that matches a particular pattern or a date chosen from a list of items. All of these can form the content of a simple type in XML. The following example shows two elements which each take one of the built-in simple types as content:

```
<?xml version="1.0"?>

<xsd:schema xmlns:xsd="http://www.w3.org/2001/XMLSchema">
  <xsd:element name="today" type="xsd:date" />
  <xsd:element name="user" type="xsd:string" />
</xsd:schema>
```

Creating new data types based on the built-in types is a straightforward process – although many different XML Schema constructs may be used. Let's change the previous example so that the date is chosen from a set of four possibilities and the user name matches a predefined pattern:

```
<?xml version="1.0"?>

<xsd:schema xmlns:xsd="http://www.w3.org/2001/XMLSchema">
  <xsd:element name="today" type="dateSet" />
  <xsd:element name="user" type="userType" />

  <xsd:simpleType name="dateSet">
    <xsd:restriction base="xsd:date">
      <xsd:enumeration value="1785-03-29">
      <xsd:enumeration value="2002-10-17">
      <xsd:enumeration value="2001-12-02">
      <xsd:enumeration value="1895-04-02">
    </xsd:restriction>
  </xsd:simpleType>

  <xsd:simpleType name="userType">
    <xsd:restriction base="xsd:string">
      <xsd:pattern value="U\w{2,6}\d{2}" />
    </xsd:restriction>
  </xsd:simpleType>

</xsd:schema>
```

Two new data types are created. The exact details don't need to detain us for long since they'll be covered later. Initially it is more important to know *what* is happening before getting caught up in the details of *how* it happens. The new data types are called `dateSet` and `userType`. Elements that contain content in these new types are declared with their `type` attribute set to the name of the new type. When setting an attribute to one of the built-in data types, the qualified name of the type is used, prefix plus local name. When user-defined types are being assigned only the local name is generally needed:

```
<xsd:element name="today" type="dateSet" />
```

In my example, the type definitions follow the element declarations. The Recommendation doesn't specify whether the definition of types should happen before or after their use. Since the W3C give some examples of usage in which the types are defined after they are first used, following this convention seems pretty safe. Difficulties would arise if tool and library vendors implement systems that require types to be defined before they are used, but you've done the opposite. Following the practice of the W3C means you are safe from this.

Defining simple types is done by taking an existing simple type and applying a restriction to it using *facets*. Facets are rules which are applied to the base type to change it in some way. The existing type may be built-in or a user-defined type that you created previously. The restriction changes the meaning of the simple type which it takes as its `base` attribute:

```
<xsd:restriction base="xsd:date">
```

That's all there is to creating a simple type: take an existing simple type and modify it to suit your needs.

4.3.2 Complex Types

A complex type is defined using the `complexType` element. Complex types may include subelements, element content and attributes, which makes designing their definitions necessarily more difficult than for simple types. A `complexType` element does not define a data type *per se*, rather it creates an association between a set of elements, each of which may be either complex or simple.

```
<xsd:complexType name="name">
  <xsd:sequence>
    <xsd:element name="title" type="xsd:string" maxOccurs="1"/>
    <xsd:element name="firstname" type="xsd:string" />
    <xsd:element name="surname" type="xsd:string" />
  </xsd:sequence>
</xsd:complexType>
```

The preceding code fragment is very similar to the one used in Listing 4.2. It creates a complex data type which is given a name and can be used elsewhere in the program through its name. The complex type is used like this:

```
<element name="from" type="name"/>
```

Wherever the data type `name` is used in the instance document, the structure *must* include all elements from the schema that are not defined as part of a group from which just one item is selected. In the example this means at most one `title` and possibly a `firstname` and a `surname`.

Controlling how often an element appears in the instance document is done through attributes:

`minOccurs`
: The minimum number of times that the element must appear in the document. This defaults to 1.

`maxOccurs`
: The maximum number of times that the element must appear in the document. This defaults to 1.

`default`
: Assigns a default value to both elements and attributes. When an attribute has a default value, this value will be used in the instance document if the attribute is not explicitly used. Elements are treated slightly differently. If an element is given a default value using this attribute but has content in the instance document, its value is set to the content. If the element is empty in the instance document, it is given the value of the default.

`use`
: Attributes must appear no more than once in a given element. Controlling how they appear is done through the `use` attribute in the schema document. This attribute takes one of three values: `required`, `optional` or `prohibited`.

`fixed`
: To force a particular value for either an element or attribute in the instance document, the `fixed` attribute is supplied in the schema.

This code shows the use of some of these attributes:

```
<xsd:complexType name="name">
  <xsd:sequence>
    <xsd:element name="title" type="xsd:string" maxOccurs="1"
       default="Miss"/>
    <xsd:element name="firstname" type="xsd:string" minOccurs
       ="2"/>
    <xsd:element name="surname" type="xsd:string" />
```

```
  </xsd:sequence>
</xsd:complexType>
```

The partial schema for the Business Letter can be rewritten using defined types as shown in Listing 4.3.

Listing 4.3 The Letter Schema Using Complex Types

```
<?xml version="1.0"?>
<xsd:schema xmlns:xsd="http://www.w3.org/2001/XMLSchema">

  <xsd:element name="header">
    <xsd:complexType>
      <xsd:sequence>
        <xsd:element name="name" type="nameType"/>
        <xsd:element name="address" type="addressType"/>
      </xsd:sequence>
    <xsd:/complexType>
  </xsd:element>

  <xsd:complexType name="nameType">
    <xsd:sequence>
      <xsd:element name="title" type="xsd:string" maxOccurs
          ="1"/>
      <xsd:element name="firstname" type="xsd:string" />
      <xsd:element name="surname" type="xsd:string" />
    </xsd:sequence>
  </xsd:complexType>

  <xsd:complexType name="addressType">
    <xsd:sequence>
      <xsd:element name="line1" type="xsd:string" />
      <xsd:element name="line2" type="xsd:string" />
      <xsd:element name="line3" type="xsd:string" />
      <xsd:element name="city" type="xsd:string" />
      <xsd:choice>
        <xsd:element name="state" type="xsd:string" />
        <xsd:element name="county" type="xsd:string" />
      </xsd:choice>
      <xsd:element name="country" type="xsd:string" />
```

```
        <xsd:element name="code" type="xsd:string" minOccurs="1"
            maxOccurs="1"/>
      </xsd:sequence>
    </xsd:complexType>

</xsd:schema>
```

4.3.3 Attributes

Attributes are defined within a `complexType` element. The definition of attributes comes after the definitions of the elements and before the closing tag of the element. Defining an attribute is very similar to defining simple types except that they occur in `attribute` tags. Here's an example:

```
<xsd:complexType name="name">
  <xsd:sequence>
    <xsd:element name="title" type="xsd:string" maxOccurs="1"
       default="Miss"/>
    <xsd:element name="firstname" type="xsd:string" minOccurs
       ="2"/>
    <xsd:element name="surname" type="xsd:string" />
  </xsd:sequence>
  <xsd:attribute name="gender" type="xsd:string" default="female
     "/>
</xsd:complexType>
```

4.3.4 References

One more method of defining XML Schemas is to create named elements that contain a `complexType`. Explicit references to those elements are used to build the schema document. The references are created using the `ref` attribute. Rather than spend a lot of time discussing this technique, since it's straightforward, Listing 4.4 gives an example.

Listing 4.4 The Letter Schema Using References

```
<?xml version="1.0"?>
<xsd:schema xmlns:xsd="http://www.w3.org/2001/XMLSchema">

  <xsd:element name="header">
    <xsd:complexType>
      <xsd:sequence>
```

```
        <xsd:element ref="name"/>
        <xsd:element ref="address"/>
      </xsd:sequence>
    <xsd:/complexType>
  </xsd:element>

  <xsd:element name="name">
    <xsd:complexType>
      <xsd:sequence>
        <xsd:element name="title" type="xsd:string" maxOccurs
          ="1"/>
        <xsd:element name="firstname" type="xsd:string" />
        <xsd:element name="surname" type="xsd:string" />
      </xsd:sequence>
    </xsd:complexType>
  </xsd:element>

  <xsd:element name="address">
    <xsd:complexType name="addressType">
      <xsd:sequence>
        <xsd:element name="line1" type="xsd:string" />
        <xsd:element name="line2" type="xsd:string" />
        <xsd:element name="line3" type="xsd:string" />
        <xsd:element name="city" type="xsd:string" />
        <xsd:choice>
          <xsd:element name="state" type="xsd:string" />
          <xsd:element name="county" type="xsd:string" />
        </xsd:choice>
        <xsd:element name="country" type="xsd:string" />
        <xsd:element name="code" type="xsd:string" minOccurs
          ="1" maxOccurs="1"/>
      </xsd:sequence>
    </xsd:complexType>
  </xsd:element>

</xsd:schema>
```

4.4 DATA IN SCHEMA

So far I've demonstrated how you can create your own data types in XML Schema. The end point of every complex type that you create is a set of simple types. Each of these simple types will either use or extend a built-in XML data type. One of the tremendous advantages that schemas of all types have when compared to DTDs is the richness of their data model. XML Schema, in particular, provides numerous useful data types which can be modified to meet specific requirements. Since the underlying model is standardized, any processing application will be able to manipulate your data. At the most primitive level your complex types are all, eventually, convertible to a set of built-in primitive XML data types.

Table 4.1: XML Schema Data Types

Type	Example or Explanation
`string`	A string of characters
`normalizedString`	Tab, return and newline characters are converted to spaces
`token`	A `normalizedString` with whitespace characters collapsed so that runs of more than one whitespace character become a single character
`byte`	–1, 125
`unsignedByte`	1, 125
`base64Binary`	Binary data in Base 64 format
`hexBinary`	Binary data in hexadecimal format
`integer`	–126789, 0, 126789
`positiveInteger`	1, 126789
`negativeInteger`	–126789, –1
`nonNegativeInteger`	0, 1, 126789
`nonPositiveInteger`	0, –1, –126789
`int`	–1, 126789675
`unsignedInt`	1, 126789675
`long`	–1, 12678967533214
`unsignedLong`	1, 12678967533214
`short`	–1, 12678
`unsignedShort`	1, 12678
`decimal`	–1.23, 0, 123.4, 78.0
`float`	32-bit floating-point numbers such as –1E4, 0, 12.3E5, NaN

Table 4.1: XML Schema Data Types

Type	Example or Explanation
double	64-bit floating-point numbers such as –1E4, 0, 12.3E53, NaN
boolean	true, false, 1, 0
time	10:35:00.00 [6]
dateTime	2002-02-16T10:35:00.00 which is 10:35 a.m. on February 16, 2002.
duration	P23Y4M2DT01H15M5S means 23 years, 4 months, 2 days, 1 hour, 15 minutes and 5 seconds
date	2002-02-16 which means February 16, 2002
gMonth[7]	– – 02 – – means February
gYear	2002
gYearMonth	2002-02
gDay	– – –16 is the 16th day
gMonthDay	– – 02 – 16 is February 16
Name	The XML name type, e.g., `recipe`
QName	A qualified name such as `from:sender`
NCName	The QName without its prefix: `sender`
anyURI	`http://www.smiggins.com`
language	Values which are valid for `xml:lang` such as en-GB
ID	An XML `ID` attribute
IDREF	An XML `IDREF` attribute
IDREFS	An XML `IDREFS` attribute
ENTITY	An XML `ENTITY` attribute
ENTITIES	An XML `ENTITIES` attribute
NOTATION	An XML `NOTATION` attribute
NMTOKEN	An XML `NMTOKEN` attribute
NMTOKENS	An XML `NMTOKENS` attribute

Table 4.1 lists the primitive XML Schema data types. It's important to notice that these are not the same data types that you would find in a programming language such as C.

[6] XML Schema uses Universal Coordinated Time which is also known as Greenwich Mean Time. Offsets are expressed after the time: 10:35:00.00-05:00

[7] The prefix g is used to denote the Gregorian calendar.

Although common data types such as unsigned integers and bytes are available, much richer types such as dates and durations are provided.

4.4.1 Regular Expression Language

The simple data types can be modified using *facets*. The complete set of facets is described in Section 4.5.4. One of the facets, `pattern`, has a simple regular expression language. The language is used to select strings and substrings and is based on the regular expression facilities in the programming language Perl. If you've programmed in Perl, you'll notice one key difference between the two languages. In Perl, the characters `^` and `$` can be used to represent the start and end of strings. In XML Schema, patterns are applied to the entire content of an element and hence `^` and `$` are not used. The character `^` is still used, but here it indicates a logical `not` in character sets.

Table 4.2: XML Schema Regular Expressions

Expression	Example	Explanation
	`recipe`	Simple strings of characters are matched exactly. Here the string `recipe` will give a successful match even if it occurs as a substring. For instance, the string `recipes` will match. All Unicode character is valid in these expressions, provided, of course, the encoding for the document supports it.
	`Espanñola`	This shows how character entities can be used to represent Unicode characters. It will match the string Española.
`\d`	`\dg`	Matches a single digit. In the example any digit followed by the letter `g` is matched.
`\d{}`	`\d{3}g`	A number in curly braces controls repetition in the match. The example matches three digits followed by a single letter `g`.

Table 4.2: XML Schema Regular Expressions

Expression	Example	Explanation
`\D`		Any non-digit. The uppercase version of a control character negates the meaning. More examples are given below.
`\s`	`\d{3}\sg`	Matches any single whitespace character. As ever in XML, whitespace is any of the characters space, tab, newline or carriage return. In the example, three digits followed by a single space then the letter `g` will match successfully.
`\w`	`\d{3}\w`	Matches any single word character. A word character is any letter or digit.
`\W`	`\d{3}\W{2}`	Matches all non-word characters. The example matches any three digits followed by two non-word characters.
`\p{Lu}`		Matches any uppercase character. `Lu` is defined within Unicode.
`\P{Lu}`		Any non-uppercase character.
`\p{IsGreek}`	λ	Any Greek Letter
`\P{IsGreek}`		Any non-Greek Letter
`*`	`c*b`	Matches the preceding character zero or more times. The example will match any of the following: `b`, `cb`, `ccb`.
`?`	`c?b`	Matches the preceding character zero or one time. The example matches `b` or `cb`.
`+`	`c+b`	Matches one or more times: `cb`, `ccb` and so on.

Table 4.2: XML Schema Regular Expressions

<table>
<tr><th>Expression</th><th>Example</th><th>Explanation</th></tr>
<tr><td>|</td><td>c|b</td><td>Separates optional items. This example matches either b or c.</td></tr>
<tr><td>[ ]</td><td>[a,b,c,d]</td><td>Creates a character set. Any of the characters in the set may match.</td></tr>
<tr><td>[-]</td><td>[a-q]</td><td>Ranges can be used in creating character sets. The example includes all letters from a to q.</td></tr>
<tr><td>^</td><td>[^a-q]</td><td>Negates the meaning of the expression. In the example, everything except the characters a through q will match.</td></tr>
<tr><td>.</td><td></td><td>Matches any character.</td></tr>
<tr><td>{,}</td><td>\d{2,4}</td><td>The comma is used to create a range. In the example the pattern will match at least two and at most four digits.</td></tr>
</table>

Approximately 100 languages can be specified in statements of the type `\p{IsGreek}`. The language name replaces `Greek` after `Is` in the example. Available languages include such diverse character sets as basic Latin, Thai, Cherokee and Byzantine musical symbols.

4.5 COMPOSITORS

Building complex types from elements and attributes is done through composition. XML Schema includes three different composition mechanisms: `sequence`, `all` and `choice`. The three can be mixed in any combination to build different types of structure. In addition, the attributes `minOccurs` and `maxOccurs` can be applied to all of them.

4.5.1 Sequence

The `sequence` compositor is used to build ordered sequences of elements and attributes. Each element in the sequence can include further subelements.

```
<?xml version="1.0"?>
<xsd:schema xmlns:xsd="http://www.w3.org/2001/XMLSchema">

  <xsd:element name="name">
    <xsd:complexType>
      <xsd:sequence>
        <xsd:element name="title" type="xsd:string" maxOccurs
           ="1"/>
        <xsd:element name="firstname" type="xsd:string" />
        <xsd:element name="surname" type="xsd:string" />
      </xsd:sequence>
    </xsd:complexType>
  </xsd:element>

</xsd:schema>
```

4.5.2 All

When an unordered set of elements is needed, the `all` composition should be used. This example creates a complex type to hold a name. The `title`, `firstname` and `surname` elements can appear in any order in the type. Since much data is inherently unordered, or has an implicit order which can be ignored, the `all` compositor has many uses.

```
<?xml version="1.0"?>
<xsd:schema xmlns:xsd="http://www.w3.org/2001/XMLSchema">

  <xsd:element name="name">
    <xsd:complexType>
      <xsd:all>
        <xsd:element name="title" type="xsd:string" maxOccurs
           ="1"/>
        <xsd:element name="firstname" type="xsd:string" />
        <xsd:element name="surname" type="xsd:string" />
      </xsd:all>
    </xsd:complexType>
  </xsd:element>
</xsd:schema>
```

4.5.3 Choice

The choice compositor creates a set of optional elements. Only one of the options may be present in the XML document. In the following example, the name may contain either a firstname or a surname.

```
<?xml version="1.0"?>
<xsd:schema xmlns:xsd="http://www.w3.org/2001/XMLSchema">

  <xsd:element name="name">
    <xsd:complexType>
      <xsd:choice>
        <xsd:element name="firstname" type="xsd:string" />
        <xsd:element name="surname" type="xsd:string" />
      </xsd:choice>
    </xsd:complexType>
  </xsd:element>
</xsd:schema>
```

4.5.4 Restriction

The creation of user-defined simple types is done using restriction of base types. The base types have certain inherent properties; for instance, an integer holds a particular range of values. If you need a special data type which holds only whole numbers in the range 7 to 3,000, you can create this by restricting the base integer type:

```
<xsd:simpleType name="myNumber">
  <xsd:restriction base="xsd:integer">
    <xsd:minInclusive value="7" />
    <xsd:maxInclusive value="3000" />
  </xsd:restriction>
</xsd:simpleType>
```

To create a new string type, for instance for a catalog number, matching a pattern such as: the string "PC", 3 integers, a hyphen then at least 3 and at most 5 letters:

```
<xsd:simpleType name="partCode">
  <xsd:restriction base="xsd:string">
    <xsd:sequence>
      <xsd:enumeration value="PC" />
      <xsd:pattern value="\d{3}" />
```

```
      <xsd:enumeration value="-" />
      <xsd:pattern value="[a-zA-Z]{3,5}" />
    </xsd:sequence>
  </xsd:restriction>
</xsd:simpleType>
```

That might also be expressed as a simple pattern:

```
<xsd:simpleType name="partCode">
  <xsd:restriction base="xsd:string">
    <xsd:pattern value="PC\d{3}-[a-zA-Z]{3,5}" />
  </xsd:restriction>
</xsd:simpleType>
```

The restriction of each data type happens through facets. Each data type can be altered in different ways. It makes sense to set a minimum length for a character string, whereas doing the same for a byte has no meaning. While most facets are pretty self-explanatory, a short description of each might be useful.

`length`

This facet determines the length of the data type. For data types based on string, this is the number of characters they contain. For binary data such as base64Binary, it is the number of octets. If the `fixed` attribute of the facet is set to true, data types derived from this type cannot specify another value for their `length`. The example creates a `partCode` which contains a maximum of 10 characters:

```
<xsd:simpleType name="partCode">
  <xsd:restriction base="xsd:string">
    <xsd:length value="10" fixed="true"/>
  </xsd:restriction>
</xsd:simpleType>
```

`minLength`

Like the `length` facet, but sets the minimum length of the data type. Where both `minLength` and `maxLength` are specified, `minLength` must be less than or equal to `maxLength`.

`maxLength`

Like the `length` facet, but sets the maximum length of the data type.

`pattern`

Specifies a regular expression which the element content must match. The XML Schema regular expression language is described in Table 4.2.

enumeration

An enumeration facet contains a set of values. Elements using an enumerated data type may only contain values which are present in the enumeration. The set of values specified in this way is not ordered. The example shows a user-defined data type which can take any one of three different values:

```
<xsd:simpleType name="partCode">
  <xsd:restriction base="xsd:string">
    <xsd:enumeration value="10" />
    <xsd:enumeration value="20" />
    <xsd:enumeration value="Part Code" />
  </xsd:restriction>
</xsd:simpleType>
```

whiteSpace

The whiteSpace facet controls how the processor should treat whitespace characters in the XML document. Three values are allowed.[8]

preserve

Normalization is not performed. The whitespace characters found in the document are preserved. This is compulsory for XML element content.

replace

The characters tab, #x9, newline, #xA, and carriage return, #xD, are replaced with space, #x20.

collapse

Sequences of more than a single space, #x20, are replaced with a single space character.

This example is taken from Part Two of the XML Schema Recommendation, which is why I haven't added the xsd prefix:

```
<simpleType name='token'>
  <restriction base='normalizedString'>
    <whiteSpace value='collapse'/>
  </restriction>
</simpleType>
```

[8] Although you can only use one in creating a particular data type.

maxInclusive

Sets an upper bound for values using the data type. The value given as an attribute is included in the set. In this example a new data type is created which restricts an order to 765 items or fewer:

```
<xsd:simpleType name="orderSize>
  <xsd:restriction base="xsd:integer>
    <xsd:maxInclusive value='765' />
  </xsd:restriction>
</xsd:simpleType>
```

minInclusive

Sets a lower bound for values using the data type. The value given as an attribute is included in the set.

maxExclusive

Sets an upper bound for values using the data type. The value given as an attribute is not included in the set.

minExclusive

Sets a lower bound for values using the data type. The value given as an attribute is not included in the set.

totalDigits

For data types derived from the decimal base type, this facet determines how many digits the data type may have. If the `fixed` attribute is set to `true`, data types derived from this may not change the value set by the facet.

fractionDigits

Sets the number of digits appearing in the fractional part of a data type derived from the decimal base type. This example creates a decimal number containing up to 6 digits, one of which is the fractional part:

```
<xsd:simpleType name="partLength">
  <xsd:restriction base="xsd:decimal">
    <xsd:totalDigits value="6" />
    <xsd:fractionDigits value="1" />
  </xsd:restriction>
</xsd:simpleType>
```

Possible values for this data type might include 23.4, 56781.9 or 0.0.

4.5.5 List

Alongside basic data types, XML Schema has a construct to define lists of values. Data in a basic type cannot be divided. The words in a character string will always be treated as a single entity. Lists are made from sequences of basic data types. The individual elements in the list have meaning on their own and can be separated out. An NMTOKEN is an atomic unit which cannot be split apart; NMTOKENS, on the other hand, is a built-in list which can be split apart into individual NMTOKEN items.

XML Schema has three of these built-in list types: NMTOKENS, IDREFS and ENTITIES. It also provides a mechanism through which user-defined list types can be created. User-defined lists contain elements which are derived from the basic types but not from existing lists or complex types. A number of different facets make sense when applied to lists. Specifically these are length, minLength, maxLength and enumeration.

```
<?xml version="1.0"?>
<xsd:schema xmlns:xsd="http://www.w3.org/2001/XMLSchema">

  <xsd:simpleType name="recipeListItem">
    <xsd:list itemType="xsd:string />
  </xsd:simpleType>

  <xsd:simpleType name="recipeList">
    <xsd:restriction base="recipeListItem>
      <xsd:minLength value="2" />
      <xsd:maxLength value="8" />
    </xsd:restriction>
  </xsd:simpleType>

</xsd:schema>
```

The preceding piece of code creates a list of ingredients for a recipe. The list contains between 2 and 8 items. The items themselves are derived from the string base type. Notice that the xsd:list element is used to create a data type which will hold the elements of the list. When creating a list based on the string type, whitespace becomes a consideration. The items in the list will be separated by whitespace, which means that none of them can contain space. Here's a legal three-item list and one that would fail.

Valid: Flour Salt Butter

Invalid: Flour Salt Olive Oil

4.5.6 Union

If you don't have much experience of the ways in which programmers sometimes see the world, a union will seem like a strange data type. The union lets an element or attribute hold data derived from more than one type. Actually, it has that potential, but only one data type will be used in a particular element or attribute. Here's how it works. The union contains a list of data types. Each of those types is appropriate for particular elements, although different types will be used in different situations. When an element, or attribute, is instantiated, it will contain data which conforms to just one of the types in the union.

You might wonder why anyone would bother with this complexity. Consider a situation in which a piece of data might be represented by a string of characters or a code. An identifier for a product in a manufacturing application is a clear example of this. Some applications, or users, might refer to a *4mm left-handed widget tensioner*, others might call the same thing *PC-4532-QW*. Rather than have XML elements for product name and product code, you might want to use a single element type to hold the product identifier.

```
<xsd:simpleType name="partCode">
  <xsd:union>
    <xsd:simpleType>
      <xsd:restriction base="xsd:string">
         <xsd:pattern value="PC\d{3}-[a-zA-Z]{3,5}" />
      </xsd:restriction>
    </xsd:simpleType>
    <xsd:simpleType>
      <xsd:element type="xsd:string" />
    </xsd:simpleType>
  </xsd:union>
</xsd:simpleType>
```

The same thing could be represented more simply by using the `memberTypes` attribute of the `union` element. This takes a space-separated list of data types as its value. Here I declare a type to hold part codes and then use it as part of the union:

```
<xsd:simpleType name="partCodeType">
  <xsd:restriction base="xsd:string">
    <xsd:pattern value="PC\d{3}-[a-zA-Z]{3,5}" />
  </xsd:restriction>
</xsd:simpleType>

<xsd:simpleType name="partCode">
  <xsd:union memberTypes="partCodeType xsd:string" />
```

```
</xsd:simpleType>
```

4.5.7 Group

It's possible in XML Schema to define groups of attributes or elements which can be treated as a single item. For example, a group of attributes may be created so that they can be used in any number of elements without having to repeat lots of code. Similarly, a group of elements may be used to create a number of different complex types. I don't want to dwell on the idea, so here's some code that shows it in action:

```
<xsd:attributeGroup name="userAttributes">
  <xsd:attribute name="username" type="xsd:string" />
  <xsd:attribute name="gender" type="xsd:string" default="female
     "/>
  <xsd:attribute name="age" type="xsd:integer" />
</xsd:attributeGroup>

<xsd:group name="room">
  <xsd:sequence>
    <xsd:element name="floor" type="string" />
    <xsd:element name="roomNumber" type="string" />
    <xsd:element name="area" type="decimal" />
  </xsd:sequence>
</xsd:group>

<xsd:complexType name="user">
  <xsd:sequence>
    <xsd:group ref="room" />
  </xsd:sequence>
  <xsd:attributeGroup ref="userAttributes" />
</xsd:complexType>
```

4.6 EXAMPLE SCHEMA

Since an XML Schema is potentially far richer than a DTD for any given application, it is also likely to be both longer and more complex. Even the relatively simple examples that I have shown throughout this chapter contain almost as much code as the complete DTDs shown in Chapter 3. The complete XML Schemas for the Recipe Book and Business Letter are an order of magnitude larger.[9] If both were included at this point, with explanatory text, the book would become almost unreadable. Rather than include ten pages of code and another five of explanation, I've included just the schema for the Business Letter. The Recipe Book is provided in Appendix D, although without explanation. Since that schema is relatively simple, you ought to be able to figure out why it has the structure it does just from the code. Before you go off and try to do that, read through the rest of this chapter. Seeing a full schema explained will give you a good start in reading others.

4.6.1 The Business Letter Schema

The complete XML Schema for the Business Letter is available, as a single piece of code, in Appendix C. Since it is so long,[10] I've split it into logical sections for this explanation. It's important to realize, at this stage, that schemas are not a drop-in replacement for DTDs. When converting a DTD into a schema, which is what I did here, some changes may need to be made to the structure of the original document. Clearly, if existing documents use the DTD, you may need to run the two definitions side-by-side for some time. With large XML structures some inconsistencies are inevitable. Taking the time and effort to minimize them will prove beneficial in the long run.

The schema starts with the XML processing instruction and a namespace definition. As I've done throughout this chapter, I'm going to use the prefix xsd for the namespace here. It is associated with the standard namespace for schemas. Remember, though, that there isn't an actual document at the end of this URI. There is a set of Recommendation documents which define XML Schema but the processing application won't be going away to find one.

```
<?xml version="1.0"?>
<xsd:schema xmlns:xsd="http://www.w3.org/2001/XMLSchema">
```

At the top of the schema, I define the document itself:

```
<!-- Define the actual document -->
<xsd:complexType name="letter">
  <xsd:sequence>
    <xsd:element ref="header" />
    <xsd:element ref="content" />
  </xsd:sequence>
  <xsd:attribute name="title" type="xsd:string" />
</xsd:complexType>
```

[9] If you'll allow me a little poetic license.
[10] It's actually over 120 lines of code.

The whole document forms a single complex type called letter. This contains a sequence of elements and can take a single attribute. The sequence must be defined before the attribute because attributes are always the last thing in a type definition. However, since the attribute is simple, let's get it out of the way now. The letter can be given a title using the attribute of that name. The title, itself, is a character string of indeterminate length. Although titles are likely to be relatively short, no restriction is imposed on the string type, since doing so might cause occasional problems for users.

The letter element contains two subelements: header and content. I could have defined these as types and created elements using those types. Since this application uses that technique everywhere else, I've used an alternative approach. I define two elements called content and header and access them using the ref attribute.

```
<!-- Define elements which are referred to -->
<xsd:element name="content">
  <xsd:complexType mixed="true" >
    <xsd:sequence>
      <xsd:element name="emphasis" type="xsd:string" />
    </xsd:sequence>
  </xsd:complexType>
</xsd:element>

<xsd:element name="header">
  <xsd:complexType>
    <xsd:sequence>
      <xsd:element ref="metadata" />
      <xsd:element name="sender" type="personType" />
      <xsd:element name="recipient" type="personType" />
      <xsd:element name="date" type="dateType" />
      <xsd:element name="signature" type="signatureType" />
    </xsd:sequence>
  </xsd:complexType>
</xsd:element>
```

The header and content elements can be considered the top level of the document. The letter element is the root below which all of the content occurs. Each of these top-level elements defines a logical section of the letter. The content element can hold mixed content. Mixed content can be either data, in DTD terms this would be PCDATA, or more elements. In this case, words or phrases in the body of the letter can be stressed using the emphasis element. Mixed content presents a topological problem if you view XML documents strictly as trees. An emphasized word isn't a subelement of the paragraph that contains it. It's part of that paragraph but a tree structure doesn't really let you conceptualize it in that way. The leaf at the end of a branch of elements will be data, but mixed content lets the final element have more than one leaf, and lets those leaves be of different types.

The header is far more straightforward. It contains a sequence of five elements. One, metadata, is a reference to an existing element. The others are elements that instantiate complex types. The important thing here is that you can mix references and elements inside the same structure. The decision on which to use often depends upon your own preferences. If you are going to modify the definition of an element in defining others, then it needs to be a type. If you always use the element *as is*, then it can be defined either as a type or as a reference.

```
<xsd:element name="metadata">
  <xsd:complexType>
    <xsd:sequence>
      <xsd:element name="keyword" type="xsd:string" />
    </xsd:sequence>
    <xsd:attribute name="value" type="xsd:string" />
  </xsd:complexType>
</xsd:element>
```

Although metadata is included through a reference, it's an ordinary element. Since it includes subelements and attributes a complex type is used. When defining a complex type *as* a type, the subelements are placed inside a complexType element. You'll see this in a moment. The metadata element *contains* complex data, but is not, itself, a new type. Despite metadata having just a single subelement, keyword, it still needs to contain a sequence. Subelements are always placed inside a container, which may be sequence, all or one of the others. This might seem like unnecessary verbiage since the structure is usually obvious to a reader. XML Schema documents are usually going to be processed mechanically, and machines need every little detail spelt out.

Once the major sections have been defined, it's time to define the types that they use. This sounds like top-down design. Those of us who teach Computer Science and related disciplines tell our students to try to work like this. Get the structure, the big picture, before starting to fill in the detail. Did I design this schema like that? No way. I defined parts of it from the top, working down, and other parts from the basement working upwards. Academic theories are very nice, and often make life easier, but sometimes you just have to be pragmatic. I mention this because this document has a neat top-down structure which yours might not. Don't worry if you're creating a mix of references, simple types and complex types as you go along. Once the schema is completed and validated, you can put the pieces together more tidily. You'll want the finished thing to be neat and tidy, especially if you're the one who's going to have to maintain it.

```
<!-- define complex types -->
<xsd:complexType name="dateType">
  <xsd:sequence>
    <xsd:element name="dayname" type="daynameType" />
    <xsd:element name="day" type="xsd:gDay" />
    <xsd:element name="month" type="xsd:gMonth" />
    <xsd:element name="year" type="xsd:gYear" />
  </xsd:sequence>
</xsd:complexType>
```

The dateType has four subelements. The first of these, dayname, takes a user-defined type. The others are all built-in types based on the Gregorian calendar. This schema was developed after the XML document and its original DTD. This structure which splits the date into pieces was already established before the schema. If I had started afresh with XML Schema, I would have used the built-in date type[11] for the whole thing. That wouldn't have included the name of the day, but letters still make sense without that particular piece of data.

```
<xsd:complexType name="personType">
  <xsd:sequence>
    <xsd:element name="name" type="fullNameType"
             minOccurs="1" maxOccurs="1"/>
    <xsd:element name="address" type="addressType"
             maxOccurs="1" />
  </xsd:sequence>
</xsd:complexType>

<xsd:complexType name="fullNameType">
  <xsd:sequence>
    <xsd:element name="title" type="titleType"
             minOccurs="1" maxOccurs="1"/>
    <xsd:element name="firstname" type="nameType"
             minOccurs="0" maxOccurs="unbounded" />
    <xsd:element name="surname" type="nameType"
             maxOccurs="1" />
```

[11] See Table 4.1.

```
    </xsd:sequence>
  </xsd:complexType>
```

Next up, the elements that hold data about either the sender or the recipient are defined. Both are, of course, people. We need the same data for each of them, basically name and address, so we can use the same structures. The `personType` contains a `name` element and an `address` element. The `name` element can only appear once. This is determined by setting both the `minOccurs` and `maxOccurs` attributes. In this schema a person has, at most, one `address`. By leaving `minOccurs` unset, the user doesn't *have* to provide data for the `address`. Similar constraints cover the structure of the `fullNameType`.

```
  <xsd:complexType name="addressType">
    <xsd:sequence>
      <xsd:element name="line1" type="addressLineType" maxOccurs
         ="1" />
      <xsd:element name="line2" type="addressLineType" maxOccurs
         ="1" />
      <xsd:element name="line3" type="addressLineType" maxOccurs
         ="1" />
      <xsd:element name="city" type="addressLineType" maxOccurs
         ="1" />
      <xsd:choice>
        <xsd:element name="county" type="addressLineType"
           maxOccurs="1" />
        <xsd:element name="state" type="addressLineType"
           maxOccurs="1" />
      </xsd:choice>
      <xsd:element name="code" type="xsd:string" minOccurs="1"
         maxOccurs="1"/>
      <xsd:element name="country" type="countryType" maxOccurs
         ="1" />
    </xsd:sequence>
  </xsd:complexType>
```

The address is more complex than anything seen so far. Since addresses differ in format and content between countries, providing a truly internationalized address structure is extremely hard. Probably the best way to do it is to create a type to define addresses for each country that you need. A single *global* address type could be created through a `union` of all the localized versions.

I've not done anything so grand. I've created an amalgamated `addressType` which is basically UK format with one change to show more aspects of XML Schemas. The UK is divided into counties[12] for either administrative purposes or historical reasons. Other nations are divided into states, regions or provinces. In giving an address, the region is usually included. So that I can select the appropriate regional type, a `choice` element is created. This contains elements that define all of the regional variants that I'm interested in. XML instance documents can use any of the subelements that are placed here. Using a choice even means that different data types can be used at the same place in a document if necessary. Perhaps paradoxically, instance documents will be simpler because the schema is more complex.

The `signatureType` contains another `choice`. This time the instance document may contain either the full name or just the first name of the sender:

```
<xsd:complexType name="signatureType">
  <xsd:sequence>
    <xsd:element name="greeting" type="greetingType" maxOccurs
        ="1"/>
    <xsd:choice>
      <xsd:element name="firstname" type="nameType" />
      <xsd:element name="name" type="fullNnameType" />
    </xsd:choice>
  </xsd:sequence>
</xsd:complexType>

<xsd:complexType name="greetingType">
  <xsd:sequence>
    <xsd:element name="greeting" type="xsd:string" />
  </xsd:sequence>
  <xsd:attribute name="type">
    <xsd:simpleType>
      <xsd:restriction base="xsd:NMTOKEN">
        <xsd:enumeration value="formal" />
        <xsd:enumeration value="informal" />
        <xsd:enumeration value="other" />
      </xsd:restriction>
    </xsd:simpleType>
  </xsd:attribute>
</xsd:complexType>
```

[12] And countries but I'm trying not to over-complicate these structures.

The greetingType which defines the salutation at the end of the letter is another interesting structure. The actual salutation varies between letters. In the UK it might be *Yours Sincerely* or *Yours Faithfully* for formal letters, or something more personal. The greeting could be included in every letter but that leads to a lot of redundant information being stored on the system. I've chosen to create an attribute which defines which type of salutation to use but leaves creating it to the processing application. The different salutations are selected using a token which is a restriction of the built-in NMTOKEN type. Possible values for the attribute are given in an enumeration.

```
<!-- define simple types -->
<xsd:simpleType name="nameType">
  <xsd:restriction base="xsd:string">
    <xsd:maxLength value="32" />
  </xsd:restriction>
</xsd:simpleType>

<xsd:simpleType name="daynameType">
  <xsd:restriction base="xsd:string">
    <xsd:maxLength value="9" />
  </xsd:restriction>
</xsd:simpleType>

<xsd:simpleType name="titleType">
  <xsd:restriction base="xsd:string">
    <xsd:maxLength value="4" />
  </xsd:restriction>
</xsd:simpleType>

<xsd:simpleType name="addressLineType">
  <xsd:restriction base="xsd:string">
    <xsd:maxLength value="48" />
  </xsd:restriction>
</xsd:simpleType>
```

Most of the complex types and elements described so far contain user-defined data types. These simple types are mostly self-explanatory. The countryCodes type is worth highlighting since, like the greetingType, it uses an enumeration to restrict the values it can contain. In greetingType, the enumeration was applied to an attribute. For countryCodes, it is applied to an element.

```
<xsd:simpleType name="countryCodes">
```

```
    <xsd:restriction base="xsd:NMTOKEN">
      <xsd:enumeration value="FR" />
      <xsd:enumeration value="UK" />
      <xsd:enumeration value="USA" />
      <xsd:enumeration value="OTHER" />
    </xsd:restriction>
  </xsd:simpleType>

  <xsd:simpleType name="countryType">
    <xsd:union memberTypes="xsd:string countryCodes" />
  </xsd:simpleType>
```

The actual country used in the address may be either the name of the country or one of the codes defined in `countryCodes`. Since both these are data types, one built-in and one user-defined, I'm using a `union` to select between them. The `union` element takes a space-separated list of data types as the value of its `memberTypes` attribute. Any type in the list is valid content for the element.

Finally, even XML Schema documents need to be ended properly:

```
</xsd:schema>
```

> **Note:**
> That's all there is to defining a non-trivial document using XML Schema. Many examples that you'll find, either in other books or on the Web, are really rather simple. They won't use the full range of possibilities that XML Schema provides. They also tend not to mix structures in the way that I have. Remember, this is a flexible technology which you can use in your own way. That's part of its beauty.

Exercises

1. Describe three advantages and three disadvantages which XML Schema have when compared to DTDs.

2. What are namespaces, and why are they needed for complex XML structures?

3. If you created the name and address document at the end of Chapter 2, write an XML Schema for the document.

4. Write a Schema for the name and address structure which you created at the end of Chapter 2. If you are unable to make your schema match the structure of your document, modify the document so that it is simpler.

5. Find software which can be used to validate documents against XML Schemas. Is your document valid?i

6. Research the structures used for addresses in the US, Japan and Brazil. Can you modify your schema so that it supports all of those forms?

7. If you modified the business letter, now modify the XML Schema so that it matches your new structure.

Part Two

Formatting XML for Display and Print

Chapter 5

Cascading Style Sheets

XML is primarily used to define formats for data structures used within applications or for the storage or transmission of data. Large XML files can look pretty fearsome. There are very few applications in which a developer would want to let users anywhere near the XML. This is a classic dilemma: the presentation of the data needs to be separated from its storage and manipulation. Applications might see XML trees but, to a user, the same data might be a document inside a word processor, an image or an email message. There's really nothing new here. Try opening a document created in a word processor such as Microsoft Word 97 inside a plain text editor such as Notepad. You'll see lots of strange characters which control the way the document looks inside Word, and somewhere deep inside the file you'll see your words.

XML presents one additional complexity that's not present with a word processor. When Microsoft developed Word 97 they were able to define what the application would do, and how it would do it. The data structure and presentation were developed side-by-side and tightly coupled to each other. The same approach could be used in XML. Define a data structure and write some code which presents that data inside your application. This immediately negates one of the benefits we get from XML since the presentation of the data now requires a particular piece of software.

What XML really needs is a platform-independent way of formatting data for presentation. Since there are different types of presentation, the XML developer has a number of technologies available. Firstly, there's Cascading Style Sheets which can be used to present XML structures in some Web browsers. Secondly, there is XSL, the Extensible Stylesheet Language. This has two aspects of its own. The first is XSLT, XSL Transformations, which is used to transform one XML structure into another. Thus, for example, a complex XML file can be converted into a set of XHTML pages for use on the Web. Unfortunately, Web pages don't print very well – especially in situations like book publishing where extremely high quality output[1] is the norm. The second part of XSL has been created to produce print quality output. XSL-FO, XSL Formatting Objects, defines transformations which can be used to produce output in PDF, PostScript, Microsoft RTF and even TEX formats. I'll cover XSLT and XSL-FO in subsequent chapters. For now, I'm going to concentrate on the simplest of the three: CSS.

5.1 CSS AND HTML

Cascading Style Sheets is an HTML technology which has been found to be compatible with XML. Although CSS became a W3C Recommendation in late 1996, it's not used as widely as it ought to be. Many Web authors prefer to embed formatting information inside their HTML files using `<font> </font>` tags. Others don't realize that this is happening, it's simply what the tools they use *do*. There's no guarantee that `<font>` tags will be rendered the same in all browsers, and if a browser doesn't understand them, downloading the document was a waste of bandwidth. Stylesheets *should* work in the same way in all browsers, and since they are separate documents, only browsers that can actually use them will download them.

Older Web browsing software won't understand XML and may struggle with CSS even when used in HTML pages. Fortunately, most people regularly update their browsers so this isn't a long-term problem. As we'll see in Chapter 8, the use of XSLT on the Web is not straightforward. As a medium-term method of presenting XML in Web browsers, CSS is a good strategy to adopt. Before examining the use of CSS with XML data, let's examine how it works with HTML.

[1]The extremely high quality output required for books has a resolution of several thousand dots per inch, compared to the several hundred dots per inch a good laser printer produces.

5.1.1 Using Styles: Simple Examples

Unfortunately, you can't really learn about stylesheets in a gradual or incremental fashion. You need to use a resource such as the list of tags in this book and then dive straight in. The following examples are just about as simple as the use of styles can get.

5.1.1.1 Changing h1 In this first example the `<h1>` tag is redefined. The text is colored in red, centered on the screen and has a thin border placed around it. Figure 5.1 shows the effect that this produces in the Konqueror browser.

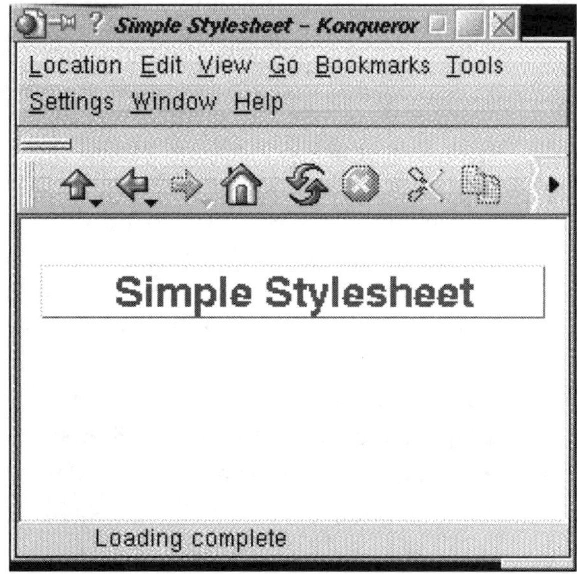

Figure 5.1 Changing `h1`

```
<html>
   <head>
      <title>Simple Stylesheet</title>
      <style>
      <!--
         h1{
            color: red;
            border: thin groove;
            text-align: center;
         }
      -->
```

```
        </style>
    </head>
    <body>
        <h1>Simple Stylesheet</h1>
    </body>
</html>
```

Notice that I'm declaring the style in the `head` of the document using the `style` tag. I place the actual style definition inside an HTML comment so that it will be ignored by browsers that don't support styles. The declaration has the name of the element that is being changed and then a definition which is placed inside braces. The attributes that are being changed are placed in a list with each term separated by a semi-colon. I usually place each attribute on a new line so that the definition is easier to read and maintain. Each definition is made from the attribute and a list of values which are separated by a colon. You might expect the values to be surrounded by double quotes in the same way that the attributes of HTML tags are. Don't do this: it isn't needed and, actually, the browser won't be able to handle the code if you include them. There are, as ever, exceptions to this. If you use a hexadecimal value to declare a color or if you use a font name that includes spaces then you can use either single quotes or quotation marks around it.

5.1.1.2 Changing More Styles This example goes slightly further by altering both `h1` and a paragraph. The paragraph is moved slightly to the right by giving it a left margin, has a colored background and a ridged border. The resulting Web page is shown in Figure 5.2.

```
<html>
    <head>
        <title>Simple Stylesheet</title>
        <style>
        <!--
            h1{
                color: red;
                border: thin groove;
            }
        -->
        </style>
    </head>
    <body>
        <h1>Simple Stylesheet</h1>
        <p>The first paragraph is left unaltered.</p>
```

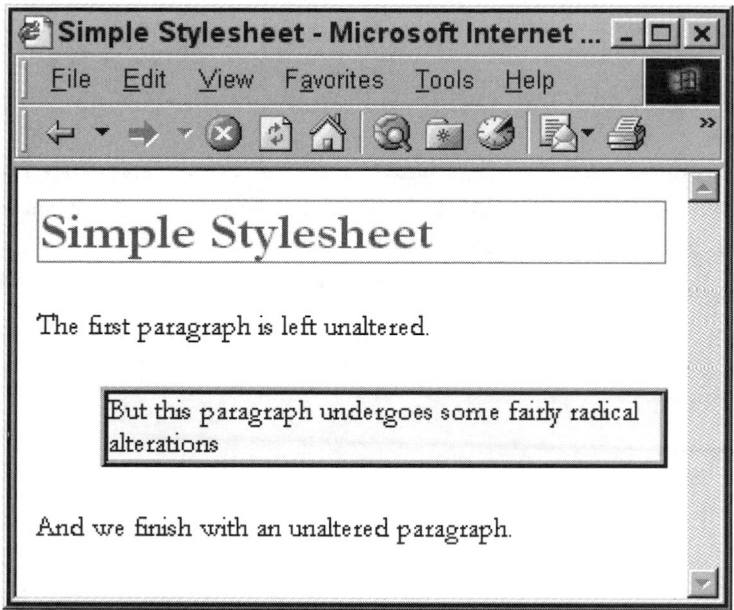

Figure 5.2 Declaring Styles Inline and in the Head

```
    <p style="margin-left: 10%; border: ridge;
       background: #ffffcc">
    But this paragraph undergoes some fairly radical
    alterations.</p>
    <p>And we finish with an unaltered paragraph.</p>
  </body>
</html>
```

The syntax of the style definition changes when it is done inside an HTML tag. The definition becomes an *attribute,* named style, of the tag. The description of the style is passed as the value of the attribute and so must follow an equals sign. The definition is placed inside quotation marks but otherwise uses the same syntax that we saw a moment ago.

Redefining elements as I've done with the paragraph in the example is unsatisfactory. There is no separation between the processing of an element and the definition of that element. Remember the markup should be logical; any physical changes, such as new formats, should appear outside of that markup.

5.2 CSS AND XML

Writing cascading stylesheets and applying them to XML documents is not very different to applying them to HTML documents. Just like HTML, the styles *can* go into the same file as the document. Unlike HTML, where this is useful when styles need to be cascaded, it doesn't provide any benefits to the XML author. If you need to know how to mix styles and XML, there are examples on the W3C Web site so I won't cover it here.

The following listing shows a simple XML document:

Listing 5.1 "Linking XML to Cascading Stylesheet"

```
<?xml version="1.0"?>
<?xml-stylesheet type="text/css" href="simple.css"?>

<document>
  <title>Simple Stylesheet</title>
</document>
```

The second line contains the link to the stylesheet file. The `<?xml-stylesheet?>` processing instruction is used to include XSL stylesheets as well as the CSS variety. It has a number of optional parameters, most of which work like those of the HTML `<link>` tag, if you're familiar with that.

`href="URI"`
: This is the URI of the stylesheet. The URI can contain a fragment identifier which points to part of the URI, thus letting the same URI contain a number of stylesheets. URIs used here can be either absolute or relative but must be accessible. If the processor is unable to access the stylesheet, the XML document will be displayed as plain text with the tags removed.

`type="text/css"`
: The MIME type for cascading stylesheets must be supplied as a value to the `type` attribute. The processor will not assume this as a default value and cannot be guaranteed to behave properly if you leave it out.

`title="string"`
: A stylesheet can be given a title if you wish.

`media="string"`
: Your XML document might be processed for many different targets. These can include Web browsers, audio devices, printers, televisions. Each will display the document differently. Specifying the output media won't guarantee sensible behavior but it might help.

charset="string"

If you use an extended character set in your XML document, you'll need to specify it here. This should be the same as the encoding given in the `<?xml ?>` processing instruction.

alternate="yes|no"

If you are providing alternate stylesheets with your document, this attribute should be set to `yes`. It defaults to `no`. Alternate stylesheets are provided so that the document can be processed differently by different applications. For example, if the XML document contains:

```
<?xml-stylesheet type="text/css" href="simple.css" title="
    normal" alternate="yes"?>
<?xml-stylesheet type="text/css" href="larger.css" title="
    large fonts" alternate="yes"?>
```

the processing application is able to choose the set of styles that are most appropriate for a particular situation.

The cascading stylesheet associated with the XML file in Listing 5.1 is shown below:

```
title {
  color:red;
  border:thick groove;
  font-size: 24pt;
  text-align: right;
  margin-top: 24pt;
  margin-left: 24pt;
}
```

Different browsers will render this in different ways. I've tried a wide variety. Konqueror running on Linux wouldn't render the document at all; Mozilla 1.0 and Opera 6 both ignored the top margin and failed to align the text to the right. Figure 5.3 shows how Internet Explorer 5.5 displayed the document. The difficulty that browsers have is that their page rendering engines are designed for HTML pages. An XML file lacks the structure of `head` and `body` sections that HTML has. When rendering XML, there's no concept of screen width or height. Treat this as a warning. You might not get what you expect. If the combination of XML and CSS doesn't work for you, use XSLT to convert your XML document into XHTML and supply a stylesheet to display that.

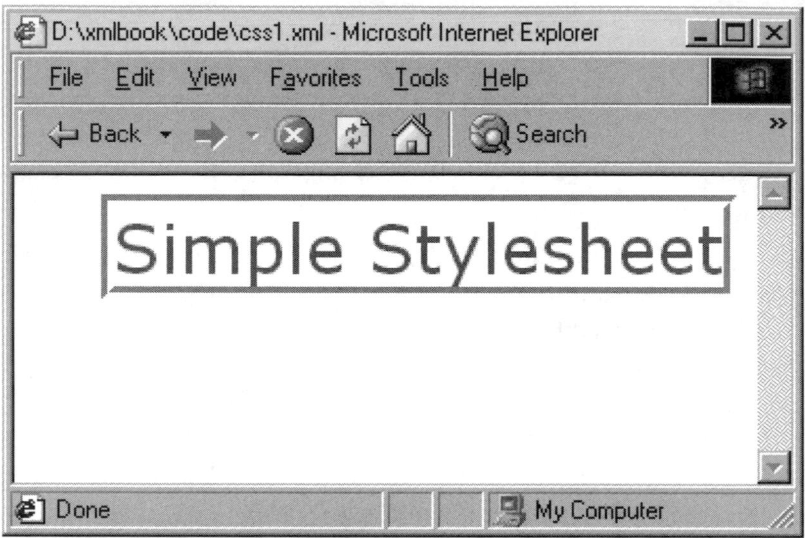

Figure 5.3 Formatting XML File Using Cascading Stylesheets

5.3 DEFINING YOUR OWN STYLES

Styles are defined by simple rules. A style can contain as many rules as you want and, as with processing HTML, if something doesn't make sense it will be ignored.

5.3.1 Cascading Styles

Conventionally, styles are cascaded. This means that you do not have to use just a single set of styles inside a document – you can import as many stylesheets as you like. This is useful if you define a set of organizational styles that can be modified by each department. The only difficulty with importing multiple stylesheets is that they cascade. This means that the first is overridden by the second, the second by the third, and so on. Of course the overriding only happens if a later stylesheet contains a definition of a style that is already defined. You can also override styles by defining styles within the body of the page as I showed in Section 5.1.1.

5.3.2 Rules

A style rule has two parts: a selector and a set of declarations. The selector is used to create a link between the rule and the HTML tag. The declaration has two parts: a property and a value. Selectors can be placed into classes so that a tag can be formatted in a variety of ways. Declarations must be separated using colons and terminated using semicolons.

selector {property: value; property: value ...}

This form is used for all style declarations in stylesheets. The declaration has three items: the property, a colon, and the value. If you miss the colon or fail to put the semicolon between declarations, the style cannot be processed. Rules do not have to be formatted as I've shown – as with HTML, you can lay the text out however you like. The rule will be more readable if you put each declaration on its own line. This is an example of a simple rule, followed by a more complex one:

```
body {
   background-color: #eebd2;
}

h1 {
   color: #eeebd2;
   background-color: #d8a29b;
   font-family: "Book Antiqua", Times, serif;
   border: thin groove #9baab2;
}
```

The detail of these style attributes will be discussed in Section 5.4.

5.3.3 Classes

The method shown above applies the same style to all examples of a given tag. That is fine if you want every paragraph equally indented or every level-one heading in the same font. If you only want to apply a style to some paragraphs, for instance, you have to use classes:

selector.classname {property: value; property: value}

<selector class=classname>

These examples show how classes should be used. In the stylesheet itself the rule is slightly modified by giving the style a unique name which is appended to the selector using a dot. In the HTML document, when you want to use a named style the tag is extended by including `class=` and the unique name.

```
h1.fred {
   color: #eeebd2;
   background-color: #d8a29b;
   font-family: "Book Antiqua", Times, serif;
   border: thin groove #9baab2;
```

```
}

<h1 class="fred">A Simple Heading</h1>
```

The benefit of classes is that they can provide a lot of variety. They are especially good if you want to redefine the paragraph style so that your introductions look different from your content.

5.3.3.1 Anonymous Classes Sometimes you want to apply a piece of formatting to many different elements within a page but not necessarily to the entire page. You could redefine every element in a stylesheet to make it use your formatting, and then redefine individual elements back to their defaults as you needed to. This is a rather awkward approach and would inevitably lead to a lot of duplication of effort. Cascading stylesheets provides a way of defining styles within reusable classes. The following code and Figure 5.4 show how this works.

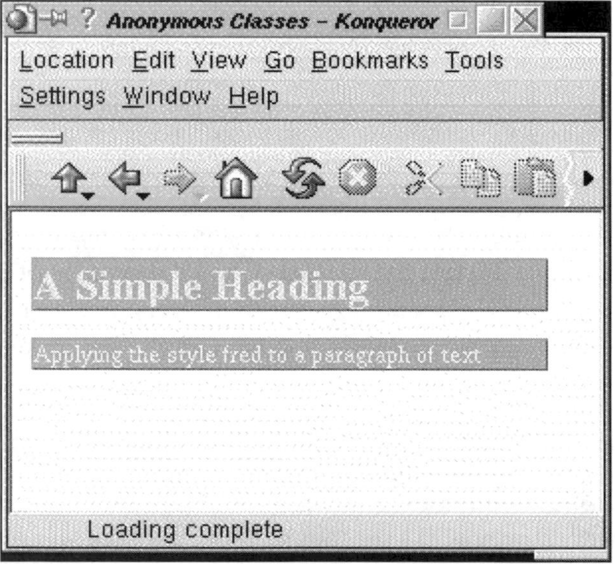

Figure 5.4 Using Classes of Style

```
<html>
   <head>
      <title>Anonymous Classes</title>
      <style>
      <!--
```

```
        .fred {
           color: #eeebd2;
           background-color: #d8a29b;
           font-family: "Book Antiqua", Times, serif;
           border: thin groove #9baab2;
        }
     -->
     </style>
  </head>
  <body>
     <h1 class="fred">A Simple Heading</h1>
     <p class="fred">Applying the style fred to a
        paragraph of text</p>
  </body>
</html>
```

5.4 PROPERTIES AND VALUES IN STYLES

A number of properties of the text can be altered. These can be grouped together. I'll list the properties in useful groups and give some of the options that you can alter. The best way of discovering how styles work is to play around with some of these properties. Try giving absurd values to elements and see what happens.

> **Rule of Thumb:**
> Don't change too many options. You're trying to present information, not give a lesson in typography and colors. Be careful, as ever, and make sure that your key changes are available to your target audience. Don't rely too heavily on styles yet – within a year or two they may be everywhere but at the moment Web surfers have to wait for the next revision of their browsers.

In the following descriptions of the properties I won't give examples; there is a large and fairly comprehensive example later in this section.

5.4.1 Formatting Elements

Styles cannot be haphazardly applied to elements, whether in XHTML or XML documents. If documents are going to be presented in a relatively uniform manner across processing agents, some rules are required which define how elements are styled. Cascading stylesheets use a box model to set out each element. Figure 5.5 shows this model.

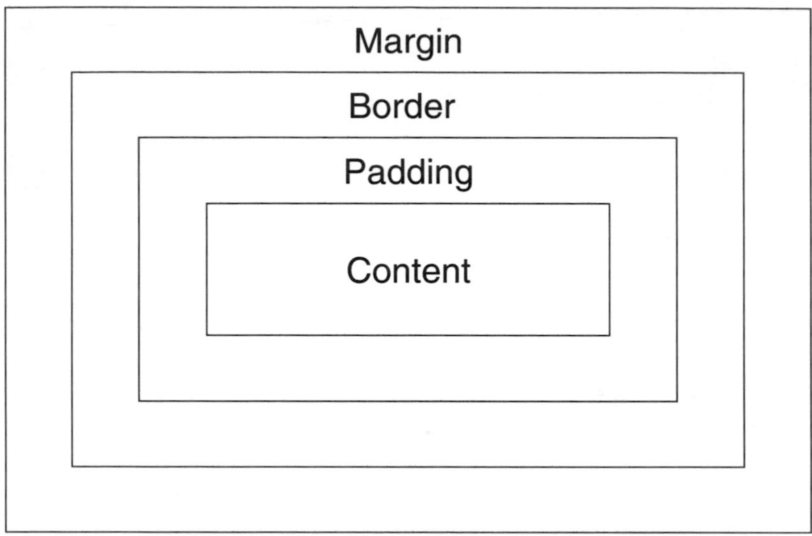

Figure 5.5 The Box Model for CSS Elements

For block-level elements, the size of the margin, padding and border can be set using CSS elements which are detailed later. Although the color of the border can be set and the padding uses the same background as the element content, the margin is always transparent.

`display: none|block|inline|list-item`

Many XHTML elements are defined as block or inline in the XHTML Recommendation. Headings and paragraphs, `<h1>` and `<p>`, for example, are always blocks. An element such as `<em>` will be inline. When defining styles for XML elements, it's necessary to specify if the element is a block or an inline element so that the browser can format it correctly. Figure 5.6 shows the effect of setting the `display` property to `block`.

By default the width of a block is not set. When formatting XML, I've found that different browsers take radically different approaches to wrapping text. Mozilla appears to *not* wrap text, while other browsers wrap it at the width of the browser on screen. If the `width` property of the block is set, the text will be wrapped in all browsers.

5.4.2 Fonts

`font-family: <family name> [<generic family>]`

Fonts are identified by giving the name of a specific font. Many Microsoft Windows and Apple systems have similar sets of TrueType fonts. Unfortunately, Unix systems use Type 1 and PostScript fonts. Therefore it is unlikely that a reader on one of those computers will have access to the fonts from your PC. The TrueType fonts look better than Type 1 fonts and the user-base of Web surfers with access to true type is far greater.

You should try to use TrueType fonts in your Web pages but provide an option for users who don't have these fonts. This can be done in two ways. First, you may specify as many fonts as you like for each style in the hope that most people will have at least one of them. Second, you can specify a default generic font which all browsers on all systems can handle. Five generic fonts are specified: *serif (times), sans-serif (arial), cursive, fantasy, monospaced (courier)*. Font names that include whitespace should be placed in quotes. Generally a list of fonts is provided, and the browser will try to use each in turn until it finds one that it recognizes:

```
p {
  font-family: "Bookman Old Style",
     "Times New Roman", Times, serif;
}
```

`font-style: normal|italic|oblique`

Fairly straightforward. Oblique fonts are slanted, italic do not have to be.

`font-weight: normal|bold|bolder|lighter|100|200|`
`300|400|500|600|700|800|900`

The weight of any font can be altered. The first four options are relative while the numbered values give absolute weights. Not all fonts support all possible weights and you may want to be careful using absolute weights. The line break here is simply so that the code fits onto the page.

`font-size: [small|medium|large]|[smaller|larger]|`
`<length>|<percentage>`

As well as changing the weight you can alter the size. Again, a choice of relative sizes is possible. Font lengths should be given in appropriate units such as pt. A discussion of units is given in Section 5.4.6. Absolute sizes include small, large, and so on, while relative sizes are larger or smaller.

`font-variant: normal|small-caps`

Some fonts are available in small capitals. When the variant is set to `small-caps`, capital letters appear as normal. Where lower-case letters would normally appear, capital letters are substituted at the same height as a lower-case vowel.

5.4.3 Backgrounds and Colors

color: <value>

background-color: <value>|transparent

background-image: URL|none

The color of any attribute can be changed. Values should be given as hexadecimal values. Backgrounds for the whole page or individual elements can have their color set from the stylesheet. Elements can also have transparent backgrounds. Instead of a color an image can be used, identified by its URL. If you set the background-color you should set the background-image to none.

background-repeat: repeat|repeat-y|repeat-x|no-repeat

When background-image is being used, the image may be tiled across the screen. The repetition is controlled by background-repeat. When set to repeat the image is tiled both horizontally and vertically. When set to repeat-x it is only tiled horizontally and when set to repeat-y only vertical tiling is used. Using no-repeat switches tiling off.

background-position: [percentage|length]{1,2}|
[top|center|bottom]|[left|center|right]

When a background-image has been specified, its initial position on the screen can be set. The position of the top-left corner of the image is specified relative to the top-left corner of the screen, with a default value of 0%,0%. If the value 100%,100% is given, the bottom-right corner of the image is placed at the bottom-right corner of the screen. A value such as 25%,33% will place the pixel at location 25%,33% across the image at the same *relative* location on the screen. Similar considerations apply to absolute length. When only a single value is given, it applies only to the horizontal positioning of the image. Finally, individual keywords or pairs of words can be given. When a pair of words is used, one is taken from each set shown in the definition, for instance top left is OK, but left right is not.

5.4.4 Text

text-decoration: none|underline|overline|line-through

Any piece of text can be decorated.

text-transform: none|capitalize|uppercase|lowercase

Allows you to set the case of text. This can be useful if you can't be sure that text will be entered appropriately. For instance if you are listing countries by their initials, create a capitalized style.

`text-align: left|right|center|justify`

One of the most useful text styles. Allows you to fully justify text in paragraphs, which many people like. By default HTML uses ragged right margins.

`text-indent: length|percentage`

Beforestylesheets were devised text could not be indented on the left side. Many people like their text indented, as this paragraph is, and would use small transparent GIFs to achieve it. Using the style is much better, as it downloads along with the text and it is flexible. Use a percentage and the amount of space will scale nicely if the browser window is resized.

`word-spacing: normal|<length>`

Specifies a distance to be added to the spacing between words. The `length` may be negative.

`letter-spacing: normal|<length>`

Specifies a distance to be added to the spacing between letters within words.

`vertical-align: baseline|sub|super|top|text-top|`
`middle|bottom|text-bottom|<percentage>`

Moves the element relative to its parent. The element may be aligned against the whole of the parent element or against the current line depending upon the value chosen. It's worth experimenting with this property – especially if you want to format mathematical expressions and don't want to investigate MathML.

`line-height: normal|<number>|<length>|<percentage>`

Changes the distance between the bottom, or baseline, of adjacent lines.

5.4.5 Boxes

Many items can be encased in boxes. This can give some very good effects although care needs to be taken. If the boxes become overwhelming or are used too much they can start to look rather odd.

`margin: length|percentage|auto {1,4}`
`border-width: thin|thick|medium|length {1,4}`
`padding: length|percentage {1,4}`

Any of the margins of a box can be changed. This time it may often be better to specify an absolute length – if you use a percentage the margins may become overly crowded when the window is resized. You can specify 1, 2, or 4 margin values. If you specify 4 they are applied in the order: top, right, bottom, and left. Specify just one value and it is applied to all four margins. Specify two values and the first will be applied to top and bottom, the second to left and right margins. As with margins, you can specify the amount of whitespace within an element. Padding and border width are applied in the same way as margins.

Individual values can be applied using attribute names built from Table 5.1. To build a name, concatenate the property name in the left column with one of the names in subsequent columns. Separate the names using hyphens, for instance, `margin-top` or `border-top-width`.

Table 5.1 Margin, Padding and Border Names

margin	top	bottom	right	left
padding	top	bottom	right	left
border	top-width	bottom-width	left-width	right-width
border	top	bottom	right	left

`border-color:   value {1,4}`
`border-style:   none|dotted|dashed|solid|double|groove|`
`ridge {1,4}`

This sets the color of the border around the element. Up to four different colors can be specified. They are applied to the borders in the same order as margins. Each edge of the border can have a different style.

`width:   length|percentage|auto`
`height:   length|auto`

Anyblock-level element can be given a specific width or height. As with so many items, it is better to specify the width as percentages to allow for resizing of the browser window. The height must be specified as an absolute size.

`float:   none|left|right`

Moves the element within the page. The value `none` leaves its position unaltered, `left` moves it to the left and `right` moves it to the right. Floating elements are treated as block-level elements even if they are not specified as such.

`clear:   none:left:right:both`

Specifies on which side, if any, the element allows floating. When set to `left`, for example, the element will be moved below any floating elements which are placed to its left.

5.4.6 Units, URLs and Colors

These can be either absolute or relative. A relative length can be either positive or negative, which is indicated by preceding the value with an optional + or –.

Relative units that can be used are:

- em: the height of the font for this element
- ex: the height of the letter "x" in the current font
- px: pixels

Allowable absolute units are:

- in: size in inches
- cm: size in centimeters
- mm: size in millimeters
- pt: points where 1 pt equals 1/72 inch
- pc: picas where 1 pc = 12 pt

URLs can be used in stylesheets just as they can in HTML documents. The format of the URL reference is:

```
url(location)
```

URLs can optionally be quoted and may be either absolute or relative. If a URL is partial it is considered to be relative to the location of the stylesheet source, not the HTML document source.

Colors are specified using either the name of the color or a numerical value in RGB form. RGB, of course, specifies a value for the amounts of red, green and blue in the desired color. RGB values can be given using either decimal or hexadecimal notation, or as percentages. Here are some examples:

```
#ff00ff, rgb(234,45,01), rgb(45%, 0%, 55%)
```

5.5 A STYLESHEET FOR THE BUSINESS LETTER

Cascading stylesheets can easily be used to format XML for presentation within a Web browser. At the time of writing this chapter, it's not really a match made in heaven. The current generation of Web browsers have great trouble making an XML file look anything other than ugly. Although CSS helps, it's not a long-term solution. The more sensible approach is to convert the XML into XHTML using XSLT and to style the XHTML using CSS.[2] There are going to be times when presenting small quantities of XML direct to a

[2] I'm really sorry about all of those acronyms, but the real names would have turned the sentence into a paragraph.

Web browser is a good idea. In this section I'm going to present a rudimentary stylesheet for the Business Letter and show you what Opera 6 makes of it.

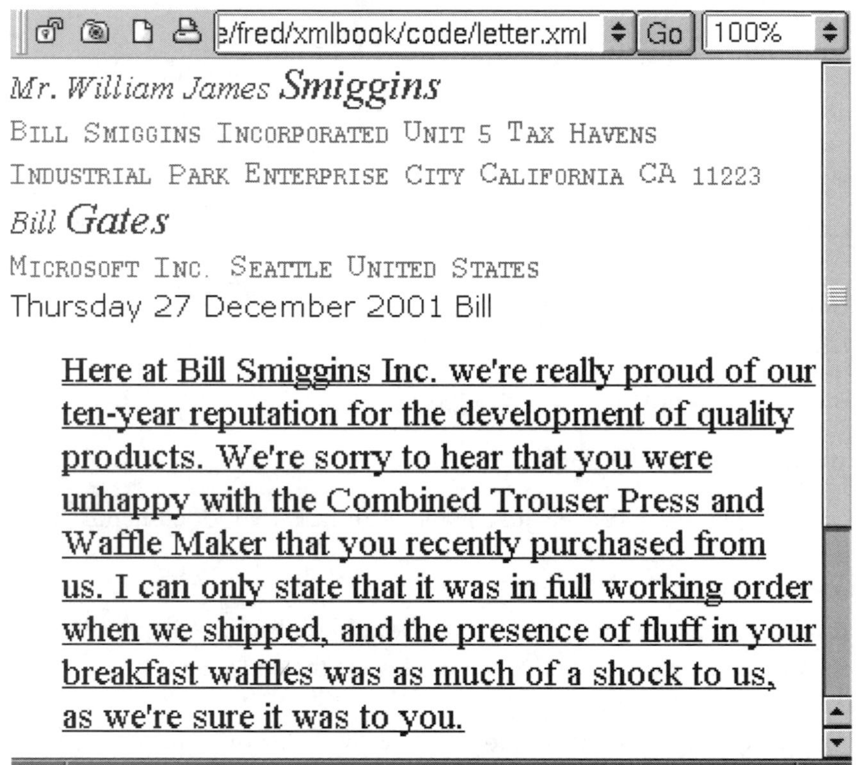

Figure 5.6 Business Letter Styled With CSS

I'm just going to style the `name`, `address` and `para` elements. Interestingly, styling an element such as `name`, which acts as a container, has the effect of applying the style to all of its subelements. Figure 5.6 demonstrates the result. Overriding the style inherited from the containing element is easy. Simply define a new style for each individual element you want to vary. Notice in the following code that the `surname` element inherits the properties of the `name` element. Some of these are then modified.

Listing 5.2 Stylesheet for the Business Letter

```
name {
  font-family: Times New Roman;
  font-size: 12pt;
  font-style: italic;
  color: blue;
}
```

```
surname {
  font-style: bold;
  font-size: 16pt;
  display: inline;
}

address {
  font-family: fixed;
  font-size:12pt;
  font-variant: small-caps;
  color: green;
  display: block;
  width: 10cm;
}

para {
  font-family: times new roman;
  font-size: 14pt;
  margin-left: 20pt;
  margin-top: 10pt;
  text-decoration: underline;
  display: block;
  width: 10cm;
}
```

There are a couple of important things to notice when comparing the code with the screenshot. The XML elements are presented by the browser in the order in which they appear in the source document. This will often be desirable behavior when the order of the elements in the XML document matches their relative positions. For the Business Letter, there is no correspondence between the position of an element in the XML and its position in a real letter. For example, the `signature` element is found in the `header` section of the XML file, yet a signature in a letter must be appended to the bottom. Where elements must be moved, or modified before presentation, XSLT is the correct approach to take.

The second important thing to notice is that the date and signature elements appear in the finished XML document in Opera yet no styles have been defined for them. CSS cannot be used to filter XML documents in any way. If it's in the document it will appear in the browser – except for comments, of course.

Exercises

1. What do Web designers mean when they talk about a *style*?

2. Although stylesheets have been a W3C recommendation for several year some browsers do not yet support them fully. How should a browser behave if it encounters formatting that it cannot handle?

3. Describe the different ways that styles can be added to an XML document.

4. What happens if you specify a formatting instruction that is unavailable?

Chapter 6

Cascading Style Sheets Two

Cascading stylesheets have proven themselves as a robust, developer-friendly technology. They are applicable to both XHTML and XML data files, they are lightweight and they work well. As defined in the Cascading Stylesheets Recommendation of 1996, and its later update in 1999, CSS is intended purely for display of data on screen. Although the Recommendation uses the term *user-agent* throughout, the fact that this means Web browser is implicit in the document. The Web has changed in any number of ways since 1996:

- Millions more people now use the Web every day.
- The technologies that underpin it, such as HTTP, are being put to a changing set of uses in areas like intranets and messaging systems.
- Web data has changed from simple HTML to XHTML and XML.
- Whole new types of application such as Web Services are being developed.
- The Web is now truly world-wide, accessed continually from every continent.

- Many pages contain a mixture of fonts and character sets.

One of the most intriguing things, from a developer's point of view, is that Web data is no longer just viewed on a computer screen. Data originating in XHTML or XML may be accessed through mobile phones or television screens, used in presentations, printed in paper documents or presented aurally. The original CSS technology doesn't allow for these myriad uses. It focused solely upon the presentation of data in a Web browser.

The Cascading Stylesheets Two, CSS2, Recommendation of May 1998 addressed the limitations of the original Cascading Stylesheets Recommendations. In particular, properties were added to:

- format printed documents,
- support the aural presentation of data,
- include formatting specifically of tables,
- aid the presentation of data to disabled users,
- allow the scripting of stylesheet properties using languages such as JavaScript.

Although the primary developer community using CSS2 is going to be Web authors working in XHTML, many aspects of CSS2 are important for other XML applications. In particular, enhancements have been made to the way that stylesheets work while remaining totally backwards compatible and usable in a variety of media. CSS2 is another one of those technologies where the specification has a significant lead over the software. At the time of writing, few, if any, applications have been developed that support more than a relatively tiny subset of CSS2. Perhaps this is not surprising since an application that uses the aural stylesheets may never need to format XML for display. It's worth remembering that CSS-compatible applications will come in a number of different types. Unfortunately, many applications do not, as yet, implement all of the properties that they could use. Most Web browsers don't even include all of the visual properties, partly due to the complexity of implementing them all, and partly due to lack of demand.

6.1 THE DESIGN OF CSS2

Cascading Stylesheets Two follows many of the same design principles that underpin the original CSS. Most importantly for developers who want to start using CSS2, the standard is totally backwards compatible with CSS. This means that browsers that only support CSS can load CSS2 stylesheets and ignore those elements that they do not understand. Since CSS2 is a super-set of CSS, any CSS2-compliant browser is also able to load CSS styles pages and render them as intended. Any user-agent such as a browser that is unable to manipulate stylesheets should be able to display the content of the file without styling it. This is more of an issue for XHTML developers than it is for XML developers. Any of the current browsers that can parse XML can also handle cascading stylesheets.

Separating the style and display information from the content brings several benefits. Different stylesheets can be created for different uses. This makes systems more maintainable, provides better utilization of network resources since browsers only download stylesheets that they can handle, and it works without affecting the structure of the markup in the XML file.

CSS2 has been designed to be simple to use. Since more properties have been added to those which are available in CSS, there has been a necessary increase in complexity. The syntax of the CSS language remains both clear and simple. Because properties have been added, the CSS2 model is extremely feature rich. Many features that Web designers had been asking for were added to CSS2. It's just a little unfortunate that the richness of the Recommendation is not equaled by the richness of use of CSS2 on the Web.

CSS2 adds many properties which are specifically designed to make content more accessible to those with disabilities. Specifically:

- the appearance of fonts can be controlled so that bitmaps which are difficult to read are eliminated,
- layout is controlled through CSS2 properties rather than through the use of tricks such as invisible images,
- using `!important` rules means that users can override aspects of stylesheets,
- media support is now provided for braille, embossed and tty terminals,
- voice and audio output can be styled using aural properties,
- attribute selectors provide alternative content within stylesheets,
- counters and numbering can be used to make document navigation easier on braille terminals.

6.1.1 Media Types

Cascading Stylesheets Two defines a number of different media types on which content might be displayed. These are given as attribute values in the `<xml-stylesheet>` element when the relationship between the XML file and stylesheet is established. The list of devices that is given in the Recommendation, and reproduced below, is not comprehensive. New devices will always appear so this list will inevitably grow as technologies change.

all
: The content is suitable for all applications.

aural
: Content is designed for speech synthesis software.

braille
: The data will be formatted for tactile braille readers.

embossed
: The data will be formatted for paged braille readers.

handheld
: Formatting for handheld devices, such as PDAs and mobile phones, which have extremely small screens.

print
: The document will be printed conventionally on paper.

projection
: The output will be displayed on a projection device or printed onto transparencies for display on a large screen.

screen
: Output will appear on a typical computer monitor capable of displaying colored output.

tty
: The output will be shown on a terminal or other device which can only display fixed fonts.

tv
: Output which will be used on a television screen.

6.2 STYLING FOR PAGED MEDIA

When information is displayed on a computer screen, it's usually available as a single long document. On modern systems, the document may be split into a series of files which are connected by hyperlinks or embedded within each other.[1] The computer provides a scrolling window onto the data within which the content is moved up or down to

[1] For instance using OLE or COM on Windows.

access different areas. Computer systems don't have the concept of paging, chunking data into screen-sized pieces and displaying a screenful at a time. That's the way that printed media works, though. Whether a newspaper, bound report, book or set of slides for a presentation, the content is split into page-sized chunks. When styling an XML file using CSS2, we don't necessarily know if the data will always be viewed on a computer screen or if it will be printed out. Fortunately, CSS2 includes properties which are designed to provide some, admittedly rather primitive, paging facilities.

CSS2 extends the box model, shown in Figure 5.5, and introduces a page box model. The page box is an abstract rendition of a page of the document in which page size, margins and layout can be specified. It does not necessarily map directly onto a physical piece of paper. Instead, once the author has defined the page layout and specified the page breaks, the processing software should be able to transfer the page boxes onto sheets of paper. CSS2 does not get involved in the details of the transfer process but the Recommendation does list the following possibilities:

- One page box is transferred to each sheet of paper. This is sometimes called *simplex* printing.
- Two page boxes are transferred to each sheet of paper. One is printed on each side of the paper. This is sometimes called *duplex* printing.
- A number of page boxes are transferred to the same side of a sheet of paper. This may be called *n-up* printing.
- A single page box is transferred across a number of sheets of paper.
- Pages may be printed on a single sheet in such order that, when the sheet is folded and cut, a book of correctly ordered pages is produced.
- A single page box or document may be printed simultaneously on a number of output devices.
- The formatted document may be written to a file in printable form.

Defining a page box involves defining the page and specifying its margins. Unlike the CSS box model, the `padding` and `border` properties do not apply to page boxes.

6.2.1 Page Rules

Page boxes are defined using the `@page` rule. This is then applied to pseudo-elements which represent the first page, all left pages, all right pages, named pages or, by default, all pages in the document. The following code defines a page box equivalent to an A4 sheet, with a 20mm margin on all four sides:

```
@page { size: 210mm 294mm; margin: 20mm; }
```

The printed area of the page is equal to the area of the page box minus the margins. The margin can be broken down and specified differently for each side of the page as shown here:

```
@page {
  size: 210mm 294mm;
  margin-left: 30mm;
  margin-right: 20mm;
  margin-top: 20mm;
  margin-bottom: 25mm;
}
```

The page size doesn't have to be defined using exact measurements. Instead it can be set to:

`auto`
: Which sets the size and orientation of the page box to the same as the target sheet.

`portrait`
: The page box will be in portrait format, regardless of the format of the target.

`landscape`
: The page box will be in landscape format, regardless of the format of the target.

When printing in book format the left and right margins change between the left and right pages. The outer margin is always set to be wider than the inner one. The CSS2 page box allows for this by letting the designer create left and right pseudo-elements which are configured differently:

```
@page {
  size: 210mm 294mm;
  margin-top: 20mm;
  margin-bottom: 20mm;
}

@page:left {
  size: 210mm 294mm;
  margin-left: 30mm;
  margin-right: 20mm;
}
```

```
@page:right {
  margin-left: 20mm;
  margin-right: 30mm;
}
```

This code sets the page size and the margins at top and bottom of the page, for *all* pages in the document. It then sets different left and right margins for left and right pages. Managing the pagination so as to decide which pages are left and which are right is left to the processing application. Setting a different page box for the first page is done through the `:first` pseudo-element.

6.2.2 Page Breaks

Although the processor will manage pagination throughout the document, there will be times when you need to force a page break. For example, if you are styling your XML so that it can be printed as a book, you will probably want to start each chapter on the right-hand page.

page-break-before: always|left|right|avoid|auto|inherit
page-break-after: always|left|right|avoid|auto|inherit
page-break-inside: avoid|auto|inherit

The values shown for these properties mean:

- `auto` Page breaks are neither forced nor inhibited.
- `always` A page break is *always* forced either before, or after, this element.
- `avoid` A page break is *never* allowed either before, or after, this element.
- `left` Page breaks are forced so that the next page will be a left-hand page.
- `right` Page breaks are forced so that the next page will be a right-hand page.

page: <name>|inherit
Use this property to give a unique identifying name to a page.

orphans: integer|inherit
widows: integer|inherit
These properties specify the minimum number of lines that must be present in a paragraph. Orphans are lines at the bottom of a page, widows are lines at the top. It's generally regarded as a *bad thing* to have one or two lines of a paragraph dangling in isolation from the rest of it. Formatting text so that widows and orphans are avoided is extremely difficult. Even well-established typesetting systems such

as TEX get it wrong. Using these two properties will, at least, give your software a start on the problem.

6.3 USING AURAL PRESENTATION

Presenting computer documents in aural form is a relatively immature technology, but one that has developed rapidly. In particular, applications intended for use by the blind or visually impaired, or others who have difficulty with text and printed material, are now widely available. Such software usually relies upon a speech synthesizer *reading* the content of the document to the user. The conversion of text into a form that a speech synthesizer can use often involves the removal of all formatting instructions so that the synthesizer receives plain text.

Clearly this is not a desirable situation, although it is preferable to having no access to the document. Structuring information conveys important meaning about the document and its content. Documents may be structured using such features as titles, sectional headers, lists or emphasized passages. Structuring a document in XML, which is basically text, and using stylesheets to format it means that both the structure and meaning of the document are preserved and can be used to aid the aural presentation of the material. Changing tone, adding sound effect and other *aural icons* can massively improve the listener's range of responses to the material.

> **Note:**
> Data may need to be presented aurally in a number of situations. Although the primary motivation is access for the disabled, access to data in situations in which reading is not possible also benefits. These may include access while driving, at work where access is restricted or in some educational situations.

6.3.1 Properties

The CSS2 properties that deal with the aural presentation of data include the ability to change sounds, volume or pitch. Sounds can be presented in three-dimensional space or spread out temporally so that one sound follows another.

`volume: <number>|<percentage>|silent|x-soft|soft|medium|loud|x-loud|inherit`

The relative volume of the output is set using the `volume` property. The volume referred to is the median value of the waveforms, at some points it may be far louder or far quieter than this median value. Its absolute volume will be determined by the settings of the output device. The dynamic range of output devices will vary greatly. Auditory output in an office environment will need to be relatively quiet, while a device such as a television will have to produce louder sounds. Therefore the CSS2 Recommendation states that the user should be able to control the setting for the `volume` from their output device. The parameters of the `volume` property have the following meanings:

- `<number>` An integer between 0 and 100. At first sight you might expect 0 to mean that the sound was off and 100 was as loud as the output device could manage. In fact, 0 means the minimum audible volume, which will be approximately as loud as whispered speech. 100 means the loudest comfortable volume – quieter than shouted speech or a rock concert.
- `<percentage>` The volume setting, which may be inherited from the containing element, is moderated by this percentage which is then converted to an integer in the 0 to 100 range.
- `silent` No sound is transmitted at all. Obviously this is not the same as setting the volume to 0.
- `x-soft` Same as 0.
- `soft` Same as a value of 25.
- `medium` The same as 50.
- `loud` As for 75.
- `x-loud` Equivalent to a volume of 100.

`speak:   normal|none|spell-out|inherit`

Specifies how the text will be rendered aurally. The `normal` setting uses language-dependent rules to read the text; `none` means that the content is not rendered aurally. Finally, `spell-out` spells the text one letter at a time.

When the `volume` is set to `silent`, the content is still rendered but no sound is generated. Doing so takes the same length of time as outputting the text at an audible volume. The time taken includes any breaks or pauses set before or after the text. Setting the `speak` property to `none` means that the text is not rendered and, therefore, no time elapses.

`pause-before:   <time>|<percentage>|inherit`
`pause-after:   <time>|<percentage>|inherit`
`pause:   [<time>|<percentage>]{1,2}|inherit`

A delay can be introduced before or after the content of the element is read. The `time` attribute sets the absolute delay in milliseconds or seconds. The `percentage` sets a delay which is relative to the `speech-rate` property. If the `speech-rate` is 60 words per minute, a delay of 100% will give a pause of one second. Generally, using relative pauses is preferred since it makes the stylesheet more transferable.

The `pause` property is a form of shorthand for `pause-before` and `pause-after`. It can receive either one or two values. If one is given, it will be applied to `pause-before`; if two are given, the second will be applied as `pause-after`.

cue-before: <uri>|none|inherit
cue-after: <uri>|none|inherit
cue: [<cue-before><cue-after]|inherit

These properties determine which, if any, *auditory icons* will be played. Auditory icons are sounds which are used to distinguish or emphasize pieces of speech. The URI must point to a valid sound file. If it points to something that cannot be handled by the application, it should be treated as if the property had the value `none`. The `cue` property works in the same way as `pause`. If it gets one URI, that is used for `cue-before`; if it gets two, the second is used for `cue-after`.

play-during: [uri [mix] [repeat]]|auto|none|inherit

A sound may be played in the background as text is being read. The `uri` must be a valid sound file. The optional `mix` value mixes sounds inherited from the parent element with the sound from the `uri`. The optional `repeat` value indicates that if the sound is shorter than the content of the element, it will be repeated for as long as required. The `auto` property indicates that the sound from the parent element continues.

azimuth: <angle>|[left-side|far-left|left|center-left|center|center-right|right|far-right|right-side]behind|leftwards|rightwards|inherit

Many systems that can give the illusion of playing sound in three dimensions are now available. Some systems, such as those for home-cinema or multi-speaker computer game systems, really do play sounds from all around the listener. The `azimuth` property is used to move sound through the horizontal plane around the listener.

- `<angle>` Indicates the position of the sound in the range −360 deg to 360 deg. A value of 0 indicates that the sound plays from directly in front of the listener.
- `left-side` Equivalent to a value of 270 deg. The directional properties can be combined with `behind` to change their value. If `behind left-side` is used, the sound plays from an angle of 270 deg.
- `far-left` An angle of 300 deg. With `behind` this is 240 deg.
- `left` An angle of 320 deg. With `behind` this is 220 deg.

- `center-left` An angle of 340 deg. With `behind` this is 200 deg.
- `center` An angle of 0 deg. With `behind` this is 180 deg.
- `center-right` An angle of 20 deg. With `behind` this is 160 deg.
- `right` An angle of 40 deg. With `behind` this is 140 deg.
- `far-right` An angle of 60 deg. With `behind` this is 120 deg.
- `right-side` An angle of 90 deg. With `behind` this is 90 deg.
- `leftwards` Moves the sound to the left of the current angle by 20 deg.
- `rightwards` Moves the sound to the right of the current angle by 20 deg.

elevation: <angle>|below|level|above|higher|lower|inherit

Moves the sound in a vertical plane. Combining this with `azimuth` gives three-dimensional movement. The value of `<angle>` specifies the angle relative to the horizontal. A value of 0 deg is horizontal with movement in the range −90 deg to 90 deg. Using `below` is equivalent to −90 deg, `above` is equal to 90 deg and `level` is 0 deg. `higher` adds 10 deg to the current elevation, while `lower` subtracts 10 deg from it.

speech-rate: <number>|x-slow|slow|medium|fast|x-fast|faster|slower|inherit

The speaking rate can be set for individual elements. Think of this rather as you might think of font size. Both relative and absolute values can be set:

- `<number>` The rate in words per minute. This may be language and application dependent. For example, software to help language learners may need to use both extremely slow and more normal speeds.
- `x-slow` 80 words per minute.
- `slow` 120 words per minute.
- `medium` In the range 180 to 200 words per minute.
- `fast` 300 words per minute.
- `x-fast` 500 words per minute.
- `faster` Adds 40 words per minute to the current rate.
- `slower` Subtracts 40 words per minute from the current rate.

voice-family: [<specific>|<generic>]|inherit

This is a comma-separated list of voices that might be used to speak the text. These are analogous to font-families. Whilst the exact meanings are likely to be application dependent, possible values for `generic` include `male`, `female` or `child`.

pitch: <frequency>|x-low|low|medium|high|x-high|inherit

Specify the *average* pitch of the speaking voice. The relative values are application dependent.

pitch-range: <number>|inherit

Specifies the variation in the average pitch of the speaking voice. This will help to add inflection and meaning to the spoken text. Values between 0 and 100 are allowed. A value of 0 gives a monotonic voice, 50 gives a normal voice.

stress: <number>|inherit

Spoken languages use stressed words to emphasize meaning. This property, in the range 0 to 100, specifies how much stress should be put into the voice.

richness: <number>|inherit

Adding richness to the voice will make it penetrate and carry better. Values in the range 0 to 100 are permitted.

speak-punctuation: code|none|inherit

When set to `code`, punctuation marks are spoken. When set to `none`, they are rendered as natural pauses.

speak-numeral: digits|continuous|inherit

If set to `digits`, the individual digits within a number are read as separate words. When set to `continuous`, the entire number is read as a single unit.

6.4 COUNTERS AND NUMBERING

It's sometimes necessary to generate additional content as a document is being rendered. The most obvious example of this is probably the creation of a table of contents and associated sectional numbering, or creating lists of numbered items. The XML document cannot, by its very nature, include such information. XML has structure, it's all about structure, but its structure is to do with the nature of the data. Numbering sections or lists is a presentational matter. This sort of content is as distinct from the raw XML as the color in which it is printed.

:before

:after

These are pseudo-elements, not properties. They are applied to existing elements to modify their behavior before styling is applied. They control the way in which generated content is added to the element as it is displayed.

Here's a quick example. I'm going to modify the stylesheet from Listing 5.2 in Section 5.5 so that the word NAME appears in red, small capitals before any name fields. This is done by adding a new element to the stylesheet specifying the text that must be added:

```
name:before{
    content: "Name";
    color: red;
    font-style: normal;
    font-variant: small-caps;
}
```

The result as displayed by Mozilla is shown in Figure 6.1.

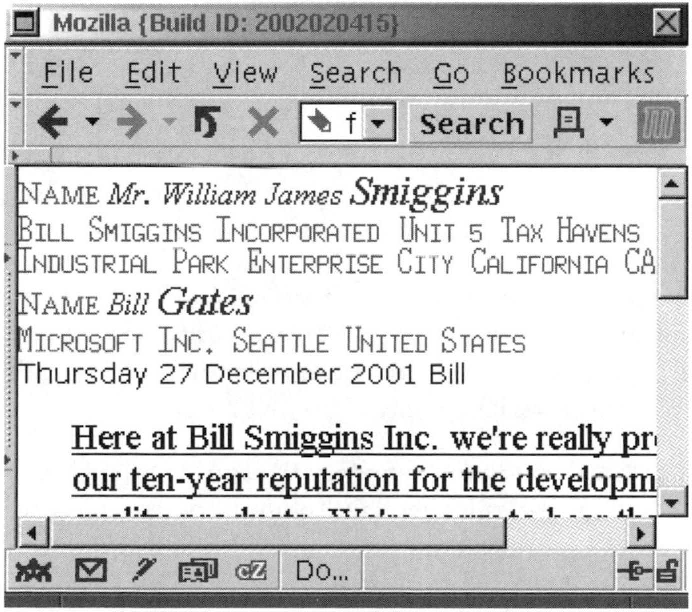

Figure 6.1 Adding Content with CSS2

content: [<string>|<uri>|<counter>|attr()|open-quote| close-quote|no-open-quote|no-close-quote]+|inherit

The `content` property is used with the `:before` and `:after` pseudo-elements to add material into the displayed version of a document. The optional values shown in the description can be mixed and repeated as needed to create the desired effect. For instance, putting quotes around the NAME string could be done with:

```
content: open-quote "Name" close-quote;
```

- `<string>` Adds text content in string format.
- `<uri>` The URI points to an external resource. If the processing application cannot handle the content there, it is ignored. Otherwise it is added to the document. This is especially useful for adding *boiler-plate* text to the content of an XML document.
- `<counter>` Adds a counter. Counters are described in detail in Section 6.4.1.
- `open-quote` and `close-quote` are replaced with the appropriate characters. These characters are likely to be application and locale specific.
- `no-open-quote` and `no-close-quote` Nothing is inserted; levels of indentation appropriate to the use of quotes are applied.
- `attr()` An attribute is given as the parameter to this function. Its content is used as the content of `content`.[2]

6.4.1 Counters

Cascading Stylesheets Two supports the automatic generation of counter values as part of the generation of content. Developers can define the counter, the elements with which it is associated and when it should be incremented. Counters have two properties:

`counter-increment [identifier [integer]]|none|inherit`
: The counter whose name is given as the `identifier` property is incremented by one. To increment by other amounts, including negative values, an optional `integer` parameter can be supplied.

`counter-reset [identifier [integer]]|none|inherit`
: The value of the counter can be reset to 0, or to any other value which is given in the optional `integer` parameter.

```
name:before{
   counter-increment: name;
   content: open-quote "Name  "  counter(name) close-quote;
   color: red;
   font-style: normal;
   font-variant: small-caps;
}
```

[2] If you see what I mean.

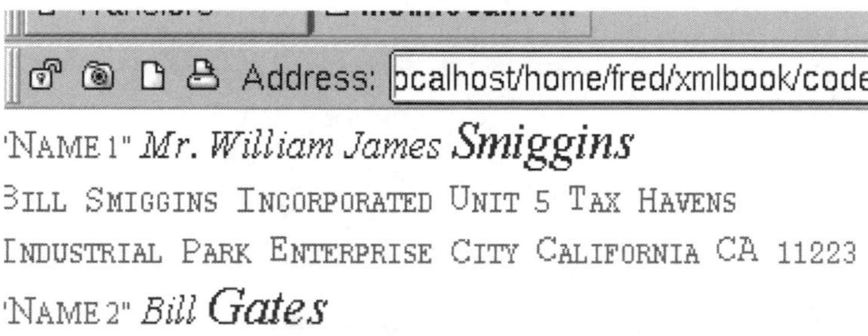

Figure 6.2 Dynamic Counters

In this code sample, a counter value now appears after the word NAME. The result, as displayed by Opera 6, is shown in Figure 6.2. Counters can be nested and modified. Nesting counters is trivial. The only thing to remember is that nested sectional counters need resetting when the outer section increments. Counters can be modified using the same properties as for bullets used with list elements. The style of counter you're using can be altered. To get a style other than the default, use `counter(name, <style>)` where the `<style>` parameter is taken from the following list:

- `decimal`
- `decimal-leading-zero`
- `lower-roman`
- `upper-roman`
- `hebrew`
- `georgian`
- `armenian`
- `cjk-ideographic`
- `hiragana`
- `katakana`

- `hiragana-iroha`
- `katakana-iroha`
- `lower-latin`
- `lower-alpha`
- `upper-latin`
- `upper-alpha`
- `lower-greek`

Exercises

1. What shortcomings of Cascading Stylesheets does CSS2 address?
2. When might you need to present data in non-textual forms such as might be found in an auditory application?
3. What are pseudo-elements? Give examples of how you might use them in preparing a document.

Chapter 7

Navigating within and between XML Documents

If there's one reason that use of the Web and markup in HTML are so popular, it must be the hyperlink. The ability to move between sections of documents or between documents that may be physically several thousand miles apart is incredibly useful to both readers and authors. HTML wasn't the first hyperlink system, it wasn't the first to become widely popular – that honor probably goes to Apple's Hypercard system. The reasons that HTML became very popular, very quickly include:

- Writing HTML hyperlinks is incredible simple.
- many different file types can be linked to.
- HTML is an open standard which anyone can implement in their software.
- HTML is a platform-neutral technology.

Whether writing for the Web or for traditional media, authors often need to refer readers to different sections of their document or to other documents. In traditional books this might be done through a table of contents, a bibliography and citations. An HTML author uses the address tag to create links directly to the referenced location:

```
To<a href="#another_section"> link </a> to sections
or<a href="http://some.site.org/doc.pdf"> documents </a>.
```

HTML links are explicit and hard coded into the document. The document has a logical structure defined through the HTML Document Object Model, DOM. Navigation through an HTML document using the DOM is the established method of finding nodes and values within JavaScript applications. Elements and structures within XML documents are also addressed using a DOM.

XML has two distinct types of navigation. Movement within a document is described in the XPath recommendation, movement between documents is covered by XPointer and XLink. I'll look at all three of these in this chapter. Before working with these technologies, you should be aware that some of them are currently in a state of flux and are likely to continue to change until significant applications arrive using particular versions.

XPath is a well-established Recommendation which is implemented in any number of XSL processing applications. Unfortunately it is not always fully implemented in these products, which means that your carefully crafted code may never be universal. You will need to read the documentation of the library or processor that you are using to check how completely it conforms to the XPath Recommendation. In addition, navigating arbitrary XPath expressions is difficult. Not all processors are equally efficient at this task. Benchmarks are notoriously unreliable indicators of true performance, but if your XPath application seems sluggardly you should first check that your code is optimized. If this doesn't improve things, try a different processor and see if that does.

As for the other two, XLink is a Recommendation of the W3C, but is not yet widely implemented. XPointer is a Candidate Recommendation as I write. This means that it remains under development but there are unlikely to be major changes between the version I'll describe in this chapter and the full Recommendation when it is published.

7.1 XPATH

XPath is an attempt to provide a universal syntax for navigation through arbitrary XML documents. The universality of XPath means that it is used as the basis of XPointer and of movement within XSLT. XPath is arbitrary since it operates on the general structure of XML documents rather than the syntax and structure of specific documents. This is a big advantage to developers as it means they do not have to construct new forms of movement for each application. They can specify XPath expressions for each and leave the problem of actually moving through the document to standard processors. Navigation through documents is complex and XPath includes data types and functions to support its main purpose.

The syntax used by XPath is unique, relatively straightforward but, as with DTDs, it is *not* XML. You may worry about this since you can easily find yourself using the different syntaxes of XML, DTD and XPath in the same project. There's no easy solution. XML developers somehow have to get used to the idea that they need to be experts in everything. Since XPath is used to address individual elements within an XML document, it can also be used as a way of comparing nodes when manipulating documents.

Generally, you will find XPath functionality hidden inside XSLT processors. Some of these expose their XPath methods as part of their API, others do not. Some DOM processing libraries include classes and methods that let you build applications that can perform any subset of the tasks normally performed by XSLT processors. Using these libraries you can embed XPath expressions in your C++, Java or Perl code.

7.1.1 Introducing XPath Constructs

XPath is based on some difficult concepts. As with many XML technologies, it brings together a variety of computer science and software engineering ideas under a single umbrella. Before examining the intricacies of XPath, it's important to have some understanding of these fundamentals.

7.1.1.1 Nodes In XPath, a document is represented as a tree structure made of nodes. The elements, attributes and content in the original XML document become element nodes, attribute nodes or text nodes. Nodes can contain other nodes, each of which can be treated as if it were the root of a subtree which might be extracted and manipulated separately. Each node can be converted to an equivalent *string-value*. For some nodes this is straightforward since the value will be part of the node. For other nodes the value is calculated by computing the values of all of the nodes below it in the tree. Each node may have a name. Since XPath supports XML Namespaces, which are described in Section 4.1, the name is actually the local name plus the namespace. The namespace part may be null if no namespace has been declared for the element.

7.1.1.2 Expressions Most of the work that is done in XPath is writing expressions. An expression can be thought of as a path through the document which terminates at another part of the document. XPath expressions are made from nodes, variables which hold values taken from nodes, functions and their return values. The value of the termination point is returned as the result of the expression. This value may be one of the four XPath data types:

- Node-set. This is an unordered collection of unique nodes. Duplicates are not put into the set and there is no sense in which the first item in the set is more important than the last.
- Boolean value representing `true` or `false`.
- Floating-point number.
- A string of Unicode characters.

Node-sets are by far the most important of the XPath data types. A node-set is formed when an XPath expression is applied to part of a document. If the expression is true for an individual node, then that node is placed into a node-set. That node-set is returned as the result of the expression and becomes available for further processing. XPath expressions can be applied to these node-sets to further refine them. If you read the XSLT and XSL-FO examples in this book, you'll notice lots of situations in which a node-set is used, refined and reused.

Evaluation of an XPath expression starts at a particular point in the document and returns a result which is relative to that point. If an expression is evaluated from a different starting point, it will give a different result even though it's being used on just one document. The point at which evaluation begins is called the *context* and thus the result of evaluating an XPath expression is always given relative to a particular context. XPointer and XSLT have their own views on how a context should be determined but, briefly, the context is composed of:

- An individual node, called the *context node*.
- Two numbers which define the position and size of the context within the document.
- A set of bindings which link variable names to variable values. The type of a variable may be any of the valid types for the evaluation of an XPath expression.
- A mapping of function names to individual functions.
- The set of valid namespaces for the current expression. The bindings in this set map namespace prefixes to URIs. Namespaces are discussed in detail in Section 4.1.

7.1.1.3 Functions XPath functions take one or more parameters and return single values. The value of a function is equal to its return value. A common set of functions which must be provided by all XPath implementations is described in Section 7.1.3. Individual implementations may, of course, extend this library. The parameters and arguments, for functions in this library, belong to the four basic types for XPath.

The functions in the library are used to manipulate the four basic data types. In fact, the functions provided by XPath seem most clearly analogous to those provided by recent ECMAScript libraries. The popular Web scripting languages JavaScript and JScript are both implementations of ECMAScript. You'll certainly be familiar with them if you've used either of those languages to manipulate the DOM of an HTML document.

Those which operate on node-sets, for instance, permit movement across the set or the selection of items from it. The string functions in the library are familiar from most modern programming languages. They permit selection of substrings, concatenation and so on. The Boolean functions give simple access to basic logical manipulations, while the number functions give limited facilities for working with numerical objects.

7.1.2 Location Paths

XPath expressions are used to identify one of the four basic XPath data types, (node-sets, strings, Boolean or number) in the document. They are evaluated relative to either the current context or the root node of the document. An XPath expression is commonly a *location path*. Location paths that start at the root node are called *absolute* paths, those that start anywhere else in the document are called *relative* paths. An absolute path starts with a forward slash, `/`, relative paths start with the name of a node. Items within the path are separated using forward slashes. The syntax used to describe location steps in XPath is quite simple but applying it to a complex document can be much more difficult. Location steps can be specified using either a verbose form or an abbreviated one. Generally the abbreviated form is used since it is much shorter and hence far easier to read and write. I'm going to begin by examining the longer form since understanding it is vital if you are going to use XPath successfully. Any decent XSLT reference manual will supply an in-depth treatment of the shorter form.

`axis::node test[predicate [predicate]]`

The verbose form of the location step has three components. Each step starts with an axis taken from the list in Table 7.1. This is separated by two colons from a node test which is optionally followed by one or more predicates. Since the predicates are optional you don't have to use them. The axis will identify a node-set, although this may be empty if the axis doesn't identify part of the document, or contain a single node. The node-set is refined by the node test which filters nodes based on either name or type, placing those that match into it. Finally the predicates add further refinement. Predicates are Boolean expressions which all nodes in the node-set are tested against. Only those nodes that evaluate to `true` against the predicate remain in the node-set.

Table 7.1: XPath Axes

Name	Description
`child`	Contains all children of the context node. Child nodes are those directly below the context node if the XML document is visualized as a tree structure.
`descendent`	Contains all descendents of the context node. Descendents include child nodes, *their* children and onwards down the tree. This axis will not select attribute or namespace nodes.
`parent`	Contains the parent of the context node. Each node has exactly one parent, although a parent node may have many children.
`ancestor`	Contains all ancestors of the context node. The ancestors include the parent node, its parent and so on back up the tree. Ancestor nodes always include the root node of the document unless the context node *is* the root node.
`following-sibling`	Holds all siblings of the context node that follow it in the node-set. Sibling nodes share a parent with the context node and appear in the node-set in the order in which they appear in the original document. Note that if the context node is either an attribute or namespace node, the result of the following-siblings axis will be an empty set.
`preceding-sibling`	Holds all siblings of the context node that precede it in the node-set. The result of this axis is empty if the context node is either an attribute or namespace node.
`following`	This holds all nodes that are in the same document as the context node and occur after it. The ordering of nodes is the same as in the original document. The result here does not include descendent, attribute or namespace nodes.

Table 7.1: XPath Axes

Name	Description
`preceding`	This holds all nodes that are in the same document as the context node and occur before it. The ordering of nodes is the same as in the original document.
`attribute`	Contains the attribute nodes, if any, of the context node.
`namespace`	Contains the namespace nodes of the context, but only if the context is an element node.
`self`	Holds the context node.
`descendent-or-self`	Holds the context node and its descendents.
`ancestor-or-self`	Holds the context node and its ancestors.

7.1.2.1 Axes XPath specifies a number of axes which are used to move through the document. Each axis returns a node-set which contains all nodes found at a particular location. The axes are listed in Table 7.1.

Simply listing the XPath axes doesn't help to understand how they are used when building location steps. Working through an example provides much more useful information. Figure 7.1 shows a tree structure which partially represents the Business Letter application from Section 2.6. I've not drawn up a tree for the full Letter simply because it would be far too large and complicated to fit onto the page of a book. Working from that diagram, let's assume that the `Name` of the `Recipient` of the letter is the context node. If you want to see the differences, applying the axes to the full document is a useful exercise when you have a few spare minutes. Use paper and pencil and try to calculate the result you would get by applying an arbitrary XPath expression to each node in your document.

The following list gives the content of the node-set when each of the XPath axes is applied. I'm only listing nodes as they appear in the tree in Figure 7.1. This gives a subset of the result that applying the axes to the full document would give.

- **`child`** contains `Title`, `Firstname` and `Surname`.
- **`descendent`** contains `Title`, `Firstname` and `Surname`. None of these nodes have children; the set here is therefore the same as for the `child` axis.

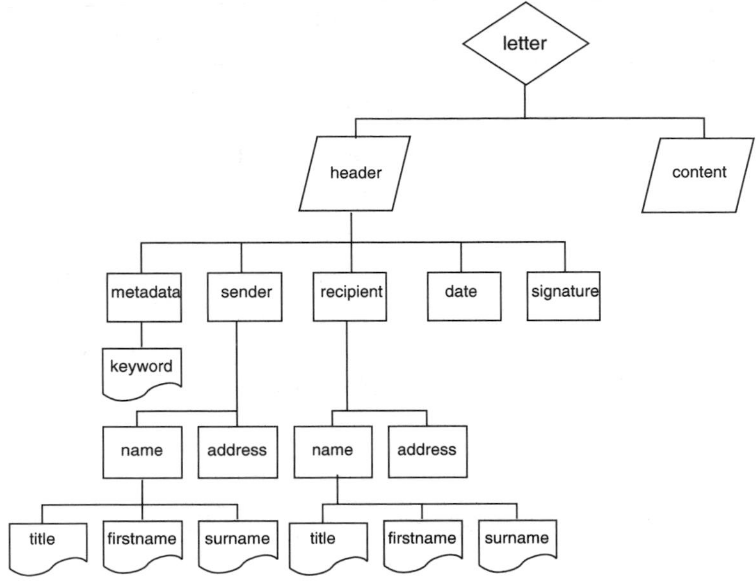

Figure 7.1 XML Tree Structure For The Business Letter Application

- **`parent`** contains `Recipient`.
- **`ancestor`** contains `Letter`, `Header` and `Recipient`.
- **`following-sibling`** contains `Address`. Only one node shares a parent with the `Name` node. The `Address` node follows the `Name` node in document order.
- **`preceding-sibling`** is an empty set since no siblings precede the `Name` node in document order.
- **`following`** contains `Address`, `Date`, `Signature` and `Content`. All these nodes follow the context node in this restricted document but none are its descendents.
- **`preceding`** contains the `Address` of the sender, the `Name` of the sender and their `Title`, `Firstname` and `Surname`, the`Sender` node, the `Metadata` node and, finally, the `Keyword`. Notice that none of these nodes are ancestors of the context node.
- **`attribute`** is an empty set since the context node has no attributes.
- **`namespace`** is empty since no namespace has been specified for the context node.
- **`self`** contains just the `Name` node.

- **descendent-or-self** contains `Name`, `Title`, `Firstname` and `Surname` nodes.
- **ancestor-or-self** contains `Letter`, `Header`, `Recipient` and `Name`.

7.1.2.2 Node tests The node test provides a simple mechanism for filtering the node-set found using the axes. The node test filters based upon the name or type of node. Only those nodes for which the test is `true` remain in the node-set after the node test has been applied. Evaluation of node tests is straightforward. The test is applied to each node in turn and is true only if the node has the same type as the principle node type of the axis and it has the same name as that specified in the test.

Phew! A lot of jargon was introduced there. This is, unfortunately, one of those times where you need to meet the jargon before the explanation makes sense.

The *principal node type* is defined for every axis.

- Those axes that can contain elements have a principal node type of element.
- An attribute axis has a principal node type of axis.
- A namespace axis has namespace as its principal node type.

Syntax and examples Some examples will clarify how node tests work. Consider the Business Letter once again. If the `Name` element of the `Recipient` is used as the context node, the axis `child` contains the `Title`, `Firstname` and `Surname` nodes. Using the node test

```
child::Title
```

will select just the `Title` node from the node-set. If the `Header` node were the context node, the expression

```
child::*/Name/Title
```

would select the `Title` nodes for both the `Sender` and the `Recipient` elements. This second example is slightly more complex. The test has two components which are separated by a slash. Think of these components as steps like those you might encounter in a URL or directory listing. The **asterisk** is used to select all nodes that have the same type as the principal node type. In this case, all nodes that are children of the `Header` node are selected. Five nodes match this: `Metadata`, `Sender`, `Recipient`, `Data` and `Signature`. Further steps in the path are separated using forward slashes. The next step selects those nodes, in this set, that contain `Name` nodes as children. This step matches the `Sender` and `Recipient` nodes. Finally the `Title` nodes for each of these are selected and remain in the node-set.

The example demonstrates that navigation through the tree is straightforward. The axis selects a region of the tree or a sub-tree, the node test selects those nodes in this sub-tree that match your criteria.

Node tests can also be used to select for particular types of content. The test `child::text()` is a call to an XPath function which will select all text nodes that are children of the context node. The `comment()` function selects all comments and `processing-instruction()` is `true` for all nodes that are processing instructions.

7.1.2.3 Predicates The final filter in building a location path is a predicate. Predicates are optional and you can include as many, or as few, as you need. Each predicate is evaluated in turn against each node on the node set. During evaluation of the predicate, the node being tested becomes the context node and the context size is set to the number of items in the node-set. Once the entire node-set has been tested, the context returns to its prior state. Nodes only remain in the node-set if the predicate evaluates to true. Strictly, a new node-set is created which contains only those nodes for which the predicate is true, but since the original node-set is discarded after evaluation the difference is really semantic.

Predicates often use XPath functions, but they don't have to. Here's a simple example which selects the second child from the context node:

```
child[2]
```

The predicate is placed in square brackets. Working from the root node of the Business Letter, the expression:

```
child::*/header/descendent::*[line2]/code
```

selects the zip code[1] below any `header` element that has a `line2` element. Working through the expression, `child::*` selects all child nodes of the root. The subpath `/header/descendent::*` will leave just the descendents of the `header` in the node set. The predicate `[line2]` selects only those nodes that have an element called `line2`. That's definitely not the easiest XPath expression, but it does show that complex selections can be made using a set of logical steps. The whole expression could also be written more simply using either of these:

```
/descendent::*/code
//code
```

A predicate can be written to filter based on the presence or value of attributes rather than elements. An attribute is specified by giving its name but preceding it with an ampersand:

```
child::*/header/descendent::[@length]
```

7.1.2.4 Examples The previous section contained a few examples of location paths. You'll probably need to see more of them before they begin to make sense. Table 7.2 shows

[1] Or post code.

Table 7.2 Sample Location Paths

Verbose	Abbreviated	Selection
`child::title`	`title`	The `title` element nodes that are children of the context node. The `child::` step is always optional.
`child::*`	`*`	The context nodes that are element nodes.
`child::node()`	`node()`	The context node, regardless of node type.
`attribute::type`	`@type`	The `type` attribute of the context node.
`/descendent::title`	`//title`	All `title` nodes below the root node.
`child::para ↩ [position()=2]`	`para[2]`	The second `para` node that is a child of the context node.
`attribute::type ↩ ="formal"`	`@type="formal"`	All `type` attributes of the context node that have the value `formal`.

some location paths in both verbose and abbreviated forms alongside an explanation of the path.[2]

The XPath Recommendation contains numerous similar examples of both verbose and concise paths which are worth reading if you need to know more. I'll be using XPaths in later chapters, so you'll get an opportunity to see them used in real applications. In particular, I'll be demonstrating how to use XPath inside XSLT and XSL-FO scripts to select node-sets in document transformations.

7.1.3 Function Library

XPath expressions include functions alongside location steps. Functions are used as part of the predicate expression and are necessary to provide the right amount of control. Functions that operate on each of the XPath data types are provided .

7.1.3.1 Working With Node-sets

number **`count(`*`node-set`*`)`**

Returns the number of items in the node-set given as a parameter.

[2]The ↩ symbol is used in Table 7.2 to show a break in code to fit it into the table. Don't break your code at the arrow.

***node-set* id(*object*)**

Selects items using their unique ID. The result is returned as a node-set. The parameter to the `id()` function may be a node-set, in which case the result is created by converting each item to its string value and applying `id()` to that. If the parameter is of any other type, it is converted to a string. This string is treated as a whitespace-separated sequence of tokens. Nodes are placed into the resulting node-set if they have a unique ID which matches *any* of those tokens.

***number* last()**

Returns a number which is equal to the context size. This may be the number of items in the node-set, for example.

***string* local-name([*node-set*])**

Some nodes have expanded names which consist of a local name and a URI. This function will return the local part of the expanded name. If the argument is omitted, the parameter defaults to being just the context node.

***string* name([*node-set*])**

Returns the expanded name, the local name plus the URI, of the item in the node-set that occurs first in document order. When the argument is omitted, it defaults to the context node.

***string* namespace-uri([*node-set*])**

Returns the namespace URI part of the expanded name of the first item in the node-set in document order. If the parameter is omitted, the context node is used as default.

***number* position()**

Returns a number which is equal to the context position. For example, this could be the position of a particular item in a node-set.

Document order simply means the order in which elements occur in the source document. This may be different to the order in which they are processed and may have no relationship to their semantic order. If we are thinking about customer addresses, for example, we normally think about the zip code *after* the name of the town or city in which the customer lives. That's the semantic order, it has real meaning, and will be specified in a DTD or XML Schema. If our document doesn't have a schema, the zip code might be stored after the customer's name and just before their telephone number. When searching the document with XPath those nodes will be returned in their stored order. If an application needs them in a different order, *it* will have to move the retrieved data around.

7.1.3.2 String Manipulation

string **concat(*string*, *string*, [*string*]**

Returns the string by concatenating the arguments given to the function.

boolean **contains(*string*, *string*)**

Returns `true` if the first argument contains the second. False otherwise.

string **normalize-space([*string*])**

Normalizes the whitespace in the string by collapsing multiple whitespace characters to a single space. The normalized string is returned.

boolean **starts-with(*string*, *string*)**

Returns `true` if the string given as the first argument starts with the string given as the second one, or false otherwise.

string **string([*object*])**

Converts the value of the object given as a parameter to a string which is returned. If the object is a node-set, `string()` returns the string value of the first item in the node-set in document order. The string value of a node may be explicitly declared. Otherwise it is calculated by converting each descendent node to a string value.

number **string-length(*string*)**

Returns the length of the string.

string **substring(*string*, *number*, [*number*])**

Returns the substring of the first argument which starts at the location given by the second. If the, optional, third argument is given the substring will stop at that position. If the third argument is omitted, the substring will continue to the end of the string. In XPath, unlike languages such as Java or C++, string positions start from 1.

string **substring-before(*string*, *string*)**

Returns the substring of the first argument which occurs before the *first* occurrence of the second argument.

string **substring-after(*string*, *string*)**

Returns the substring of the first argument which occurs after the *first* occurrence of the second argument.

string **translate(*string*, *string*, *string*)**

Returns a copy of the first argument with occurrences of the characters in the second string replaced by the corresponding character in the third string, For example:

```
translate("A sample string", "abcde", "ghijk")
```

would return the string `A ogmplk string"`.

7.1.3.3 Boolean Functions

boolean **boolean(*object*)**

Converts its argument to either `true` or `false`.

boolean **false()**

Returns `false`.

boolean **not(*boolean*)**

Returns `false` if the argument is `true`, `true` otherwise.

boolean **true()**

Returns `true`.

7.1.3.4 Numerical Functions

number **ceiling(*number*)**

Returns the largest integer value that is not smaller than, or equal to, the argument.

number **floor(*number*)**

Returns the largest integer value that is not larger than, or equal to, the argument.

number **number([*object*])**

Converts the argument to a number. If the argument is omitted, the context node is used. If the argument is a node-set, the first item in the node-set in document order is converted.

number **round(*number*)**

Returns the nearest integer value to the argument.

number **sum(*node-set*)**

Returns the sum of the values in the node-set. Each item in the node-set is converted to its string value which is then converted to a numerical value.

7.1.4 Data Types

The data types used in XPath include some common ones which are used in most programming languages, alongside unique types such as node and node-set. The details of how nodes and node-sets are designed and work are really only required if you plan to implement software that manipulates XPath expressions. If you are just using software such as libraries which others have written, these details can safely be ignored. It's important to take a quick look at the more common data types so that you can see how they relate to data types which you may know from languages such as C++ or Java.

7.1.4.1 The Boolean Data Type Boolean objects take the values `true` and `false`. As you would expect, an object can either be `true` or `false` at any one moment. Boolean objects cannot exist in both states at the same time. The Boolean data type is supported by a number of logical operators.

`expression`* `and` *`expression`

Each expression is converted to a Boolean value. The result is `true` if both expressions are `true`, otherwise it is `false`. Note that if the left-hand side evaluates to `false`, the right-hand side is not converted to a Boolean.

`expression`* `or` *`expression`

Each expression is converted to a Boolean value. The result is `true` if either expression is `true`, otherwise it is `false`.

=, !=, <=, <, >=, >

Operators are supplied for standard Boolean comparisons. The expressions being evaluated are converted to common types where possible. If node-sets are involved the comparisons become somewhat more complex. If both operands are node-sets, the result is `true` if there are items in each node-set whose string values are equal. If one item is a node-set, the other is converted to a string value and the result is `true` if that value equals the string value of any item in the node-set.

A more comprehensive description of these comparisons, including some detailed examples, can be found in the XPath Recommendation. Broadly, though, these Boolean operators work just as you would expect from using more conventional languages.

7.1.4.2 The String Data Type XPath strings are one or more characters, where a character is as defined in the XML Recommendation. These characters are abstractions of Unicode characters rather than standard Unicode values.

7.1.4.3 The Number Data Type The XPath number type is a floating-point number. There is a special number value, `NaN`, which represents those data items that are *Not a Number*. Conventional numerical operators are supplied. These convert their operands to the number type.

+

Adds the operands.

-

Subtracts the operand on the right-hand side from the one on the left.

`*`
: Multiplies the two operands.

`div`
: Performs floating-point division of the left-hand side by the value on the right side

`mod`
: Returns the remainder from an integer division. Floating-point operands are converted to integers internally.

7.2 XLINK

The XML Linking Language, XLink, is used to specify links from one XML document to another. It uses pure XML to supply functionality that extends far beyond the sort of hyperlink that is found in HTML documents. The conventional HTML hyperlink is unidirectional. It starts from one document, or location within a document, and terminates at another. Hyperlinks are usually controlled by the person reading or viewing the document through a mouse click. Some hyperlinks are followed automatically by browser software as it loads pages, for instance when fetching images or stylesheets.

While the HTML hyperlink generally provides sufficient expressiveness and power, there are times when more complex linking schemes are desirable. Since XML does not rely upon a particular implementation, and does not make assumptions about what technology can actually achieve, XLink can be used to describe far more complex linking schemes.

In XLink, a link is more than a simple connection between two documents. Links can be used to express relationships between multiple resources, metadata can be associated with each link and links can be separated from the documents to which they apply. There is no assumption built into XLink that a defined link will be implemented as a hyperlink to be followed dynamically. The use of links in XML documents, how they are processed and followed is really left to an individual implementation. Some generic functionality is desirable, and tools are starting to appear which can be used to move across links and access the documents to which they point. These types of tool do not attempt to access the underlying richness of the link within individual applications. For example, data at the end of a link may never be accessed directly by users, they may simply need to know that the data exists. An application which uses this link may do so by querying the application at the other end in a manner similar to a traditional programmatic structure such as a remote procedure call.

Examples of different uses of links include:

- A link may be followed when a static document is built from a set of XML sources with links followed just once.

- Where data is being transmitted between remote applications, links may refer to resources or applications which are necessary before the data can be properly processed.

- A link may perform the same role as a foreign key in a relational database.

So what is a link? At the most basic level, an XML link is a relationship between two resources. A resource is anything that can be addressed by a URI. While we are used to the idea of a resource as a text file, often in HTML, or an image, it may also be something diverse such as a program or a dynamically created data set.

Applications that are to process links need to be able to recognize them. To guarantee this recognition, XLink specifies the use of a particular namespace. The namespace to be used with XLink is:

```
http://www.w3.org/1999/xlink
```

This namespace must always be declared in documents that use XLink; see Section 4.1 for more information on using and defining namespaces.

XLink is used to express relationships between resources. A relationship might be used for something as simple as the citation of a reference, where the cited document is not going to be accessed by the reader. On the other hand, the link might involve the remote processing of data from a number of sources, its downloading and presentation. How is the local application to know when data should be downloaded and when the link is simply for reference? The answer is in the XLink concept of an *arc*.

The HTML hyperlink has a single starting point, the source, and a single destination, the target, which might be a document or a location inside a document. Since XLink simply describes a relationship between resources, it does not permit the notions of source and target. Moving across links, a process called *traversal*, is a different thing altogether. In XPath this is described using *arcs*. Each link can have zero or more arcs, each of which may lead to a different target resource. Thus a node can be at the center of a Web of links, each of which means something different and is processed differently. No software currently exists to harness more than a fraction of this expressivity.

7.2.1 An XLink Scenario

Spending a few moments thinking about how XLink might be used is a useful exercise. Once you've seen a few examples I'm sure you'll be able to dream up scenarios of your own. Here's one from me to get you started. I'm going to keep away from code, and just imagine how inter-document links might be used. Implementation[3] of these ideas in XLink may not even be possible – that depends upon the expressive power of the language. Implementation of the whole thing in a development language may be even less feasible. Let's start by dreaming up the ideas and worry about the details later.

Imagine someone reading a computer-based recipe book. The recipes may be stored locally on the same machine, on a near-by server, probably on a local network, or remotely to be accessed across the Internet. The "computer" being used to read the recipes might be a desktop machine, a laptop with wireless networking, a PDA or even a conventional household TV set. Our budding chef starts by selecting a recipe. This is conventionally done using a search system or a series of menus. Let's assume the latter, in this case. The chef moves down the menu but is unsure about the meaning of some of the entries. He or she notices that when the menu items are being viewed they display in a different color. If the chef waits for a short time on each menu item, some text is presented as an overlay on the screen, which describes the menu item in more detail. This text can be navigated and some of the words and images within it bring up yet more overlays.

Having eventually chosen a recipe, the chef starts to read through it. Some unfamiliar ingredients are listed. Fortunately, the system displays descriptive text for each item. But where can the chef purchase these ingredients? By selecting each item, a list of local suppliers appears, and where no supplier is known, an alternative ingredient is shown.

Different types of link are happening here. The menu system may be using simple links with each item linking to one other. The descriptive information which appears when the user hovers over the ingredients is another form of simple link. Both will be familiar to Web users as they can be implemented using conventional HTML and JavaScript techniques, and in fact these often are used.

More complex ideas are needed to create additional links from the descriptive text in the menu system. There are many ways that this might be implemented, but XLink can also be used to create dynamic links while the user is accessing the document. Finally, bringing up lists of suppliers requires knowledge about the chef and his or her needs and data about the recipes.

All of this functionality *could* be provided using technologies such as HTML, JavaScript and CGI. One problem that developers would face today would be simply expressing the relationships between all of the different data items. This is where XLink comes in. Complex, possibly unique, relationships among disparate data items can be described succinctly. Building software implementations that can manipulate those relationships is, of course, a different, and far more complex, proposition.

[3]A wise man once told me that any implementation is *mere detail*. While I don't agree, getting the ideas right before you start to develop is certainly important in the long run!

7.2.2 XLink Attributes

Writing an XLink is not simply a matter of adding a new tag to a document. If XLink worked in a similar way to the HTML <a> tag, which is used to create hyperlinks, something like the following code might be used:

```
<ingredient>
  <name>Sugar</name>
  <quantity amount="20" />
  <xlink href="http://foodlink.org/ingredient/sugar.xml" />
</ingredient>
```

This would simply add an xlink element to the document. In fact, this isn't how XLink works. Since links have to carry more information than just an address, the structure of the linking element becomes a little more complex.

```
<ingredient xmlns:xlink="http://www.w3.org/1999/xlink">
  <name
    xlink:href="http://foodlink.org/ingredient/sugar.xml"
    xlink:type="locator" >
      Granulated Sugar
  </name>
  <quantity amount="20" />
</ingredient>
```

Firstly, notice that the ingredient tag has changed. I've added a *namespace declaration*. This can be done at the root of the document, if you're going to be using the same namespace in many places, or, as here, it can be done to declare a namespace for part of a document. The link itself is not a separate element in the document. Instead the link, and associated information become attributes of an existing element. You could add a new element to the document to contain this information, but it usually makes sense to alter an existing one. Here the name element becomes the source of the link. The link itself is a straightforward declaration of a URI. XLink provides a set of attributes which can be added to elements to provide varying degrees of functionality.

> **Note:**
> Before the XLink attributes can be used in a document, the XLink namespace, http://www.w3.org/1999/xlink, must be declared. Only if the namespace is used will applications recognize the attributes as part of an XLink.

actuate="onLoad|onRequest|other|none"
Applications need to know when to traverse an arc.

- `onLoad` The application should traverse the arc as soon as the document that contains the link is loaded. When one source links to several targets, application behavior is not defined by the XLink Recommendation. This leaves implementors to find their own way of handling the data from all the targets.
- `onRequest` The arc is only traversed following some action from the user. For instance, the user may click on a link using a mouse to initiate the traversal.
- `other` The way that the application handles the traversal is defined elsewhere. The application must hunt for that definition itself.
- `none` No behavior is defined for the traversal of the arc. Since the document does not help the application decide how to proceed, it is likely that a default behavior will be used, although that behavior will have to be built into the processing software.

`arcrole`

This is an absolute URI that identifies a resource. The resource should describe the property in a form which the processing application can use.

`from`

The `from` attribute identifies the source of the link. The value given to this attribute *must* correspond to the value of the `label` attribute in the source document.

`href`

This attribute provides addressing for remote resources. It is optional for links of type `simple` and mandatory for those of `extended` type. The value of the `href` must be a URI. The URI may be absolute or relative, but relative URIs will be computed by the processor before they are used.

`label`

Provides a textual label which identifies the link. Unlike the `title` attribute, the `label` is not necessarily descriptive.

`role`

Identical to the `arcrole` attribute but used in different types of link.

`show="new|embed|other|replace|none"`

This attribute defines how the target resource should be presented once the traversal has been completed. The attribute values have the following effects:

- `new` The target resource is presented as a separate item. This may mean opening a new window on the desktop, a new pane within an application, or starting a new page in a printed document. The exact details will depend upon the nature of the application and of the target data.

- `embed` The target resource replaces the link definition in the presentation of the source document. The target data is usually presented inline within the document, for instance as a new paragraph.
- `other` The application must look for additional instructions within the markup on how it is to process the data.
- `replace` The target resource replaces the existing resource in the window or frame or other presentational device.
- `none` No guidance is given to the application on how it should process the target data.

`title`

Provides a human-readable label which describes the link. The label should be a text string rather than an image or other resource.

`to`

The `to` attribute identifies the target of the link. The value given to this attribute *must* correspond to the value of the `label` attribute in the target document.

`type="simple|extended|locator|arc|resource|title|none"`

This attribute must be used when the XLink namespace is used. The `type` identifies which of the various types of link this one is. Each type offers a different level of functionality:

- `simple` These links describe a relationship between exactly two resources. One resource is the source and the other the target. Simple links are always outward from the source document, which contains the link element, to the target.
- `extended` Links of this type may use the full functionality of XLink. They can have complex structures since they may be describing many-to-many relationships among remote and local resources.
- `locator` These links provide addressing for remote resources.
- `arc` Provides rules defining how traversal among the resources for this link occurs.
- `resource` Provides addressing for local resources.
- `title` Gives a label for the link in a human-readable form.

The chosen `type` restricts which of the other attributes can be used in the link. Table 7.3 shows the permitted combinations.

Table 7.3 Relationships Between XLink Attributes

	Simple	Extended	Locator	Arc	Resource	Title
`title`	Required	Required	Required	Required	Required	Required
`href`	Optional		Required			
`role`	Optional	Optional	Optional		Optional	
`arcrole`	Optional			Optional		
`title`	Optional	Optional	Optional	Optional	Optional	
`show`	Optional			Optional		
`actuate`	Optional			Optional		
`label`			Optional		Optional	
`from`				Optional		
`to`				Optional		

7.2.3 Simple Links

A unidirectional point-to-point relationship, similar to an HTML hyperlink, is called a simple link in XLink. Generally a simple link consists of an `href` and `title`, although the latter may be omitted. In some circumstances the `title` may be implied from the context, for instance the content of the element may be used as the title. This implicit relationship should be specified in the DTD or XML Schema associated with the XML document.

7.2.3.1 The Business Letter To demonstrate how simple links might be used, I'm going to show some possible modifications to the Business Letter from 2.6. A somewhat simplified tree structure for this application is shown in Figure 7.1. The letter comprises a `header` section, which holds control data such as the names and addresses of the sender and recipient, and a `content` section which holds a series of paragraphs of text. If the Business Letter had been developed for presentation on the screen of a networked device, its structure could be modified to link to external resources. These modifications would simplify the structure of the document, while making the processing of the document more complex. At the moment we can be more concerned with the structure than the processing – that will be examined later.

The `header` of the document contains three elements which might profitably be replaced with links:

- `metadata` Each of the `keyword` elements within the metadata could become a link to a resource which gives an explanation of it. The target would only be presented following some action from the user such as selecting a highlighted word in the document.

- `sender` Why place the name and address of the author in every letter? That information is common to many documents and could be held in an external resource. When the reader accesses the letter, this resource is accessed automatically. The reader will not know that these details are being pulled from a different document to the one that holds the content of the letter.

- `recipient` If each author has a file that contains their details, that data can be used to create the content for the `recipient` element. Rather than storing the data locally on the author's system, it could be accessed dynamically from the recipient's own system. One thing to note about this is that the address will always be current. For archival, the address to which the letter was originally sent would be more important than the current address. Since I'm simply outlining a possible scenario here, such problems do not concern me.

The `metadata` element might change to something like the following:

```
<metadata>
   <keyword
      xlink:href="http://smiggins.com/products.asp?waffle%20maker
         "
      xlink:actuate="onRequest"
      value="waffle maker" />
</metadata>
```

The alterations there are quite limited. Basically a couple of new attributes have been added to the existing element. No other changes are made to the overall structure of the document and it can still be processed perfectly without access to the target resource. The changes to `sender` and `recipient` would necessarily be more drastic since they require access to the target resources if the document is to remain coherent. Here they are:

```
<header>
  <sender
    xlink:href="http://smiggins.com/signatures/billsmig.xml"
    xlink:actuate="onLoad" />
  <recipient
    xlink:href="http://microsoft.com/signatures/billg.xml"
    xlink:actuate="onLoad" />
</header>
```

7.2.4 Extended Links

A link that carries more information than a simple relationship is called an extended link. Extended links may involve multiple resources, be at least bidirectional, and contain information that controls how they are processed.

7.2.4.1 The Recipe Book The simple links demonstrated for the Business Letter could easily be applied to the Recipe Book from Section 2.5. The Recipe Book lends itself to more complex relationships between data items. In Section 7.2.1 I outlined a scenario in which a chef was using an online system to access recipes.

```
<supplier
  xlink:type="locator"
  xlink:href="http://foodsRus.com"
  xlink:role="http://foodsRus.com/supplier"
  xlink:label="foodsRus" />

<description
  xlink:type="locator"
  xlink:href="http://foodlink.org/ingredient.xml#xpointer(//
     sgflour)"
  xlink:label="sgflour-def"
  xlink:role="http://foodlink.org/descriptions" />

<ingredient
  xlink:label="sgflour"
  xlink:type="extended">
    <quantity amount="450" />
    <name
      xlink:type="locator"
      xlink:label="sgflour-name">
        Stoneground Wholemeal Flour
    </name>
</ingredient>

<go
  xlink:type="arc"
  xlink:from="sgflour"
  xlink:to="foodRus"
  xlink:arcrole="suppliers.xml"
```

```
    xlink:actuate="onRequest" />

<go
    xlink:type="arc"
    xlink:from="sgflour-name"
    xlink:to="sgflour-def"
    xlink:arcrole="definitions.xml"
    xlink:actuate="onRequest" />
```

That XML fragment is significantly more complex[4] than the original code which looked like:

```
<ingredient>
    <quantity amount="450" />
    <name>Stoneground wholemeal flour</name>
</ingredient>
```

It also has vastly more functionality. The XLink code defines two relationships for the `ingredient`. Firstly, two new elements are added to the document which define a `supplier` and a `description`. These could be used throughout the recipe, so the additional overhead is not too great at this stage. Both `supplier` and `description` point to remote resources but their use isn't clear. So that the processing application knows how to handle these resources, I have included `role` attributes for both. These direct the application to resources, probably programs such as Java Servlets, on remote servers. These resources would provide information on the role of the resource when processing the document.

Each target resource has an address specified as a URI. The `description` has an extended URI which includes an XPointer expression:
`xlink:href="http://foodlink.org/ingredient.xml#xpointer(//sgflour)"`
pointing to a fragment of the document. XPointer is an implementation of XPath and has broadly the same syntax and semantics. If I wanted to use the same `description` element for multiple ingredient names, I would find a different way of expressing this relationship. Using the current structure, a new `description` must be added to the document for each `name`. The `ingredient` and `name` elements in the original document have been modified with some XLink attributes. The `ingredient` becomes an extended link, and both are given identifying labels. Finally I include two elements called `go`. Each of these defines an arc from the local document to a remote resource. The `ingredient` element is linked to the `supplier`, and the `name` is linked to the `description`.

[4] I *could* have written less code but it might not have been as clear as this sample.

In a real application, each ingredient would probably be linked to a number of suppliers. If the first was too expensive or didn't have the item in stock, the user could then order from the next one in the list. This is easily achieved. A new `supplier` element is added for each supplier, and a `go` element for every ingredient–supplier relationship that needs to be established.

7.2.5 Linkbases and Generic Links

There are time when readers would like to be able to annotate documents but can't because those documents are read-only. Annotations could be used in many ways. They might be useful for all readers or just for the person who made them, they might be editable or read-only, they might be hidden or always visible. Adding and using annotations is an incredibly useful facility, but it's not one that is available with current systems. XLink provides a mechanism by which such annotations can at least be described. Implementing them is a different problem...

When a document is read-only, annotations cannot be added into it directly. The solution here is to store the annotations in a separate file, which is usually called a *linkbase*, and have the processing software include them as it displays the original document. The application needs to be able to find the linkbase, which cannot be directly linked from the source document. Many different schemes can be imagined, ranging from using a default linkbase, analogous to the Web browser bookmark file, through to asking the user for the URI of the file they wish to use. These are application-specific problems which, again, need not detain us here.

The XLink version of the Recipe Book provides a suitable application to demonstrate how a linkbase might be used. The Recipe Book needs to be returned to its original form. A linkbase is created which looks something like the following:

```
<!xml version="1.0"?>
<definitions>
  <xref type="extended"
    <ingredient
      xlink:type="locator"
      xlink:href="#xpointer(string-range(//name, 'Stoneground
         wholemeal
      flour'))"
      xlink:label="sgflour-name" />
    <description
      xlink:type="locator"
```

```
xlink:href="http://foodlink.org/ingredient.xml#xpointer(//
    sgflour)"
xlink:label="sgflour-def" />

<go
  xlink:type="arc"
  xlink:from="sgflour-name"
  xlink:to="sgflour-def"
  xlink:arcrole="definitions.xml"
  xlink:actuate="onRequest" />
</xref>
</definitions>
```

This code creates a relationship between the ingredient name and the definition. The application is able to find individual names because they are expressed using XPointer. This could be implemented as a regular expression search or using SAX events depending upon the internal representation of the document that the application used. Whenever the application finds the text string `Stoneground wholemeal flour` in the document, it creates an arc to the appropriate definition.

The linkbase concept is useful when building systems that support generic links. A generic link is created by defining a set of conditions which, if met, are used to establish a relationship. The conditions are described using XPointer expressions just as in the last example, but they can be much less precise. For instance, XPointer would allow selection based upon:

- the element type,
- the value of particular attributes of given elements,
- pattern matching within element names.

The node-set which is created from the XPointer expression can have multiple entries. If these are extended XLinks, they can be sources or targets for the arc, which means that very complex relationships can be built almost automatically. Why automatically? The developer will not know what relationships are going to arise when the code is written. The creation of those relationships depends upon the application software, although the developer may have a good idea what the result will be. Imagine how complex these generic relationships might become in, for example, technical documentation where sets of elements are being linked to other sets. Such documents truly become webs of information.

7.3 XPOINTER

The XPath recommendation describes a generic set of facilities which can be used to navigate through XML documents. XPath is not intended to be used *as is*, instead it forms the basis of other languages. Common uses of XPath include XSLT, XSL-FO and XPointer. XPointer adds facilities to XPath so that complex expressions can be built and fragments of documents, for instance over a range of nodes, addressed. XPointer expressions are commonly used with extended XLink links to address fragments of remote documents. This can be done because XPointer is able to select based upon string comparisons, element names and attributes even when those items do not have specific IDs.

> **Note:**
> This discussion of XPointer is based upon the Candidate Recommendation published in September, 2001. By the time you read this, the Recommendation will have been released – but it will be broadly the same.

XPointer extends XPath in three important ways:

- XPointer expressions can be appended to URIs to address fragments of remote documents.
- Ranges of elements and individual points within a document can be addressed.
- XPointer includes facilities for matching with character strings.

In XPointer, a point is an individual location within an XML document. The addressing scheme allows for selection of points before or after any individual node or character. The location of a point is an integer position within a node or string. Given that both XPath and other XPointer functions number from one, it is somewhat surprising that points number from zero. XPointer expressions can address fragments of XML documents where those fragments span across a range. A range is defined as being all of the XML between two points. The XPath concept of a node is extended in XPointer to become a *location*. Location is a more flexible concept since it subsumes nodes, points and ranges into a single idea.

Since XPointer is based upon XPath, evaluation of expressions must take place within a context. When addressing a fragment of a resource which is identified through a URI, the context is taken from the root node of the remote resource.

XPointer provides some additional functions beyond those supplied by XPath.

`location-set range-to(location-set)`

This function operates on each node in the current context. It returns a range for the location. The start of the range is determined by calling the `start-point()` function, the end by calling the `end-point()` function. The following code fragment, which is based on an example in the XPointer Recommendation, finds the range from the start of the `Sugar` element to the end of the `Salt` element.

```
xpointer(id("Sugar")/range-to(id("Salt")))
```

***location-set* string-range(*location-set, string,* [*number*], [*number*])**

This function works on each element in the location-set given as first argument. The location is converted to a string value which is searched for the substring given in argument two. The third argument, which is optional, selects part of the string. The final argument will select the end of this part. For instance, in the following example, the string *Stoneground wholemeal flour* is matched in an ingredient name. The result is truncated to start before the letter at position 7 and terminate after the character at position 14.

```
string-range(//ingredient/name, "Stoneground wholemeal flour", 7, 14)
```

which results in `round wh`.

***location-set* range(*location-set*)**

This returns ranges for each location in the location-set given as a parameter.

***location-set* range-inside(*location-set*)**

Returns locations for all the contents of the location-set given as an argument.

***location-set* start-point(*location-set*)**

Returns the starting point of each location in the location-set given as an argument to the function.

***location-set* end-point(*location-set*)**

Returns the end point of each location in the location-set given as an argument to the function.

***location-set* here()**

Returns the location of the node that contains the XPointer. If the XPointer is inside a text node, the location of the element that contains that text node is returned.

***location-set* origin()**

This function returns a single location which is the element from which traversal to the current location was initiated.

Exercises

1. Briefly describe the purpose of XPath, XLink and XPointer.
2. Why is a dedicated navigation language needed for the traversal of XML documents? Why not simply use the techniques which are available in languages such as Java?
3. What is meant by the *context* of an XPath expression?
4. What is a node-set?
5. Download the XPath Recommendation from the W3C Website. Using it, list and describe the functions which XPath provides.
6. What do the following XPath axes mean? Give suitable supporting examples:
    - `child`
    - `parent`
    - `following`
    - `preceding-sibling`
    - `self`
7. Write an XPath expression which returns the third ingredient of the fourth recipe in the second category of the recipe book. Can you find an alternative way of navigating the same path?

Chapter 8

XSL Transformation Language

As you've already seen in this book, XML is a powerful way of structuring data. It is relatively simple and, thanks to its verbosity, very easy to read and write. Data rarely just sits unused on a forgotten and neglected system. Even if the values don't change, the data set will be queried and tested over time. Often this involves sharing data between applications, although it's rare for both applications to need exactly the same data. Usually one application will require just a subset of the data available to the other. For example, an application that is creating an invoice will not need to know the details of every customer in the database, just the one being billed. When applications share data, they may use different structures to meet their differing needs. Sometimes data may even be added, or removed, from a structure as it is processed.

On other occasions the application may need to present data to a human reader. Although XML is moderately readable, few end-users would be happy seeing it on their screens. When data is going to be displayed on screen it may be formatted using cascading stylesheets, as we've seen. This is only a partial solution since the entire data set must be presented to the user and we are relying upon the browser software performing the transformation correctly. A better alternative is to convert just the required parts of the XML into a format such as XHTML or Adobe's PDF which can be viewed on screen or printed out.

The process of changing the structure of an XML document is called *transformation* and is done using the Extensible Stylesheet Language, XSL. Originally XSL was envisaged as a single language which could perform all possible transformations. This was impractical as the language would have been exceptionally complex. In software development complexity is often the enemy of usefulness – once languages reach a certain level of complexity developers will prefer to find other, simpler solutions. The solution to the complexity of XSL was to split it into two smaller, though still pretty complex, languages. XSLT, the XSL Transformation language, was developed for the purposes of transforming between XML structures. The XSL Formatting Objects, XSL-FO, language was developed for transformations into printed or aural forms. I examine XSL-FO in Chapter 10; *this* chapter will concentrate on XSLT.

> **Note:**
> Since XHTML is an XML application, transformations into Web pages are usually done through XSLT rather than XSL-FO. Web browsers can display XHTML, thus in common with most XML books, the examples here will transform from XML to XHTML.

8.1 INTRODUCING XSLT

Transformations require a source document, in XML, and an XSLT stylesheet. These are given as input to the XSLT processor which outputs a new XML document. Figure 8.1 shows how this works.

The XSLT processing software includes an XML parser which transforms the two input documents into an internal representation. The parser may use either DOM or SAX technologies and the internal format may be a tree, a list or something more exotic. Most commonly, tree structures are used since they mirror the logical structure of the XML document, but parsers written in Lisp, or its variants such as Scheme, are more likely to use list structures. The XSL Recommendation describes the handling of XSL as a process of transforming between tree structures and, conceptually, this is the easiest way of understanding the process.

When writing XSLT code, you'll process node-sets using XPath expressions. The node-set will often contain part of the XML *tree* but visualizing it as such won't help you develop the correct expressions. If you think about node-sets, parent nodes, child nodes and so on,

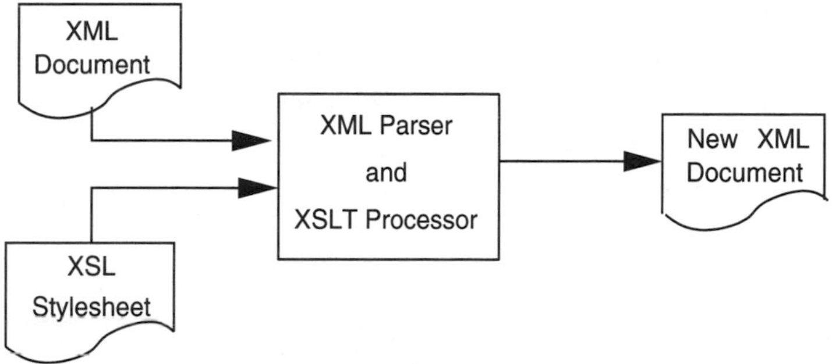

Figure 8.1 XML plus XSLT Produces XML

you'll find writing XPath easier. Look at Chapter 7 for a detailed explanation of how to navigate within XML documents.

8.1.1 Why Use XSLT?

Developers who are new to XML often wonder why they need to use XSLT. Given the existence of APIs such as SAX, discussed in Chapter 13, or DOM, which is outlined in Chapter 12, why not write custom applications? Imagine this scenario: You spend weeks writing an application which transforms your XML structure, works quickly and effectively and uses some neat programming tricks. Days before the system goes live the system architect adds a new XML element and three new attributes to the structure you are working with. Suddenly, your code doesn't work and you have to restart the whole development process. Six months after rolling out the system, your company gets a new supplier who will provide XML data in a new format. You have to rewrite your application yet again. Once you've sorted that little lot out, the IT director decides that you need to move from Java Enterprise Beans to the .Net framework. Yet again all of the transformation code has to be altered and now neither the user documentation[1] nor the design matches the running system.

How would XSLT help? Firstly, XSLT processors are designed to be generic applications which all comply with the same W3C Recommendation. If the underlying system changes, you ought to be able to plugin a new processor and carry on running without too much change to the stylesheets.

Secondly, because XSLT systems are generic and extensible, if you need to handle a new structure, you can. Easily. All you need do is to write a new stylesheet which you then feed into your system. When the company changes supplier, your system can handle

[1] You did write documentation, didn't you?

their data with minimal effort. How does this work? XSLT is one of many *declarative* languages. The programmer specifies *what* they want from their application, not *how* the application should work. Effectively your stylesheet simply says that given a particular XML structure as input, you'd like a different one as output. Changing a transformation is achieved by rewriting the stylesheets without altering any of the application programs.

> **Note:**
> Many XSLT processors let you write your own *extension functions* or provide libraries of functions which extend beyond the XSLT Recommendation. If you use these, you won't be able to change processor very easily.

8.1.2 An Example Transformation

The best way to learn about any new language is to see it in action. Classically, the example programming tutorials always start with is the display of the message *Hello World*. That's just where I'm going to start with XSLT. In Listing 2.1, I showed you a simple XML file. I'm going to use an even simpler file this time so that I can create the most straightforward of transformations.

Listing 8.1 Hello World in XML

```
<?xml version="1.0"?>
<?xml-stylesheet type="text/xsl" href="hello.xsl"?>
<message>Hello World</message>
```

That's a one-element XML file which contains a simple message. The second line is a processing instruction which tells the processor to use the stylesheet `hello.xsl` to transform the file. Listing 8.2 shows the XSLT stylesheet that will transform the XML shown in Listing 8.1.

Listing 8.2 Hello World

```
<?xml version="1.0"?>

<xsl:stylesheet
  xmlns:xsl="http://www.w3.org/1999/XSL/Transform"
  version="1.0">

  <xsl:template match="/message">
    <html>
      <head><title>Test</title></head>
      <body>
```

```
        <h1><xsl:value-of select="."/></h1>
      </body>
    </html>
  </xsl:template>

</xsl:stylesheet>
```

The essence of this script is to place the code for an XHTML file inside an XSLT template. As the template is processed, the contents of elements from the original *XML* document are placed inside the XHTML tags. Once processing has been completed, the HTML is output. The details of the XSLT will become clear throughout this chapter. The tags that start with the namespace prefix `xsl:` are XSLT tags, the other tags are XHTML tags. The two attributes `match` and `select` are XPath expressions which are selecting the parts of the document that are going to be processed. The result of applying that stylesheet to the XML file is shown in Figure 8.2.

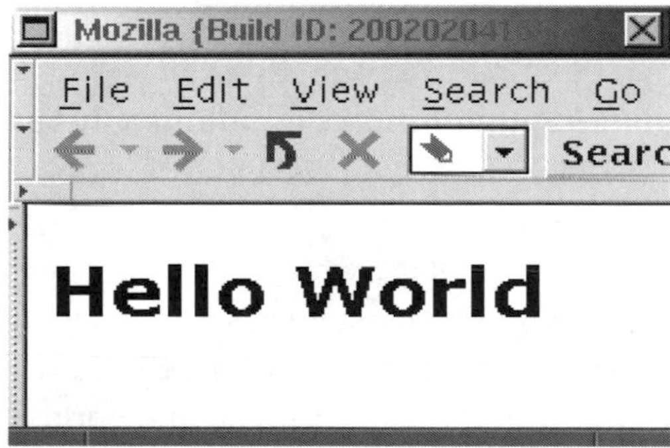

Figure 8.2 Hello World Transformed

In a production environment[2] the results of an XSLT transformation are likely to be either:

- passed to another application for further processing,
- saved in a file or database,
- or streamed across a network as XHTML, for display in a Web browser.

The examples in this book are handled rather differently. All the transformations that I'll show convert XML into XHTML. Some modern Web browsers, such as Mozilla and Internet Explorer, include both XML parsers and XSLT transformation engines. This means

[2]Often referred to as the *real world*.

that given an XML file and an XSLT stylesheet, they can display the result of the transformation. Since I use Linux, I'll be showing the result of using Mozilla,[3] but you should get similar results from Internet Explorer.

8.2 STARTING THE STYLESHEET

An XSLT stylesheet is a valid XML document. This simple fact cannot be stated too often or too clearly. Everything that applies to the XML files that you, yourself, write also applies to XSLT stylesheets. At the top of the file, therefore, you will find an XML declaration. Also at the top of the file, there is a namespace declaration:

```
<xsl:stylesheet
     xmlns:xsl="http://www.w3.org/1999/XSL/Transform"
     version="1.0">
```

The namespace for XSLT version 1.0 stylesheets must be:
`http://www.w3.org/1999/XSL/Transform`
This is defined in the XSLT Recommendation and can only be altered if you use a later version of XSLT. The namespace can only be used for XSLT documents; it cannot be used in XML source documents.

XSLT is a large and complex language which contains many different elements. It's highly probable that large stylesheets in complex systems will use XSLT tags which are the same as elements within either the source or target documents. This makes the use of a namespace prefix vitally important. Even if you are working exclusively with small documents, using a prefix is a good habit to get into. Other authors will use them, and if *you* do the same, reading *their* code will be much easier.

In programming, life is often easier if you stick to *idiomatic* structures. An idiomatic structure is one that all programmers use and recognize instantly. By using well-known, established forms, code is clearer and easier both to read and to write. Namespace prefixes are a little like that. The use of `xsl` as the prefix for XSLT elements has rapidly become established as the *de facto* standard. This is probably both because it is the prefix used in the XSLT Recommendation and because it's obvious and memorable. Each developer could invent their own prefix but that would be yet another piece of information to remember when reading a stylesheet. Psychologists tell us that most people can manage and manipulate five pieces of information at one time.[4] If you use a prefix other than `xsl`, that's just one more thing to be remembered by anyone reading your code to maintain,

[3]Which is available for many different operating systems and hardware platforms.
[4]The normal range is said to be from three to seven.

verify or improve it. On small projects that person is likely to be you, and you're likely to use different prefixes on different projects. Be boring and normal. Don't try to be clever. Use the `xsl` prefix and save everyone's sanity.

The elements that follow the `stylesheet` element are called *top-level* elements. Any of the following are permitted:

- `attribute-set`,
- `decimal-format`,
- `import`,
- `include`,
- `key`,
- `namespace-alias`,
- `output`,
- `param`,
- `preserve-space`,
- `strip-space`,
- `template`,
- `variable`.

This book is an introductory guide which gives an overview of the capabilities of many different technologies, so that you can start writing code straight away. If each technology were comprehensively described, the book would be a thousand pages too long and three years late. I'm not, therefore, going to discuss every XSLT element. Once you understand how XSLT works, you can learn more from reading the Recommendation or a comprehensive reference work. This is all a round-about way of saying that I won't be looking at all of those elements. I make no apologies for not even mentioning some of them after this section.

8.3 TEMPLATES

XSLT stylesheets are made of templates. A template contains an XPath expression which is used to select elements from the source document, and a set of transformations which are applied to the selected elements. Since element selection is performed using XPath expressions, the results are held in node-sets which contain matched elements plus their subelements. Logically, these form a set of partial tree structures to which further matches can be applied. Patterns are applied within a particular context which will be the node that is being evaluated or one of its ancestors. The expression will not be applied to nodes that are outside the context. This is one of the commonest causes of problems when writing XSLT: the expression may appear to be correct, but if the context is wrong at runtime, results will be incorrect.

Using a series of *templates* and *pattern matches* it is possible to drill down into the source document searching for particular nodes and performing transformations along the way.

`<template match="expression" name="qname" priority="n" mode="qname"/>`

Templates must be defined before they can be used. Template definitions are placed inside `template` elements. A `template` element has a number of attributes. Usually the template will contain a rule which can be matched against the content of the XML document. The rule is described using the `match` attribute which accepts an XPath expression as its value.

In a completely declarative programming style, templates would be selected solely because the value of their `match` attribute was successfully matched against content in the source document. In reality, though, there are many occasions on which this is not possible. Stylesheets can be made much tidier if the author controls the order in which templates are used. This level of control also means that the structure of the output document is not dependent upon the structure of the source document. Elements can be transformed in the order in which they are eventually required. Templates can be identified using the `name` attribute which accepts a valid XML name as its value.

Sometimes the same content must be processed several times, in different ways. The templates that are used for this sort of processing will all match the same pattern which means that the processor needs to decide which template to use at a particular time. This is where the `mode` attribute is used. Each of the templates that will match a particular expression is given a different identifier as the value of the `mode` attribute. The processor uses the value of `mode` to select the correct template. You'll see examples of the different ways that templates can be used later in this chapter.

`<apply-templates select="expression" mode="qname" />`

Defining templates is only part of the story. The processor needs to be told which templates to use. This is done through two different XSLT elements. The `apply-templates` element is used to process the children of the context node. The value of the `select` attribute is an expression which creates a node-set of matching elements. The rules inside the apply-templates element will be applied to each element in the node-set in turn.

<call-template name="qname" />

Named templates can be invoked using the call-template element. This has a single attribute which is the name of the target template. It's important to note that templates do not have to be named. When the call-template element is used, it overrides the match and mode attributes of the template element.

8.4 XSL ELEMENTS

XSL specifies many different elements. There isn't space here to describe them all, instead I'll just look at some of those that you are likely to use on a regular basis. The template element contains a small tree of nodes which are used to generate content and control how it is generated.

<for-each select="expression" />

Given a node-set containing elements of a single type, or identically structured subtrees, the same processing can be applied to all of its elements. In a typical programming language such as Java, iteration across a set of values is normally achieved using the for loop. In XSLT the same effect is achieved using the for-each element. This takes an expression as its parameter, which may match the context node or any of its subelements, and applies transformations to all matching elements.

The following code fragment is taken from a stylesheet, presented in Chapter 9, which is used to transform the Business Letter application. The code finds all firstname elements that are subelements of the element contained in the variable $nom. Matching elements are then placed in the output document.

```
<xsl:for-each select="$nom/firstname">
   <xsl:value-of select="." />
</xsl:for-each>
```

<if test="boolean expression" />

The if element has a single test attribute. This attribute takes an expression as its value. Once the expression has been evaluated, its result is converted to a Boolean value. For those nodes for which the expression evaluates to true, the processing contained in the template is performed.

The following fragment is, once again, taken from the stylesheet for the Business Letter. It shows nested if elements performing string comparisons:

```
<xsl:if test="$tmp='informal'">
   <xsl:if test="$msg=''">
      Yours Sincerely,
   </xsl:if>
</xsl:if>
```

```
<output
method="xml" | "html" | "text"
version="nmtoken"
encoding="string"
omit-xml-declaration="yes" | "no"
standalone="yes" | "no"
doctype-public="string"
doctype-system="string"
indent="yes" | "no"
media-type="string" />
```

The XSLT processor has no way of knowing what output format it should use for a transformation. Processors default to producing XHTML, but where a different format, such as XML, is required, the `output` element should be used. This is a top-level element which should be placed after the `stylesheet` element and before any templates. Using the `output` element gives tight-grained control over exactly how the output will be presented so that, for example, your input document might be in UTF-8 and the output in UTF-16.

<param name="qname" select="expression" />

A `param` element binds a value to an identifying name so that it can be passed to a template or stylesheet. Parameters may hold data of any type that can be returned from an XSLT or XPath expression. The `parameter` element must be have a value assigned to its `name` attribute.

<preserve-space elements="tokens" />
<strip-space elements="tokens" />

These two elements provide partial control over the handling of whitespace within source documents by the XSLT processor. Whitespace handling in XSLT is discussed in Section 8.9.

<text disable-output-escaping="yes" | "no" />

When text that does not occur in the source document has to be written to the output, it can originate directly from the XSLT. This may give unpredictable or unexpected results where whitespace characters are concerned. To ensure that what appears in the output is *exactly* what is intended, the text can be placed inside a `text` element.

<with-param name="qname" select="expression" />

The `with-param` element is used to pass parameters into templates and stylesheets. The parameters must be declared and have values assigned to them before they are passed. Parameters can be passed in either `apply-templates` or `call-template` elements. The parameter value can be chosen either using the name of the parameter, or using the `select` attribute. Using named parameters will be more familiar to most programmers, and is easier to read.

<value-of select="expression"
disable-output-escaping=["yes"|"no"] />

This element is used to create a text node in the output document. The result of the expression given to the `select` attribute is converted to a string and placed directly into the output.

<variable name="qname" select="expression" />

A `variable` element binds a value to an identifying name. Variables can hold data of any type that can be returned from an XSLT or XPath expression. The `variable` must be given a value for its `name` attribute.

8.5 XSL FUNCTIONS

XPath and XSLT provide a number of functions which can be used in expressions. The XPath functions were described in Section 7.1.3. I'll highlight some of the ones that you are most likely to use in XSLT, in this Section. Comprehensive details can be found in that earlier section.

boolean()

This function converts its argument to a Boolean value. Conversions are based upon four simple rules:

- The number zero is converted to `false`. All other numbers are converted to `true`.
- A string of length zero becomes `false`. All other strings are converted to `true`.
- Boolean values pass through the function unchanged.
- An empty node-set is converted to `false`. All other node-sets become `true`.

ceiling()

Given a numeric argument, this function returns the smallest integer that is equal to, or greater than, its argument.

`concat()`

Takes two or more arguments, converts each to a string and returns a new string which is the result of concatenating the converted strings.

`count()`

Given a node-set as its parameter, this function will return the number of nodes which it contains.

`floor()`

When given a numeric argument, this function returns the largest integer that is equal to, or smaller than, the argument.

`last()`

Returns the number of nodes in the current context.

`name()`

Returns a qualified name, a Qname, which represents the name of a node. Generally, this will be the name that the node has in the XML document.

`normalize-space()`

Takes a string as its argument, removes leading and trailing whitespace, and replaces all internal sequences of whitespace characters with a single space.

`not()`

Negates the Boolean value of its argument and returns this value. If given the value `true`, this function will return `false`.

`number()`

Converts its argument to a number using the following simple rules:

- When given a Boolean value, `false` is converted to zero and `true` to one.
- If given a number, it is unaltered.
- When given a string, leading and trailing whitespace is removed. If the string is then an XPath number, optionally preceded by a minus sign, its value is returned. If the value of the string is not an XPath number, `NaN` is returned.
- If given a node-set as an argument, the node-set is converted to a string and then processed as for string arguments.

`position()`

Returns a number that represents the current position in the context. Nodes in the context are numbered from one.

round()

Returns the integer value that is closest to the value of its, numeric, argument.

string()

Converts its argument to a string which it returns. The following rules apply:

- The Boolean value `false` is converted to the string *false*. The value `true` is converted to the string *true*.
- The number `NaN`[5] is converted to the string *NaN*. The value zero is converted to *0*, infinity to the string *infinity*. All other numeric values are converted to strings which are valid XPath numbers. The conversions happen exactly as you would expect.
- Strings are returned unchanged.
- The rules for processing node-sets are rather complicated.
  - An empty node-set becomes an empty string.
  - A non-empty node-set is represented by the value of its first node, in document order.
  - A text node is converted to a string equal to its content.
  - A comment node becomes a string which is the same as the comment.
  - A processing instruction becomes a string which represents its data part.
  - A namespace node becomes a string representing the namespace URI.
  - An attribute node becomes the value of the attribute.
  - A root node, or element node, becomes a string which represents the concatenation of all of its descendent text nodes in document order.

substring(value, start[, length])

Returns a substring of the parameter `value`. The start of the substring is the character at position `start`, with the first character of the string having position one. An optional `length` attribute specifies how many characters the substring should include. If this number is greater than the length of `value`, the substring terminates at the end of the original string.

translate(string, from, to)

The `translate()` function changes characters within a string. It takes three parameters, the first of which is the string that will be changed. The second and third parameters are lists of characters. All characters in the `value` string that occur in

[5] If Nan can really be considered a numeric value, since it means *not a number*.

the `from` list are replaced by the character in the `to` list that is at the same position. Take, for example, the following code fragment:

```
<xsl:value-of
   select="translate(., 'abcde', 'EDCB7')"/>
```

Each lower-case `a` is replaced with an upper-case `E`, lower-case `e` with the number `7`, and so on. One common use of `translate()` is to convert all lower-case letters to upper-case or vice versa as XSLT does not provide `toLowerCase()` or `toUpperCase()` style functions.

```
<xsl:value-of select="translate(.,
                            'abcdefghijklmnopqrstuvwxyz',
                            'ABCDEFGHIJKLMNOPQRSTUVWXYZ')"/>
```

8.6 USING VARIABLES

Variables are an essential part of the programmer's toolkit. They simplify code and make it more efficient. XSLT includes a limited type of variable. The XSLT `variable` element is really somewhat misnamed because in XSLT variables don't vary. Once a value has been assigned to a `variable` element, it cannot be changed. Therefore, in XSLT, variables are really constants.

Unvarying *variables* may seem terribly limiting. How can you write real, meaningful code if you can't manipulate data? It's important to remember that XSLT is not a procedural language, it's declarative. When you write XSLT, you are telling the processor what result you would like once it has finished transforming the source document. You are *not* telling it *how* to achieve that result. If this seems like a strange idea, it really isn't. If you've written database code in SQL, tried your hand at Lisp programming or taken a functional programming course using a language such as Haskell, then you've used this idea before. In fact, since Lisp is one of the oldest programming languages in use today, programming without variable assignment must be one of the oldest ideas in computing. You're probably wondering why, if this is such an old and well-established idea, the vast majority of code is written in languages such as Java and C++ which use variables. Many answers could be offered to that question, but in the end it probably all comes down to control and complexity. As programmers, we like to be in control of the machine. Programming in a language such as Lisp often seems to leave the computer in charge.[6] A

[6]It isn't, but that's not how these languages feel.

more realistic reason for the popularity of variables is that programming without them can be very complicated. Learning to write XSLT stylesheets will take some time but it's not an impossible task.

XSLT variables are declared using the `variable` element. Each variable must be given a name that is unique at its level of scope. Within each template, all variable names must be unique and must not clash with a global variable. The same name can be used for a local variable in every template if you wish. Variables are accessed by placing a dollar sign before their name. If the value of the variable is to be assigned to an attribute, it is placed inside curly brackets, even if, as in this example, it is an attribute of a CSS style:

```
<some_element attr={$variable} />
```

Listing 8.3 modifies the *Hello World* stylesheet to use variables. The code now displays an HTML page which shows the message `Chris Says Hello World` when transformed using a Web browser.

Listing 8.3 Hello World Using Variables

```
<?xml version="1.0"?>

<xsl:stylesheet
  xmlns:xsl="http://www.w3.org/1999/XSL/Transform"
  version="1.0">

<xsl:variable name="msg">
  <xsl:value-of select="/" />
</xsl:variable>

  <xsl:template match="/">

    <xsl:variable name="greeter">
      <xsl:text>Chris</xsl:text>
    </xsl:variable>

    <xsl:variable name="col">
      <xsl:text>purple</xsl:text>
    </xsl:variable>
    <html>
      <head><title>Test</title></head>
      <body>
        <h1 style="color: {$col}">
```

```
            <xsl:value-of select="$greeter" />
            Says
            <xsl:value-of select="$msg"/>
          </h1>
        </body>
      </html>
  </xsl:template>

</xsl:stylesheet>
```

The code shows a global variable, msg, which is available throughout the stylesheet. This contains the root node of the XML source document. Inside the template, a local variable is declared which holds a text element containing the string Chris. I *could* simply have placed the string inside the variable element; the text nodes are not strictly required here. Using them in your stylesheet guarantees control over whitespace inside text content. The third variable, col, is given a string value which represents the color of the text. This is used in styling the <h1> level heading. Notice that because the variable is being used in an attribute, its name is placed in curly brackets.

8.7 PARAMETER PASSING

When a piece of data is needed in more than one template, it *could* be declared as a global variable and used freely. Global variables cannot, though, be used if the data item is going to be generated during the processing of the script. This may happen when, for instance, a numerical value is being created which is based on the value of elements in the source document. Fortunately, XSLT includes a parameter passing mechanism. Values can be created as the stylesheet is executed, and passed to those templates that require them. This is far safer than using global variables. If you have to pass a parameter explicitly, you know that you need it. Global variables can be used accidentally, which will lead to incorrect outputs.

Parameters are created using the with-param element. Parameters are passed into named templates which are being processed through the call-template element. Each parameter is given an identifier using the name attribute, and a value using either the select attribute of the with-param element, or using a nested value-of element. Parameters are extracted in the template using the param element. This takes a single parameter which is the identifying name of the parameter. The names used in the param element must be identical to those used in the with-param element. The extraction of parameter values is done using direct comparison of names rather than, for instance, the order in which parameters are passed.

Listing 8.4 code modifies the *Hello World* example to use parameters.

Listing 8.4 Hello World Using Parameter Passing

```
<?xml version="1.0"?>

<xsl:stylesheet
  xmlns:xsl="http://www.w3.org/1999/XSL/Transform"
  version="1.0">

  <xsl:template match="/">

    <html>
      <head><title>Test</title></head>
      <body>
        <xsl:call-template name="makeBody">
          <xsl:with-param name="content" select="." />
          <xsl:with-param name="greeter">
            <xsl:value-of select="'Chris'" />
          </xsl:with-param>
          <xsl:with-param name="color" select="'purple'" />
        </xsl:call-template>
      </body>
    </html>
  </xsl:template>

  <xsl:template name="makeBody">
    <xsl:param name="content" />
    <xsl:param name="greeter" />
    <xsl:param name="color" />

    <h1 style="color: {$color}">
      <xsl:value-of select="$greeter" />
      Says
      <xsl:value-of select="$content"/>
    </h1>
  </xsl:template>
```

```
</xsl:stylesheet>
```

The stylesheet has two templates. A top-level template sets up the structure of the result document, which is an XHTML page. A second template, named `makeBody`, is called from this one and three parameters are passed to it. The first parameter is node-set which contains the body of the XML source document. The context in the first template is the root node of the XML document. Giving the value `'.'` to the `select` attribute will, therefore, pick all nodes in the document.[7] The second parameter contains a text node which has the value `Chris`, and the third is a text node which holds `purple`. Notice that the parameters `greeter` and `color` are declared using the two different syntactic options. In the called template, `makeBody`, the parameters are extracted and used as if they were local or global variables.

8.8 MODES

Sometimes the same XML element, or subtree, needs to be processed more than once. Good examples of this include the creation of a table of contents at the start of a book, and the placing of footnotes on a printed page. In each case content must be placed into the flow of the output document and later placed in the document but outside of its main flow. The two pieces of processing must be treated independently of each other. A table of contents cannot be created until the rest of the document has been produced because chapter, section and page numbers depend upon the structure of the whole document.

XSLT provides control over repeated code using *modes*. Modes work with the `apply-templates` element which passes control to templates using matching expressions rather than calls to named templates. The same template can be matched by repeatedly using `apply-templates` elements that have the same context and use the same pattern in their `select` attributes. The name of the mode is supplied using the `mode` attribute. Listing 8.5 shows this in action.

Listing 8.5 Hello World Using Modes

```
<?xml version="1.0"?>

<xsl:stylesheet
  xmlns:xsl="http://www.w3.org/1999/XSL/Transform"
  version="1.0">

  <xsl:template match="/">
```

[7] In this trivial example, the values `'*'` and `'/'` would have the same effect.

```
    <html>
      <head><title>Test</title></head>
      <body>
        <xsl:apply-templates select="/" mode="makeHead" />
        <xsl:apply-templates select="/" mode="makeBody" />
      </body>
    </html>
  </xsl:template>

  <xsl:template match="/" mode="makeHead">

    <h1 style="color: purple">
      Chris Says
      <xsl:value-of select="."/>
    </h1>
  </xsl:template>

  <xsl:template match="/" mode="makeBody">
      <p>Fred Says
      <xsl:value-of select="."/>
    </p>
  </xsl:template>

</xsl:stylesheet>
```

A set of templates is created which match the expression. In the `template` element of each, a different mode is supplied. When the processor successfully matches the expression in a `select` attribute of an `apply-templates` element, it will search for a template whose `mode` matches that of the element. Figure 8.3 shows what happens when Listing 8.5 is applied to the code from Listing 8.1 using Mozilla.

8.9 HANDLING WHITESPACE

Processing whitespace is one of the most complex and problematic parts of XSLT. This might seem peculiar at first sight. After all, whitespace is just whitespace and it ought to be copied straight from the source document to the output document, shouldn't it? Actually no. The complexity arises because some whitespace is significant and some isn't.

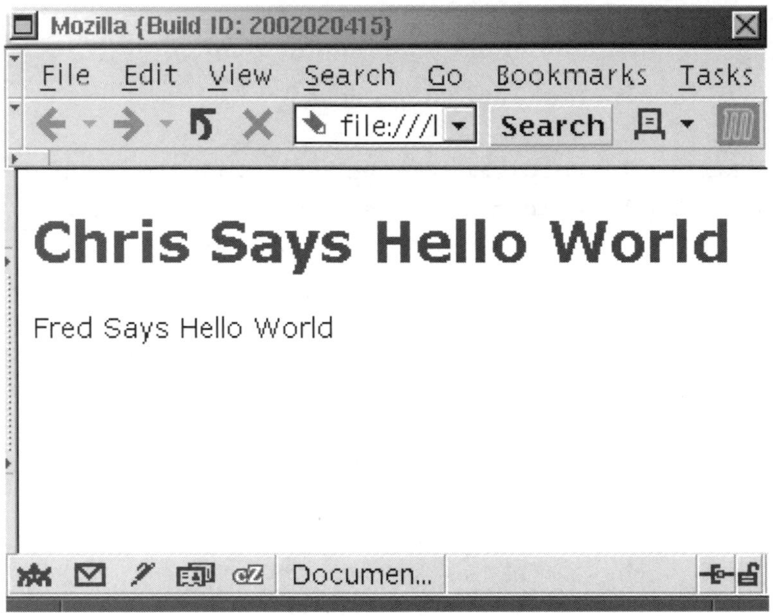

Figure 8.3 Styling Hello World Using Modes

Significant whitespace is found in the content of the elements in the source document. As a general rule this should be passed straight through to the output document. Whitespace that is not significant includes those newlines, tabs, spaces and carriage-returns used to format XML documents so that humans can read them. When the output of a transformation is destined directly for a Web browser, another set of problems is created. Browsers normalize whitespace in element content. This means that where a piece of content has a run of more than one adjacent whitespace characters, those characters are reduced to a single space. XSLT provides us with a number of techniques which can be used to control the appearance of documents.

`<preserve-space elements="tokens" />`

By default, any space that is present in the content of an element is left there by the XSLT processor. This doesn't guarantee that you'll notice it in the output, especially if you are transforming to XHTML. Sometimes, where nested stylesheets are being used, or where one stylesheet is including or importing another, whitespace may be removed by an earlier instruction. If you need to guarantee that space will be left alone, use the `preserver-space` element. It takes a list of element names as the value to its `elements` attribute. The names in the list must be separated by spaces.

<strip-space elements="tokens" />

When you need to guarantee the removal of insignificant whitespace, use the `strip-space` element. Again this takes a space-separated list of element names as the value for its `elements` attribute.

<text />

The content of `text` elements is placed directly into the output document. This makes them a very convenient way to add whitespace where it would otherwise not appear. You've previously seen Table 8.1 in Chapter 2, but it's reproduced here to refresh your memory. The table lists the Unicode values that can be used in XML entities to get space in your output. These entities are understood by all XSLT and XML processors and will always work.

Table 8.1 XML Whitespace Characters

Character	Unicode Value
tab	`#x9`
newline	`#xA`
carriage return	`#xD`
space	`#x20`

normalize-space()

This function is used to remove leading and trailing whitespace from the text content of elements. The element name is placed inside the parentheses of the function during selection:

```
<xsl:value-of select="normalize-space(elementName)" />
```

I've tried to illustrate the handling of whitespace in the example which occupies the rest of this chapter. This is a straightforward, and relatively common, application. I've created an XML file which holds a poem. The poem is *Elegy written in a Country Churchyard* by the English poet Thomas Gray who lived from 1716 to 1771. The poem itself is quite long so I'm only using the first three stanzas in this example. Listing 8.6 shows the contents of the XML document.

Listing 8.6 An XML Formatted Poem

```
<?xml version="1.0"?>
<?xml-stylesheet type="text/xsl" href="poem.xsl"?>

<poem>
```

```
  <title>Elegy written in a Country Churchyard</title>
  <author>
    <first>Thomas</first>
    <last>Gray</last>
  </author>
  <content>
    <stanza>
      The Curfew tolls the knell of parting day,
      The lowing herd wind slowly o'er the lea,
      The plowman homeward plods his weary way,
      And leaves the world to darkness and to me.
    </stanza>
    <stanza>
      Now fades the glimmering landscape on the sight,
      And all the air a solemn stillness holds,
      Save where the beetle wheels his droning flight,
      And drowsy tinklings lull the distant folds;
    </stanza>
    <stanza>
      Save that from yonder ivy-mantled tow'r
      The moping owl does to the moon complain
      Of such as, wand'ring near her secret bow'r,
      Molest her ancient solitary reign.
    </stanza>
  </content>
</poem>
```

The simplest transformation will display the name of the author, title of the poem and place each stanza in a separate paragraph. I'm using XHTML as the output format so that I can display the result in a Web browser. To avoid anomalies caused by the implementation of software, I transformed the XML to XHTML, saved it in a file, using Xalan-J, and opened the result directly in Mozilla. Doing this not only verified the transformation, it also meant that the HTML output was available so that its structure could be examined.

Listing 8.7 shows the first transformation.

Listing 8.7 Stylesheet For A Poem

```
<?xml version="1.0"?>
<xsl:stylesheet
  xmlns:xsl="http://www.w3.org/1999/XSL/Transform"
  version="1.0">
```

```
  <xsl:template match="/poem">
    <html>
      <head>
        <title><xsl:value-of select="title" /></title>
      </head>
      <body>
        <h1><xsl:value-of select="title" /></h1>
        <h3>By
          <xsl:value-of select="author/first" />
          <xsl:value-of select="author/last" />
        </h3>
        <xsl:for-each select="content/stanza">
          <p><xsl:value-of select="." /></p>
        </xsl:for-each>
      </body>
    </html>
  </xsl:template>

</xsl:stylesheet>
```

The result of the initial transformation is shown in Figure 8.4. Notice how the poet's names have been run together into a single word, and the stanzas, which were neatly formatted, are now presented as long lines of text. The obvious question is which of these are artifacts of the way that the browser handles text, and which are XSLT problems. Looking at the HTML code will give us the necessary answers. Listing 8.8 shows the HTML code.

Listing 8.8 Transformed XML Poem

```
<html>
<head>
<title>Elegy written in a Country Churchyard</title>
</head>
<body>
<h1>Elegy written in a Country Churchyard</h1>
<h3>By
           ThomasGray</h3>
<p>
       The Curfew tolls the knell of parting day,
       The lowing herd wind slowly o'er the lea,
```

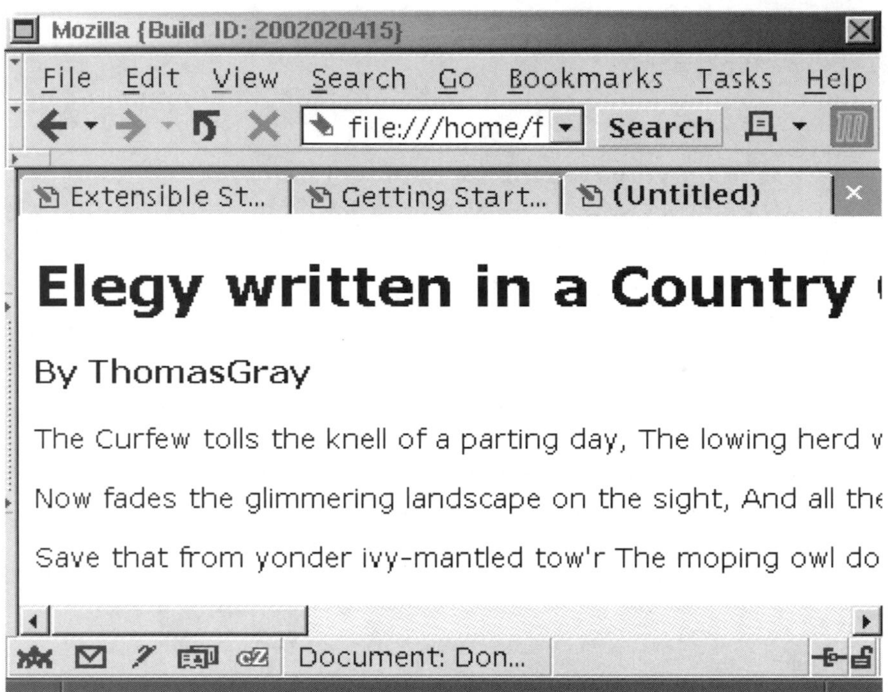

Figure 8.4 Styled Poem

```
      The plowman homeward plods his weary way,
      And leaves the world to darkness and to me.
    </p>
<p>
      Now fades the glimmering landscape on the sight,
      And all the air a solemn stillness holds,
      Save where the beetle wheels his droning flight,
      And drowsy tinklings lull the distant folds;
    </p>
<p>
      Save that from yonder ivy-mantled tow'r
      The moping owl does to the moon complain
      Of such as, wand'ring near her secret bow'r,
      Molest her ancient solitary reign.
    </p>
</body>
</html>
```

Two separate problems are now clearly identified. The XSLT processor has run the poet's names together but it has preserved the whitespace in the stanzas of the poem. This is exactly the default behavior that was expected. Now that the problems have been identified, they are easily solved. A space entity, , can be placed between the names and the HTML <pre> element can be used to format the poem. The default behavior of <pre> is to use a fixed pitch font such as Courier, but I'm going to apply a style to get a more reader-friendly version.

Listing 8.9 A Better Stylesheet For A Poem

```
<?xml version="1.0"?>
<xsl:stylesheet
  xmlns:xsl="http://www.w3.org/1999/XSL/Transform"
  version="1.0">

<xsl:output method="html" indent="yes" />

  <xsl:template match="/poem">
    <html>
      <head>
        <title><xsl:value-of select="title" /></title>
      </head>
      <body>
        <h1><xsl:value-of select="title" /></h1>
        <h3>By
          <xsl:value-of select="author/first" />
          <xsl:text>&#x20;</xsl:text>
          <xsl:value-of select="author/last" />
        </h3>
        <xsl:for-each select="content/stanza">
          <p><pre style="font-family:helvetica">
            <xsl:value-of select="." />
            </pre>
          </p>
        </xsl:for-each>
      </body>
    </html>
  </xsl:template>

</xsl:stylesheet>
```

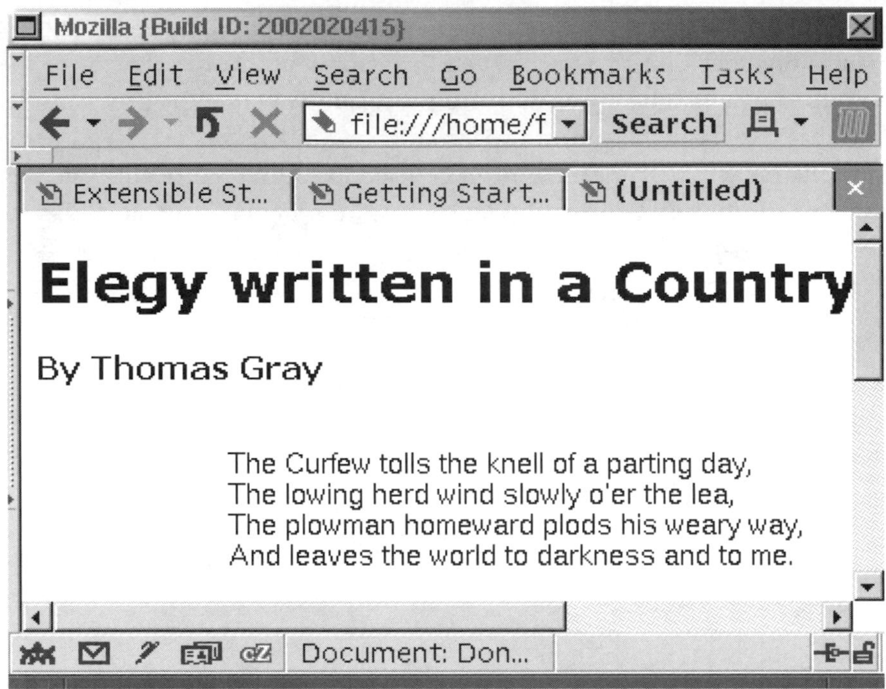

Figure 8.5 Styled Poem With Whitespace Handling

Figure 8.5 shows the resultant output. The structure of the code is demonstrated in Listing 8.10. A space now appears between the names. The stanzas remain as they were yet they now display exactly as intended.

Listing 8.10 Transformed XML Poem

```
<html>
   <head>
      <title>Elegy written in a Country Churchyard</title>
   </head>
   <body>
      <h1>Elegy written in a Country Churchyard</h1>
      <h3>By
           Thomas Gray</h3>
      <p>
         <pre style="font-family:helvetica">
       The Curfew tolls the knell of parting day,
       The lowing herd wind slowly o'er the lea,
       The plowman homeward plods his weary way,
```

```
         And leaves the world to darkness and to me.
            </pre>
         </p>
         <p>
            <pre style="font-family:helvetica">
         Now fades the glimmering landscape on the sight,
         And all the air a solemn stillness holds,
         Save where the beetle wheels his droning flight,
         And drowsy tinklings lull the distant folds;
            </pre>
         </p>
         <p>
            <pre style="font-family:helvetica">
         Save that from yonder ivy-mantled tow'r
         The moping owl does to the moon complain
         Of such as, wand'ring near her secret bow'r,
         Molest her ancient solitary reign.
            </pre>
         </p>
   </body>
</html>
```

This chapter has introduced many new ideas. Learning XSLT is an incremental process which can be extremely infuriating. Most people transform using a Web browser, at least during development. This is quick and convenient but difficult to debug. The main difficulty is that the output file never really exists. The output is only in the memory of the browser. If you are having debugging problems with something like whitespace, transforming your code using software such as Xalan or Saxon will give you an output file that you can examine.

In Chapter 9 I demonstrate two large and complex transformations. The Recipe Book becomes an online application. Readers get to select a recipe from a menu and see it displayed on screen. The Business Letter is transformed into XHTML which displays on screen just like a printed letter – it even includes footnotes.

Exercises

1. Find and install at least one application which can be used to transform XML documents using XSLT. be sure to run any test suites which come with the application so that you know it installed properly.
2. Describe three problems which might be encountered when using CSS to format XML documents. How does XSLT address these problems?
3. What output formats are commonly created by XSLT processors?
4. Think of two output formats which are not currently supported by XSLT processors. Outline why you think these ought to be added to popular processors.
5. Write an XSLT stylesheet which converts your name and address document into XHTML. View the resulting document in a Web browser.
6. List, and briefly describe, three pieces of XSLT processing software.
7. Why don't all Web browsers support automated transformation of XML to XHTML using XSLT?
8. Outline why XML to XHTML transformations using XSLT are normally performed on a server rather than at the client.
9. What is an XSLT template element? Why are XSLT stylesheets formatted as sets of templates?
10. What other XML technology is used in XSLT to navigate through documents.
11. If a stylesheet needs to add information into an output document, that information is placed inside an XSLT element. Using a code fragment describe how this is done.
12. Describe how XSLT variables differ from those in programming languages such as Pascal.
13. How are parameters passed into XSLT templates?
14. Why are modes needed in XSLT stylesheets? Give an example of their use.
15. Create an XSLT stylesheet which creates an XHTML document containing a calendar of the current month. Place the calendar in a table with the names of the days in blue text.
16. Modify the calendar so that, using selection and iteration, it produces a calendar for the current year. You may ignore the problem of leap years, for this exercise.

Chapter 9

XSLT in Use

I've said it before, but this point is worth emphasizing: XSLT is an extremely complex and awkward language. The complexity is magnified because using XSLT requires in-depth knowledge of XML, namespaces and XPath, as well as an understanding of the desired transformation. Understanding can only really be gained through experience, but writing non-trivial stylesheets without seeing others is far from easy. To help you get enough knowledge to write your own stylesheets, this chapter is composed of two substantial examples in which the Recipe Book and Business Letter are transformed to XHTML-format Web pages for display in a traditional browser. Since XHTML is an application of XML, a valid XHTML page is also a valid XML page. XSLT is commonly used to transform one XML structure into another. The commonest of these transformations is probably XML to XHTML, as shown here. In previous chapters, I've placed the examples in the chapter which they refer to. These XSLT examples are too long and complicated to fit comfortably in Chapter 8, which is why I've split them into a chapter of their own.

The code that follows is, on the whole, straightforward. Having said which, it's only straightforward if you read and understand XML, XSLT and XPath. Plenty of explanation accompanies and illuminates the code. Often, when faced with a programming example, readers dive straight for the code, bypassing the explanation. I'm not sure that approach will work in this case. The examples demonstrate a variety of XSLT constructs and approaches. The reasons for choosing this particular set of techniques are not always obvious from the source so it's worth spending some time finding out *why* certain design decisions were made. When you read through these examples, notice that the XPath expressions are rather simple. XPath can be used to construct fearsomely complex expressions but, often, that code can be broken down into a series of much simpler steps. The advantage of writing simple code is that you are far less likely to make mistakes during development and, just as importantly, you will be able to maintain your code in the future.

9.1 THE RECIPE BOOK

The Recipe Book is going to become a traditional Web-style application. This has two parts. First, a list of categories and the recipes they contain is shown to the user. The user selects an item from the list which is then displayed, nicely formatted.

I've only built sample code. All of the processing is performed by the Web browser which in my case is Mozilla. If I were building a real application, the XSLT would remain virtually unchanged. I would add hyperlinks to the list of recipes, so that user-driven selection worked, but the rest of the code would remain the same. The largest change would be in the way that the XML and XSLT are processed. Rather than sending a large XML file and a complex stylesheet to the browser, the processing should be performed on the server. The browser then receives HTML and, probably, a stylesheet. This is an important difference. Web browsers do not all process XSLT properly. Even the latest revisions of browsers can have problems. Figure 9.1 shows what happened when I loaded the Recipe Book XML file into Opera which supports XML but not XSLT.

I consider these examples to be demonstrations of what the technology can do, rather than sensible applications. Web browsers are designed to display XHTML, that's what they do well. XHTML sent using the Web-standard HTTP protocol is a relatively lightweight, fast and extremely simple way of communicating data. XML is none of these things. Sending XML between processing applications, for instance within an e-commerce environment or to replace a technology such as EDI[1], is sensible. Using it when you really need to pass XHTML around is simply foolish.

That's quite enough proselytizing for now, though. Let's see what XSLT can do for us, wherever and however we choose to use it.

9.1.1 Selecting a Recipe

The Recipe Book is a single XML file which contains many recipes. These are placed into categories, each recipe appearing in only one category, making a simple non-relational database. Presenting this data to a user is typical of the requirements of many different

[1]Electronic Data Interchange. A long-established standard for sharing transactional information between businesses.

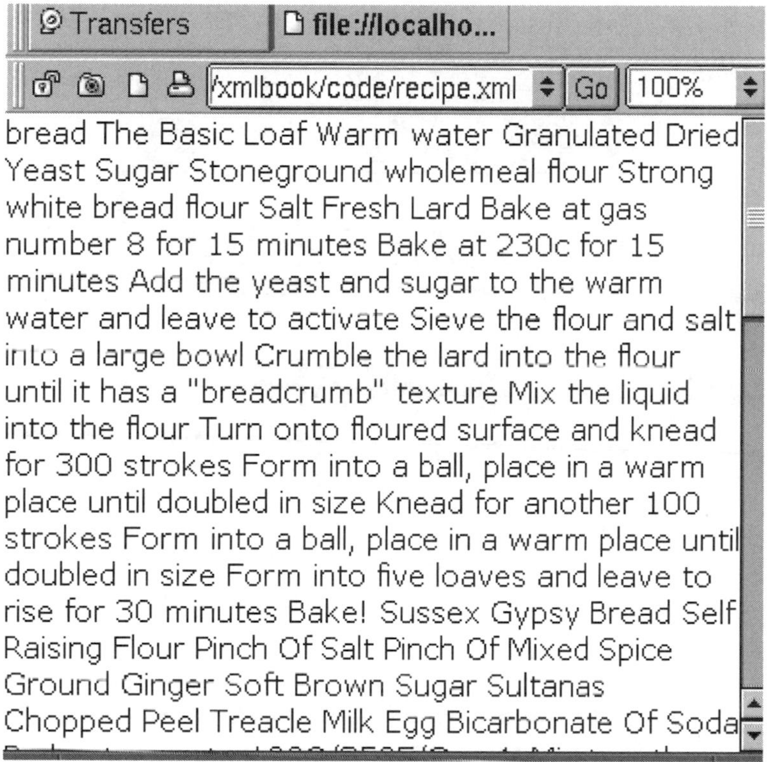

Figure 9.1 XML plus XSLT in Opera

Web applications. Users will want to see a small selection of the recipes from the database. They will, typically, select recipes either from a menu system or through a search script. Searching may be based on category, the name of the recipe, ingredients or regular expressions which can match against anything in the database.

Two possible transformations suggest themselves immediately. The first is a search through the XML file which pulls out categories and recipes. The information is formatted into a table inside an XHTML page. The result is shown in Figure 9.2.

Since the stylesheet that creates the list is relatively straightforward, I'll show all of the code in a single block. Later examples are more complex and have been split so that they are more readable. Read through the code first, try to make sense of it, then look at the explanation which follows.

Listing 9.1 Selecting a Recipe

```
<?xml version="1.0"?>

<xsl:stylesheet
```

Figure 9.2 The List of Categories and Recipes

```
  xmlns:xsl="http://www.w3.org/1999/XSL/Transform"
  version="1.0">
<xsl:template match="/cookbook">
  <html>
    <head>
      <title>Available Recipes</title>
    </head>
    <body>
      <h1>Available Recipes</h1>

      <p style="margin-left:2cm">
        <table border="3" cellspacing="10">
          <xsl:for-each select="category">
          <tr>
            <td style="font-size:20pt;
                       color:maroon;
```

```
                    background:pink;
                    text-align:center">
                <xsl:for-each select="title">
                  <xsl:value-of
                    select="translate(.,
                        'abcdefghijklmnopqrstuvwxyz',
                        'ABCDEFGHIJKLMNOPQRSTUVWXYZ')"/>
                </xsl:for-each>
              </td>
            </tr>
            <xsl:for-each select="recipe/name">
              <tr>
                <td style="color:navy; font-style:italic">
                  <xsl:value-of select="."/>
                </td>
              </tr>
            </xsl:for-each>
            </xsl:for-each>
          </table>
        </p>
      </body>
    </html>
</xsl:template>
</xsl:stylesheet>
```

The first thing to notice is that the transformation results in a well-formed[2] XHTML page. The XHTML tags are not given a prefix. The output from this transformation, if it were executed on a server, would be redirected to a browser. Although many of the more modern Web browsers understand at least some XML, assuming that the browser would understand namespaces and prefixes is extremely dangerous. To allow for the possibility that the reader is using Internet Explorer 3 or Navigator 2, the output doesn't include anything that older browsers can't handle.

The gimlet-eyed among you will have spotted two potential flaws here. This output is XHTML, but older browsers only understand HTML. What happens to the additional features, such as empty tags, that XHTML provides? Easy – since they look like tags, they get ignored. Web browsers have always ignored everything inside an element that they can't process. It's a safety mechanism since most Web pages are badly formed. But

[2] I don't include a Document Type Declaration since most Web browsers assume one anyway.

what about the `style` attributes? They're treated in just the same way. Since the browser knows they're attributes that it can't handle, it ignores them. An old browser will show a simple, unadorned, Web page that functions perfectly. Isn't backwards-compatibility great?

```
<xsl:template match="/cookbook">
```

The stylesheet starts with the selection of all `cookbook` elements into a single node-set. Although there's only one of these elements in the file, making it into a node-set simplifies the XPath expressions in later selections. Once the infrastructure of the XHTML page has been established, the `category` elements are selected into another node-set. Since the selection process is working upon the context node, the `select` attribute only requires the name of the target node:

```
<xsl:for-each select="category">
```

The finished page is going to display all categories in the XML file. Using the `for-each` element means that they are all selected into a node-set which the processor then moves across, handling one element at a time. Although `for-each` looks like a typical programmatic loop control, it isn't. Remember XSLT is a purely declarative language. This statement is telling the processing application that it must operate on all `category` elements but it does not say *how* it should do that. The software may implement the operation as a `for` or `while` loop, may handle the process recursively, or manage the whole thing through a tree structure. The great thing is that *we don't care.* So long as all `category` elements are selected and processed in reasonable time, we can be satisfied.

```
<xsl:for-each select="title">
   <xsl:value-of
       select="translate(.,
                   'abcdefghijklmnopqrstuvwxyz',
                   'ABCDEFGHIJKLMNOPQRSTUVWXYZ')"/>
   </xsl:for-each>
```

Next up, the `title` element of the `category` is pulled out for display. Unfortunately, there's no way of knowing if the content here is upper-case, lower-case or a mixture of the two. Displaying these as upper-case letters makes them stand out and, coincidentally, shows another neat aspect of XSLT. The `translate()` function can be used to convert items in one string into something different. In this example the function is applied to the *content* of the current node, represented by a dot. The lower-case English alphabet is given as the second parameter, the upper-case version as the last one. As each lower-case letter is encountered in the content, it is replaced by the letter that appears at the same position in the upper-case set. Performing the same thing when the content may contain any Unicode character is rather less straightforward since it requires the use of extension libraries. The

XSLT Standard Library, which is available from `http://xsltsl.sourceforge.net`, provides functions to do this.

At this point, the node-set contains all of the `category` elements and their subelements. The next part of the processing is the extraction of recipe names for each category. The code is still inside the `for-each` element, which means that whatever follows will be applied to each `category` in turn. The first step is to extract the name of each recipe:

```
<xsl:for-each select="recipe/name">
```

This XPath is expressed relative to the context node, `category`, and heads straight down to the `name` element. The selected `name` becomes the new context node. Its content is placed into the table using:

```
<xsl:value-of select="."/>
```

That's it. The entire database of recipes can be traversed and the desired nodes extracted with this simple script. If you look back at the code, roughly eight XML elements are used. Most of the script is XHTML. Try writing the same thing as simply using Java or Active Server Pages and you will start to appreciate the power of XSLT. If it is used appropriately, a compact, yet powerful, solution can be built.

9.1.2 Displaying a Recipe

Once visitors to the site have selected a recipe, it needs to be presented to them as a neatly formatted Web page. The desired output is shown in Figure 9.3.

The page contains a table of ingredients, a numbered list of notes and a series of paragraphs delimited by bullet points. The table and bullet-pointed list are standard HTML constructs. The creation of the numbered list *could* have been done using a simple HTML enumerated list. In this example it's created using some of the more powerful features of XSLT. The stylesheet that creates this simple page is far too long to present as a single block of text in a book. Instead it has been split it into small pieces which, if assembled in the same order in which they are presented, combine to make the whole stylesheet.

In the previous example, the entire stylesheet was wrapped inside a single `template` element. That is the most straightforward way to write a stylesheet. The structure of the input mirrors exactly the structure that will be found in the resulting XML. If the transformation is simple, this is probably the best way of writing the XSLT, if possible. It certainly makes for readable code, requires relatively little documentation, and can be maintained easily. The problem with this simple approach is that it is incredibly restrictive. Achieving complex results inevitably requires duplication of code throughout the stylesheet. That's not how complicated programs are written and it needn't be how complex XSLT scripts are created.

In XSLT templates can be written for each operation and called from a main template, or from each other. In fact, templates can be used in a very similar way to functions in

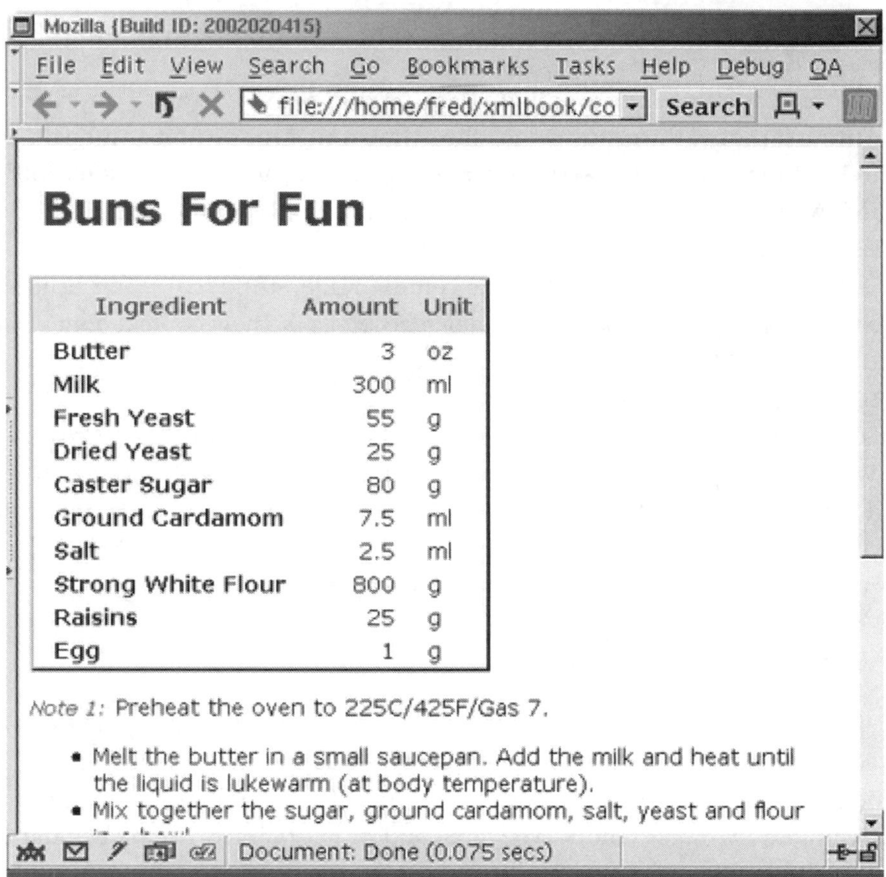

Figure 9.3 A Selected Recipe Displayed in Mozilla

traditional programming languages. It's important to remember that XSLT is a declarative language; templates don't work like functions and variables aren't really variable. If you forget these things, the results that you get can sometimes be unexpected.

```
<?xml version="1.0"?>
<xsl:stylesheet xmlns:xsl="http://www.w3.org/1999/XSL/Transform"
   version="1.0">

<xsl:variable name="recipe" select="//category[1]/recipe[3]"/>

<xsl:template match="/cookbook">
  <html>
    <head>
```

```
      <title><xsl:call-template name="showTitle"/></title>
    </head>
    <body>
      <h1 style="color:maroon; background:lemon; padding:5pt">
        <xsl:call-template name="showTitle"/>
      </h1>
      <table border="2">
        <tr style="background:wheat; color:darkgreen">
          <th style="padding:5pt">Ingredient</th>
          <th style="padding:5pt">Amount</th>
          <th style="padding:5pt">Unit</th>
        </tr>
        <xsl:call-template name="showIngredients" />
      </table>
      <xsl:call-template name="showNotes"/>
      <ul style="width: 12cm">
      <xsl:call-template name="showMethod" />
      </ul>
    </body>
  </html>
</xsl:template>
```

The stylesheet starts with a main template which calls all of the others. Before this, though, the selected recipe is extracted into a single-element node-set and assigned to a variable. The recipe that we want to display is the third one in the first category. The array indexing syntax of square brackets may be familiar from other programming languages.

```
  <xsl:variable name="recipe" select="//category[1]/recipe[3]"/>
```

The recipe is going to be used repeatedly throughout the transformation. Searching for it or making it into the context node for each template is going to cause a massive performance hit. The code is simplified, which means that development and maintenance are also easier. In the example, I assume that the user has asked for the third recipe in the first category. In my small database this is a recipe called *Buns For Fun*.

```
<xsl:template name="showTitle">
  <xsl:value-of select="$recipe/name"/>
</xsl:template>
```

All of the templates work in the same way. Each has a unique name so that it can be called from the top-level template and so that, if needed, it can be reused throughout the program. Each template displays subnodes of the selected recipe. The `showTitle` template is used to display the name of the recipe. It is called to create content for the title of the page, which displays in the frame of the browser, and to create a large heading at the top of the page. When the entire XML file is sent to the browser for a client-side transformation, the title is *not* displayed since the browser doesn't have a complete HTML page. Getting at the subnodes is very simple. Because they are subnodes of the node which is held in the variable `recipe`, a simple XPath expression will pick them out. The XPath starts at the contents of `recipe` which are available when a dollar sign is placed in front of the variable name.

```
<xsl:template name="showIngredients">
  <xsl:for-each select="$recipe/ingredient">
    <tr>
      <th align="left" style="padding-left:8pt">
        <xsl:value-of select="name"/>
      </th>
      <td align="right" style="padding-right:7pt">
        <xsl:value-of select="quantity/@amount"/>
      </td>
      <td align="left" style="padding-left:7pt">
        <xsl:value-of select="quantity/@unit"/>
      </td>
    </tr>
  </xsl:for-each>
</xsl:template>
```

Creating the table of ingredients is more complex than getting the name of the recipe, but not greatly so. The template iterates across the `ingredient` subnodes of the recipe. During each iteration the `ingredient` being processed becomes the context node. This means that selection of *its* subnodes such as the `quantity` element is relative to `ingredient`. The `name` of the `ingredient` is selected first and placed in a cell of the table. The `quantity` element never has content but it *does* have two attributes whose values interest us. Accessing the content of the attributes is done by placing an ampersand in front of the attribute name within the XPath expression:

```
quantity/@unit
```

Notice that the code that creates the table includes styles so that each cell is neatly formatted. Using a combination of text-justification and padding within each cell means that some visually interesting effects can be created. In fact, there's no reason why HTML tables can't be as interesting as those found in print media.[3]

[3] Although I'm not going to claim that this table is in any way interesting.

```
<xsl:template name="showNotes">
  <xsl:variable name="tmp" select="$recipe/cooking/note"/>
  <xsl:for-each select="$tmp">
    <p>
      <span style="font-style:italic;
              color:purple;
              font-size: 10pt">Note
        <xsl:value-of select="position()"/>:
      </span>
      <xsl:value-of select="."/>
    </p>
  </xsl:for-each>
</xsl:template>
```

Recipes often include information which, while instructional, is not part of the method. This information may include cooking times or temperatures, the number of people served by the recipe or details of special equipment that might be required. In the Recipe Book XML example, this class of information is called a `note`. I decided to display `note` data in a numbered list. I didn't use the built-in HTML ordered list since I wanted to show another feature of XSLT. The template starts by selecting all of the notes into a node-set:

```
<xsl:variable name="tmp" select="$recipe/cooking/note"/>
```

The code iterates across this node-set placing each item into a styled paragraph. Writing out the contents of the node is a simple matter of using:

```
<xsl:value-of select="."/>
```

But a number needs to be shown before the contents are displayed. I do this using the `position()` function. Each node is numbered by showing its position in the node-set which is held in \`$tmp`:

```
<xsl:value-of select="position()"/>
```

I'll use the same idea in Section 9.2 to produce numbered footnotes and references to them.

```
<xsl:template name="showMethod">
  <xsl:for-each select="$recipe/method/instruction">
    <li><xsl:value-of select="." /></li>
  </xsl:for-each>
</xsl:template>

</xsl:stylesheet>
```

Displaying the instructions is another easy step. Again the XPath has three steps but once each item has been selected it is placed into a `<li>`, list item, element. The browser will automatically place bullet points in front of these and arrange them on the page. None of the complexity that was required to format the notes is needed here.

When the stylesheet is considered as a piece of code, and when it's compared to alternatives such as PHP or Java, XSLT begins to look like an excellent transformation language. Problems may arise because of its succinctness, but they are easily surmounted given enough practice.

9.2 THE BUSINESS LETTER

Generally, styling content for display on a screen is very different to styling for print. Screens are far more flexible than pages when displaying layered or formatted content. Physical pages are subject to many different constraints such as the need for margins and the limited amount of transparency that can be applied to text or images. When content is displayed on screen it can be far more fluid; most people expect that when they resize an application, its content will flow around into a new configuration. Despite this, many Web designers create pages that are so rigidly sized that they often leave the user's screen part empty. When writing the XSLT for the Business Letter, I decided to try to mimic a typical printed layout using XHTML as the target output format. In part, this example shows more features of XSLT, but it also demonstrates that XML can be transformed into almost any form. Figure 9.4 shows the end product of the transformation.

The XSLT code that accomplishes these whole-scale changes is long and complicated. As with the Recipe Book, I've separated the processing into a set of templates which are called from the top-level template. Each template transforms part of the source code into XHTML. Although XSLT is a declarative language, we can exercise some control over how it works. By calling templates in a particular order, XHTML is generated in the correct order.

Read through the code for the first template, then I'll explain it. Many of the ideas that I used to style the Recipe Book are reused here. In this explanation I'll skip over this familiar territory. This transformation introduces a lot of new, and more complex, ideas which I want to look at in some detail.

```
<?xml version="1.0"?>
<xsl:stylesheet version="1.0"
            xmlns:xsl="http://www.w3.org/1999/XSL/Transform">

<xsl:variable name="footnotes" select="//content/para/footnote"/>

<xsl:template match="/letter">
```

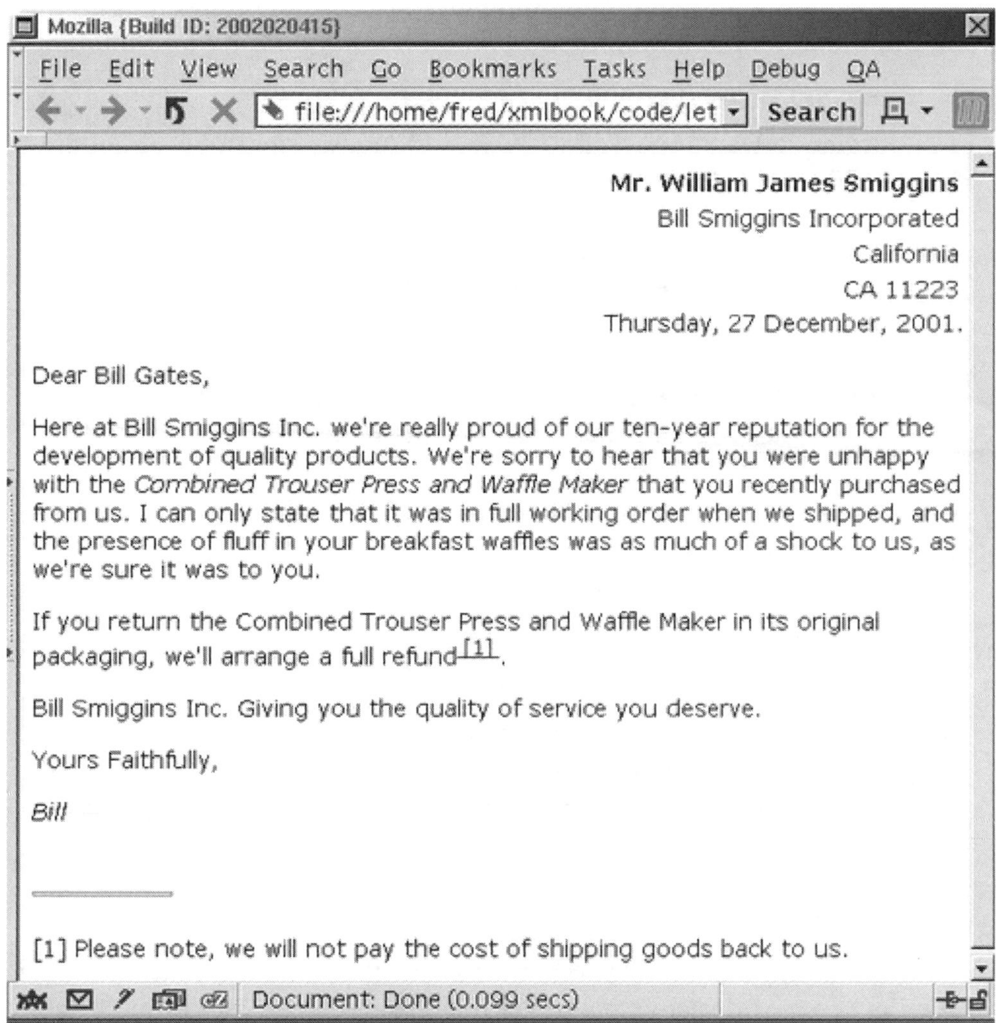

Figure 9.4 Mozilla Displaying the Styled Letter

```
<html>
  <head>
    <title>To:
      <xsl:value-of select="recipient/name/firstname"/>
      <xsl:text>&#x20;</xsl:text>
      <xsl:value-of select="recipient/name/surname"/>
    </title>
  </head>
```

```
    <body style="width: 15cm">

      <xsl:call-template name="address_table">
        <xsl:with-param name="side" select="'right'" />
        <xsl:with-param name="add"
                    select="header/sender/address" />
        <xsl:with-param name="nom"
                    select="header/sender/name" />
      </xsl:call-template>

      <xsl:call-template name="address_table">
        <xsl:with-param name="side" select="'left'" />
        <xsl:with-param name="add"
                    select="header/recipient/address" />
        <xsl:with-param name="nom"
                    select="header/recipient/name" />
      </xsl:call-template>

      <xsl:call-template name="dater"/>
      <xsl:apply-templates select="//content"/>
      <xsl:call-template name="salut"/>
      <xsl:call-template name="footnotes"/>
    </body>
  </html>
</xsl:template>
```

A variable called `footnotes` is declared at the very top of the template. Later in the template I'm going to create footnotes which are placed at the foot of the letter,[4] and referenced from the body of the text. I need to be able to access all footnotes which are defined in the XML structure. Since footnotes can only occur inside paragraphs inside the content of the letter, I can select them into a node-set just once. The following line of code performs the selection:

```
<xsl:variable name="footnotes" select="//content/para/footnote"/>
```

Because this node-set is created before any templates are defined, it is effectively a global variable which can be used in all of the templates inside the stylesheet. Creating a global variable means that I don't have to worry about passing the variable as a parameter to

[4]Of course!

each template that needs it. This makes the code both more readable and, hopefully, easier to process.

The `title` element of the XHTML document should contain the names of the recipient with a space character between each part of the name. A brute-force approach to creating the content for this element would be simply to select all `firstname` and `surname` elements from below the `recipient` element. This causes problems with the handling of whitespace. Simply placing a space between the content of each node as it is selected does not guarantee that there will be a space in the output. Remember that whitespace is treated in different ways at different times. In this situation we are neither preserving whitespace from the source document, nor removing it. Rather, we are adding *new* whitespace to the output of the document as it is created. The problem, therefore, is one of forcing the processor to place whitespace characters where it would not, by default, do so.

The solution is something that is obvious when you've seen it, but extremely difficult to figure out the first time. Since the XML is being transformed into XHTML, the most obvious answer is to place the XHTML non-breaking space character into the output. This character has a standard XHTML entity: `&#nbsp;` which all HTML processors understand and which they convert into a single space character. Unfortunately, with this transformation we're dealing with an XML parser and an XSLT transformation engine. They do not, by default, understand the meaning of `&#nbsp;`. XML software understands the meaning of the Unicode space character which is represented by the entity ` `. This is one of four such entities which were listed in Table 2.4. Having identified the correct character, it has to appear in the transformed document. This *could* be done by placing the entity directly into the stylesheet, but this doesn't guarantee that the space will appear in the output. Output can be forced using the `<xsl:text>` element whose content will always be placed into the transformed document:

```
<xsl:text>&#x20;</xsl:text>
```

Having sorted the `title`, the body of the letter itself can be created. The letter starts with the names and addresses of the sender and recipient. I'm using a typical British structure here in which the sender's details are placed on the right side, and the recipient's on the left of the page.[5] Since both transformations use the same data structures, I'd like to be able to use the same template for them both. None of the browsers I've tried have any concept of page width when transforming XML. Content placed on the right side of the page will disappear way over to the right so that the page must be scrolled to view it. This behavior can be negated by setting the width of the page:

```
<body style="width: 15cm">
```

[5]The screenshot in Figure 9.4 omits the recipient's address so that the image fits on a printed page.

The only difficulties in this transformation will be identifying the correct elements and telling the template which side of the screen to place the content. I'll solve both problems by passing values into the stylesheet as parameters. I create a template named address_table and call it with three parameters: the side on which I want the content, a node-set containing the address and a node-set containing the name. Each parameter is passed in using the xsl:with-param element. This has two attributes: a parameter name and the value which is assigned to the select attribute.

```
<xsl:with-param name="nom" select="header/sender/name" />
```

The address_table template, shown below, starts by extracting the parameters so that they can be used in the same way as variables. The parameter names in the template *must* match those in the with-param element inside the call-template element that called the address_table template.

```
<xsl:template name="address_table">
  <xsl:param name="side" />
  <xsl:param name="add" />
  <xsl:param name="nom" />

  <div align="{$side}">
    <table border="0">
      <tr>
        <th align="left">
          <xsl:if test="$nom/title">
            <xsl:value-of select="$nom/title" />
            <xsl:text>&#x20;</xsl:text>
          </xsl:if>
          <xsl:for-each select="$nom/firstname">
            <xsl:value-of select="." />
            <xsl:text>&#x20;</xsl:text>
          </xsl:for-each>
          <xsl:value-of select="$nom/surname" />
        </th>
      </tr>
      <xsl:for-each select="$add/child::*">
        <tr>
          <td align="{$side}">
            <xsl:value-of select="."/>
          </td>
        </tr>
```

```
      </xsl:for-each>
    </table>
  </div>
</xsl:template>
```

The address_table template formats a name and address using an HTML table. Aligning the text on screen is a simple matter of aligning the cells in each row of the table, and of correctly placing the table on the page. To align the table the content of the side parameter must be extracted and used as the value for HTML attributes:

```
<div align="{$side}">
```

To obtain the value of a parameter as text, the parameter reference is placed inside curly brackets. A reference to a parameter is created by placing a dollar sign before the parameter name. If the parameter is a node-set, its content is accessed by creating XPath expressions which start with the parameter reference such as $nom/surname. Selecting and displaying subelements of the address could be done in a number of ways. A crude approach would be to select all subelements, items such as line1 or country, and place them inside an HTML table. Doing that is going to require a significant amount of code. In this example a more compact approach has been taken:

```
<xsl:for-each select="$add/child::*">
```

The stylesheet iterates across all children of the address node, extracting the content of each and placing it in a new row of the table. This approach is far less selective. With the brute-force approach, if it was decided that line3 elements should not be shown the appropriate lines could be removed from the stylesheet. Using the iterative approach a conditional expression would have to be written to selectively remove line3 elements as they were encountered.

```
<xsl:template name="dater">
  <xsl:variable name="dy" select="//header/date"/>
  <div align="right">
    <xsl:if test="$dy/dayname">
      <xsl:value-of select="$dy/dayname"/>,
      <xsl:text>&#x20;</xsl:text>
    </xsl:if>
    <xsl:if test="$dy/day">
      <xsl:value-of select="$dy/day"/>
      <xsl:text>&#x20;</xsl:text>
    </xsl:if>
    <xsl:if test="$dy/month">
      <xsl:value-of select="$dy/month"/>,
      <xsl:text>&#x20;</xsl:text>
```

```
      </xsl:if>
      <xsl:if test="$dy/year">
        <xsl:value-of select="$dy/year"/>.
      </xsl:if>
    </div>

    <xsl:call-template name="greet"/>
  </xsl:template>
```

Once the addresses have been displayed, the date is placed on the right-hand side of the page. The code in the `dater` template is pretty simple. It works by testing the type of each element below the `date` element and displaying its contents. Why not use a simple loop to iterate across these elements? When the date is displayed the order of the parts is important. When the data is stored, that order doesn't matter. An iterative approach to processing the date may give the output we want, but it's more likely not to.

Once the date has been formatted, the body of the letter starts. Letters always begin with a greeting of the form `Dear Miss Smith`. The `greet` template formats the greeting.

```
  <xsl:template name="greet">
    <xsl:variable name="nom" select="//header/recipient/name" />
    <p>Dear<xsl:text>&#x20;</xsl:text>
      <xsl:if test="$nom/title">
        <xsl:value-of select="$nom/title" />
        <xsl:text>&#x20;</xsl:text>
        <xsl:value-of select="$nom/surname" />
      </xsl:if>
      <xsl:if test="not($nom/title)">
        <xsl:for-each select="$nom/firstname">
          <xsl:value-of select="." />
          <xsl:text>&#x20;</xsl:text>
        </xsl:for-each>
        <xsl:value-of select="$nom/surname" />,
      </xsl:if>
    </p>
  </xsl:template>
```

Once the recipient's title has been shown, we want to output their name. They may have several `firstname` elements and they will have just one `surname`. Yet again, iteration across the node-set held in `$nom` is not going to work since we have already processed the title.[6] Using the `not()` function means that only `firstname` and `surname` fields will be processed.

```
<xsl:if test="not($nom/title)">
```

Actually, I could have written the template without this particular test. It's included to show you a different way of using XSLT and, of course, similar tests could be useful in many circumstances.

After processing the recipient's name, control returns to the main template. The body of the letter is going to be processed next. This presents more complications as the text of the letter is contained in a series of paragraphs which may each contain text, footnotes or emphasized text. Since the XSLT processor cannot know, in advance, how the contents of letters will be nested, processing the letter must be done in a properly declarative manner. The easiest technique here is to create a series of templates which match the elements found below the `content` element and leave the processor to sort out how it should call them. Processing is initiated using the `<xsl:apply-templates>` element:

```
<xsl:apply-templates select="//content"/>
```

Handling basic paragraphs and emphasized text is not a problem. The next two templates should need no explanation.

```
<xsl:template match="para">
  <p><xsl:apply-templates /></p>
</xsl:template>

<xsl:template match="emphasis">
  <span style="font-style: italic">
    <xsl:value-of select="."/>
  </span>
</xsl:template>
```

Footnotes are a more complicated story, though. Processing a footnote has two stages. First, it must be identified and a marker placed in the text. Secondly, the markers must be reproduced at the bottom of the letter, along with the content of the footnotes. It's obviously vital that markers are placed next to the footnote to which they refer. These footnote handling templates are based upon those supplied with the XSLT stylesheets which are used to process the XML version of DocBook. Chapter 17 describes the DocBook XML structure and stylesheets.

```
<xsl:template match="footnote">
  <xsl:variable name="tmp" select="para"/>
```

[6] A less formal letter can be created if the title is not processed.

```
    <xsl:for-each select="$footnotes/para">
      <xsl:if test="$tmp=.">
        <xsl:variable name="var" select="position()"/>
        <sup><a href="#ftn.{$var}">
          [<xsl:value-of select="$var"/>]
        </a></sup>
      </xsl:if>
    </xsl:for-each>
  </xsl:template>
```

Each time that the processor encounters a `footnote` element, it uses this template. The template starts by selecting the content of the `footnote`, which is contained in a single `para` element, and placing it into the `$tmp` variable. All of the `footnote` elements in the document were collected into a node-set referenced by the `$footnotes` variable at the very top of the stylesheet. The stylesheet next iterates across this node-set, comparing the `para` subelement of each `footnote` with the value held in `$tmp`. If the two are the same, the position of the item in `$footnotes` is saved in the variable `$var` using the built-in `position()` function. The position is going to be used to create the marker for the footnote and is used to create a hyperlink from the marker to the footnote.

```
<xsl:template name="footnotes">
  <div><br/><hr width="15%" align="left"/>
  <p>
    <xsl:apply-templates select="$footnotes" mode="showem" />
  </p></div>
</xsl:template>

<xsl:template match="footnote" mode="showem">
  <xsl:variable name="var" select="position()"/>
  <a name="ftn.{$var}">
    [<xsl:value-of select="$var"/>]
  </a>
  <xsl:text>&#x20;</xsl:text>
  <xsl:value-of select="para"/><br/>
</xsl:template>
```

Displaying the footnotes uses almost the same process as creating the markers. The `footnotes` template is called at the very end of processing the letter. It uses the `<xsl:apply-templates>` element to process the contents of `$footnotes` once more. The `<xsl:apply-templates>` element causes the processor to search for a template that has the same name as the element it applies to. In this example, that is a template called footnote. Unfortunately, that template was the one was used to create the markers in the text, and it can't perform both tasks. The solution is to use a *mode*. XSLT modes provide a way to apply different templates, with the same name, to the same content. In this case, when the processor has to apply a template to a footnote element without the mode attribute, it creates a marker. If the mode attribute has the value showem, it prints the markers and the content of the footnote.

The last piece of the letter before the footnotes is a signature and closing message. These are created using the salut template.

```
<xsl:template name="salut">
  <xsl:variable name="msg"
            select="//header/signature/greeting" />
  <xsl:if test="$msg">
    <p>
    <xsl:if test="$msg/@type">
      <xsl:variable name="tmp" select="$msg/@type"/>
      <xsl:if test="$tmp='formal' ">
        <xsl:if test="$msg=''">
          Yours Faithfully,
        </xsl:if>
      </xsl:if>
      <xsl:if test="$tmp='informal' ">
        <xsl:if test="$msg=''">
          Yours Sincerely,
        </xsl:if>
      </xsl:if>
      <xsl:if test="not($msg='')">
        <xsl:value-of select="$msg"/>,
      </xsl:if>
    </xsl:if>
    </p>
  </xsl:if>

  <xsl:variable name="nom" select="//header/signature" />
  <p style="font-style: italic">
    <xsl:if test="$nom/firstname">
      <xsl:value-of select="$nom/firstname"/>
    </xsl:if>
```

```
        <xsl:if test="not($nom/firstname)">
          <xsl:if test="$nom/name/title">
            <xsl:value-of select="$nom/name/title" />
            <xsl:text>&#x20;</xsl:text>
            <xsl:value-of select="$nom/name/surname" />
          </xsl:if>
          <xsl:if test="not($nom/name/title)">
            <xsl:for-each select="$nom/name/firstname">
              <xsl:value-of select="." />
              <xsl:text>&#x20;</xsl:text>
            </xsl:for-each>
            <xsl:value-of select="$nom/name/surname" />
          </xsl:if>
        </xsl:if>
      </p>
    </xsl:template>

</xsl:stylesheet>
```

Three types of message are allowed, with the appropriate one controlled by the `type` attribute of the `greeting` element. The first test determines if a `greeting` element exists:

```
<xsl:if test="$msg">
```

the `greeting` having already been selected into the `$msg` variable. If there is a `greeting`, its `type` attribute is tested:

```
<xsl:if test="$msg/@type">
```

This can take the values `formal`, `informal` or `other`. If the attribute has not been set, processing transfers to the sender's name. The stylesheet then selects the appropriate message based on the value of the `type` attribute:

```
<xsl:if test="$tmp='informal'">
```

Generally, when the attribute is set to either `formal` or `informal`, the element will be empty. If, however, the `greeting` element has content, that content will override the default messages.

Again, this transformation shows the simplicity and power of XSLT. When combined with an efficient transformation engine, it's an extremely useful tool which every XML developer should have in their toolbox.

Chapter 10

XSL Formatting Objects

XSLT is a powerful and comprehensive mechanism for transforming between XML structures. It can be used to select elements and subtrees, modify the content of elements and create entirely new structures. The biggest problem with XSLT is that the end result of all that processing is either plain text or another XML structure.[1] XML structures are great when pieces of software are communicating with each other but they are virtually unreadable to humans. What is needed is the ability to transform XML into formats that can be printed in the same way as conventional books, memos or articles, printed as braille documents or read by synthesizer software. These ideas should be familiar to you because they were first introduced in Chapter 6 which examined Cascading Stylesheets Two.

The differences between XML to XML transformations and XML to presentation format transformations were recognized right at the beginning of the development of XSL. The same difficulties had already been encountered and, at least partially, overcome when styling HTML documents. That knowledge could be usefully applied to the development of a technology for the transformation and styling of XML. In fact, the original version

[1] Don't forget that XHTML is an XML application.

of the Extensible Stylesheet Language included both transformation and styling under a single banner. This was cumbersome and so complex that no one would ever use it, hence the two functions were split into distinct languages. XSLT was developed for the transformation process, andXSL Formatting Objects, XSL-FO, for styling.

If you struggled with some of the ideas involved in designing XSLT stylesheets, you may not wish to know that XSL-FO is, if anything, more complex. Working with XSL-FO involves the creation of a stylesheet which is broadly similar to those that are created in XSLT. The stylesheet is applied to XML documents using an XSLT processor which outputs a new document containing a set of Formatting Objects. The formatting objects are converted into the end document, which may be PDF, PostScript, audio or braille, using a formatting objects processor. From the developer's point of view, the complexity of XSL-FO occurs because to be able to write even the simplest of stylesheets you need to understand:

- XML,
- the use of Namespaces,
- Cascading Stylesheets Two,
- Extensible Stylesheets Language,
- XPath expressions,
- XSL Formatting Objects,
- The structure and composition of your finished document.

Fortunately, if you've worked through this book so far and grasped at least the basics of each idea, you will know enough to make some progress here. The new ideas are XSL-FO and document structures. Before introducing XSL-FO, I'm going to look at document structuring, particularly as it is used with XSL-FO.

> **Note:**
> Throughout this chapter, I'm only considering text in Western languages such as English or French. In these languages text runs from the top left corner of the page in horizontal lines. Document content starts at the front of a book, page one, and continues to the end. Other families of languages use different structures such as running text vertically down the page. XSL-FO has been designed to accommodate all possible structures and to use Unicode characters.

10.1 DOCUMENT STRUCTURE

Writing a formatting object processor is a highly complex software engineering task. Not only does the software need to understand XML and process XSLT, it also needs to be able to work with the output format. I'm not going to consider the areas of braille or audio output since these are, to the best of my knowledge, still theoretical applications for which no software has yet been released.

Although printed documents come in a wide variety of shapes and sizes, we can extrapolate some general structures that hold for many applications. If you are seriously considering the use of XSL-FO for a project, it's probable that you have a fairly typical document structure in mind. I'm going to look, briefly, at two widely used structures: a report which might be printed on a typical office printer, and a book structure. One thing I'm not thinking about here is *inline* formatting. That's the sort of thing that is used when text color or fonts for individual words or phrases are changed.

10.1.1 Structuring a Report

Most of the reports and memos circulating in businesses today have a single, somewhat boring, logical structure. This structure results from the use of word processors to create the report, and laser printers to publish it. The limitations of both the hardware and software, and often, the relative lack of knowledge of most users mean that complicated documents cannot reasonably be expected from them. It's unlikely that XML and XSL-FO could ever replace the output from desktop publishing software such as Quark Express, but they certainly can replace a word processor. If you are suddenly wondering *why* anyone would want to replace their word processor, remember all of the advantages that XML provides, such as platform independence, multiple output formats, reuse, easy indexing and so on.

The typical business report includes some, or all, of the following features:

- It is printed on just one side of the paper.
- The content is split into sections.
- A table of contents is used.
- The title appears on a separate page.
- Page numbers are used on all pages.
- Footnotes are used sparingly.
- Version control information such as the author, date of creation and version number, appear in either the page header or footer.

- Images, including charts and diagrams, appear in the flow of the text.

All of those features can be implemented using XSL-FO. The great thing about using XSL to format your reports is that a single corporate style can be created. Users will no longer be tempted to spend hours changing fonts or colors in their reports – the stylesheet will do all of that for them. The downside is that, at the time of writing, no usable software exists for the creation of styled documents. Programmers don't mind using plain text editors and command-line tools, but to expect ordinary office workers to do the same is to be extremely unrealistic.

10.1.2 Structuring a Book

Producing a book is different to producing a report. Once the author has created the content it goes off to the publisher who finds a typesetter[2] to style the book for printing. Books have a more intricate structure than business reports:

- The book has three logical parts.
  - The front matter contains title pages, copyright and catalog information, and tables of contents and figures.
  - The body of the book consists of the chapters of content.
  - The back matter contains the glossary, appendices and index.
- Chapters always start on the right hand page, which has an odd number.
- Chapters may contain sections, subsections and so on.
- Images and tables are placed in the flow of the text, although systems such as LaTeX float them to the top of a page.
- All pages are numbered except the first page of each chapter.
- Page numbering in the front matter often uses Roman numerals.
- Even pages have the chapter title in the header.
- Odd numbered pages have section titles in their page header.
- The first page of each chapter has nothing in its header.
- Margins at the inside of the page, by the binding, are often smaller than those on the outer side of the page.

[2]Some authors, me included, prefer to produce the finished *camera-ready* copy themselves.

- Footnotes may be placed either at the bottom of the page or in the outer margin.

A book requires a number of different formats: the front matter, the first page of a chapter, odd-numbered pages, even-numbered pages and back matter. This type of structure looks difficult but *can* be created using XSL-FO.

10.1.3 Page Structure

Whatever type of document you are creating, the same logical structure is used for all pages. Figure 10.1 shows what the structure looks like. A page is divided into two areas: the margin in which no text will appear, and the body in which all content, headers and footers appear. It is important that you understand the difference between the page margin and any headers, footers or marginalia which you use in your work. The margin is whitespace which surrounds all of the text on the page. Generally a small amount of whitespace is provided at the top and bottom of the page with larger areas at the sides. Traditionally the outside, edge of the page has a wider margin area than the bound side, although in modern books this distinction has been lost.

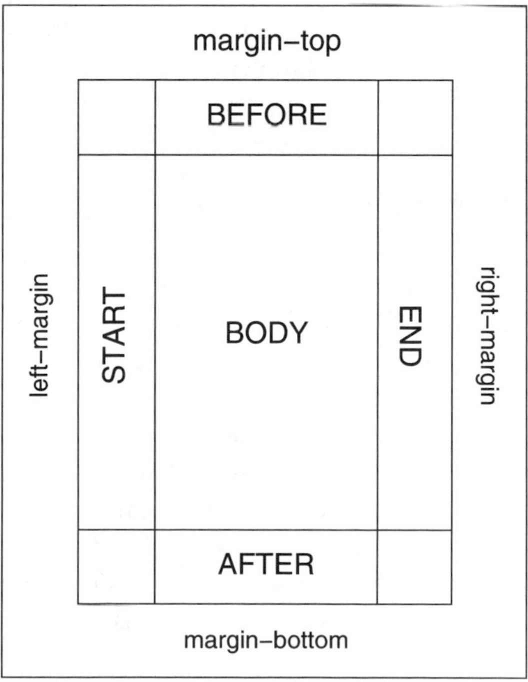

Figure 10.1 XSL FO Page Structure

In Section 10.3 I'll show how to define the structure of a page using XSL-FO. Although it requires some complex code, defining page structures is a logical process once you get into it.

Page headings, page numbers, footnotes and any ruled lines used to give them distinction appear as part of the body of the page. They are always separated from the main page content using a small area of whitespace. Some book designs use notes in the margin rather than footnotes. These look good, and may be more useful to readers when notes are being used extensively. One can think of many such applications, from scientific or mathematical works, through to annotated pieces of literature.

The designer has to tell the processor where all of the page components will appear, and how much space to use for them. The first thing to specify is the page size. This is done with the `page-height` and `page-width` properties. In common with all XSL lengths, these take either absolute or relative values. Generally, you will specify absolute lengths using `px`, `em`, `mm`, `cm` or `inches`. The amount of whitespace around the page is defined using the `margin` property, although individual values can be specified for each side using `margin-left`, `-right`, `-top` and `-bottom`.

The area of the page that holds all of the content is called the `region-body`. If your document includes headers, footers or marginalia, you must tell the processor how much space to leave *inside* the `region-body` for them. The amount of space that is made available must be at least as large as the *extent* of these areas. The extent of an area is the amount of space that it will occupy within the `region-body`. There are examples and detailed description in Section 10.3.

10.2 PROCESSING XSL-FO

One problem which currently faces would-be XSL-FO developers is the lack of supporting software. Although editing the XSL-FO file can be done using the same tools that you use for your other XML development, processing those files to achieve a finished document is not easy. As I write these words, no application that can take an XML document, an XSL-FO stylesheet and interactively display the formatted XML exists. In fact there is no software available that even understands all of the XSL-FO elements and functions. It is currently not possible to process an arbitrary XML document and XSL-FO stylesheet with any guarantee of complete success. Contrast that with XSLT which can be viewed in some recent Web browsers and you will start to see why XSL-FO has not been widely adopted. Because the development of XML and XSL applications is a complicated piece of software engineering, developers are loathe to build tools before a market exists, yet users will not adopt a standard that lacks the support of high-quality tools. There's also the problem that XML is widely, if incorrectly, seen as being a *Web thing*. People expect to view XML in a Web browser, but XSL-FO is targeted at producing output in print formats such as PDF. Many potential users see this task as the domain of other types of software such as word-processors.

> **Warning:**
> XSL-FO can produce auditory output, similar to that which CSS2 allows. Applications that can handle this are a remote possibility at the moment. For this reason I am going to ignore all of the auditory aspects of XSL-FO, although they are comprehensively documented in the W3C Recommendation.

I've found three applications that can process XSL-FO. These are commonly cited on mailing lists and Web sites and appear to be the sum total of such software. The applications are:

- XEP which is made by RenderX Inc. This is a commercial program, although an evaluation version can be downloaded from `http://www.RenderX.com/`, and academic licenses are available. XEP is a Java application, so you will need to install a Java Runtime Environment if you don't already have one.
- PassiveTeX which uses XSL-FO stylesheets to convert XML into TeX. If you want to process this output to get printable documents, you will need to install a version of TeX. The PassiveTeX macros are available from `http://www.ctan.net`.
- FOP which is produced by the Apache project and can be downloaded free of charge from their Web site at `http://www.apache.org`. This is a Java application so you'll need one of the many Java Runtime Environments, which are freely available, on your machine.

Each of the XSL-FO processors that I've listed shares a common failing. They do not implement all of the Recommendation. In fact, important parts may be omitted – FOP doesn't properly create tables, for instance. XEP is probably the best of the bunch but it's not perfect. Many users claim that the printed documents they can produce from XSL-FO do not look very nice. Certainly this is true when compared to the output that can be generated using a dedicated typesetting system such as LaTeX, or a modern word-processor. Writing software that can format printed documents is a massive task. The algorithms required to place content on a page and produce output which looks pleasing are fearsomely complex. If the user-base for XSL-FO grows, I'm sure that the tools will improve and that output quality will start to rival that of other systems.

I tend to use FOP for my XSL-FO work. I'm going to show you how I use it to process the XSL-FO, described in Section 10.4, which prints a recipe from my Recipe Book application. The aim is to produce output in Adobe PDF format, which is the default output for FOP. The stylesheet is an XSL application and is stored in a file called `recipe.xsl`. The first stage is to transform the XML into *formatting objects* that match the instructions in the XSL file. Since the formatting objects are valid XML, this is an XML-to-XML transformation which can be handled by any XSLT processor. I use Xalan like this:[3]

```
java org.apache.xalan.xslt.Process
      -in recipe.xml -xsl recipe.xsl -out recipe.fo
```

Xalan takes a number of possible parameters. You'll always need to specify the XML source file, an XSL file and the output file. The formatting objects must then be processed by FOP. I use a batch file to do this. In fact I use batch files to run most of my Java applications since I have no desire to continually reconfigure my system. If you are not familiar with Java, the use of batch files might seem like common sense. After all, it's how many applications are launched. In Java, though, applications can be launched in several different ways. Each application tends to require its own libraries[4] which must be found on either the `PATH` or `CLASSPATH` environment variables, or placed in special directories. If you use a lot of Java, as I do, bypassing all of this with a batch file is far simpler. Here's the one I use to run FOP on a Linux system:

Listing 10.1 Batch File to Run FOP 0.20.3

```
java -cp /opt/fop-0.20.3/build/fop.jar:/opt/fop-0.20.3/lib/batik.
   jar:/opt/fop-0.20.3/lib/xalan-2.0.0.jar:/opt/fop-0.20.3/lib/
   xerces-1.2.3.jar:/opt/fop-0.20.3/lib/jimi-1.0.jar:/opt/fop
   -0.20.3/lib/avalon-framework-4.0.jar:/opt/fop-0.20.3/lib/
   logkit-1.0.jar:.:/opt/jbuilder5/jdk1.3/jre/lib/rt.jar org.
   apache.fop.apps.Fop "$@"
```

The batch file is called `fop`, and lives in a directory that can be found on my `PATH`. Batch files similar to those shown here can be created on systems such as Windows 2000 or MacOS X. FOP requires the name of the file that holds the formatting objects, and the name of the PDF document you want it to create:

```
fop recipe.fo recipe.pdf
```

If you've used FOP, or read the information provided on the Apache Web site about it, you may wonder why I bother to use Xalan. FOP can take the XML and XSL files and produce a PDF document itself. The formatting objects do not need to be stored in a file, and the entire transformation can happen in a single step. That's fine of you know that

[3]The code is wrapped so that it will fit onto the printed page.
[4]Java calls these packages.

the process works. If you are still debugging or developing your XSL-FO code, you'll find the error messages that FOP produces almost useless. I prefer to use Xalan, or sometimes Saxon, since the information these give back to me is more meaningful when I'm trying to track down an error. Once I've got valid formatting objects, I know that any errors I get from FOP are problems with the way that it is transforming the formatting objects rather than problems with the creation of those objects.

10.3 FORMATTING OBJECT ELEMENTS

The XSL Formatting Object Recommendation describes a great number of elements and attributes. I'm not going to cover them all here; if you need more detail you should either download the Recommendation[5] or buy a reference book dedicated to the topic. This chapter is just an introductory guide, which is why I shall only be describing a few of the available elements and attributes. Unfortunately, descriptions of elements can be rather dry and dusty. You may find that looking at the example stylesheets in Appendices E and F makes this material more meaningful.

`<root>`

All XSL-FO documents must start with a `root` element. This provides the root of the tree from which the document will be created. The `root` element can have up to three types of children: a single `layout-master-set`, a set of `page-sequences` and, optionally, a `declaration` element. I'm ignoring the latter in my quest for some simplicity.

`<layout-master-set>`

This element is used to define the sequence in which pages appear, and their geometry. The geometry of the page includes its size and margins and the positioning of headers, footers and so on within the page. Each child of the `layout-master-set` is an element which defines part of the structure of the document. These elements all have names that end in `-master`. The `page-master` elements describe the structure of the page, while `page-sequence-masters` describe the order in which the `page-master` elements are used.

`<page-sequence-master master-name="string">`

This element is used to specify the order in which pages are created. Each page can have a different structure since they can all have different `page-masters`. As a general rule of thumb, in designing a book, the front matter, main content and back

[5] Actually, everyone working with any of these W3C Recommendations should download and read the ones they are using.

matter have different structures. The page-sequence-master would be used to define the use of those different page layouts. As an aside, front matter is the table of contents, copyright information, preface and so on, and back matter includes the glossary, index and appendices.

Each page-sequence-master in the document must be uniquely identified using the master-name attribute. Even if your document includes just a single page-sequence-master, you'll need to name it so that it can be referred to when it is used.

The page-sequence-master has four possible child elements. These are listed below, along with their attributes. For details of how they are used, consult the Recommendation.

- <single-page-master-reference master-reference="name">
- <repeatable-page-master-reference master-reference="name" maximum-repeats="integer">
- <repeatable-page-master-alternatives maximum-repeats="integer"> This element has conditional-page-master-reference elements as children.
- <conditional-page-master-reference master-reference="name"
  page-position="first|last|rest|any|inherit"
  odd-or-even="odd|even|any|inherit"
  blank-or-not-blank="blank|not-blank|any|inherit">

Remember that the page is divided into an outer margin and an inner region, which acts as a container for page content. The page layout is defined in a page master. At the time of writing, only the simple-page-master, which describes a standard rectangular page, is available. In the future, different types of page-master are likely to become available.

<simple-page-master master-name="name" page-height="length page-width="length" margin-top="width|percentage" margin-left="width|percentage" margin-right="width|percentage" margin-bottom="width|percentage">

Often the layout-master-set will have just one page master element. When all pages in the document have the same structure, as they do in most word-processed documents, a simple-page-master is used. The page is divided into five regions, although only those that are being used need to be specified.

The simple-page-master may be given a name so that it can be referenced from elsewhere in the stylesheet. The page size is given using the page-height and page-width attributes. If these are omitted, the processing application *may* assume a default, which is likely to be 8.5 inches wide by 11 inches high. The page margins may be given as absolute lengths or as percentages of the page size. If these are not used, text will be printed as close to the edge of the paper as possible.

```
<region-body clip="shape|auto" column-count="integer"
column-gap="length|percentage"
overflow="visible|hidden|scroll|error-if-overflow"
region-name="xsl-region-body|xsl-region-start|xsl-region-end|
xsl-region-before|xsl-region-after|name"
writing-mode="lr-tb|rl-tb|tb-rl|lr|rl|tb"
margin-top="length|percentage" margin-bottom="length|percentage"
margin-left="length|percentage" margin-right="length|percentage">
```

The region-body element defines an area in the center of the page which may be offset if the page margins are not all identical. This description is quite complex. Page layout is non-trivial and XSL-FO attempts to cover most eventualities. I've tried to simplify the information provided here, but it will probably only make sense once you see an example.

The region-body must be large enough to accommodate the page content plus any side regions. The region may be uniquely identified through its region-name attribute. Those optional values that start xsl- are defined within the Formatting Objects Recommendation.

When headers, footers or marginalia are being used, space must be allocated to them. This space is specified twice: first in the margin-top, -bottom, -left and -right attributes of the region-body element. Each of these can be given an absolute size or a size expressed as a percentage. These values must be at least as large as the value given to the extent attributes of the other four regions. The margins here are separate to, and different from, the page margins which were specified in the simple-page-master-element. *These* margins exist so that content can be placed inside them. If you are not using a region, there is no need to specify a size for it. It will be subsumed into the region-body and used for the main content of the page.

If the content in an element is too large for its containing region, it will overflow it. Overflowing content may be clipped or displayed in full. The clip attribute is used when the overflow attribute has any value apart from visible. The shape given as the value for this attribute can currently only be specified as a rectangle. Don't expect complex behavior from current generations of processors. Overflowing content is likely simply to disappear.

Using multiple columns in documents is a common requirement. By default, XSL-FO places text into a single column. If multiple columns are needed the number should be specified using the column-count attribute. The gap between columns is set to 12pt if the column-gap attribute is not given an alternative value. Formatting multi-column output seems to be one area in which the current generation of processors is particularly deficient, but it's such a common requirement that it will be well supported at some point in the near future.

The writing-mode attribute specifies the direction in which text is written. In the definition given here, l means left side of the page, r means right, t means top and b is the bottom of the page.

The following CSS2 background, border and padding attributes, and possible values for them, may be used with the region-body element:

- background-attachment=scroll|fixed
- background-color=<color>|transparent
- background-image=uri|none
- background-repeat=repeat|repeat-x|repeat-y|no-repeat
- background-position-horizontal=percentage|length|left|center|right
- background-position-vertical=percentage|length|left|center|right
- border-*side*-color=color
- border-*side*-style=style
- border-*side*-width=width
- padding-*side*=padding-width

Note:

- In the listed items, the text *side* is replaced with one of the values: before, after, top, bottom, start, end, left or right.
- The border-style may be one of: none, hidden, dashed, solid, double, groove, ridge, inset, outset.
- Widths take the values thin, medium, thick or may be given a specific size such as 1pt.

<region-before extent="length|percentage">
region-after extent="length|percentage"
region-left extent="length|percentage"
region-right extent="length|percentage"

These elements specify areas inside the `region-body` element that can be used to hold content. They are all optional. The `region-before` element is used for page headers, `region-after` for page footers, `region-left` for content in the left margin of the page and `region-right` for the right margin. Each must have an `extent` which specifies the size of the region. This must be smaller than the equivalent margin of the `region-body` element.

The following attributes from `region-body` may also be used with these elements:

- `clip`
- `overflow`
- `region-name`
- `writing-mode`
- `background-attachment=scroll|fixed`
- `background-color=<color>|transparent`
- `background-image=uri|none`
- `background-repeat=repeat|repeat-x|repeat-y|no-repeat`
- `background-position-horizontal=percentage|length| left|center|right`
- `background-position-vertical=percentage|length| left|center|right`
- `border-`*`side`*`-color=color`
- `border-`*`side`*`-style=style`
- `border-`*`side`*`-width=width`
- `padding-`*`side`*`-padding-width`

In version 1.0 of the Recommendation, the border-width and padding attributes *must* be given the value 0. When using the `border` elements, replace the word *side* in the descriptions with the appropriate choice from top, left, bottom and right.

Listing 10.2 shows how a page can be defined. In this case the page is a typical A4 sheet with 25mm margins on three sides and a smaller, 10mm, margin at the top. The `region-before` and `region-after` elements are used to define space within the `region-body` for page headings and a footer. This page definition is taken from the Recipe Book example which is described in Section 10.4.

Listing 10.2 A Page Definition

```
<fo:simple-page-master master-name="recipeContent"
       page-height="297mm" page-width="210mm"
       margin-left="25mm" margin-right="25mm"
       margin-top="10mm" margin-bottom="25mm">
  <fo:region-body margin-top="10mm" margin-bottom="25mm"/>
  <fo:region-before extent="10mm" />
  <fo:region-after extent="25mm" />
</fo:simple-page-master>
```

Having created structures for the page and the document, content can be added to those pages. Each document must contain at least one `page-sequence` element which is used to define a sequence of pages within the document. These are associated with a page master and contain `flow` and `static-content` elements which hold the content of the page. Again this appears complicated but once you start to grasp the hierarchy it makes a lot of sense. The structure of the hierarchy is shown in Figure 10.2. I've simplified it by ignoring `page-sequence-master` elements. This shouldn't present too much of a problem since no examples I've ever seen actually use them. This may be because these elements are too complex, redundant or simply beyond the capabilities of processors.

page-sequence id="string" master-reference="master" initial-page-number="number|auto|auto-odd|auto-even"

A `page-sequence` is an ordered set of pages. All pages within the `page-sequence` have the same structure as they will all use the same page master. The page master is selected using the `master-reference` attribute. If you need to refer to a `page-sequence` later in a stylesheet, it needs to be uniquely identified. This is done by giving a unique value to the `id` attribute. If the `page-sequence` does not need to be referred to elsewhere, the `id` attribute can be ignored.

When creating a complex document such as a book, different parts of the book may have different page numbering schemes. The page number can be specified using the `page-number` attribute. A particular value can be given, or one of the `auto` options can be used. The simplest case is to use `auto` where the processor will assign a default page number – usually incrementing the preceding value. The `auto-odd` value increments the number of the preceding page and, if the result is even, adds one to it. Clearly `auto-even` works in the same way as `auto-odd` but ensures that the new page number is an even value.

The `page-sequence` element can have up to three child elements. These define containers which will be used to hold parts of the page.

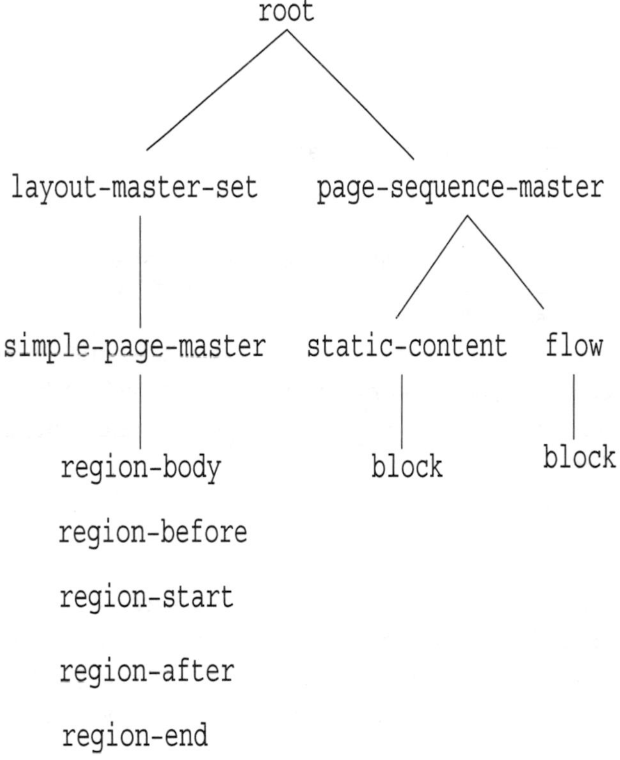

Figure 10.2 A Simple Hierarchy of Formatting Object Elements

`title`

A `page-sequence` may, optionally, be given a title. When transforming to a format such as HTML, the content of the `title` element would be used as the content of the HTML `title` element in the `head` of the page.

`static-content flow-name="region"`

The `static-content` element holds content which will be used on every page within a `page-sequence`. Typically, `static-content` is used to create page headers or footers which are placed in `region-before` or `region-after` elements. The same content will appear each time that the `static-content` element is included. The element takes a single parameter, `flow-name`, which is the name of the region in which it should be placed. XSL reserves the following names:

- `xsl-region-body`,
- `xsl-region-before`,

- `xsl-region-after`,
- `xsl-region-start`,
- `xsl-region-end`,
- `xsl-region-before-float-separator`,
- `xsl-region-footnote-separator`.

Only `block` elements may be placed as children of `static-content`.

`flow flow-name="region"`
The main text of the document, including tables, lists, images and so on, is placed inside `flow` elements. As for `static-content` elements, the `flow` element takes the name of a region as the value of its `flow-name` attribute, and has `block` elements as its children.

10.3.1 Blocks

The content of the document is logically separated into constructs such as paragraphs, title, sectional headings, lists, tables, figures and so on. Within the source XML file these will all be marked up using tags which are, hopefully, meaningful to document authors. When XML is transformed to XHTML, simple transformations can be made so that, for instance, an XML element such as:

```
<section title="Blocks" />
```

becomes the following XHTML:

```
<h2>Blocks</h2>
```

XSL-FO cannot supply such simple transformations. Output languages such as PDF do not include concepts such as generic section headings. Since a language like PDF is intended to reproduce arbitrary output ranging from text documents through to complex graphics, they describe the *form* in which content will be displayed rather than the *meaning* of the content. In some ways this is the reverse of XHTML which gives meanings[6] to tags and relies upon stylesheets to describe how they are displayed.

XSL-FO removes all meaning from the document, hopefully just at the structural level, and replaces it with instructions for formatting output for display. Formatting instructions are supplied using the attributes of the `block` element. The permissible set of attributes that `block` can take includes virtually all of the properties described for Cascading Stylesheets Two, CSS2, as well as additional XSL-FO properties which are listed in Section 10.3.2. If you want to display an element separately, as for instance must be done

[6]Yes, I know that XHTML tags carry no useful meanings, but they do supply a useful distinction between, for instance, different types of heading.

for each paragraph, that element will need to be placed inside a `block`. Useful ways of doing this use the XSL `for-each` and `call-template` elements. You'll see examples of both later in this chapter. Given the XML element:

```
<section title="Blocks" />
```

this `block` will format it as 14-point green text which is horizontally centered within the flow, and which has a 16-point deep space below it:

```
<fo:block text-align="center" font-size="14pt"
                        color="green" space-after="16pt">
       Blocks
</fo:block>
```

Displaying a Poem In Section 8.9, I transformed an XML version of Thomas Gray's *Elegy Written in a Country Churchyard* into HTML. The same poem can be converted into PDF using XSL-FO. The code, as shown in Listing 10.3, is slightly longer and more complicated than the XSLT code. The additional length is partly explained by the need to set up the page structure. The complexity has grown because of the use of `static-content` and `block` elements. One interesting thing, though, is that most of the code is either XSLT which is being used to control the transformation, or CSS2 properties which are being used to style the output. To achieve a simple XML-to-PDF transformation relatively few XSL-FO elements are needed.

Listing 10.3 XSL-FO to Convert Gray's Elegy

```
<?xml version="1.0"?>
<xsl:stylesheet version="1.1"
            xmlns:xsl="http://www.w3.org/1999/XSL/Transform"
            xmlns:fo="http://www.w3.org/1999/XSL/Format">

<xsl:variable name="Ptitle" select="/poem/title"/>

<xsl:template match="/poem">
  <fo:root>
    <fo:layout-master-set>
      <fo:simple-page-master master-name="poemContent"
             page-height="297mm" page-width="210mm"
             margin-left="25mm" margin-right="25mm"
             margin-top="10mm" margin-bottom="25mm">
        <fo:region-body margin-top="25mm" />
        <fo:region-before extent="25mm" />
      </fo:simple-page-master>
```

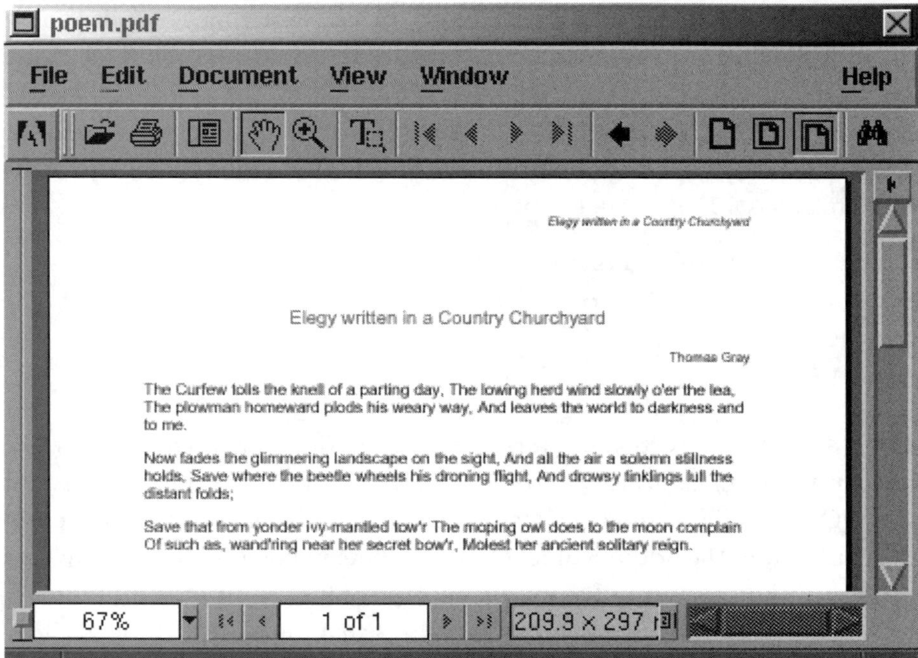

Figure 10.3 Gray's Elegy Formatted for Print

```
</fo:layout-master-set>
```

The first task is to extract the name of the poem and save this in a variable. The name will be used in a few places within the stylesheet, but searching for it will be time-consuming so it's important to get that done as early as possible – and to do it just once. Formatting is performed within an XSL template element which is used to select the root node of the poem. The page is set to A4 size with a small margin at the top of the page and larger margins on the other sides. A margin is set within the body of the page so that a header can be printed within it.

Listing 10.4 XSL-FO to Convert Gray's Elegy

```
<fo:page-sequence master-reference="poemContent">
  <fo:static-content flow-name="xsl-region-before">
    <fo:block text-align="end" font-style="italic"
          font-size="9pt" color="navy">
      <xsl:value-of select="$Ptitle" />
    </fo:block>
  </fo:static-content>
```

The page header is the name of the poem, printed in small blue, italic text. This header is aligned to the right-hand edge of the region-body. Content for this region is taken from the variable which was initialized earlier.

Listing 10.5 XSL-FO to Convert Gray's Elegy

```
<fo:flow flow-name="xsl-region-body">
  <fo:block text-align="center" font-size="14pt"
        color="green" space-after="16pt">
    <xsl:value-of select="$Ptitle" />
  </fo:block>
```

The title is displayed once more, this time as the document title. Formatted in large text and colored green, the title is followed by some vertical whitespace. Notice how everything that is written to the page is placed inside block elements.

Listing 10.6 XSL-FO to Convert Gray's Elegy

```
<fo:block text-align="end"
      font-size="10pt" space-after="12pt">
  <xsl:value-of select="author/first" />
  <xsl:text>&#x20;</xsl:text>
  <xsl:value-of select="author/last" />
</fo:block>
```

Formatting the name of the author uses some techniques which were demonstrated in Chapter 9. The names of the author are held in two elements in the source XML file. When displayed we want a space between those names. If I used code like this no space would appear:

```
<xsl:value-of
    select="author/first" /> <xsl:value-of
                                 select="author/last" />
```

The whitespace has to be forced with the   entity. Writing that into the document is done by placing it inside an XSL text element.

Listing 10.7 XSL-FO to Convert Gray's Elegy

```
<xsl:for-each select="content/stanza">
  <fo:block text-align="start"
        font-size="12pt" space-after="12pt"
        linefeed-treatment="preserve">
    <xsl:value-of select="." />
  </fo:block>
```

```
        </xsl:for-each>
      </fo:flow>
    </fo:page-sequence>
  </fo:root>
</xsl:template>

</xsl:stylesheet>
```

Individual stanzas are selected and formatted inside a `for-each` element. Whitespace is placed after each stanza to separate them on the page. It is important that the line structure of the stanza is maintained. Within the XML file each line of the poem is separated from the following line by a newline character. By default, the processor would collapse these so that the stanza appeared on a single line. Using the `linefeed-treatment` attribute of the `block` element, and setting its value to `preserve`, keeps the correct structure.

That code produces the output shown in Figure 10.3. Here the PDF file is being displayed in Adobe Acrobat which has scaled the text so that it fits in the window.[7] Notice that the line structure has *not* been preserved. That's because FOP 0.20.3 doesn't support `linefeed-treatment` yet. Instead it gives this warning:

```
[WARN]: property - "linefeed-treatment" is not implemented yet.
```

and places the text incorrectly.

10.3.2 XSL-FO Properties

The Formatting Objects Recommendation is, in some ways, a synthesis of all of the preexisting W3C Recommendations that deal with content presentation and formatting. It brings together formatting properties which were described in the Cascading Stylesheets Recommendation, properties from CSS2[8] alongside elements and functions from XSLT. I've already described many properties from Cascading Stylesheets and since I don't want to repeat myself, I will not be describing them again here. The easiest way of discovering those CSS properties that can be used with XSL-FO is trial and error. If a property makes sense within a printed document as, for example, `font-family` does, then use it and see what effect it has.

`space-before="length"`
`space-after="length"`
Almost inevitably `block` elements need to be separated from each other so that they

[7] But you don't need to read the poem again, do you?
[8] And CSS2 is an extension of the CSS Recommendation.

can be differentiated. In most word-processed documents, a whitespace of approximately the depth of a single line is left between paragraphs. These two properties can be applied to the `block` element to achieve this effect. The two can be combined so that the first block has a value for its `space-after` property and the second one has a value for `space-before`. Since this will probably not give the desired result, using one property or the other rather than a mixture of the two is advisable.

start-indent="length|percentage"

This element indents the start edge of a block within its containing flow. Notice that this is different to indenting just the first line, and provides an alternative to increasing the margin or adding padding before the start edge.

break-after="auto|column|page|even-page|odd-page"
break-before="auto|column|page|even-page|odd-page"

Typesetters apply a set of complex rules to text at those places where page or column breaks occur in a document. Having the last two or three lines of a paragraph at the top of a page, or the first few lines at the bottom of a page is considered *a bad thing*. Tables and lists should, wherever possible, be placed on a single page even if that moves them some distance from their *natural* location in the document. Typesetting software such as $\TeX$ includes many complex algorithms which automatically implement the rules of good layout. Generally they do a surprisingly good job, too. The `break-after` and `break-before` properties let XSL-FO stylesheets specify some of the same rules. `break-after` means that the `block` that follows the current one should start a new context such as a page or column. `break-before` means that *this* element is the first one of the new page or column. The list of values that these properties can take is self-explanatory apart from `auto` which means that no breaking is performed. The default value for both these properties is `auto`.

hyphenation-keep="auto|column|page"

This element controls how the final word of a context is hyphenated. When given the value `auto`, the final word of a page or column may be hyphenated even if this breaks basic typesetting rules. When set to `column`, both parts of the hyphenated word must be placed in the same column. `page` means that both hyphenated parts lie on the same page.

id="name"

Any `block` can be given an optional unique identifier using the `id` property.

keep-together="auto|always|integer"
keep-with-previous="auto|always|integer"
keep-with-next="auto|always|integer"

The processor can spend time and resources paginating the document and moving elements around so that elements fit where they naturally occur. Given a formatting object which *may* be too large to fit on a page or within a column, the processor will generally break the content once one page is full and resume processing on the next page. These three properties can be used to give the processor some indication of how much effort it should expend on layout and pagination. `keep-together` is used to try to force the content of the `block` to be placed together as a unit. `keep-with-previous` is used to try to ensure that the current `block` is placed on the same page, or column, as the previous one. `keep-with-next` tries to place the element on the same page as the one that follows it.

The default value for all of these properties is `auto` which imposes no constraints on the processor. The value `always` means that the processor must do everything possible to keep the content together. An integer value can be given which indicates the relative amount of effort that the processor should take. Sometimes the `block` will hold so much content that it has to be split. Even in these circumstances the processor will do all that it can to give the desired result.

`orphans="integer"`

`widows="integer"`

I've already noted that good practice in typesetting indicates that whenever possible one or two lines of a paragraph should not escape onto a page of their own. The `orphans` property specifies the minimum number of lines from a paragraph that should be grouped at the bottom of a page. The `widows` property indicates the minimum number of lines that can be processed at the top of a page. Both default to the value two.

`linefeed-treatment="ignore|preserve|treat-as-space|treat-as-zero-width-space"`

Sometimes you want to preserve the linefeed characters found in the content of an element, when it is converted for printing. The PDF version of Gray's *Elegy* was a classic example of this. At other times, you will want the processor to treat linefeeds in the source as whitespace characters. In this context a linefeed is the entity `�A;` or its Unicode equivalent `U+000A`.

The `linefeed-treatment` property can be given one of four values. `ignore` tells the processor to remove linefeeds, `preserve` tells it to do nothing special with them. When `preserve` is used they should be left in the document and should, usually, be expected to appear in the printed document.

`white-space-treatment="ignore|preserve|ignore-if-before-linefeed|ignore-if-after-linefeed|ignore-if-surrounding-linefeed"`

This property specifies how the processor should handle all whitespace characters *except* linefeed characters. The value `ignore` indicates that the whitespace characters are discarded. `preserve` means that they are converted to the XML entity ` `, or an equivalent.

`white-space-collapse="true|false"`

If this property is set to `true`, runs of more than one consecutive whitespace character are converted to a single whitespace.

`text-align="start|center|end|justify|inside|outside left|right|<string>"`

This property controls how text within the `block` is aligned across the horizontal axis of the page.

`text-indent="length|percentage"`

This element is used to control the indentation of the first line of text within a block. It can be given an absolute length or a percentage of the length of the enclosing region.

10.3.3 Inlines

Text that is part of a block may be styled independently from the rest of the block. This may be done for emphasis, using *italic* or **bold** fonts, or simply to add colors or other effects. Formatting instructions which are placed in the flow of text are called *inline* instructions. Inline formatting is created using the `inline` element. This accepts any of the properties that the `block` element accepts. If you have written XHTML code, `inline` works like the `<span>` tag, whereas `block` elements are analogous to `<div>` tags.

10.3.4 Footnotes

Annotations to the body of a text[9] are created using the footnote element. The processor can be instructed to place the content of `footnote` elements wherever you require. Although they can appear at the foot of the page, they may be displayed at the end of a chapter or as margin notes.

The `footnote` element is placed into the flow at the point at which the reference to the footnote is needed. References may be symbols, such as ♣, or numbers. The character that will be used for the reference is not described within the `footnote` element, but must be created using normal XSLT code. A `footnote` has two parts: an `inline` element which is used to create the reference marker, and `footnote-body` which holds the content. The content of a footnote must be placed inside a `block` if you want it to appear on the page.

[9]Such as this.

The following code shows a technique which I use to create numbered footnotes within documents such as memos and letters. It may not be directly applicable to documents such as books which have complicated internal structures. I start by selecting all footnotes into a variable:

```
<xsl:variable name="footnotes" select="//content/para/footnote"/>
```

The template shown below is used to process the footnotes.

```
<xsl:template match="footnote">
  <fo:footnote>
    <xsl:variable name="tmp" select="para"/>
    <xsl:for-each select="$footnotes/para">
      <xsl:if test="$tmp=.">
        <xsl:variable name="var" select="position()"/>
        <fo:inline>
          <xsl:value-of select="$var" />
        </fo:inline>
      </xsl:if>
    </xsl:for-each>

    <fo:footnote-body>
      <fo:block>
        <fo:inline>
          <xsl:value-of select="position() div 2" />
        </fo:inline>
        <text>&#x20;</text><xsl:value-of select="para" />
      </fo:block>
    </fo:footnote-body>

  </fo:footnote>
</xsl:template>
```

Numbered references are created by comparing the content of the current `footnote` element with all of the nodes in the variable. When the two match, the position of the element in the node-set is used as the reference number. Creating the number in the `footnote-body` is slightly different. The template has matched all `footnote` elements in the document. It creates a node-set which contains the body of each footnote and a reference to it. The position of the footnote within the node-set is not, therefore, the same as its numerical order within the document. The reference number is, in fact, the current position divided by two. This slight quirk is obvious when the code is executed: remove the division and your footnote references will be wrong; include it, and they're correct.

10.3.5 Tables

Tables are widely used both to present structured data, and to present unstructured data within a tidy format. The latter use is more widely used when developing Web sites and other forms of output in which the data is displayed on a computer screen. Printed documents are usually formatted around columns rather than a table as might be used on a Web page. An XSL-FO table is created in roughly the same way that an HTML table is, although the names of the tags are different. If you've worked with tables in Web pages then you will be aware that they require lots of tags and attributes. Even if you spend a long time tweaking a Web table, it will often look *wrong* when displayed in the browser. This is simply because when the table is designed, it must be created for a generic device. The screen size and resolution are unknown until the page is actually displayed. Since tables created using formatting objects are going to be printed, factors such as page size are no longer variables, but are defined in the stylesheet. This means that the designer can spend much more time working on the table layout to get the best possible result.

> **Note:**
> Table support in XSL-FO processors seems to be particularly weak as I write this. The Apache FOP processor, for example, cannot process the basic `table-and-caption` element. Tables with captions must be built using other techniques. Check what your formatting software can handle before you invest too much time and effort in table design.

`table-and-caption caption-side="before|after|start|end|top|bottom|left|right"`

The root element from which tables are created is `table-and-caption`. This creates a block on the page which contains two areas. One is used for the caption, the other for the table itself. The `caption-side` attribute is used to define where the caption will be placed relative to the table. This element also takes the following attributes, which have been described previously:

- all border, padding and background properties,
- all margin properties,
- `break-after`,
- `break-before`,

- `id`,
- `keep-together`,
- `keep-with-next`,
- `keep-with-previous`,
- `text-align`.

This element only *has* to be used when the table is going to have a caption, although many stylesheets will also use it to aid in numbering, indexing and in creating a *list of tables* at the front of a document.

`table-caption height="length" width="length"`

This element is used to define a caption for the table. The content of the caption must be placed inside a `block` element within the `table-caption`. The commonly used border, background and padding properties can be applied to a `table-caption` element.

If your table is simple and will display neatly inline within a document, it can be defined within a `table` element rather than a `table-and-caption` element. If the table is going to be floated and appear away from where it is being referenced, you'll need to provide some form of captioning so that readers can find the table.

Before showing an example of a table, I'll describe the elements and some of their attributes which are needed to define tables.

`table table-layout="auto|fixed"`
`table-omit-header-at-break="true|false"`
`table-omit-footer-at-break="true|false"`
`height="length|percentage" width="length|percentage"`

The `table-layout` attribute is used to select one of the layout algorithms which are used to place content within the table. Not all processors are guaranteed to support both algorithms. When a table spans more than a single page, reproducing the header and footer on each page may not be desirable. Their presence is controlled by the `table-omit-header-at-break` and `table-omit-footer-at-break` attributes. If set to `true`, the header, or footer, will appear on only one page. The table element also accepts border, background, padding and margin attributes, and those dealing with the relationship between pages and elements. These include `break-before`, `break-after`, `keep-together` and so on.

`table-column column-width="length|percentage"`
`number-columns-repeated="number"`

Defining the width of columns when the table is created may be important. The layout algorithm will generally be able to do this automatically, but that may lead to results that are visually unsatisfactory. Much better, therefore, to use a `table-column` element for each column and determine a fixed width. Any `table-column` elements are placed as direct children of the `table` element. If a number of columns are to have the same width, the `number-columns-repeated` attribute can be used in preference to repeating code.

`table-header`

This element is used to define the table header. It accepts `table-row` and `table-cell` elements as children, and can be formatted as a mini table in its own right. If `table-cell` elements are being used without first being placed into `table-row` elements, the `starts-row` and `ends-row` properties of the `table-cell` *must* be used.

`table-footer`

This defines a footer for the table and works exactly like the `table-header` element, except that it appears at the bottom of the table.

`table-body`

This element contains the main body of the table. It has `table-row` or `table-cell` elements as its children. Although the normal background properties can be applied, those relating to padding, borders and margins cannot be used here.

Defining the overall structure of tables is not overly complicated. The main difficulty comes when content is being added. Although the content of a table is simply a set of cells which are placed into rows and columns, those cells need not be uniform. Cells can be made to span horizontally across columns, or vertically across rows. Cells can even contain whole tables. Nesting and spanning are awkward, so planning ahead by drawing the expected table on paper always provides a useful aid.

`table-row`

This element defines the structure of the table by grouping cells into horizontal rows. Every cell defined in a given row will have its top edge at the same level, but some may span vertically across more than one row.

`table-cell starts-row="true|false" ends-row="true|false" height="length|percentage width="length|percentage" number-rows-spanned="number" number-columns-spanned="number"`

The real work of creating a table is done using `table-cell` elements.

Not all cells have to be in rows. If `table-cell` elements are placed directly into `table-body`, `table-header` or `table-footer` elements, the formatter must be told which cells start and end the row. Setting the `starts-row` element to `true` means that the cell starts a row, `false` means it doesn't. Of course, the same meanings apply to the values of the `ends-row` attribute.

The size of a cell can be determined using the `height` and `width` properties. Spanning of rows and columns is determined by the remaining attributes shown here, both of which take the number of rows, or columns, spanned as their value.

The code in Listing 10.8 shows a simple table. In fact, it's part of a more complex table which you will encounter in Section 10.4. The full table is used to display the ingredients for a recipe. This just shows some headings.

Listing 10.8 A Sample Table

```
<fo:table border-width="1pt" border-color="purple"
      border-style="groove" table-layout="fixed">

   <fo:table-column column-width="60mm"/>
   <fo:table-column column-width="15mm"
              number-columns-repeated="2"/>

   <fo:table-body>
      <fo:table-row text-align="center" border-width="1pt"
              border-color="purple" border-style="solid">
         <fo:table-cell padding="4pt" border-bottom="solid">
            <fo:block>Ingredient</fo:block>
         </fo:table-cell>
         <fo:table-cell padding="4pt" border-bottom="solid">
            <fo:block>Amount</fo:block>
         </fo:table-cell>
         <fo:table-cell padding="4pt" border-bottom="solid">
            <fo:block>Unit</fo:block>
         </fo:table-cell>
      </fo:table-row>
   </fo:table-body>
</fo:table>
```

10.3.6 Lists

A list is described using a small tree of elements. The entire list is placed inside a `list-block`. Each item within the list is placed in a `list-item` element. This, in turn, has two parts: a `list-item-label` which holds the label, and a `list-item-body` which holds the content of the item. Formatting of the components of the list, including the amount of separation between the label and the contents can be finely controlled. I'm only going to show the most basic of structures here.

`list-block provisional-distance-between-starts="length" provisional-label-separation="length"`

A list is not enclosed in a normal `block` element. Instead lists are placed inside `list-block` elements. The two attributes shown here control the amount of separation between the label and body of each item in the list. The leading edge of an element is its start and the `provisional-distance-between-starts` attribute controls how far apart these edges should be for the label and body. This distance includes the complete length of the label plus any whitespace that is needed after the label and before the body text. The `provisional-label-separation` attribute gives some degree of control over the depth of the whitespace between the label and the body.

These two attributes are both *provisional* because circumstances within the document may call for the processor to expand or shrink them, for instance to fit in a larger number if the label is numeric. The normal properties for padding, margins and spacing may also be applied both to, and within, the list.

`list-item`

Each item within the list is placed inside a `list-item` element.

`list-item-label`

The label in a list is usually a symbol or number. Numbers are used in enumerated lists in which each successive item is given a higher number to indicate ordering or precedence. Symbols are used for lists in which items are unordered. Since the label is being created using XSL-FO, it can actually be anything that your processor can handle, including an image from an external file. The content of the `list-item-label` must be placed inside a `block` element.

`list-item-body`

The text or image, or even a sublist, is placed inside the `list-item-body` element. Again, the content must also be wrapped inside a `block` element.

In the following example, I've included values for `start-indent` and `end-indent` which I haven't described here. These are needed to get FOP to format the list properly, and are one way of overcoming the limitations of pre-beta software. This code fragment iterates across a node-set. It extracts each item from the node-set in turn and formats it into a new list item. The label is the number of the position of the item within the node-set. This is acquired using the XSL `position()` function.

Listing 10.9 A Simple List

```
<fo:list-block provisional-distance-between-starts="15mm"
          provisional-label-separation="5mm">
  <xsl:for-each select="instruction">
    <fo:list-item>
      <fo:list-item-label start-indent="7mm"
                     end-indent="label-end()">
        <fo:block>
          <xsl:value-of select="position()"/>.
        </fo:block>
      </fo:list-item-label>
      <fo:list-item-body start-indent="body-start()">
        <fo:block>
          <xsl:value-of select="." />
        </fo:block>
      </fo:list-item-body>
    </fo:list-item>
  </xsl:for-each>
</fo:list-block>
```

10.3.7 Images

Printed documents often include images. Typically the data used to draw those images is stored in an external file as a bitmap or a vector image. I say typically, because XML solutions such as SVG pictures may be placed in the body of the XML document. Using images in XSL-FO is very simple.

external-graphic id="name" src="uri" clip="shape" content-height="auto|scale-to-fit|length|percentage" content-width="auto|scale-to-fit|length|percentage" content-type="string" height="length|percentage" width="length|percentage" scaling="uniform|non-uniform" scaling-method="auto|integer-pixels|resample-any-method"

Images are included using the `external-graphic` element. The image may be given a unique identifier within the document using the `id` property. The image file is identified using a URI which is supplied to the `src` property. This property must *always* be used. The processor also needs to know what type of image is being used so that it can process it correctly. The image type is defined using the `content-type` property which takes either a valid MIME type or a namespace as its value. The MIME type should be expressed using a string of the form `content-type: image/bmp`. The full property is given as:

```
content-type="content-type: image/bmp"
```

The processor must be told how much space to allocate for the image – often the processing of the image itself will be off-loaded to another application. The size of the image can be given using the `height` and `width` properties which accept absolute lengths or percentages. If given a percentage value, the space allocated to the image is calculated relative to other objects within the flow. Generally, absolute lengths should be given.

The image can be scaled; it doesn't have to be displayed at its original size. Better results come from scaling images which are defined as vector graphics than from bitmaps or as encapsulated PostScript. The easiest way to scale an image is to define its height and width using the `content-height` and `content-width` properties. When given the value `scale-to-fit`, the processor should scale the image to fit into the available space. Image scaling may happen equally along both horizontal and vertical dimensions. This preserves the *aspect-ratio* of the image, but is not always desirable or necessary. The `scaling` image is used to select `uniform` or `non-uniform` scaling.

In addition to the properties listed above, all padding, margin and space properties may be applied to the image to alter its appearance and position on the page.

The next code sample shows how to include an image in an XSL-FO stylesheet:

```
<fo:block text-align="center">
  <fo:external-graphic id="StructureFig1"
                src="'file://images/struct1.eps"
                content-type="content-type: image/eps"
                height="90mm" width="70mm" />
  The Structure of an XSL Processor
</fo:block>
```

10.3.8 Floats

Some typesetting systems, notably TEX, move the content of the document around to get the best fit. Tables and images, in particular, do not always fit easily on the page at the point at which they are defined. For example, if there is just 3cm left at the bottom of the page and an 8cm tall image to fit in, how should the processor behave? An application such as TEX will put the image at the top of the next page and move some text forward onto the current page. Working like this means that authors always need to provide labels which can be used to create references to images or tables from within the text. In fact, in typesetting this book, I'm using $\LaTeX$ macros which could be used to float all of the program listings as well. If the processor you are using works well and includes a good set of heuristics for this sort of thing, using floats is an excellent idea. It removes a lot of decision making from authors so that they can concentrate on content creation.

> **Note:**
> Whenever possible, floated regions will appear at the top of the page. They *can* be floated sideways to become margin notes but this is difficult with large items.

float float="before|start|end|left|right|none"
clear="before|start|end|left|right|none"

The `float` element is placed around elements to be floated. It takes an attribute, which is also called `float`, which controls how floating should happen. The rules that the processor is required to follow are too complex, and uninteresting, to describe here. They can be found in the Recommendation if you really need them. When `float` is set to the value `none`, the block will not be floated. The other values should be obvious.

The `clear` attribute controls how objects near the floated element are moved around it.

Here's a declaration of an image which the processor is now free to move around the page:

```
<fo:float float="before">
  <fo:block text-align="center">
    <fo:external-graphic id="StructureFig1"
                  src="'file://images/struct1.eps"
                  content-type="content-type: image/eps"
                  height="90mm" width="70mm" />
    The Structure of an XSL Processor
  </fo:block>
</fo:float>
```

10.4 THE RECIPE BOOK

As with XSLT and XML Schema, the relationships between XSL-FO elements can only be understood by seeing them used in a moderately complex example. In Section 9.1 a sample recipe was extracted and displayed inside a Web page. The extraction and transformation were performed using XSLT. In this section I'm going to show the same process of extraction and transformation. This time, though, the extraction will be performed using XSLT and the transformation will use XSL-FO. The result, after processing using Xalan and FOP, will be a PDF file which can be viewed on screen or sent to a printer.

I've endeavored to use the same colors and fonts in the printed version that I used in the XHTML one so that you can more easily see similarities and differences between the two approaches. Astute readers should be able to skip over those formatting instructions that describe the fonts and colors, and dive headlong into understanding those elements that actually create the document. Which might all make you wonder why the formatting instructions haven't simply been removed. They are important, and it's really vital that you know how to include them in your stylesheets. If I were going to give some advice, I'd say that readers should first understand the new XSL-FO material, then learn how to relate the text formatting commands to it.

The code in this section was run through Xalan to create a formatting objects file. That was then processed using FOP 0.20.3 to get a PDF file. The output from all that processing is shown in Figure 10.4. The fonts look a little ugly because the image has had to be scaled down to fit on the page.

```
<?xml version="1.0"?>

<xsl:stylesheet version="1.1"
            xmlns:xsl="http://www.w3.org/1999/XSL/Transform"
            xmlns:fo="http://www.w3.org/1999/XSL/Format">

<xsl:output method="xml"
         version="1.0"
         indent="yes"
         encoding="iso-8859-1"/>

<xsl:variable name="recipe" select="//category[1]/recipe[3]"/>
```

The stylesheet has been split into a set of pieces here so that brief explanations can be filtered in. It can be re-created by concatenating all of the code fragments in this section. Each code fragment represents approximately one template.

The stylesheet starts in a conventional way with an XML declaration. All valid XSL stylesheets are also valid XML documents. XSL-FO stylesheets need two namespace declarations: one for the XSLT elements and one for the XSL-FO elements that they use. You can, of course, add further namespaces of your own if you need to. XSL processors tend to default to producing HTML if not given alternative instructions. In this case I want to

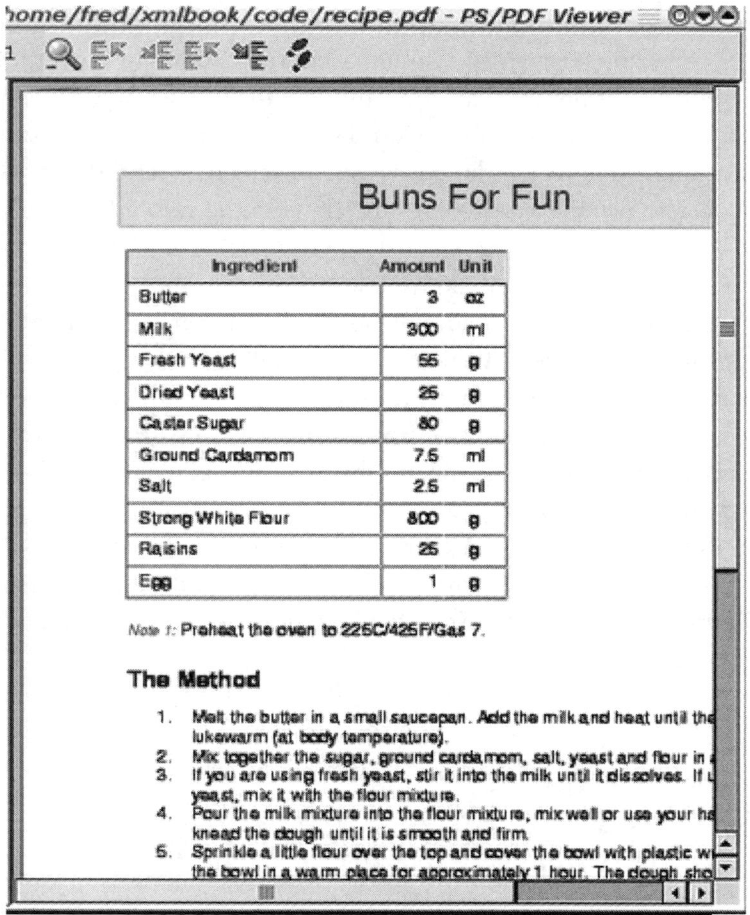

Buns For Fun

Ingredient	Amount	Unit
Butter	3	oz
Milk	300	ml
Fresh Yeast	55	g
Dried Yeast	25	g
Castar Sugar	80	g
Ground Cardamom	7.5	ml
Salt	2.5	ml
Strong White Flour	800	g
Raisins	25	g
Egg	1	g

Note 1: Preheat the oven to 225C/425F/Gas 7.

The Method

1. Melt the butter in a small saucepan. Add the milk and heat until th
   lukewarm (at body temperature).
2. Mix together the sugar, ground cardamom, salt, yeast and flour in
3. If you are using fresh yeast, stir it into the milk until it dissolves. If
   yeast, mix it with the flour mixture.
4. Pour the milk mixture into the flour mixture, mix well or use your h
   knead the dough until it is smooth and firm.
5. Sprinkle a little flour over the top and cover the bowl with plastic w
   the bowl in a warm place for approximately 1 hour. The dough sho

Figure 10.4 The Recipe Formatted Using XSL-FO

produce another XML document, the formatting objects file, so I use an `<xsl:output>` element to specify XML output. Finally, before the top-level template starts, I extract the recipe I want to process and store it in a global variable.

```
<xsl:template match="/cookbook">
  <fo:root>
    <fo:layout-master-set>
      <fo:simple-page-master
            master-name="recipeContent"
            page-height="297mm"
            page-width="210mm"
            margin-left="25mm"
```

```
        margin-right="25mm"
        margin-top="10mm"
        margin-bottom="25mm">
    <fo:region-body margin-top="10mm" margin-bottom="25mm"/>
    <fo:region-before extent="10mm" />
    <fo:region-after extent="25mm" />
  </fo:simple-page-master>
</fo:layout-master-set>
```

The top-level template matches the root element of the Cookbook. The template has to match the root element of the source document, even though the content that will be processed is already stored in a variable. The XSL-FO code starts with a compulsory `root` element. The first thing declared inside that is a `layout-master-set` which consists of a single `simple-page-master`. The formatted recipe will display on just a single page, but even if it spread over a number of pages, a more complex document layout is not needed. I've set the page size to the same size as A4 paper, but that is easily changed if you are working with US letter-sized sheets. Margins are declared on all four sides. Remember, these will be the blank areas between the text and the edge of the paper. Finally, regions are declared for the body, a header and a footer. The margins in the `region-body` are set to the same size as the `extent` attributes of the `region-before` and `region-after` elements. Those elements will be placed in the margins of the `region-body`.

```
<fo:page-sequence master-reference="recipeContent">
  <fo:static-content flow-name="xsl-region-after">
    <fo:block text-align="center" font-style="italic"
            font-size="9pt" color="navy">
      Page <fo:page-number/>
    </fo:block>
  </fo:static-content>

  <fo:static-content flow-name="xsl-region-before">
    <fo:block text-align="end" font-style="italic"
            font-size="9pt" color="navy">
      <xsl:call-template name="showTitleSmall"/>
    </fo:block>
  </fo:static-content>
```

The page footer is going to hold the page number, and the header will hold the name of the recipe.[10] Both these would appear in the same form on every page, although the page number would, of course, change. This means that they can be declared using `static-content` elements which are associated with a particular region using default values for `flow-names`. These defaults are specified in the Recommendation document.

The page number is inserted using the XSL-FO `page-number` element which hasn't been mentioned before. The processor will work out page numbers as it processes the document. They cannot be calculated in advance for anything apart from the simplest of documents. Content for the page header is created by calling a template named `showTitleSmall` which I'll look at it in a short while.

```
        <fo:flow flow-name="xsl-region-body">
          <xsl:call-template name="showTitle"/>
          <xsl:call-template name="showIngredients" />
          <xsl:call-template name="showNotes"/>
          <xsl:call-template name="showMethod" />
        </fo:flow>
      </fo:page-sequence>

  </fo:root>
</xsl:template>
```

The body of the page is created by calling a set of templates. This is the same approach that I took when converting to XHTML using XSLT. It gives much tighter control over which content is processed at a given time. It also seems more natural to me since I rarely program in declarative languages; if I hacked around in Scheme all day, I'm sure that I would feel differently.

The page body is placed in a `flow`. This element is going to hold the content of the page which will vary throughout the document. This `flow` is associated with the `region-body`. Its content will be placed in that area of the page.

```
<xsl:template name="showTitle">
  <fo:block text-align="center" font-size="24pt"
        space-after="16pt" font-family="sans-serif"
        color="purple" border-color="purple"
        border-style="groove" border-width="thin"
        padding="5pt" background-color="wheat">
    <xsl:value-of select="$recipe/name"/>
```

[10]This has, unfortunately, been cut off in the screenshot.

```
  </fo:block>
</xsl:template>

<xsl:template name="showTitleSmall">
  <fo:block>
    <xsl:value-of select="$recipe/name"/>
  </fo:block>
</xsl:template>
```

The main document title and page header are created in the same way. The name of the recipe is selected using the `xsl:value-of` element which you ought to be familiar with by now. This is placed inside `block` elements and styled.

```
<xsl:template name="showIngredients">
  <fo:table border-width="1pt" border-color="purple"
         border-style="groove" table-layout="fixed"
         space-after="16pt">

    <fo:table-column column-width="60mm"/>
    <fo:table-column column-width="15mm"
                 number-columns-repeated="2"/>

    <fo:table-body>
      <fo:table-row text-align="center" color="darkgreen"
                 background-color="wheat" font-weight="bold"
                 border-width="1pt" border-color="purple"
                 border-style="solid">
        <fo:table-cell padding="4pt" border-bottom="solid">
          <fo:block>Ingredient</fo:block>
        </fo:table-cell>
        <fo:table-cell padding="4pt" border-bottom="solid">
          <fo:block>Amount</fo:block>
        </fo:table-cell>
        <fo:table-cell padding="4pt" border-bottom="solid">
          <fo:block>Unit</fo:block>
        </fo:table-cell>
      </fo:table-row>
```

Tables can be pretty complex. Although the table containing the list of ingredients looks simple, it actually needs quite a large amount of code to define it. The table is defined using a `table` element since no caption is required. It has three columns, two of which have the same width. This means that only two column-width elements are needed – the second is simply going to be repeated.

The remainder of the code fragment given above creates the table header. I've done this using an ordinary row and applied lots of styling to it. Notice that content is placed inside block elements which are placed, in turn, inside table-cell elements.

```
      <xsl:for-each select="$recipe/ingredient">
        <fo:table-row border-width="1pt" border-color="purple"
                  border-style="solid">
          <fo:table-cell padding="4pt" padding-left="8pt"
                  text-align="start" border-bottom="solid"
                  border-right="solid" border-color="purple">
            <fo:block>
              <xsl:value-of select="name"/>
            </fo:block>
          </fo:table-cell>
          <fo:table-cell padding="4pt" text-align="end"
                  border-bottom="solid" border-color="purple">
            <fo:block>
              <xsl:value-of select="quantity/@amount"/>
            </fo:block>
          </fo:table-cell>
          <fo:table-cell padding="4pt" text-align="center"
                  border-bottom="solid" border-color="purple">
            <fo:block>
              <xsl:value-of select="quantity/@unit"/>
            </fo:block>
          </fo:table-cell>
        </fo:table-row>
      </xsl:for-each>
    </fo:table-body>
  </fo:table>
</xsl:template>
```

Once the header has been created, the stylesheet iterates across all of the ingredients. The ingredient element has a name child which is extracted and placed into a table-cell. It also has a quantity child which never holds content of its own. Instead, quantity has two attributes: amount and unit. Their content is extracted and placed in table-cells. The value of the attributes is extracted using the xsl:value-of element and passing it an XPath expression which points to the attribute like this:

```
<xsl:value-of select="quantity/@unit"/
```

Although the table needs lots of code, once you've read through it, understanding what is happening, and how it happens, shouldn't be too difficult.

```
<xsl:template name="showNotes">
  <xsl:variable name="tmp" select="$recipe/cooking/note"/>
  <xsl:for-each select="$tmp">
    <fo:block space-after="4pt">
      <fo:inline font-style="italic"
             color="purple"
             font-size="10pt">
        Note <xsl:value-of select="position()"/>:
      </fo:inline>
      <xsl:value-of select="."/>
    </fo:block>
  </xsl:for-each>
</xsl:template>
```

The recipe notes are additional instructions which are not part of the main method. They are formatted into a numbered list using a simple, but effective method. There are many different ways of achieving the same result here. Try to find other ways of getting this output.

The template starts by extracting all of the notes into a variable called `tmp`. Each note is formatted in turn by iterating across the node-set using an `xsl:for-each` element. Each note is placed inside a block, with a small gap placed after the block to give a neater presentation. Notes are numbered using their position in the node-set as the number value. Notice that the word *Note* and the number are styled using an `inline` element.

```
<xsl:template name="showMethod">
  <fo:block space-after="10pt" font-size="16pt"
         font-weight="bold" font-family="sans-serif"
         color="navy" space-before="16pt">
    The Method
  </fo:block>
  <fo:list-block provisional-distance-between-starts="15mm"
             provisional-label-separation="5mm">
    <xsl:for-each select="$recipe/method/instruction">
      <fo:list-item>
        <fo:list-item-label start-indent="7mm"
                        end-indent="label-end()">
          <fo:block>
```

```
            <xsl:value-of select="position()"/>.</fo:block>
        </fo:list-item-label>
        <fo:list-item-body start-indent="body-start()">
          <fo:block><xsl:value-of select="." /></fo:block>
        </fo:list-item-body>
      </fo:list-item>
    </xsl:for-each>
  </fo:list-block>
</xsl:template>

</xsl:stylesheet>
```

The method is formatted using another numbered list. The same numbering technique used to number the notes is applied here. Each item in the list has two parts, a number and some content. The number is created using the `list-item-label`, while content is created with the `list-item-body` element. The amount of space allocated to the label is set using the `start-indent` and `end-indent` attributes. The end of the label is calculated by the `label-end` function. This should mean that even if labels became large numbers, they would not run into the body of the item.

Exercises

1. Download and install an XSL-FO processor such as FOP from the Apache project.
2. Describe three problems which might be encountered when using CSS to format XML documents for printed output. How does XSL-FO address these problems?
3. What output formats are commonly created by XSL-FO processors?
4. Why don't current XSL-FO processors support the full Recommendation?
5. Give one reason that XSL-FO compatibility is not built into common XML-enabled applications such as Internet Explorer.
6. What are page masters?
7. List those elements which may be used in XSL-FO documents to control the appearance of text.
8. What is an XSL-FO block element used for?
9. Describe how whitespace is controlled in XSL-FO.

10. Create an XSL-FO stylesheet which creates a PDF document containing a calendar of the current month. Place the calendar in a table with the names of the days in blue text.

11. Modify the calendar so that, using selection and iteration, it produces a calendar for the current year. You may ignore the problem of leap years, for this exercise.

Part Three

Handling XML in Your Own Programs

Chapter 11

Java and XML

Some technologies seem to fit together so naturally that thinking about one automatically leads to consideration of the other. XML and Java appear to be two such. Many developers who are tasked with creating an application that uses XML will readily think about writing it in Java. In this part of the book I am going to look at how software that uses XML as one of its data formats can be written. The techniques and APIs[1] that I'll be using are all Java solutions. Before getting involved in too much technical detail, I'd like to attempt to justify my use of Java.

The first thing to realize is that you don't have to use Java with XML, or indeed, XML with Java. You can write programs that use and manipulate XML in any programming language. Each language has its good points and its bad points, and each tends to be suitable for a different type of problem, or for a different type of developer. Let's take a moment to look at some of the alternatives, and a few of my personal thoughts on why you might want to avoid them.

Visual Basic This high-level language from Microsoft is used to build many, perhaps most, desktop applications for Microsoft Windows systems. Using it to create applications with neat, standard graphical interfaces is simplicity itself. The language has access to an excellent range of libraries through the `dlls` that come with the

[1] Application Programmer Interface, the available routines in a code library.

operating system. Handling XML in VB is done through the parser that comes with Internet Explorer 6. The problems with VB, for me, are that it becomes pretty wordy, and it is a platform-specific system. I'm not using it here because I've only ever dabbled with it.

C++ The world heavyweight champion of programming languages. You name a problem that can be solved computationally and someone, somewhere will be solving it in C++. Many different XML parsers can be accessed from C++ programs, including Xerces which I'll be using later, and Internet Explorer. All of that power comes at a price. In the case of C++ the price is fearsome complexity. The C programming language is often describe as *write-only*; C++ is worse.

Perl If you need to manipulate text then Perl is the language to choose. Perl is a great language for hacking together a quick solution to a problem. It has an incredibly rich set of freely available libraries within which you can find code to do almost anything. For many people Perl is the perfect solution for Web development, but its XML libraries are equally powerful. The problem with using Perl in a textbook is that not everyone can read it, and its peculiar syntax *can* make even simple programs look like spaghetti.

Python Like Perl, Python is a scripting language. Originally developed for system administration, it too has a rich set of libraries. Python is a very simple language, yet it's also very powerful. Unfortunately, it has quite a low public profile at the moment which means that you are unlikely to have used it. Not ideal for examples in a book, although I did think long and hard about using it, regardless of that.

Scheme Not just Scheme, really, but all languages from the Lisp family. Most Lisp dialects have good XML libraries available. They also tend to be very fast. I've seen benchmarks which claim that Scheme outperforms C++ when parsing XML. That's impressive stuff. Most readers who have graduated in Computer Science will have taken a Lisp course, and those of you who are still studying *will* be taking one at some point. Almost every programmer can read these languages, but not everyone *wants to*. Scheme, like Python and Perl, is a language to consider for your own projects.

Processing speed is important. Even in these days of multi-processor, multi-gigahertz servers, and equally powerful desktop workstations, some applications can still bring a machine to a crashing halt while it crunches data. An unfortunate reality which all XML developers face at some point is that XML is definitely one of those things. Small files of a few kilobytes will stress-test the parser in a browser such as Mozilla. Industrial-sized files which contain many tens of megabytes of raw data can bring a powerful server grinding to a halt for several seconds. These delays matter a lot. If your server is restricted to a single task every time that it has to parse some data as part of a transaction you will soon start to lose business.

Everyone is looking for an instant response, which you might think would mean that all organizations are going to use the fastest parsers they can. It *might* mean that, but in reality it doesn't. Raw speed is just one factor to consider in this equation. Others include system resources, development time, lifetime maintenance costs, availability of suitably skilled staff, licensing and similar costs. Sometimes, personal preference even creeps in there too. If execution speed were all that mattered, everyone would choose C for everything. Much enterprise-level development of server applications and XML processors is done using Java. XML parsers written in Java all seem extremely slow to me. I haven't performed accurate benchmarking, but they introduce delays that can be timed on a wristwatch.

Why use Java with XML? I really don't have a definitive answer to that question. I guess there probably isn't one, but here are a few of the things that *might* be part of it:

- Many developers switched to Java because it was a *better* C++. It's not really, but the syntax of Java is instantly familiar to anyone who knows C++. Java is also popular because it automates some of the complexities of C++ such as pointers and garbage collection.

- XML and Java were developed at roughly the same time. People who wanted to learn one of them might also have wanted to try the other.

- Both Java and XML are perceived, rightly or wrongly, as being Web technologies.

- Many XML users are relatively new to document markup. Their background is more likely to be in HTML than SGML so they look for Web-type solutions to problems. SGML has always had a closer relationship with Lisp.

- The two technologies work well on similar types of problem. These are, broadly, applications that are networked, require interoperability and are based around heterogeneous systems where the platform really doesn't matter. In part, it's the availability of Java that has made these applications so common today.

- The performance problem doesn't exist for many developers. If you are building an enterprise-scale system that uses Java to manipulate XML, you're likely to be using something like Enterprise Java Beans, EJBs. A Java Bean is a special type of object which can be loaded dynamically by a running system. Beans adhere to a particular *design pattern* which means they can be queried by running systems and are *toolable*.

> An EJB takes the idea of a bean and adds business logic to it. EJBs are run using special server processes which keep them in memory once loaded. Using a Java Hotspot compiler, EJBs can execute almost as quickly as compiled code written in C++.

Why use XML in your programs? By now you'll be aware that XML is an excellent way of describing data structures. It works really well as an intermediate data format between, for example, a database and a Web page. XML structures can be searched, modified or transformed into HTML or another XML structure. Even more relevantly, XML can be parsed by both machines and humans, although the chances of a person bothering to read a large complex XML structure are remote. This means that if your data has been structured using XML it will be converted into other formats by machines before being used by people.

Machines are really very good at handling complex structured data such as XML files. Once data is in an XML tree, using it for more complex tasks is relatively light on resources and easy to achieve. The possibilities are many-fold. Some of the most exciting uses of XML can be found in the field of distributed computing. Broadly, distributed computing is the use of more than one processor in an application, with those processors connected by a network rather than a system bus. Although some people claim that the Internet is an example of distributed computing, it isn't really. It's an example of distributed *data*. Once machines on the Internet start to share processing as well as data, and begin to talk to each other automatically, distributed computing can be talked about. Among the XML technologies that will facilitate the distribution of processing are SOAP, which provides a lightweight messaging infrastructure, and the resource description framework, RDF. RDF lets applications describe their services to each other using common metadata. Moving a stage further towards automation, agent technologies present the possibility that intelligent software applications can begin to navigate the Internet in their own right, gathering and processing data for human users without being directly controlled by them. Any *next-generation* applications such as intelligent agents will mandate the use of common data formats on networked servers. XML is really the only player in this particular game at the moment.

Of course, if machines are going to share information, they need to be programmed. This is where the conjunction of Java and XML comes from. Java isn't the only language which can be used to build network-enabled, powerful general-purpose software applications. The .NET platform and the C# programming language from Microsoft promise similar capabilities on their operating systems. Java currently has millions of developers who have invested time, effort and money into learning its intricacies. C#, on the other hand, is new and untested in large production environments.

11.1 JAVA PACKAGES FOR PROCESSING XML

In subsequent chapters I'm going to show briefly how Java can be used to manipulate XML. Doing this requires additional libraries which aren't shipped with a default Java Software Development Kit, SDK. Borland, whose Java IDE I use for my development work, provide many XML processing libraries alongside their IDE software. While other vendors may do the same thing, I haven't used their products so I'm not qualified to comment. The libraries that Borland supply can be integrated easily and quickly into any project. The world of XML library development moves far more quickly than the world of IDE development. The consequence is that the libraries supplied by your vendor may be out of date by the time you use them. This may not matter if the changes are to parts of the code that you don't use. It will matter, though, if the API undergoes major changes. An example of this is the SAX API, described in Chapter 13. Several methods, including many that were widely used, were deprecated between versions one and two. Libraries implementing SAX had to undergo significant rewrites, leading to many deprecated methods. This isn't important if your code is never going to be used or maintained by other people, but relatively few developers are in that position.

There are significant differences between libraries that perform the same type of processing. JAXP and Xerces can both use either SAX or DOM but they are not directly interchangeable since their package structures differ. While it's not important that users know the detail of the differences, knowing that they exist definitely is useful.

I don't intend to provide detailed descriptions of every Java library that can be used to process XML. I'm mainly going to introduce the ones that I've used. All of these libraries, plus the myriad others that are available on the Internet, include documentation. Once you know how DOM and SAX work, understanding the correct way to use a new library is surprisingly easy.

11.1.1 Java API for XML Processing

A large number of Java processors have been created. When you write your own Java applications you will normally expect to use one of these processors within it. Rather than going to the effort of writing your own code to create a DOM tree or a SAX parser, you will use one that already exists. If you are a good programmer, or an overly self-confident bad programmer, you might think that writing your own parser is a good idea. As an exercise in learning to program it probably is, but as part of the development of another application, using someone else's code is almost always better. Basically, if the parser is any good, the developers will have taken the time to optimize their code, to make using it as easy as possible, and to include all of the necessary functionality. If you are writing an e-commerce system, for example, any parser that you create for yourself is likely to be as minimalist as possible since you will need it quickly. You are not going to be able to test it thoroughly or reuse it in other applications simply because the parser is not your main focus.

The best of the available parsers, such as Xerces, have comprehensive APIs which fully implement SAX and DOM. Such software can often be used as a standalone application for one-off needs, but it can also be linked in to other programs. Some parsers use APIs that have been developed by their creators to meet specific needs. You might wonder why more than one XML processor has been written in Java; after all once someone has written the code, everyone else can simply reuse it. Processing XML is very complicated, and doing so efficiently is difficult. Parsers may run at different speeds or require different system resources across platforms. What works well on a sub-mainframe server may be totally impractical on a PDA.

Many XML parsers are either volunteer efforts or are created and donated by large software houses in addition to their core business. There are relatively few that are fully supported with guaranteed futures. Ideally developers would use only those parsers that they know will be supported for as long as their own application is in use. In reality this is not possible. It may even be necessary to change parser at least once during the lifetime of a product. This is where the Java API For XML Processing, JAXP, becomes useful.

JAXP is an attempt by Sun Microsystems to create an API that is processor and data structure independent. There is a close relationship between TrAX, which is introduced in Section 11.1.3, and JAXP. While TrAX is an API for transformations, JAXP presents a standard API for all XML and transformation needs, and subsumes TrAX within it. Sun do not, themselves, supply a complete implementation of JAXP. A JAXP compliant parser called Crimson ships with Java 2 version 1.4 and has been donated to the Apache Foundation. The code from Crimson has been integrated into the Xerces project. Sun appear to recommend using the JAXP implementations in Xerces, Xalan and Saxon for parsing and transformations.

JAXP supports both DOM and SAX parsers. Rather than shipping with a single parser, JAXP defines a set of methods which act as hooks that can be used to plug in any compliant processor. Parsers and XSLT processors are loaded at runtime by *factory* classes. A factory is a design pattern describing how classes can be instantiated and loaded as a program runs. The key factories within JAXP are:

- `javax.xml.parsers.SAXParserFactory` which loads a SAX parser,
- `javax.xml.parsers.DocumentBuilderFactory` which loads a DOM tree builder, and
- `javax.xml.parsers.TransformerFactory` which is used to instantiate an XSLT engine.

Each factory uses either an environment variable or a value within the file `$JAVA_HOME\lib\jaxp.properties` to find a parser. Changing parser is achieved by changing the value of one of those settings.

11.1.2 Xerces

Xerces is the Apache Foundation's XML parser. It fully complies with the XML Recommendation and, in version 2, is made into separate components with a new interface which makes programming it easier. Xerces 2 adds support for XML Schema – as with the XML parser it fully conforms to the W3C specification. Finally the working draft of DOM 3 is partially supported.

Xerces 2 supports the following W3C Recommendations:

- XML 1.0 second edition,
- Namespaces in XML,
- DOM level 2,
- SAX 2,
- JAXP 1.1, and
- XML Schema 1.

The Xerces parser forms the basic foundation of all of the other XML processing technologies that the Apache Foundation has. You'll see it in use throughout the remaining chapters of this book.

11.1.3 Xalan-Java

Xalan is a transformation engine developed by the Apache Foundation and available for C++ and Java. The latest release of the Java implementation, version 2, is based around the Transformation API for XML, TrAX.

Having a simple API which Java developers can use to transform between XML structures is clearly important. Much of the development work within Java-XML communities focuses upon the area of transformations, and other products described in this chapter are also used specifically for transformation. Inputs to, and outputs from, transformations may be URIs, DOM trees, streams of SAX events, text documents or other formats. Tools must be able to transform between any possible combination of input and output. Having a specialized API to deal with each possible transformation is possible but complex. Imagine if separate APIs were needed to transform from DOM trees to SAX events, from URIs to text documents and from DOM trees to URIs. As the uses of XML grow, more XML structures will be developed and the combination of possible transformations will lead to unmanageable APIs. TrAX tackles this problem by presenting a single API which can be used in Java applications whichever transformation underlies the process.

Xalan implements XPath for navigation through XML documents and XSLT for transformations, and is able to perform most types of transformation to XML formats. Transformations into printable formats such as PDF are handled by another Apache project called FOP, described in Section 11.1.5. Xalan does not include its own XML parser. The default configuration is that Xalan passes parsing to Xerces which is supplied with it however, any suitable XML parser may be plugged in as a replacement. Since Xalan is based on TrAX, input can come from a URI, a DOM tree, or a stream of SAX events and the result can be output to any of the same types of location. Transformations can be chained to give more complex results. Xalan exposes an API which means that developers can base their own applications around it or it can be used as a standalone application from the command-line.

11.1.4 Saxon

Saxon is an XSLT processor which is written and developed by Michael Kay, the author of *XSLT Programmer's Reference*. Version 7.2, the latest release at the time of writing, introduces support for XPath 2.0 and XSLT 2. This is, at best, a beta quality release since the specifications continue to change. The stable version, 6.5.2, supports version 1 of both XPath and XSLT. Many people prefer Saxon over Xalan, and it is often described as both smaller and faster. Like Xalan-Java, Saxon is a pure Java solution which implements the TrAX API. Using this API the processor can be included within other applications but Saxon can also be used as a command-line application. If you are looking for an XSLT processor, installing both Xalan and Saxon is a good idea so that you can use whichever works best for you. If you use TrAX in your applications, swapping between the two processors is done in the same way as for other JAXP-compliant APIs.

11.1.5 FOP

FOP is one of the few transformation engines currently available that can process XSL Formatting Objects. At the time of writing, the latest version of FOP is 0.20.4. This provides only a partial implementation of version 1.0 of the XSL-FO Recommendation and not all of the properties and objects which it implements are complete. FOP works well for simple and small documents, the sort that might be normally be prepared using a word processor. It *can* be used with complex DTDs such as DocBook, described in Chapter 17, but will not give perfect results.

FOP is mainly intended as a way of producing PDF documents from XML sources using XSL-FO stylesheets. It can also produce output in print, SVG, PCL, PostScript and text formats. FOP is distributed with Cocoon so that PDF documents can be produced directly for distribution across the Web. Because of internal problems within the design and code base, FOP is currently undergoing a complete redesign. A branch was made in the project at version 0.20.2. Updates will continue to be released based upon this branch but at some point a totally new FOP will appear to replace them.

I mention FOP here only because you are likely to want to use it if you are going to try using XSL-FO.

11.1.6 Oracle XDK

Oracle is probably the largest supplier of relational database software in the world today. It's certainly one of the largest companies in the world, with tremendous power and influence outside of the database development community as well as within it. No company gets to dominate an entire sector of the computer industry without being able to spot, and react to, major changes almost before they happen. Oracle has done just this with XML in exactly the same way that Microsoft, IBM and Sun have done. Unlike those other companies the primary focus of Oracle is, of course, data storage. The latest versions of Oracle's main products support XML in key areas, allowing for the storage, management and querying of XML within a database.

Oracle*9i* has a number of components that can be used with XML, XML Schema, XSLT and XML Query and programmed in Java, C, C++ and PL/SQL. The main components are the Oracle XML Developer's Kit, XDK, which contains libraries that allow the development of many different types of XML-based application; and the XML SQL Utility, XSU, which is used to generate and store XML through normal database queries, sets and tables. XDK is supplied under a license which means it can be used within other commercial products. XSU maps XML structures onto relational structures during queries and updates.

Table 11.1, which is based on data from the Oracle XML Developer's Kits Guide found at `http://otn.oracle.com`, lists the parts of the XDK. Different subsets of this list of components are available in C, C++ and PL/SQL. The full set is only available for Java applications.

11.1.7 Cocoon

If XML and XSLT become wide-spread in e-commerce and other Web domains, simple server-side applications that support high-volume processing will be required. These will not be the Web-server and CGI script combo which was widespread in the late 1990s, nor

Table 11.1 Components of the XDK

Component	Description
XML Parser	Parse XML documents. Can use either DOM or SAX and supports version 2.0 of both. The parser also supports XPath which can be used in XSLT, XQuery and XLink applications.
XSLT Processor	Transform XML into other text formats such as XHTML using XSLT stylesheets. This processor is fully compliant with version 1.0 of the W3C Recommendation
XML Schema Utility	Understands XML Schema and can be used to validate XML documents against it.
XML Class Generator	Generates Java, or C++, classes from DTDs and XML Schema.
XML Transviewer	A set of JavaBeans which can be used to transform and view XML documents.
XML SQL Utility	Generates XML, DTDs and XML Schema from SQL queries.
XSQL Servlet	Within the server XML, SQL and XSLT can be combined to deliver dynamic content for Web applications. The servlet has been tested with a wide range of commercial and Open Source servlet engines, including those from Apache, Sun and Oracle.
TransX Utility	Loads XML formatted data into a database.
Oracle SOAP server	A SOAP Server which is based upon the one developed by the Apache Foundation.
XML Compressor	Compresses XML documents into a smaller binary format for easier storage and transmission.

will they be based around proprietary technologies such as Enterprise JavaBeans or .Net. Content producers, who may be authors, publishers or multinational corporations, will want to produce their content in XML and have it transformed into XHTML, PDF or even video streams simply and cost-effectively. Cocoon from the Apache project is an attempt to build just such a server.

Cocoon is a framework that uses XML and XSLT to publish XML formatted data on the Web. The content of a document is separated from its logical structure and from the presentation of that content in a completed document. Cocoon undertakes the same decoupling of content and presentation that Cascading Stylesheets does for HTML, but rather than expecting that the client undertakes styling, the server does this. Cocoon integrates well with other Apache projects such as Tomcat, and in fact is usually installed with Tomcat.

You might wonder why a special server is needed to perform all of this processing. Other pieces of software such as Saxon or Xalan can be used to apply XSLT stylesheets to XML documents to produce PDF, XHTML or other outputs. The big win that Cocoon brings is that it simplifies team working. Each member of staff, be they developer, artist, analyst or system administrator, is able to work on their own part of the system without impacting on the work of others. Of course, there needs to be management and control of the whole process but because document structure, design and presentation are separated, each person can concentrate on their own specialty. Using pure XHTML technologies, the code that controls the presentation of the document and the data it contains tend to exist in the same files. If the business logic changes, all of the presentation code has to be accessed so that the data can be changed to match the new design.

Unlike the other technologies in this chapter, Cocoon *uses* XML. It isn't used to create or manipulate XML *per se*. Similar ideas such as Websphere from IBM and some of the developments happening to Java may dominate the marketplace in the future. If you want to find out what is possible and where the future of e-commerce and Web applications may lie, download Cocoon and spend some time playing with it.

Chapter 12

The Document Object Model

When thinking about the structure and content of documents, many people will naturally think about tree structures. Documents usually comprise some combination of parts, chapters, sections, subsections, tables, images and footnotes. Even documents written using a word-processor include meta-information such as the time and date the document was created, the name of the author and some form of revision history. Not all documents are directly created by a human author. In business, using documents created automatically by software applications is common. These may be reports generated from batch-processing software, the output of a database query, or a system log-file. However they are generated, all of these documents have an internal structure. If readers were asked to draw schematic diagrams of those structure, they would produce variants on trees.

I'm emphasizing, although some might say belaboring, the tree structure of documents because it is central to this chapter. Few documents are really written as trees. How many people ever use the outlining feature in Microsoft Word, for example? Even fewer are stored as trees in memory, and larger documents are not typically rendered as a single entity in memory in any format. By thinking about documents as abstract, logical trees and developing APIs that can be used to manipulate those trees, software development is vastly simplified. A single model can be applied in many different applications which means that developers can concentrate on using data, not merely manipulating it.

12.1 THE W3C DOCUMENT OBJECT MODEL

The standard representation for HTML and XML documents is the Document Object Model. This has been a W3C Recommendation since 1997 and is well established. The current release, at the time of writing, is version two. This is the version I'll be concentrating on throughout this chapter. The Recommendation states that the DOM is an API that

> ...defines the logical structure of documents and the way a document is accessed and manipulated

The DOM defines the API but leaves the implementation to the developers of parsers and other low-level XML manipulating software. DOM provides a standard within which those developers must work as they create libraries, parsers and other tools. Application developers who use those tools will expect them to present documents to their applications in DOM-compliant fashion. That implies that the *logical* view of the document is going to be as a tree and that writing applications that traverse that tree should be technically possible. It definitely does not mean that DOM-compliant parsers have to *implement* the document structure as a tree. Any data structure can be used internally. Provided it is presented to the rest of the world as a tree, the parser will be complying with the Recommendation.

In this book, I'm not interested in writing XML parsers. I am interested in using them, and in this chapter I am especially interested in using parsers written in Java, by other people, in my own Java applications. How the DOM can be used, through a typical parser such as Xerces, is more relevant here than how the parser is implemented.

12.1.1 What is the DOM

The first consideration is what the DOM is *for*. Why define an API for generic XML documents? Applications need to be able to access elements, attributes, processing instructions and other nodes that comprise the document. Applications have to be able to navigate between those nodes, accessing their content, modifying it, deleting nodes and adding new nodes. If the DOM had not been defined, each parser would implement the same set of features in its own way. Changing parser would mean learning a totally new API and a different way of working. Software houses would then start to add their own features which would require extensions to XML, or changes in it. The XML community would fragment as developers became locked-in to particular suppliers, and the attraction of XML as a platform-independent, non-proprietary data format would be lost. If that seems far-fetched, in the mid-1990s both Netscape and Microsoft tried exactly the same thing with HTML. Each started to add proprietary tags, hoping that if developers used those extensions, surfers would be forced to use a particular browser. To some extent that has happened, not with HTML, but with JavaScript and JScript. Although the two languages are supposed to be compatible with a standard called ECMAScript, and to implement the DOM, they differ in their compliance. This has led to numerous Microsoft-only or Netscape-only Web sites which are inaccessible to users of other browsers.

The XML community seems far more standards aware than the Web development community. Possibly because XML developers are either software engineers or have a background in information management, they recognize the dangers of non-compliance. It's also true that the DOM is extremely useful which probably has more than a little to do with its popularity.

12.1.2 What the DOM is Not

First, and foremost, let's be clear about what the DOM is not. The W3C document object model is not a product such as a piece of software. It's an idea, or rather it's a set of ideas. The Recommendation document lists the following things that the DOM isn't:

- The DOM also does not specify any sort of binary format; application interactivity is not specified.
- The DOM does not specify any data structures, it is purely logical.
- DOM is not a way of serializing data from other formats into XML.
- DOM does not define how important the data within a document is.
- Although DOM structures can be used in interoperating environments, DOM is not the same as middleware technologies like COM or CORBA.

12.1.3 DOM Nodes

In the DOM, everything that is part of a document is defined as a node. The leaves and branches of the DOM tree are all implemented as different types of node. The DOM is an *object* system; trees and nodes are represented as objects which contain both data and processing. In the theory of object orientation, common functionality is defined in a generic *base* class which can be used to derive other classes with more tightly specified functionality.

Describing everything in the document using a single object type means that only one set of operations is required to manipulate the entire tree. Individual nodes such as elements and attributes have important differences. These can be built into the program if they are implemented as subclasses which *inherit* and extend the functionality of the basic node class. The document object model Recommendation includes the following definition of a node:

```
interface Node {
  const unsigned short      ELEMENT_NODE                = 1;
  const unsigned short      ATTRIBUTE_NODE              = 2;
  const unsigned short      TEXT_NODE                   = 3;
  const unsigned short      CDATA_SECTION_NODE          = 4;
  const unsigned short      ENTITY_REFERENCE_NODE       = 5;
  const unsigned short      ENTITY_NODE                 = 6;
  const unsigned short      PROCESSING_INSTRUCTION_NODE = 7;
  const unsigned short      COMMENT_NODE                = 8;
  const unsigned short      DOCUMENT_NODE               = 9;
  const unsigned short      DOCUMENT_TYPE_NODE          = 10;
  const unsigned short      DOCUMENT_FRAGMENT_NODE      = 11;
  const unsigned short      NOTATION_NODE               = 12;

  readonly attribute DOMString        nodeName;
           attribute DOMString        nodeValue;

  readonly attribute unsigned short   nodeType;
  readonly attribute Node             parentNode;
  readonly attribute NodeList         childNodes;
  readonly attribute Node             firstChild;
  readonly attribute Node             lastChild;
  readonly attribute Node             previousSibling;
  readonly attribute Node             nextSibling;
  readonly attribute NamedNodeMap     attributes;
  readonly attribute Document         ownerDocument;
  readonly attribute DOMString        namespaceURI;
  attribute DOMString                 prefix;
  readonly attribute DOMString        localName;

  Node insertBefore(in Node newChild,
                    in Node refChild)
                    raises(DOMException);
  Node replaceChild(in Node newChild,
```

```
                    in Node oldChild)
                    raises(DOMException);
  Node removeChild(in Node oldChild)
                   raises(DOMException);
  Node appendChild(in Node newChild)
                   raises(DOMException);
  boolean hasChildNodes();
  Node cloneNode(in boolean deep);
  void normalize();
  boolean isSupported(in DOMString feature,
                      in DOMString version);
  boolean hasAttributes();
};
```

Although the definition of the `Node` type is written using IDL, it should be clear in its intent if you've ever programmed in Java or C++. Interface Definition Language, IDL, is a language developed by the Object Management Group to describe the interfaces of objects in distributed systems. It is designed to be neutral about implementation language although it has a clear C++ heritage. The `Node` types should be obvious. If they aren't, you should review Chapter 4 which describes XML Schema in some detail.

Some nodes have children while most have parents[1]. The `Node` type includes methods which are used to manipulate the structure of the tree through parents and children. The `cloneNode` method is used to make an exact copy of the node. If the parameter `deep` is set to `false`, just the one node is cloned. If it set to `true`, a subtree is created by recursively copying all nodes below the current one. This process is called a *deep copy*. If you need to copy a node and any `text` nodes that contain the content of the node, a deep copy is required.

12.2 THE XERCES DOM API

Xerces includes a complete implementation of version 2 of the W3C document object model. The classes and interface that comprise this model are packaged into a whole slew of packages:

- `org.w3c.dom`
- `org.w3c.dom.events`

[1] All except the document root.

- `org.w3c.dom.html`
- `org.w3c.dom.ranges`
- `org.w3c.dom.traversal`

Each of these packages contains many different classes which, in turn, have many more methods. There are far too many of these to document here. If you are going to be using Xerces, the complete API documentation is supplied as part of the binary download. To get you started with all that documentation I am going to briefly examine the `Node` interface which is found in `org.w3c.dom`. The DOM is totally based around nodes. Almost everything in the DOM is either a node or a subclass of a node which adds specialized features. Subclasses are available for node types such as attributes, elements and processing instructions, each of which has its own additional requirements and uses. The DOM has some public fields and lots of methods which we'll look at first.

12.2.1 Fields

The fields are implemented as static short integers. They all identify the specific node type of the current node. The fields are:

- `ATTRIBUTE_NODE`
- `CDATA_SECTION_NODE`
- `COMMENT_NODE`
- `DOCUMENT_FRAGMENT_NODE`
- `DOCUMENT_NODE`
- `DOCUMENT_TYPE_NODE`
- `ELEMENT_NODE`
- `ENTITY_NODE`
- `ENTITY_REFERENCE_NODE`
- `NOTATION_NODE`
- `PROCESSING_INSTRUCTION_NODE`
- `TEXT_NODE`

12.2.2 Methods

`Node appendChild(Node newChild)`

Each node has a list containing its children. Not all nodes will actually have children, but they all have the list. The node that is referenced by the `newChild` argument is appended to the end of the list of children.

`Node cloneNode(boolean deep)`

This method returns a copy of the current node. If the value of `deep` is set to false, only the current node is returned. If `deep` is set to `true`, a subtree that contains a copy of the current node and all of its children is returned.

`NamedNodeMap getAttributes()`

This method returns the attributes of the node. If the node doesn't have any attributes `null` is returned.

`NodeList getChildNodes()`

This returns a list containing all of the children of the node.

`Node getFirstChild()`

Returns the first child of the node. This node is the first one in the list of child nodes. The list of child nodes is not logically ordered or sorted.

`Node getLastChild()`

Returns the last child in the node list.

`String getLocalName()`

Returns the local part of the qualified name of the node.

`String getNamespaceURI()`

Returns the namespace of the node. If a namespace has not been specified, `null` is returned.

`Node getNextSibling()`

Each node, except for the root of the document, belongs to a list of nodes which is held by its parent. This method returns the node which following the current one in that list.

`String getNodeName()`

Returns the name of the node.

`short getNodeType()`

Returns an integer which identifying the type of the node. The integer matches one of those shown in the fields list given above.

`String getNodeValue()`
Returns the value of the node where this can be calculated.

`Document getOwnerDocument()`
Returns the Document to which this node belongs.

`Node getParentNode()`
Returns the parent of the node.

`String getPrefix()`
Returns the namespace prefix. If the prefix has not been set, this method will return `null`.

`Node getPreviousSibling()`
Return the item before this one in the node list of its parent.

`boolean hasAttributes()`
Returns `true` if the node has any attributes. Otherwise it will return `false`. Only `element` nodes can give `true` with this method since other nodes cannot have attributes.

`boolean hasChildNodes()`
Returns `true` if the node has children, `false` otherwise.

`Node insertBefore(Node newNode, Node ref)`
This method inserts the node identified by `newNode` into its node list. The node is placed before the node identified by `ref`.

`void normalize()`
All nodes in the subtree below this node are converted into normal form.

`Node removeChild(Node old)`
Removes the node identified by `old` from the node list.

`Node replaceChild(Node old, Node newNode)`
Replaces the node that is identified by `old` with the node identified by `newNode`. The method returns the node identified by `old`.

`void setNodeValue(String val)`
Sets the value of the node to that given in `val`. Not all nodes can contain values. This method only applies to those that *can* take a value.

`void setPrefix(String prefix)`
Sets the prefix for the node.

12.3 USING THE DOM TO COUNT NODES

The remainder of this chapter includes two examples of how the DOM can be used in simple applications. I've taken the same approach here that I use with the SAX examples in Chapter 13. The original programs process the XML Recipe Book and display their results in a simple Java GUI. All the code for these applications is available from the supporting Web site. The only code shown here is that which deals directly with the XML document.

The two SAX applications which I show in Chapter 13 read through the document and counted some of the nodes it contains. The sensible place to start exploring the DOM is with a program that does the same thing. The result of executing the code is shown in Figure 12.1.

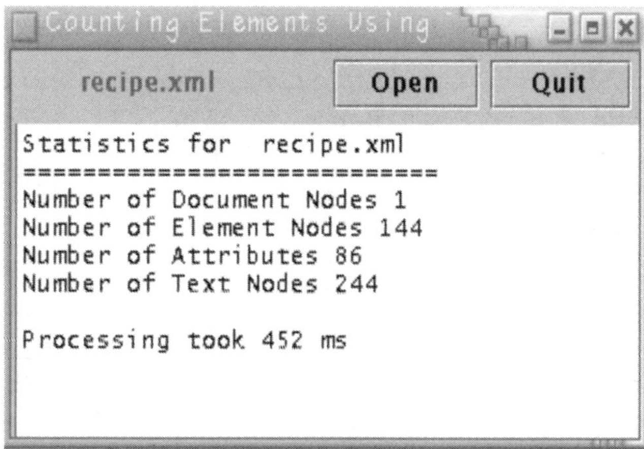

Figure 12.1 Counting Using the DOM

Parsing using the DOM requires a different set of packages to the DOM. The main package which needs to be imported is `org.w3c.dom` which contains all of the interfaces and classes that the application needs to use or implement. The SAX package, `org.xml.sax` is imported because the parser can throw an exception which it defines. Finally, the application must import the parser it is going to use. In this case I'm using a parser which was implemented by the Apache project. If you have already looked at Chapter 13, you might remember that switching from one parser to another was not straightforward. The same is true of the DOM. Although two libraries implement the same API, they do not have to do so in the same way. Provided the interfaces are consistent with the Recommendation, the APIs are compliant.

```
import org.xml.sax.*;
```

```
import org.w3c.dom.*;
import org.apache.xerces.parsers.DOMParser;
```

Counting nodes using the DOM requires only two methods. The first creates a parser, parses the document and builds a string which is returned to the graphical part of the application for display. The parser in this example is the Xerces DOMParser which can be created directly using `new`. If you refer back to the SAX examples, you'll see that they need to be created using a factory class. Extracting the data from the document and building the tree is performed using the `parse` method of the `DOMParser` object. This method takes the name of the file, or a `File` object, as its argument.

Having parsed the XML document, its content is available through the `Document` interface. This interface represents the root node of the document tree, which is a sensible place to start traveling across the tree. The `Document` is created using the `getDocument` method of the `DOMParser`.

```
private void countDom() throws SAXException, IOException {
  DOMParser domp = new DOMParser();

  startTime = System.currentTimeMillis();
  domp.parse(srcFile);
  finishTime = System.currentTimeMillis();

  Document doco = domp.getDocument();
  this.count(doco);
  StringBuffer msg = new StringBuffer("Statistics for ");
  msg.append(srcFile);
  msg.append("\n============================\n");
  msg.append("Number of Document Nodes " + documentNd);
  msg.append("\nNumber of Element Nodes " + elementNd);
  msg.append("\nNumber of Attributes " + numAtts);
  msg.append("\nNumber of Text Nodes " + textNd);

  String timeTaken = Long.toString(finishTime - startTime);
  msg.append("\n\nProcessing took " + timeTaken + " ms");

  jTextPane1.setText(msg.toString());
} // countDom
```

Having created a `Document` object, it is passed to the methods that perform the specific processing for the particular application. In this small program, the method that does this is called count. Notice that it receives a Document object as an argument, but its parameter list specifies a Node object.

```
private void count(Node nd) {
  NodeList offspring;

  if(nd == null)
    return;
  int type = nd.getNodeType();

  switch(type) {
   case Node.DOCUMENT_NODE:
     documentNd++;
     offspring = nd.getChildNodes();
     for(int i = 0; i < offspring.getLength(); i++)
       count(offspring.item(i));
     break;

   case Node.ELEMENT_NODE:
     elementNd++;
     NamedNodeMap atts = nd.getAttributes();
     if(atts.getLength() > 0)
         numAtts = atts.getLength();

     offspring = nd.getChildNodes();
     for(int i = 0; i < offspring.getLength(); i++)
       count(offspring.item(i));
     break;

   case Node.TEXT_NODE:
     textNd++;
     break;
  } // switch

} // count
```

The processing here is a simple switch statement in which the next piece of processing is chosen through the type of the node. This code sample is very primitive since it only handles three different types. If the node is of a type that *may* have children, the program iterates across the list of children and recursively calls the count method with the child node as parameter. If the node is an element, its attributes are extracted into a `NamedNodeMap`, and the number of attributes stored in a global variable.

12.4 USING THE DOM TO DISPLAY A DOCUMENT

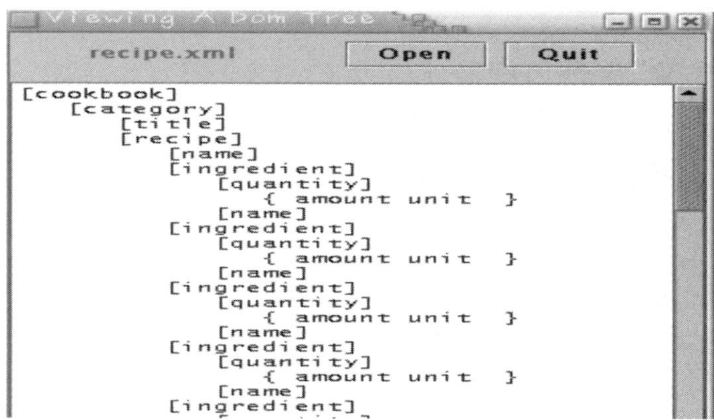

Figure 12.2 Displaying a DOM Tree

Using the DOM to count the elements in the tree isn't an especially effective use of resources. Being honest, it's a complete and utter waste of resources. A much better use of the DOM is shown in this section. This example moves across the DOM tree and displays each node in square brackets and each attribute in curly brackets. The tree is neatly indented so that its structure is clearly visible.

This code uses the same set of the packages as the previous example, and is controlled by the same code.

```
import org.xml.sax.*;
import org.w3c.dom.*;
import org.apache.xerces.parsers.DOMParser;

private void printDom() throws SAXException, IOException {
  DOMParser domp = new DOMParser();
  domp.parse(srcFile);
  Document doco = domp.getDocument();
  this.print(doco);

} // printDom
```

The big changes occur in the method that moves across the tree. I've renamed it as print so that its function is obvious.

```
private void print(Node nd) {
  StringBuffer sb = new StringBuffer();
  NodeList offspring;

  if(nd == null)
    return;
  int type = nd.getNodeType();
  switch(type) {
    case Node.DOCUMENT_NODE:
      offspring = nd.getChildNodes();
      for(int i = 0; i < offspring.getLength(); i++)
        print(offspring.item(i));
      break;

    case Node.ELEMENT_NODE:
      for(int j = 0; j < indent; j++)
        sb.append(spacer);
      indent++;
      displayNode(sb.toString() + "[" + nd.getNodeName()+ "]");
      NamedNodeMap atts = nd.getAttributes();
      if(atts.getLength() > 0) {
        StringBuffer at = new StringBuffer(sb.toString() + " { "
            );
        for(int j = 0; j < atts.getLength(); j++) {
          at.append( ((Attr)atts.item(j)).getNodeName() );
          at.append(" ");
        }
        at.append(" }");
        displayNode(at.toString());
      }
      offspring = nd.getChildNodes();
      for(int i = 0; i < offspring.getLength(); i++)
        print(offspring.item(i));
      break;

    case Node.TEXT_NODE:
```

```
        break;
    } // switch

    if(type == Node.ELEMENT_NODE)
      indent--;
} // print
```

The changes should be obvious. The class that contains all of this code has an integer variable called `indent`. It is used to output blank spaces; three are displayed for each increment of `indent`. The names of element nodes are extracted using the `getNodeName` method of the `Node` class. Attributes are, once again, extracted into a `NamedNodeMap`. The program iterates across this and extracts each attribute in turn. The attributes come out of the data structure as `Nodes` and have to be cast to the `Attr` node type before their name can be accessed.

Exercises

1. What is a document object model?
2. Describe three advantages which using the DOM has over writing your own custom document handler.
3. When is the DOM a better API than SAX?
4. What performance and system constraints might force the use of SAX rather than DOM?
5. Make a list of DOM-aware processors and libraries which are available for your favorite programming language. Give one positive and one negative point about each of them.
6. Write a Java application which lets the user select a recipe, and which then displays the ingredients and quantities it requires. Use a DOM library.

Chapter 13

The Simple API for XML

The Document Object Model, DOM, is a well-established description of an abstract document. It has all the authority of a W3C Recommendation which means it was created with both the support and direct involvement of many major companies in the Web sphere. The DOM is an extremely important concept which has a great many applications on the Web, in XML processing and elsewhere. In common with many standards documents, though, the DOM shows its heritage. It was clearly designed by a committee which, one assumes, had to make many compromises during that design process.

The DOM expresses a document as a tree which is held in memory. Any processing on the document means that the tree has to be traversed and, often, subtrees need to be extracted for further work. This model is one that is clearly familiar from the XML we have examined so far. Selecting and manipulating subtrees is performed using XPath, XLink and XPointer. These complex tools are used within XSL stylesheets as part of the transformation process and are well understood by experienced XML developers. That's fine because trees are familiar to all software developers and the concept is not a difficult one even for non-specialists. Trees present two big problems which prevent them being the ideal data structure in every circumstance.

The first problem with a tree is that of size. The infrastructure required to build and store a tree in memory means that any tree will be significantly larger than the total size of the raw data it holds. If your XML files are a few kilobytes, or even a few tens of megabytes, the size of tree required to hold them may not be an issue. A modern PC or server usually has RAM to spare and can process many XML trees, holding them all in memory without having to resort to using swap space. If your documents are business letters or small databases of recipes, the DOM provides a simple and intuitive API for your projects. Industrial-strength applications which are handling hundreds of megabytes of data cannot possibly use the DOM and be executed efficiently.

The second problem is efficiency, or to be more exact, speed. Developers and users are always hunting for more speed. Near-instant response from an application is never fast enough. The fact that the computer is lying idle most of the time while the user stares out of the window wondering what to do next[1] doesn't matter. When data has to be processed, the results must be available *right now*. Networked applications suffer from a magnified version of this effect. Although most users will tolerate some delays loading data across a network, they are not prepared to wait while that data is processed and presented to them once it has arrived.

Alternatives to the DOM are clearly needed in some circumstances. This is why SAX was developed. SAX, the Simple API for XML, was created by Dave Megginson and his fellow subscribers to an email list called XML-DEV.[2] SAX is now in version two, which is supported by the majority of implementations and is the version I am going to discuss. Whenever I use the term SAX in this chapter I shall be referring to SAX version 2. It's important to note that SAX is neither an official standard nor a Recommendation of the W3C. It has, though, become a *de facto* standard since so many XML products support it. SAX is so unofficial that there isn't even a standards document that specifies what it does. Instead SAX, which was developed specifically for Java, is specified through its Java API. There is no need to worry about SAX being a Java-only API, as it has been implemented in many programming languages. The structure of the API and the way that it operates are the same in C++, Python, Java or any other language.

The popularity of SAX stems from the way in which it works. It is fast, requires relatively little memory and can be used to process any size of document. This is made possible because, unlike the DOM, SAX doesn't build an in-memory representation of the data set. It performs its processing in response to *events*.

[1] It's not just me doing this, is it?

[2] XML-DEV can be found at `http://www.xml.org.xml-dev`.

13.0.1 Event-Driven Processing

Applications can process data in many different ways. One common approach is to create a data structure which the program then moves across from one data item to the next. Each item is checked against one or more criteria and processing is performed if they are satisfied. Historically this is probably the commonest type of application. A second approach is exemplified by languages such as SQL and XSLT. Using these *declarative* languages, programmers specify the result that they want but not how to achieve it. Instead the program manipulates the data in whatever ways it needs to in order to achieve the desired result.

Event-driven programming presents a third paradigm. This type of program only processes data in response to events. It's the model used by SAX, but will be familiar to you because it is used by graphical user interfaces, GUIs. A typical GUI, such as the interface for Microsoft Windows, runs in a loop. Applications are made from myriad *widgets* such as menus and buttons. Each time that a user manipulates one of these widgets or presses a key or moves the mouse, an event is generated. The application searches through its code looking for an event handler. Event handlers are methods which are assigned to particular events. When the event is *raised*, the code inside the handler method is executed. If a handler hasn't been written for an event, that event is ignored.

Event handling is efficient because although the program performs a series of tasks, it only has to manage the data for one task at a time. You are probably wondering how this idea can be applied to parsing an XML document. XML documents are composed of different types of node: elements, attributes, text, CDATA sections, processing instructions etc. In a SAX-based program an event handler is written for each node type, rather, for those nodes that the program needs to handle. The XML document is then passed through the parser. Each time the parser finds a node it searches for an appropriate handler. If a handler is found, the node is passed to it for processing. If there isn't a handler, the parser moves along to the next node. Event-driven processing like this is especially useful when data is being streamed over a network, or when only some nodes are interesting.

13.1 THE SAX API

The SAX API is divided into three Java packages. This section contains descriptions of two of those packages. The third, `org.xml.sax.ext`, is for extension functions which I'm not going to examine. The API altered slightly between versions 1 and 2; this description concentrates on version 2.

SAX is event-driven and makes the nodes of the document available through callbacks. Each component of an XML document triggers a different event. The parser finds a method within the implementation that can handle the event. Those methods must have the same *signature* as the ones given here. Method names and parameters have to be given in the exact form that the API specifies. If this is not done, the events will still occur but a handler will not be found and the application will ignore the event.

13.1.1 org.xml.sax

This package contains a number of interfaces and classes which handle different parts of the document.

Interfaces

`Attributes`

This class manages a list of attributes. Attributes can be accessed by their index,[3] by their fully namespace-qualified name or by a prefixed name. Any attributes specified as being `#IMPLIED` are omitted from the list.

The following methods are available:

`int getIndex(String qName)`
returns the index of a node which is identified through its locally qualified name.

`int getIndex(String uri, String localPart)`
returns the index of an attribute which is identified by its namespace qualified name.

`int getLength`
returns the number of attributes in the list.

`String getLocalName(int index)`
returns the local name of an attribute which is identified by its index.

`String getQName(int index)`
returns the qualified name of an attribute which is identified by its index.

`String getType(int index)`
returns the type of an attribute. The index can be replaced by the local name or fully qualified name by changing the parameter type to match those of the appropriate `getIndex` method.

`String getValue(int index)`
returns the value of the attribute. The index can be replaced by the local name

[3] Location within the list.

or fully qualified name by changing the parameter type to match those of the appropriate `getIndex` method.

`ContentHandler`

is the main class in the package. It is used to receive events which are triggered by the structure of the XML document. If this class is being implemented by an application, an instance of it must be registered with the parser so that the parser knows where to pass structural events. The registration is done using the `setContentHandler` method of the XMLReader class. It's worth noting that the `ContentHandler` class is namespace aware.

The following methods are available:

`void characters(char[] ch, int start, int length)`
handles character nodes.

`void endDocument()`
handles the end of the document.

`void endElement(String namespaceURI, String localName, String qName)`
handles tags that close elements.

`void ignorableWhitespace(char[] ch, int start, int length)`
handles ignorable whitespace in the *content* of a node.

`void processingInstruction(String target, String data)`
handles processing instruction nodes.

`void startDocument()`
handles the start of a document.

`void startElement(String namespaceURI, String localName, String qName, Attributes atts)`
handles the start of an element.

`DTDHandler`

Applications that need to handle events relating to unparsed entities or notations subclass this interface. The only events handled are those that the XML Recommendation requires of parsers. Those events relate to entities of the type `NOTATION`, `ENTITY` and `ENTITIES`.

The following methods are available:

`void notationDecl(String name, String publicId, String systemId)`
handles events triggered by notations.

`void unparsedEntityDecl(String name, String publicId, String systemId, String notationName)`
handles events triggered by unparsed entities.

EntityResolver

This interface must be implemented in those applications which need to resolve external entities. Since relatively few applications actually need to do this, don't worry too much about it. Read the API documentation if you ever actually need to implement this one.

ErrorHandler

Applications that need to customize the way they handle errors should implement this interface. Although this interface is not required, if it is not implemented the behavior of the application may be unpredictable.

The following methods are available:

void error(SAXParseException exception)
receives errors from the parser.

void fatalError(SAXParseException exception)
receives fatal errors from the parser. The application will not be able to recover from these errors.

void warning(SAXParseException exception)
receives warnings from the parser.

Locator

This interface is implemented by application, that want to know where in the document the parser currently is. Since parsers are not required to implement this functionality, I'm going to skip by it.

XMLFilter

An instance of this interface receives events from `XMLReader` objects rather than from a document. An `XMLFilter` is used to preprocess events before they are passed on to other objects.

The following methods are available:

XMLReader getParent()
returns a reference to the `XMLReader` object that is actually performing the parsing.

void setParent(XMLReader parent)
sets up a reference to the parsing object.

XMLReader

All SAX2-compliant parsers must implement this interface. It is used to configure the parser, register event handlers with it and start the parsing process. The application cannot perform other processing until the `parse` method of the `XMLReader` implementation returns, and new events are not raised until the preceding one has been fully processed. The `XMLReader` class is namespace aware.

The following methods are available:

`ContentHandler getContentHandler()`
: returns a reference to the `ContentHandler` that has been registered with the parser for the current document.

`DTDHandler getDTDHandler()`
: returns the registered `DTDHandler`.

`ErrorHandler getErrorHandler()`
: returns the registered `ErrorHandler`.

`void parse(InputSource input)`
: tells the parser to parse the document identified by an `InputSource` object.

`void parse(String URI)`
: tells the parser to parse the document identified by the URI.

`void setContentHandler(ContentHandler handler)`
: is used to register a handler for document content with the parser.

`void setEntityResolver(EntityResolver resolver)`
: is used to register an object that will be used to resolve entities.

`void setErrorHandler(ErrorHandler handler)`
: is used to register a handler for parser errors.

Other methods are available which can be used to set properties and features of the parser, and to query it about its features and properties. Since the features and properties that can be set are specific to individual parsers I'm not going to look at them.

13.1.1.1 Classes Class interfaces define the structure, the signature, of the class. Its methods are defined through their names, the parameters that they will accept and any data types that they will return. The methods defined within Java interfaces do not contain any implementation code. Classes, on the other hand, contain full implementations of their methods. When a class is inherited, some, or all, of its methods can be overridden through new implementations.

`InputSource`
: This class is used to wrap information about the input document which is being

passed to the parser. This information includes public identifier, system identifier, byte stream or character stream. An object of this class may be passed as an argument to the parse method. The parser uses the information contained within the object to decide how to handle the input.

The class has four different constructors:

```
InputSource()
InputSource(java.io.InputStream byteStream)
InputSource(java.io.Reader characterStream)
InputSource(String systemId)
```

The following methods are available:

```
java.io.InputStream getByteStream()
java.io.Reader getCharacterStream()
String getEncoding()
String getPublicId()
String getSystemId()
void setByteStream(java.io.InputStream byteStream)
void setCharacterStream(java.io.Reader characterStream)
void setEncoding(String encoding)
void setPublicId(String URI)
void setSystemId(String URI)
```

13.1.1.2 Exceptions The SAX API defines these exceptions which applications must handle:

`SAXException`
: Contains the most basic errors and warnings from the parser. Such exceptions include any thrown to the parser from other classes. These must be wrapped within a `SAXException` and made available to the calling class or its designated handler.

`SAXNotRecognizedException`
: This is thrown if an application tries to set a feature or property of the parser that is invalid in some way.

`SAXNotSupportedException`
: Thrown if the parser recognizes a feature or property that an application is trying to set, but is unable to perform the operation.

`SAXParseException`
: If the parser finds an error in the XML source document, it throws this exception.

The controlling application does not have to throw this exception onwards, but can choose to take action based upon the content of the exception.

13.1.2 org.xml.sax.helpers

Helper classes provide functionality that applications need but the base classes don't provide. For example, if the base class is an interface, it cannot be directly instantiated. Instead a factory class is used to create an object. One good example of this process is the `XMLReader` interface which encapsulates the functionality needed to talk to the SAX parser. An `XMLReader` object cannot be directly created; instead an identifier for the parser implementation is passed to a factory which creates an `XMLReader` object.

`AttributesImpl`

This class provides a default implementation of the `Attributes` interface. It can be used to take a more permanent representation of the attributes found within a `startElement` event, or to build a list of attributes which can then be added to an element.

The following methods are provided in addition to those found in the `Attributes` interface. These are use to manipulate the list of attributes that an object of this class holds.

`void addAttribute(String uri, String localName, String qName, String type, String value)`
adds an attribute to the end of the list.

`void clear()`
is used to empty the list.

`int getIndex(String qName)`
`int getIndex(String uri, String localName)`
these are used to find the index of an attribute within the list.

`int getLength()`
returns the number of attributes in the list.

`String getLocalName(int index)`
returns the local name of an attribute.

`String getQName(int index)`
returns the fully qualified name of an attribute.

`String getType(int index)`
`String getType(String qName)`
`String getType(String uri, String localName)`
return the type of the attribute.

String getURI(int index)
returns the namespace of an attribute.

String getValue(int index)

String getValue(String qName)

String getValue(String uri, String localName)
return the value of an attribute.

void removeAttribute(int index)
deletes an attribute from the list.

void setAttribute(int index, String uri, String localName, String qName, String type, String value)
sets the value of an attribute.

void setLocalName(int index, String localName)
sets the local name of an attribute.

void setQName(int index, String localName)

void setType(int index, String type)

void setURI(int index, String uri)

void setValue(int index, String value)
set the properties of an attribute.

DefaultHandler

This class provides a default event handler. It can be used instead of the four event handling classes:

- EntityResolver
- DTDHandler
- ContentHandler
- ErrorHandler

It implements the same methods as those four interfaces. Look back at the descriptions of ContentHandler and ErrorHandler to see what those methods are.

XMLReaderFactory

This is a factory which is used to create an XMLReader. It contains a single method:

static XMLReader createXMLReader()

static XMLReader createXMLReader(String className)
The second version of the method takes the name of a class which contains a parser as its argument. Clearly when working with Java it is important that the class is available on the system CLASSPATH if it's going to be loaded and used.

13.2 A SAX EXAMPLE

SAX presents a standard but complicated API. Using it in programs is difficult without seeing examples because of the problem of choosing the *right* class and the *best* method. Often, of course, there is no right class or best method, and what's important is choosing those components that you understand and can use successfully.

All of the Java implementations of SAX that I've seen come with API documentation in HTML format, and a few sample programs. In the rest of this chapter I'm going to present my interpretation of a typical SAX exemplar. The application I present here has almost no practical use, but it does rather neatly demonstrate how to handle event using SAX. I'm going to read through the code for the XML Recipe Book and count the number of elements, attributes, characters and the amount of ignorable whitespace in the document. I'll do this in two ways, using different parsers from the Apache project: firstly, Xerces 1.2.2, as supplied with Borland JBuilder 5 Professional, and secondly, Crimson 1.1.3 downloaded from the Apache Web site. I'm also going to time how long each parser takes to process the document and display the results in a little GUI.

13.2.1 Using Xerces

This sample application reads through the XML document, counts some of its properties and displays the results in a GUI. The output it produces is shown in Figure 13.1. The GUI was developed in JBuilder 5 using its form designer. I've removed those parts of the code that created it since leaving them in might be confusing.

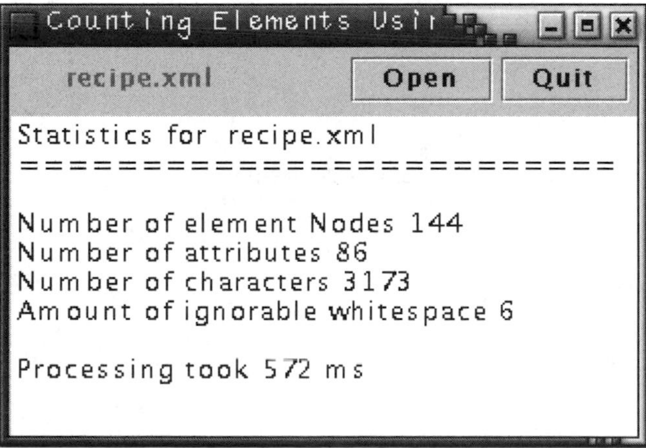

Figure 13.1 Processing Using Xerces

The GUI code was placed in a class called `SaxFrame`. When the `Open` button is selected a standard file selection dialog opens. The name of the source file is passed to another class for parsing. The complete code for this application is available from the supporting Web site.

All Java applications start by importing necessary packages. I've removed from the list all those needed by the GUI, or those such as `java.io` which most applications need to import. If you're familiar with Java, you'll know what's required. If you're a Java novice, the code will be confusing enough without them. Notice that the code for this application is in a package structure. Using packages for your Java applications keeps them tidy since it enforces a sensible directory structure.[4]

```
package sax;

import org.xml.sax.XMLReader;
import org.xml.sax.Attributes;
import org.xml.sax.SAXException;
import org.xml.sax.SAXParseException;
import org.xml.sax.helpers.DefaultHandler;
import org.xml.sax.helpers.XMLReaderFactory;
```

The `org.xml.sax` package contains a number of interfaces. These are Java classes whose publicly available methods are specified but not implemented. Applications that use the interface must implement those methods they require. The interface mechanism is used because Java doesn't support multiple inheritance. Look back at Section 13.1 if you want to know about the functionality of the classes I'm using.

```
class Counter extends DefaultHandler {
  private String srcFile;
  private int elements, attributes, characters,
     ignorableWhitespace;
  private long startTime, finishTime;


  Counter(String src) {
    super();
    srcFile = src;
  }
```

[4] It's also the default mode of operation for many IDEs.

The class that will count the nodes in the document is called `Counter`. It is a subclass of `DefaultHandler`. This provides implementations of methods which are called as the parser generates events in response to the content of the XML document. The methods in `org.xml.sax.helpers.DefaultHandler` do nothing by default. Application developers must override them if their applications are going to respond usefully to events.

The private class variables in the `Counter` class are mostly integers which are used to count items in the file, and two long integers which will hold the times that processing starts and finishes. The name of the file that is to be processed is passed into the constructor as a parameter. Once the GUI has successfully called the constructor for the `Counter` class, it calls the `processSax` method to actually parse the document.

```
public String processSax() {
  String msg;

  try {
    XMLReader parser = XMLReaderFactory.createXMLReader(
           "org.apache.xerces.parsers.SAXParser");
    parser.setContentHandler(this);
    parser.setErrorHandler(this);

    startTime = System.currentTimeMillis();
    parser.parse(srcFile);
    finishTime = System.currentTimeMillis();
    msg = makeMsg();

   } catch (SAXParseException spe) {
     msg = spe.toString();
   } catch (SAXException se) {
     msg = se.toString();
   } catch (Exception e) {
     msg = e.toString();
   }

  return msg;

} // processSax
```

The `processSax` method attempts to parse the XML document. If it succeeds it builds a message which it returns to the calling `SaxFrame` class for it to display. If an exception is raised during parsing, *it* is returned for display.

The first thing to do, before the document can be parsed, is to create a parser and tell it that the `Counter` class is going to handle some of the events it generates. The parser is an instance of the `XMLReader` class but it isn't created directly through the use of a constructor. Instead, an `XMLReaderFactory`, based on the popular *factory* design pattern, is used. Many parsers may be present on a system, and the `XMLReaderFactory` is able to use any of them in an application. The parser is chosen either by giving its class name as a parameter string to the factory's `createXMLReader()` method, or by setting an environment variable called `org.xml.sax.driver`. The factory will dynamically instantiate the parser class at runtime. In my code, I am using `org.apache.xerces.parsers.SAXParser` which is supplied as part of the Xerces download.

Once the parser has been created, the `Counter` class is registered with it to accept content events and error events. If the parser doesn't have a handler for an event type, it simply throws those events away. Parsing of the document is performed by calling the `parse()` method of the XMLReader instance.

In this sample program, the event handlers are exceptionally straightforward, since all that they do is increment some class variables.

> **Note:**
> The signatures of the event handlers in the following code fragments are important. Their methods are defined in `org.xml.sax.helpers.DefaultHandler` which is being extended by the implementation.

```
public void startDocument() {
    elements         = 0;
    attributes       = 0;
    characters       = 0;
    ignorableWhitespace = 0;
}

public void startElement(String uri, String local, String raw,
                         Attributes attrs) {
    elements++;
    if (attrs != null)
        attributes += attrs.getLength();
}

public void characters(char ch[], int start, int length) {
    characters += length;
```

```
    }

    public void ignorableWhitespace(char ch[], int start,
                                    int length) {
       ignorableWhitespace += length;
    }
```

The final method in the class builds a message string and returns it so that it can be displayed by the GUI.

```
    public String makeMsg() {
      StringBuffer msg = new StringBuffer("Statistics for ");
      msg.append(srcFile);
      msg.append("\n========================\n");
      msg.append("\nNumber of element Nodes " + elements);
      msg.append("\nNumber of attributes " + attributes);
      msg.append("\nNumber of characters " + characters);
      msg.append("\nAmount of ignorable whitespace " +
          ignorableWhitespace);

      String timeTaken = Long.toString(finishTime - startTime);
      msg.append("\n\nProcessing took " + timeTaken + " ms");

      return msg.toString();

    } // makeMsg

} // class Counter
```

13.2.2 Using Crimson

SAX defines a standard API which you might expect means that changing the parser used by an application is simply a matter of plugging a different one in. Experience of using computer systems will tell you that life is never *quite* that simple. Fortunately, changing SAX parsers is relatively painless. To demonstrate just how it works I've altered the code from the previous section so that instead of using the Xerces toolkit, I'm going to use Crimson. The proof that it really works can be seen in Figure 13.2. Notice the different values for the amount of whitespace and the number of characters compared to the implementation using Xerces. The total number of characters processed is the same with both processors but they classify some of them differently.

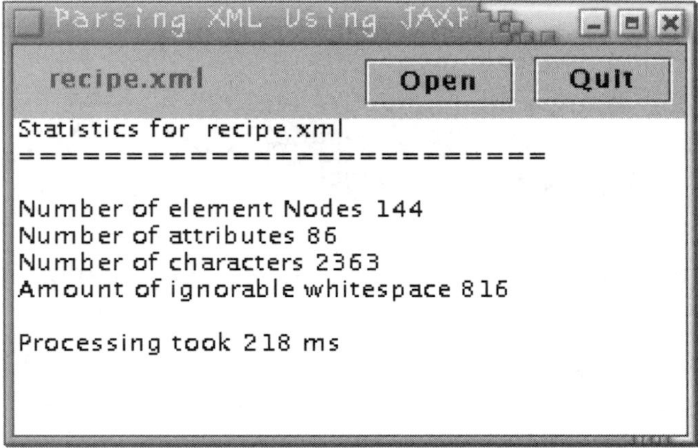

Figure 13.2 Processing Using Crimson

The first thing to change is the list of packages and classes which are being imported into the program. Although the generic parts of the SAX API remain in a package called `org.xml.sax`, other packages are implementation specific.

Listing 13.1 Package Imports Required to Use Crimson

```
import org.xml.sax.*;
import org.xml.sax.helpers.DefaultHandler;
import javax.xml.parsers.SAXParser;
import javax.xml.parsers.SAXParserFactory;
import javax.xml.parsers.ParserConfigurationException;
```

That's actually the bulk of the work achieved. The remaining changes are in the code which instantiates the parser. The documentation for Crimson includes an `XMLReaderFactory` class, that ought to mean that no changes need to be made to the code. When I tried to use that factory I got a slew of runtime exceptions. The following code fragment works with both Crimson and Xerces 2.0.1.

Listing 13.2 Code Changes Required to Use Crimson

```
public String processSax(String src) {
  String msg;

  try {
    SAXParserFactory factory = SAXParserFactory.newInstance();
    XMLReader parser = null;
    SAXParser saxParser = factory.newSAXParser();
    parser = saxParser.getXMLReader();
```

```
parser.setContentHandler(this);
parser.setErrorHandler(this);
```

The approach here is to use a `SAXParserFactory` to create a `SAXParser` then use that to create an `XMLReader`. The problems that I've had with interchanging packages and parsers might be due to the way that my system is configured or with the particular libraries I've been using. Fortunately, few alterations were needed to the code to get it working. All of the event handling code works in both applications without being changed. In the end most of the code can be transferred directly between applications which saves a lot of work.

Exercises

1. What is meant by the term *event-driven processing*?
2. Why is event-driven processing particularly suitable for the handling of XML documents?
3. Where, and when did SAX originate?
4. Describe the role of a ContentHandler in SAX applications.
5. What is meant by the term *exception*, in a SAX application?
6. Describe the exceptions which SAX processors may create.
7. Write a Java application which lets the user select a recipe, and which then displays the ingredients and quantities it requires. Use a SAX library.

Part Four

Some Real-World Applications of XML

Chapter 14

Introducing XHTML

The World Wide Web has changed the world more than anyone could possibly have imagined ten years ago. We now live with technology that gives access to volumes of knowledge and data that have reached ridiculous proportions. The vast majority of that data is structured using HTML. HTML is a markup language, just like applications of XML are, and shares a common parentage with XML. HTML was developed as a very simple subset of SGML, with additional features added so that pages could link to each other and to non-HTML data sources such as image files, scripts or stylesheets.

Most people who author HTML by hand make a terrible mess of it. Their code is unstructured, badly arranged, often incomplete and sometimes just plain wrong. Using HTML editing tools often produces code that is not much better. Tools such as Dreamweaver let authors decide exactly how their pages will look. To create exact layouts these tools may litter source files with empty tables, line breaks and incomplete paragraphs. Web browsers are incredibly flexible pieces of software. They take all of the garbage code thrown at them and attempt to create meaningful Web pages from it. If you don't believe me, try saving the following code fragment in a file called `test.html` and opening it in your favorite Web browser.

```
<p>This isn't an HTML file
```

Although there is a well-defined structure for HTML files, that code was rendered as if it were a proper Web page. That happens despite its having *none* of the standard structure. If Web browsers were as rigorous[1] as XML validators, large areas of the Web would suddenly stop working. It's quite likely that future generations of Web browsing software will be much more rigorous. The Web is moving from being simply an application of desktop PCs. Games consoles, handheld computers and mobile phones are all becoming multi-purpose devices which can be used to surf the Web. These devices may not have enough spare processing power to display broken HTML.

To address these and other concerns, W3C has reformulated HTML as an XHTML application. XHTML doesn't add anything new to HTML; there are no new elements to learn about, and elements do not do anything that they didn't do before. Documents which are valid XHTML must be more tightly authored, with elements nested correctly, attribute values quoted and cascading stylesheets used to give platform-independent styling. This new version is called XHTML.

One of the bonuses that developers get from using XML to structure data is that elements can be given real meaning. In HTML this has never applied. Elements such as `<h1>` or `<h5>` may be used to indicate levels of heading in a document, but they don't have to be used in that way. Web browsers apply built-in styles to those elements so that fonts and colors indicate titles or sectional headings to a typical reader. If an author wants something that looks like a heading but isn't one, they're free to use one of the *heading* elements such as `<h3>`. If you were to search through an arbitrary HTML document trying to find all section headings, how would you do it? Typically you might use a utility such as `grep` or the search facility in a file manager to look for all instances of each of the heading elements. This might return all of the headings, then again it might not. Try the same thing on a document structured using an XML application such as DocBook, and you could guarantee that what came back was just heading elements.

What about XHTML then? Since it refactors HTML as proper XML, it must add meaning to elements. Well no, it doesn't. XHTML has to remain backward compatible with HTML. If elements had been altered drastically so that an `<h1>` element really was a title or a section heading, a fundamental change would have been made to the way that authors could work with the language. Instead, XHTML has altered HTML so that it can be processed by XML-compliant tools without them producing reams of error messages. It's now possible for Web developers to create XML-compliant documents which applications can process automatically, without having to re-learn their existing skills.

[1] I almost wrote *fussy* there.

I don't have space in this book to provide a complete how-to guide to writing Web pages. Plenty of those exist in dedicated textbooks and on myriad sites around the Web. I feel that it's likely that most readers of an XML textbook can already write at least some form of Web page, but that's not guaranteed. To help those who might want to write Web pages of their own I'm going to provide a brief primer which introduces the more basic and common XHTML elements and gives a couple of examples of how they are used.

14.1 XHTML DOCUMENT TYPE DEFINITIONS

We know by now that XML documents usually have Document Type Definitions or schemas, and XHTML pages are no exception. These DTDs are used by validating parsers to check that the markup has been used correctly. DTDs are available for versions of HTML but have rarely been used by authors. Some of the HTML editing tools automatically include an appropriate DTD in the document but few authors pay much attention to its presence. If you want to provide some future-proofing then your XHTML documents have to specify a DTD.

All XHTML document type declarations take the same format. The following code can be placed on a single line in your documents, if you prefer.

```
<!DOCTYPE html
   PUBLIC "-//W3C//DTD XHTML 1.0 Transitional//EN"
   "DTD/xhtml1-transitional.dtd">
```

Notice that the `html` element, the document root, is specified in lower case. HTML was not case-sensitive, XHTML *is*. All element and attribute names must be in lower-case text. There are three different DTDs to choose from. Replace `transitional` from the example with the one you want to use:

- `transitional` should be used in pages that include some presentational markup such as `<font>` tags. These documents will be accessible to browsers that don't understand stylesheets, for instance.

- `strict` is used when you want your document to be fully compliant with the standard. All presentational control is done through the use of cascading stylesheets.

- `frameset` lets you partition the screen into a number of separate frames.

14.2 AN XHTML PRIMER

All HTML documents follow the same basic structure. They have a head which contains control information used by the browser and server and a large body. The body contains the content that displays on the screen and tags that control how that content is formatted by the browser. The basic document is shown in Listing 14.1. The result of opening that file in a Web browser is shown in Figure 14.1.

Listing 14.1 A Minimal XHTML Document

```
<?xml version="1.0"?>
<!DOCTYPE html
  PUBLIC "-//W3C//DTD XHTML 1.0 Transitional//EN"
  "DTD/xhtml1-transitional.dtd">

<html xmlns="http://www.w3c.org/1999/xhtml"
  xml:lang="en" lang="en">
    <head>
      <title>A Minimal XHTML document</title>
    </head>

    <body>
      <h1>The Largest Heading</h1>
      <p>A sample paragraph showing formatting and
      followed by a line across the screen.</p>
      <hr/>
    </body>
  </html>
```

Despite its simplicity, this document needs a little explaining for novices. The entire document is surrounded by<html>...</html> which tell the software that it is now processing HTML. Most Web browsers can display a number of types of content. At the very least they are able to display plain text and HTML. If the page were not enclosed in html tags the page might be displayed as plain text with both content and formatting information on display.

XHTML document must have both a <head> element and a body element. The <head> is used to hold control information which affects how browsers, and other applications, process the document. It has to have a <title> element as a child even if it contains no other elements. The page content which will be displayed by the browser is placed inside the <body> element.

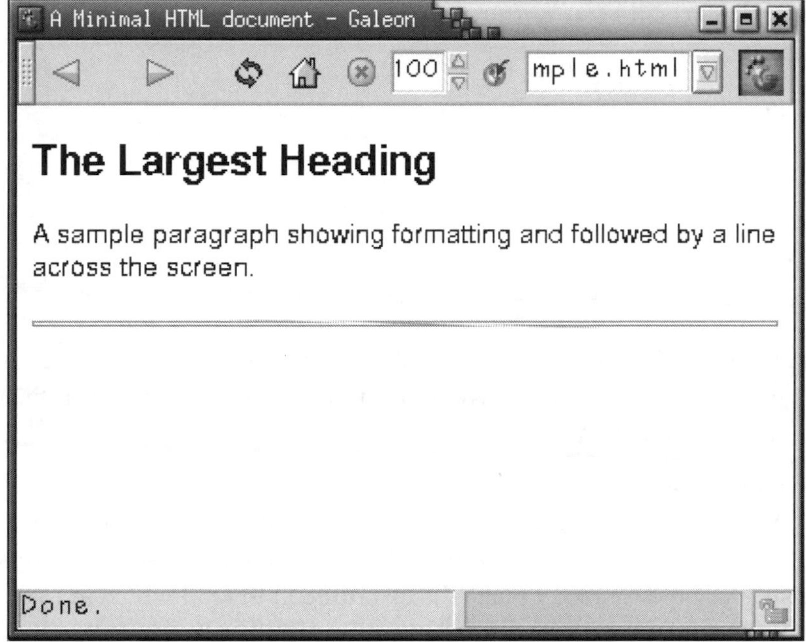

Figure 14.1 The Minimal Web Page

14.2.1 The Expanded HTML Element

The top-level node of an XHTML document *must* be an `<html>` node. In previous versions of HTML this tag was used to carry control information about formatting and events such as `onLoad`. It now holds information about the page itself.

```
<html xmlns="http://www.w3c.org/1999/xhtml"
   xml:lang="en" lang="en">
```

The `html` tag declares the namespace for the document through the `xmlns` attribute. The valid namespace for XHTML 1.0 is as shown above. The language of the document is also declared inside the `html` tag. The `xml:lang` attribute takes precedence over any other language declarations.

14.2.2 Text Formatting

Most text within Web pages is placed inside paragraphs. These are denoted using the `<p>` element. Text within paragraphs may be styled in a number of ways. Major alterations such as changes of font or color are usually taken care of by using CSS. Relatively minor changes such as italicization are performed with the following elements, which are placed inline within paragraphs.

```
<b>...</b>
<i>...</i>
<strong>...</strong>
<tt>...</tt>
<sub>...</sub>
<sup>...</sup>
```

> Altering the appearance of text can subtly change its meaning. If text is in a bold typeface then it is often read with added emphasis. When you are writing Web pages that present information you'll need to use standard typographical methods of changing the appearance of text.
>
> These should all be used with care as they can make the text unreadable. For instance you may want to emphasize something such as a warning or a special offer on a commercial site. The best way to do that is often by using color; using something such as bold font may make the text difficult to read which in turn may cause visitors to pass on, ignoring your message. On the other hand browsers on platforms such as mobile phones or PDAs, or browsers used by the disabled, may not be able to display your colors. These browsers depend upon the standard text formatting commands, as shown here, to change the way they display content.
>
> The bold and italic tags should be self-explanatory. The `<strong>` tag is used as a form of emphasis, usually rendered as a bold-faced font. The browser will choose an alternative if bold is not available. Therefore use `<b>` when you want a boldface and `<strong>` to ensure the text is always emphasized. The `<tt>` tag lets text be rendered using a monospaced font to simulate typewriter output which can be useful if you want to include program code, for instance, on a Web page. Finally `<sub>` renders text as a subscript, `<sup>` as superscript. These can be useful when rendering mathematics,[2] for instance, or symbols such as @ or ©.

The code in Listing 14.2, shown in a browser in Figure 14.2, demonstrates these elements.

Listing 14.2 Varying Font Styles

```
<html>
  <head>
    <title>Font Variations</title>
```

[2]Although browsers are now starting to provide support for the MathML maths markup language.

```
  </head>
  <body>
    <h1>Font Variations</h1>
    <p>We can use <b>simple</b> tags to <i>change</i> the
    appearance of <strong>text</strong> within <tt>Web
    pages</tt>. Even super<sup>script</sup> and sub<sub>
    scripts</sub> are <em>supported</em></p>
  </body>
</html>
```

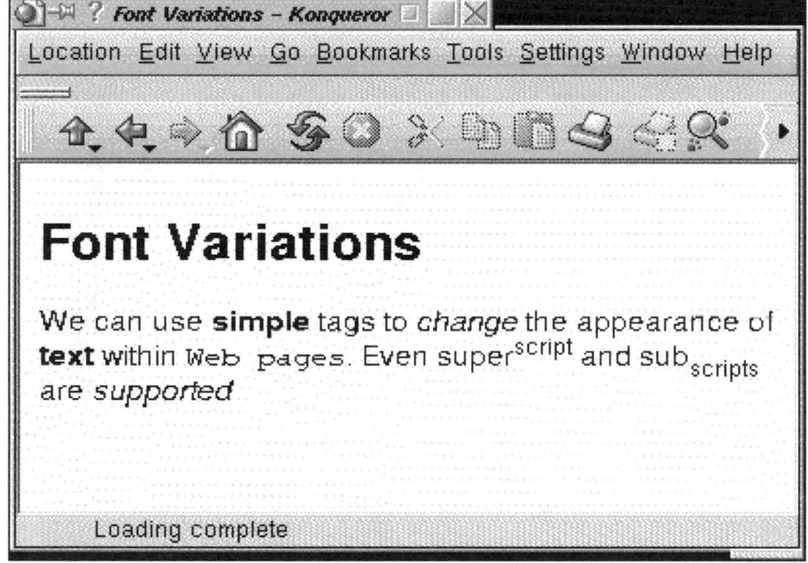

Figure 14.2 Font Variations

**
**

Forces a line break within a passage of text where a paragraph is not desirable. On complex pages it is sometimes useful to put a `<br/>` before and after tables, lists, or `<hr/>` as this simplifies rendering for the browser.

<pre>...</pre>

Sometimes you will want to include ready-formatted text on a Web page, for instance program code, recipes, or poetry. Inside a `<pre>` tag the text is only wrapped when the source has a line break and tabs or multiple whitespaces are not converted to a single space.

`& < > "   ©`

These are character escape sequences which are required if you want to display characters that HTML uses as control sequences. When HTML finds a character such as < in the text of a page, it treats it as an instruction. Therefore you cannot display such a character simply by using it in your page. Instead you must use one of the alternatives shown here. All of these replacement sequences start with an ampersand, `&`, and are terminated with a semicolon.

Although double quotes usually display normally, this behavior is not guaranteed, so it is safer to use `"` which always behaves correctly. If you want to force a whitespace where one would not be used by default you should use ` `. Figure 14.3 shows the effect of these sequences.

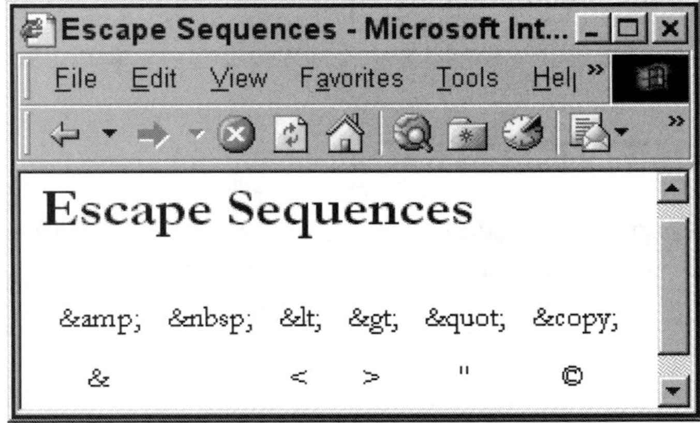

Figure 14.3 Escape Sequences

14.2.3 Hyperlinks

The power and flexibility of HTML comes from the simple method it uses to link documents together. A single tag is used for all types of links. Links should be used freely within documents where they either add to the understanding of the work or can be used to reduce download times. It is better to have many links to medium-sized documents containing about a screenful of information rather than forcing readers to download a single massive document. When structuring a Web site always consider that most users will be accessing your site via 56 Kbps modems rather than their own ISDN or T1 link. If a page takes a long time to download these users will go elsewhere for their information or business.

<a href="address">...</a>

The link tag has three sections: the address of the referenced document, a piece of text to display as the link, and the closing tag. The link text can be formatted using any of the text formatting options. Hypertext references, the `href` part of the tag, can be: links to documents or services at other Internet sites; links to documents within the same Web site; or links to a specific part of either the current page or another page. For example:

<a href="pagetwo.html">Next Page</a>

Links to another page in the same directory. The browser displays Next Page on the screen and highlights it so that readers know it is a hyperlink. Usually this highlighting takes the form of displaying the link in blue text and underlining it.

<a href="http://www.somesite.co.uk/index.html">Some Site</a>

Links to another Web site. This time Some Site is displayed and highlighted.

A sample hyperlink is shown in Figure 14.4.

Figure 14.4 Hyperlinks

14.2.4 Lists

One of the most effective ways of structuring a Web site or its contents is to use lists. Lists may be for something as simple as supplying a piece of information or for providing a straightforward index to the site, but could become highly complex. As an example, a commercial Web site may use pictures of its products instead of text in hyperlinks. These can be built as nested lists to provide an interesting graphical interface to the site.

HTML provides three types of list: the basic bulleted list, a numbered list, and a definition list. Each has a different use but generally the definition list is the most flexible of the three as it easily incorporates images and paragraphs of text while keeping an obvious structure.

<li>...</li>
: The ordered and unordered lists are each made up of sets of list items. Elements of a list may be formatted with any of the usual text formatting tags and may be images or hyperlinks.

<ul>...</ul>
: The basic unordered list has a bullet in front of each list item. Everything between the tags must be encapsulated within `<li>...</li>` tags.

<ol [start="n"]>...</ol>
: An ordered list has a number instead of a bullet in front of each list item. A list can number from any value that you desire: the starting value is given by the `start` attribute. As with the unordered list, all items in an ordered list must be enclosed within `<li>...</li>` tags.

<dl>...</dl>
: Definition lists are different to the previous types in that they do not use list items to contain their members. Elements within a definition list are either items being defined or their definitions.

<dt>...[</dt>]
: Definition terms mark items whose definition will be provided by the next data definition.

<dd>...[</dd>]
: Definitions of terms are enclosed within these tags. The definition can include any text or block formatting elements. The text of a definition is usually rendered indented and on the line below the preceding item.

Lists – a worked example The basic unordered list and the numbered list are fairly intuitive to anyone who has used a word processor. Almost everyone will, at some point, have created a list of items or the outline of an essay or report using them. What about the definition list, though? That's not quite so easy to understand. The following code shows all three lists in action; hopefully you'll see from its structure that the definition list is actually a very powerful construct with many applications.

Listing 14.3 Using Lists

```
<html>
  <head>
```

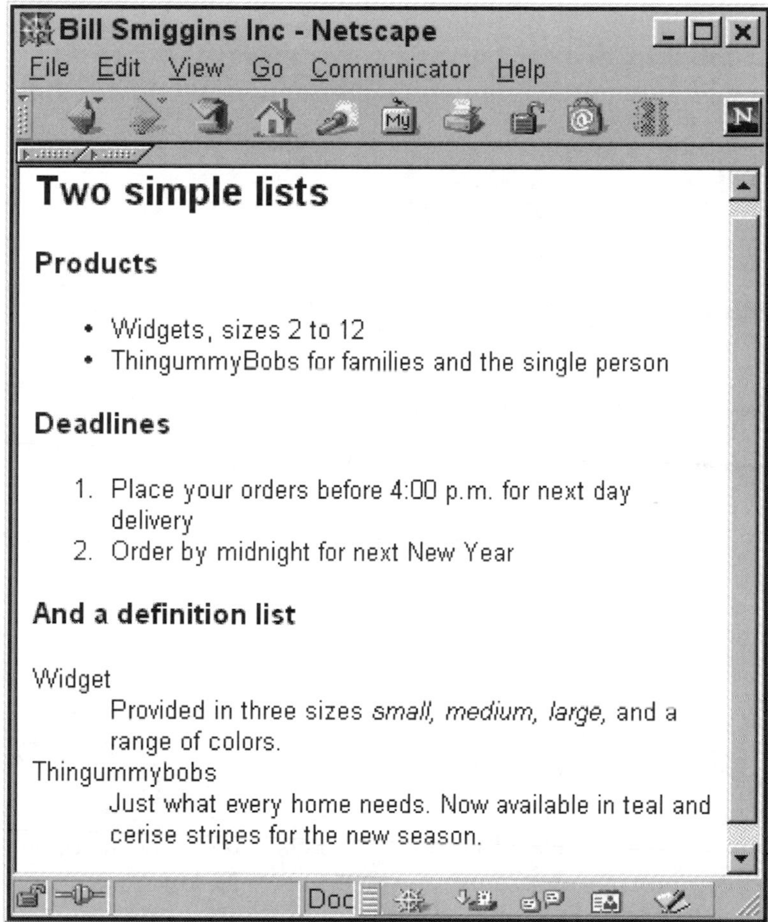

Figure 14.5 Lists

```
  <title>Bill Smiggins Inc</title>
</head>
<body>
<h2>Two simple lists</h2>

<h3>Products</h3>
<ul>
  <li>Widgets, sizes 2 to 12</li>
  <li>ThingummyBobs for families and the single
  person</li>
</ul>
```

```
  <h3>Deadlines</h3>
  <ol>
    <li>Place your orders before 4:00 p.m. for next
    day delivery</li>
    <li>Order by midnight for next New Year</li>
  </ol>

  <h3>And a definition list</h3>
  <dl>
    <dt>Widget</dt>
      <dd>Provided in three sizes <i>small, medium,
      large</i>, and a range of colors.</dd>
    <dt>Thingummybobs</dt>
      <dd>Just what every home needs. Now available in
      teal and cerise stripes for the new season.</dd>
  </dl>
  </body>
</html>
```

14.2.5 Tables

The table is one of the most useful HTML constructs. You'll find tables all over the Internet. Often you don't even know that the page you're looking at is awash with tables; instead it just appears to be a very well-structured site.

The only consideration that you must think about is processing – some browsers may struggle to process complex tables. Web browsers have a *layout engine* which arranges the pieces before the Web page is displayed. Where the page is difficult to lay out there will be a noticeable delay before your content appears. This problem is made worse by the use of images within tables, especially where the size attributes of the image have not been set.

Figure 14.6 shows how simple a table can be. The code that created it is pretty simple too:

Listing 14.4 A Simple Table

```
<html>
  <head>
    <title>A Simple Table</title>
  </head>
```

```
  <body>
    <h2>A Simple Table</h2>
    <table border="1">
    <tr>
      <th>Left Column</th>
      <th>Right Column</th>
    </tr>
    <tr>
      <td>A little bit of data</td>
      <td>Rather more data in this cell which will
      wrap around...</td>
    </tr>
    </table>
  </body>
</html>
```

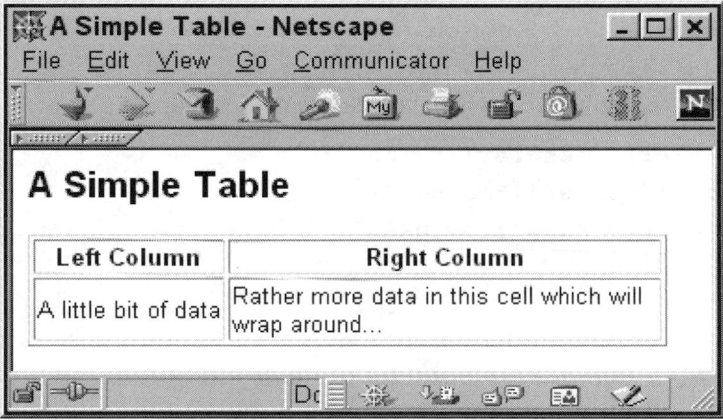

Figure 14.6 A Simple Table

<table [align="center"|"left"|"right"] [border[="n"]] [cellpadding="n"] [width="nn%"] [cellspacing="n"]> ...</table>

Everything between these two tags will be part of the table. These attributes control the formatting of the table as a whole, not that of the items in each cell. Tables can be aligned on the screen like most other items; usually they are centered for impact and clarity. A table can have a border, which includes a border between the cells. If the `border` attribute is not set the table has no border. When the `border` attribute is set but a valid value is not given, a single pixel-wide default border is drawn. For wider borders you must give a positive integer value.

`Cellpadding`, in pixels, determines how much space there is between the contents of a cell and its border; `cellspacing` sets the amount of whitespace between cells. The `width` attribute sets the amount of the screen that the table will use. This is best given as a percentage so that if the browser is resized the table will continue to make sense.

> **Rule of Thumb:**
> Tables can, if used carefully, provide the best way of structuring a Web page. If you are using a table to format the whole page it is best to avoid using a border and to play around with cellpadding and cellspacing to see what effects you can achieve.

<tr [align="left"|"center"|"right"] [valign="top"|"center"|"bottom"]> ...</tr>

Each row of the table has to be delimited by these tags. The row can be aligned horizontally and vertically within the table if you want. Although the `</tr>` tag is strictly optional since it is obvious when rows end, you should always use it. If you are creating a complex table which has other tables nested within it these may be rendered incorrectly if all rows are not explicitly closed.

<th [align="left"|"center"|"right"] [valign="top"|"center"|"bottom"] [nowrap] [colspan="n"] [rowspan="n"]>...</th>

These are table cells which are to be used for headings. Typically a table header will be rendered in emphasized text such as **<strong>**.

The contents of the cell can be aligned vertically and horizontally within their row; these attributes override any that were set for the row. If `nowrap` is set, the contents of the cell will not be automatically wrapped as the table is formatted for the screen. To prevent long lines messing up the look of your tables use `<br/>` to force text wrapping.

The `colspan` and `rowspan` attributes allow individual cells to be larger than a $1x1$ grid. It is often useful to have a heading that spans more than one column, for instance if you are nesting headings, in which case you should use `colspan`. Similarly, some data cells may need to be more than one cell deep and `rowspan` should be used.

<td [align="left"|"center"|"right"] [valign="top"|"center"|"bottom"] [nowrap] [colspan=n] [rowspan=n]>...</td>

The basic data cells. For explanations of the options see `<th>`.

Advanced Table Elements

<caption>string</caption>
This optional element is used to provide a string that describes the contents of the table. If used it *must* immediately follow the `table` element.

<thead>...</thead>
<tfoot>...<tfoot>
<tbody>...<tbody>
The rows in a table *can* be grouped into one of three divisions. This grouping is optional. The idea is that browsers will be able to scroll the `tbody` section of the table without moving either the `thead` or `tfoot` sections. When long tables extend over more than one page the information in `thead` and `tfoot` can be automatically replicated on each page.

<colgroup [span="n"] [width="n"]>...</colgroup>
Columns within a table can be logically grouped together. Each group of columns can be assigned a default `width` which will apply to all columns that do not set one of their own. The span indicates the number of columns in the group.

col [span="n"] [width="n"]>...</col>
The attributes of individual columns are set using the `col` element. The `span` and `width` attributes work in the same way as for the `colgroup` element.

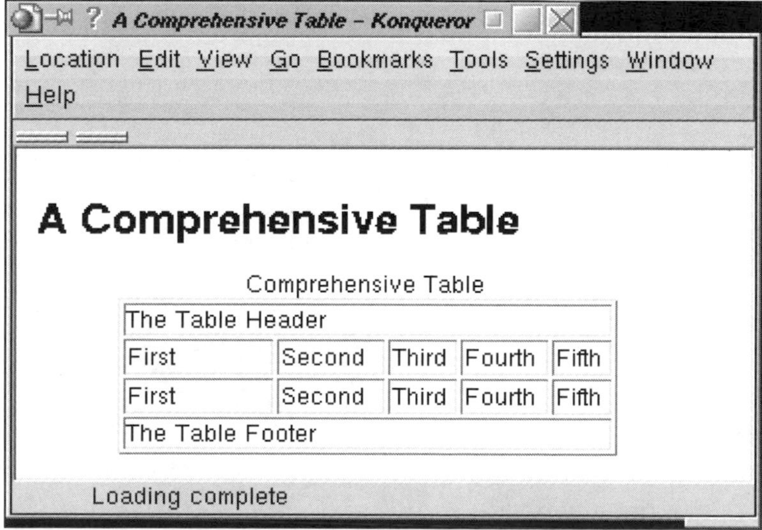

Figure 14.7 A Comprehensive Table

The following code shows a table which, while admittedly uninteresting in itself, shows how to use all of the table elements. The result is shown in Figure 14.7.

Listing 14.5 A Comprehensive Table

```
<html>
   <head>
     <title>A Comprehensive Table</title>
   </head>
   <body>
     <h1>A Comprehensive Table</h1>
     <table align="center" width="75%" border="1">
       <caption>Comprehensive Table</caption>
       <colgroup width="30%" span="2">
       </colgroup>
       <colgroup span="3">
       </colgroup>
       <thead>
         <tr><td colspan="5">The Table Header</td></tr>
       </thead>
       <tbody>
         <tr>
           <td>First</td>
           <td>Second</td>
           <td>Third</td>
           <td>Fourth</td>
           <td>Fifth</td>
         </tr>
         <tr>
           <td>First</td>
           <td>Second</td>
           <td>Third</td>
           <td>Fourth</td>
           <td>Fifth</td>
         </tr>
       </tbody>
       <tfoot>
         <tr><td colspan="5">The Table Footer</td></tr>
       </tfoot>
     </table>
```

```
  </body>
</html>
```

14.3 THE RULES OF XHTML

Although the XHTML contains the same set of elements as HTML 4, the ways in which they may be used have been tightened up considerably.

- Nested tags must be terminated in the reverse of the order in which they were declared. You will no longer be able to have overlapping tags. The following example shows incorrect code followed by the correct version:

  ```
  <tr><td>Some <b>Data</td></b></tr>
  <tr><td>Some <b>Data</b></td></tr>
  ```

- XML is case-sensitive. All XHTML tags and attributes *must* be in lower-case.

- All tags which have, or may have, content must have end tags. Again I'll show some incorrect code and then the correct version:

  ```
  <p>
  <p>Here's a paragraph of text

  <p></p>
  <p>Here's a paragraph of text</p>
  ```

- Empty elements, tags that do not contain content, must either have end tags or be terminated properly. A space should be placed before the terminating slash. This example shows valid alternatives:

  ```
  <hr></hr> <hr />
  ```

- All attribute values must be placed inside quotes. This applies equally to numerical and textual arguments:

  ```
  <hr width="50%"></hr>
  <p align="center">Content</p>
  <table rows="3">
  ```

- Block-level elements such as headers, paragraphs or lists cannot be nested inside each other. If you want to include a list within a paragraph, you must end the paragraph before you start the list. Lists can still be nested inside each other but item tags, `<li />`, must now be closed properly.

- Scripts and styles must be *wrapped* so that they are not parsed as markup. Even inside `<script>...</script>` tags the characters < and & will be treated as part of the XHTML markup. To avoid this, scripts and styles are declared as containing #PCDATA. The script element is included like this:

```
<script>
   <![CDATA[
      // your script goes here
   ]]>
</script>
```

- Some HTML elements have had a `name` attribute with which they could be uniquely identified by scripts. This has been particularly important for forms and for elements such as `div` which have been manipulated through scripting. In XHTML 1.0 the `name` attribute has been deprecated to be replaced by `id`. According to the Recommendation document the `name` attribute will be removed from a future version of XHTML altogether.

14.3.1 Validation

When you author a Web page using XHTML you are going to make mistakes in the way that you nest elements or in the attributes that you use. If you want your pages to work with all browsers, be future proof and comply with all of the relevant Recommendations of W3C, these mistakes need to be removed. Spotting simple errors in large pages is often near-impossible. What authors need is a piece of software that will do the validation for them, supply a list of their errors or certify that their page adheres to its DTD. I recommend to my students that they use a page on the W3C Web site for validation.

`http://validator.w3.org`

This page contains a form in which you enter the URL of your page. If you've specified a DTD or an encoding within the file, the validator will use those. If you haven't, you'll need to specify which DTD you want your page validated against. When you submit the form your page will be validated. You'll get either a page containing errors or a message saying that your page is valid. I've only found one program that will do the same validation to files that are not kept on Web servers. I edit XHTML using Emacs and PSGML mode. These can validate any XML file for which the DTD is available on the local filesystem. If you're not an Emacs user, other editors may offer the same facilities.

If your code is messy, or if it contains a lot of errors once you've validated it the answer is HTML Tidy. This is a downloadable application which was originally developed by Dave Raggett. It's now maintained by a group of volunteers. The home page is currently:

`http://www.w3.org/People/Raggett/tidy/`

Since the volunteers are using Sourceforge, `http://www.sourceforge.net`, to host their project, there is sure to be a more recent homepage there too. HTML Tidy can do fantastic things to code, and it's far more patient and accurate than most humans. If your code is a mess, give it a try.

Exercises

1. Try putting a `title` and an `h1` level header into an new file. Save the file as `test.html` remembering to use the `.html` extension. Now try to open the file inside your favorite Web browse
2. How can page content be formatted horizontally across the screen?
3. Why has W3C developed the XHTML specification?
4. Write an XHTML document which conforms to the XHTML recommendation.
5. Search the Web for an XML validator. Does your XHTML page pass the validation process?
6. Why does the browser ignore white space and newline characters in the source text for XHTML documents?
7. The Web started out as a text-only medium. Now many sites are unusable if you can't see their images. How has the increased use of images affected different groups of Web users?
8. Think about the colors that you see on Web sites. Which combinations of colors work well together, and which are unpleasant and make sites difficult to read?

Chapter 15

Web Services – The Future of the Web?

The World Wide Web may well be the most successful tool for communication that has yet been invented. Access points can be found almost anywhere on the planet, and where static access is unavailable the Web can be used through battery-powered computers and satellite dishes. Beyond its ubiquity, the Web is based on simplicity. Compared to the vast majority of computer applications, using a Web browser is very easy. Editors such as Frontpage and Dreamweaver mean that anyone who is prepared to invest some time and effort can write their own Web site. The content found on the Web exists largely beyond the control of governments and corporations, even if they own the underlying infrastructure.

The Web combines simplicity and freedom. It also taps into, possibly unexpected, desires that many people have to communicate, learn and cooperate. The great power of the Web is also becoming a restriction on how it can be used. Two difficulties are commonly encountered:

- The vast amount of data available on the Web makes finding the most relevant items very difficult. Search engines, such as Google or Northernlight, are helpful but their indexes are either created by a staff of editors or built using complicated algorithms. There is no guarantee that the pages they list are actually the ones that you want.

  Page authors *ought* to be able to improve the way that their pages are listed using metadata. For a long time now, HTML has included a `meta` tag which was meant to be used to include information that describes the content of the page. This metadata could then be used by search engines when they build their indexes. Unfortunately, the `meta` tag has been widely abused by authors who want to move their page to the top of the index, or who want to get their page indexed in more than one place. Most search engines now ignore metadata instead they base their indexes on the content of the page and how it fits into the hyperlinked superstructure of the Web.

- Automated transmission of data using simple protocols such as HTTP has been attempted since the early days of the Web. Machine-to-machine communication lies at the heart of distributed processing and is generally achieved through application-specific structures and protocols. Using an open system such as the Web requires a different approach since any client may wish to deal with any server. Generic protocols and structures are required, which must be low-cost and widely available. HTML seems to provide the solution. In fact it doesn't because HTML structures data according to the way it will be presented on screen rather than the meaning of the data.

15.1 SOME TYPICAL SCENARIOS

For most current users, the Web of today is more powerful than they need. Many millions of people have access to more information and to more communities than they could have imagined possible only a decade ago. For business people, developers and academics the Web has become a vital tool but that doesn't stop them asking *what if....* What if applications could talk to each other? What if some of their more mundane tasks could be offloaded to machines? What if they simply had more computing power available?

Before describing some of the XML technologies which may help to change the way we think about, and use, computing, I'm going to outline a couple of scenarios. These might seem like science fiction today, but they could rapidly become tomorrow's reality.

15.1.1 The Evening Meal

Shopping for a meal is simply a matter of choosing a recipe and buying the ingredients, but when communication is involved, even this can become fraught with problems.

Today Chris, sitting in his office, decides to make a vegetable curry for the evening meal. He starts up his Web browser and points it at a site he has bookmarked where hundreds of recipes are listed. Searching through the vegetarian and Indian categories, he finds a recipe that looks appealing and prints it off. Someone needs to buy the ingredients that aren't in the store cupboard at home, but Chris won't have the time. He phones his wife, Julie, to tell her what he is making and to discuss what needs to be bought. Once Chris has a list, he sends an SMS text message to his daughter at college. After her class Sophie reads the message and replies that she'll pick up the vegetables, some Basmati rice and naan breads on her way home.

When Chris gets home he hunts through the cupboards and refrigerator for his ingredients. Unfortunately, neither sunflower oil nor cumin seeds were on the list that was sent to Sophie, and neither he nor Julie had remembered that both were needed. Sophie, not having seen the recipe, didn't know that she ought to buy some.

It seems that dinner is going to be late again.

Tomorrow In the future things may start in the same way but they'll soon differ. Chris, sitting in his office, decides to cook vegetable curry for the evening meal. He asks his desktop agent to sort it out for him. The desktop agent is a software application which includes a degree of intelligence. It understands Chris's preferences, is able to find Web sites that may be of interest to him, sorts his email by topic and priority and manages his appointments. The agent retrieves a set of menus, presenting those that use ingredients that Chris and his family like, and ignoring those that, on past experience, it suspects they won't like.

When Chris gets a few moments of free time he chooses a recipe and tells the agent that the family will be eating rice and naan breads with it. Chris can now forget about the evening meal: the ingredients will be ready when he needs them. The agent prints the recipe and sends a request to Chris's refrigerator and store cupboards to discover which of the ingredients they contain – and in what quantities. The missing ingredients, including oil and cumin seeds, are formed into a shopping list.

The agent knows where Chris prefers to shop. It connects to the online catalogs of one shop, ordering the vegetables and spices, and authorizing a payment. The agent then goes to another store and orders the remaining items, adding a bottle of wine which the store's system suggests will complement the meal. Once again, payments are authorized automatically by the agent. The agent sends an SMS message to Sophie asking when she expects to arrive home and arranges for delivery fifteen minutes after that time.

Dinner looks like it will be on the table good and early, tonight.

15.1.2 Ordering Goods and Services

Less than ten years ago most people would not have dared to purchase goods or services using a computer system. Ordering and billing online were the strict province of large companies that could afford to use Electronic Data Interchange, EDI. Since then, retailing has been revolutionized by cheap and simple e-commerce applications.

Today Chris decides that he is fed up with constantly having creased trousers. Although he has an iron and ironing board, using them satisfactorily on a pair of trousers is beyond his skill levels. The solution must be to buy a trouser press just like the ones they have in all those fancy hotels. Since Chris doesn't want to go to any shops,[1] he'll have to buy online. After searching the Web, Chris locates Bill Smiggins Inc. who claim to make the best trouser presses money can buy.

Unfortunately, they are located in the USA and Chris is in Great Britain, they don't sell direct and their Web site doesn't list any European dealers. After a lengthy exchange of emails, Chris is told that a dealer has recently been appointed in Italy to cover Europe. More emails follow, but our intrepid shopper neither reads nor writes Italian and the dealer has only rudimentary English.

The deal falls through and Chris learns to iron properly.

Tomorrow In the online world of the future, the desktop agent finds Bill Smiggins Inc. It searches out a suitable trouser press and looks for a local dealer. Although no local dealer is listed, Bill Smiggins Inc. recommends trying again at a later date. Some weeks later the agent returns to the site where the Italian dealer is now listed. The agent places an order and authorizes payment.

15.1.2.1 But How... Clearly both the situations described above require some intelligence on the part of all of the computer systems. Whether artificial intelligence will work to the extent that those applications require is a moot point which I'm not going to discuss here. Let's assume that intelligent systems really can be built. A number of questions should have occurred to you:

[1] Shopping without shops is just so much less hassle.

- How can they share data structures which are as complex as invoices, shopping lists and catalogs?
- Why might software work when different human languages are involved?
- Can we trust software to understand what we mean and to do the right thing?

It may be that none of these things will ever come to pass, but if they do, the underlying structures will require a common grammar and standard meanings for terms. A large amount of work has been done in this field, but perhaps the best-known initiative is called the Semantic Web.

15.2 SEMANTIC WEB

Finding things on the Web as it is today can be surprisingly difficult. If you know what you want and where to start looking, you can browse across the Web moving from place to place following hyperlinks. If you don't know where to begin browsing, a search engine such as Google will provide numerous potential starting points. Even if you are an experienced and selective Web surfer, finding the information that you want can be difficult.

The Web is driven by hyperlinking. Currently most hyperlinks point to Web pages, images, sounds or movies but they don't have to. Because of the universal nature of the URI, a hyperlink can point to a location, a person, a device or an entry in an X.500 directory. If you were to search for `Bill Smiggins`,[2] you might find references to the man himself, his role as husband and father, the address of his office, his company or reviews of his products. If you want to email him, most of this information is useless to you, but the volume of it makes finding the piece that you want more complicated. Many search engines rank *hits* according to the degree to which the page satisfies the search criteria. If the search engine returns ten hits per page and Bill's email address appears in hit 34, you may have given up reading before you find it. Of course you may narrow your search by extending the term to `Bill Smiggins email`, but doing that requires some understanding of how the search is being performed.

Ideally, page authors would be able to describe the meaning of key terms in their pages based upon the context within which they occur. That might sound complicated but actually it's something that we do all the time. As readers we can tell the difference between Bill Smiggins the man and Bill Smiggins the company because we understand the sentences that contain those words. It would be great if an author could add an annotation

[2] I've never checked, but I really hope that Bill is a figment of my imagination.

to their page that would help readers discern the meaning of key terms. These annotations might be hidden unless specifically requested, or might only be available to software applications such as desktop agents. As an added refinement, the annotations could be hyperlinks pointing to URIs which define the terms. This would mean that everyone writing about Mr. Bill Smiggins would reference the same URI which would provide a standard Internet-wide definition for him.

Let's consider at a different example: ordering a trouser press using e-commerce. There are few difficulties searching for products online, ordering them and paying for them automatically. Suppliers can easily interact with customers: receiving orders and sending invoices and dispatch notes. But if we try to automate parts of the process or get software to perform decision making on behalf of users, problems start to appear. One problem which can easily derail the whole process is the definition of terms. Both vendor and customer use the word *payment* but for customers that is money that moves from them to the retailer, for the retailer it is money that comes to them from a customer. Humans have no problem with this since the way in which the word is used makes its meaning obvious. Software has no way of knowing what the word means in a particular situation.

Tim Berners-Lee, the co-inventor of the World Wide Web, is the driving force behind W3C's Semantic Web initiative. Semantic Web is an attempt to build structure into the *meaningful* content of Web pages. Software agents should, the theory goes, be able to use those structured meanings to perform relatively complex tasks for their users. Furthermore, the whole system can remain decentralized with just as much *redundancy* as the existing Web. Semantic Web is intended to be an addition which is easily bolted on to the existing Web infrastructure.

The problem that Semantic Web addresses is essentially one of *meaning*. Applications can only interact if they are giving the same meanings to things. Meanings can be expressed in many ways; in this case they will be described using *ontologies*.

15.2.1 Ontologies

If you look in a dictionary, you will see that an ontology is a theory about the nature of existence. Researchers in artificial intelligence have adopted the word to mean a formal definition of the relationships among a set of terms. Typically in Web research an ontology has two parts: a taxonomy and a corresponding set of inferences.

Taxonomy is, unsurprisingly, another borrowed term. In biology it means a classification of species, on the Web it describes classifications of *things* and their interrelationships. For example, in manufacturing or retailing an *order* contains *order lines* which, in turn, contain *part numbers*, *descriptions* and a *quantity*.[3] Whether you are working in the United States, Britain or Japan these structures remain universal. Even language is no barrier; an order placed with a Japanese company but written in English by an American is structured according to these universal rules.

Inferences extend the descriptive power of taxonomies. An inference is a logical rule in which a conclusion is linked to a premise by deduction. For example an inference rule may state that:

> If an order line contains a part number and a description then the description applies uniquely to the product which is identified through the part number.

Software that had access to a suitably encoded version of this rule could now search for parts based upon descriptions, safe in the knowledge that the relationship between the two could be guaranteed. Confusion can still arise when apparently identical terms are defined differently in different ontologies. Part number might be used to enumerate issues of magazines or volumes within an encyclopedia. To ensure that standard definitions are used each ontology must be identified with a URI which provides the same features as an XML Schema namespace.

15.3 RESOURCE DESCRIPTION FRAMEWORK

The Resource Description Framework, RDF, is one way of encoding metadata. RDF takes ideas from information scientists, librarians, catalog authors and Web developers to create a set of simple, generic rules which can be used to describe almost any metadata. RDF is a framework, not a grammar. It can be implemented in many ways, although XML is probably the most commonly used representation.

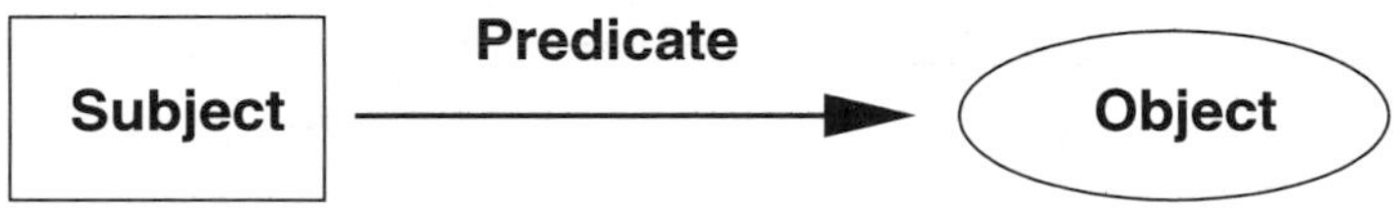

Figure 15.1 The Generic RDF Statement

RDF has three components:

- **Resource** RDF expressions describe resources which are identified by URIs. A resource may be part of a Web page, an XML file or the result of a database query. Since library catalogs, entire Web servers or even people can be identified with URIs, these can also be described with RDF.

[3]Each italicized term indicates a member of the taxonomy.

- **Property** A property is a particular aspect or character of a resource. Properties have particular meanings with defined sets of values.
- **Statement** The basic RDF statement has three components:
  - its subject is a resource,
  - its predicate is a property of the resource,
  - and its object is a particular value for that property.

  Figure 15.1 shows these three elements. The value of the object of an RDF statement may be a text string, a valid XML expression or another RDF statement. If the RDF is marked up in XML and the object value is also XML, the application that is processing the RDF does not have to be capable of processing the object value. It may simply retrieve it and pass it to other applications for their use.

Consider a simple statement such as *Bill Smiggins Inc. is owned by Mr. Bill Smiggins*. Figure 15.2 shows how this can be conceptualized in RDF.

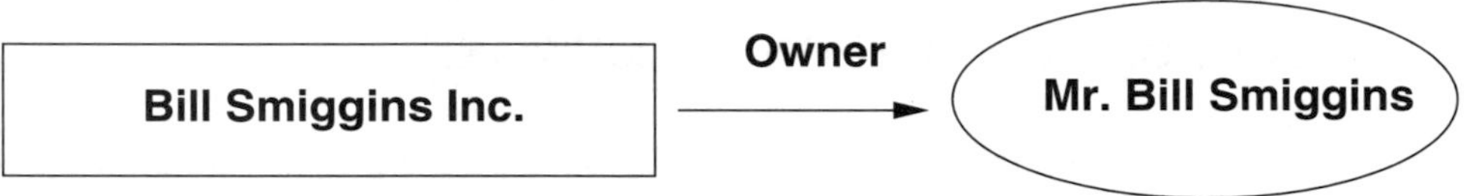

Figure 15.2 A Simple RDF Statement

Such a simple statement can be easily processed by software. If an application were reading through some form of online database searching for information about companies it could readily retrieve the name of the owner of `smiggins.com`. The RDF statement is a one-way relationship. An application that is processing it will, in all likelihood, not *understand* the data with which it is working. Software is, therefore, unable to work backwards along the arc from the object to the subject. It may be clear to us that if Mr. Bill Smiggins is the owner of Bill Smiggins Inc., then Bill Smiggins Inc. is owned by Mr. Bill Smiggins. The reverse relationship cannot be automatically inferred by processing applications. If the reverse relationship is important it must be described in a separate RDF statement.

A compound RDF statement can be built from a number of smaller RDF statements. Figure 15.3 shows an example of this. Mr. Bill Smiggins is a complex entity. We may want to store and access data such as his salary or the location of his office. This data can be linked indirectly to the company name so that having found the name of the company and its owner, we can then contact him directly.

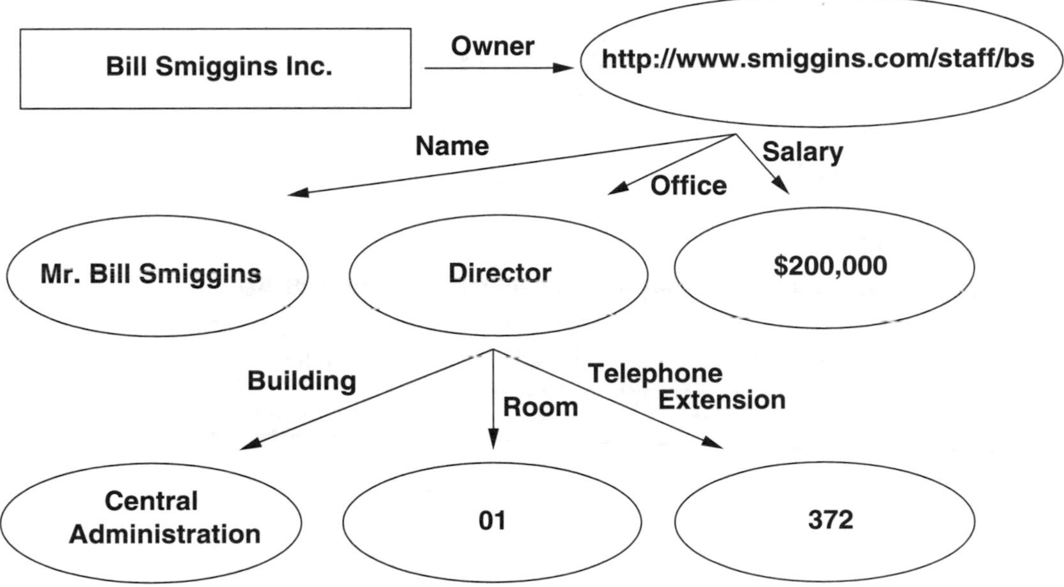

Figure 15.3 A Compound RDF Statement

15.3.1 Representing RDF Statements in XML

RDF is defined using a simple schema. The root element of an RDF document is `RDF` which contains a `description` element. This contains elements which describe a property of the item that is being described. These property elements are not defined by the RDF schema but are part of the schema of the application. Listing 15.1 shows how the simple RDF statement given in Figure 15.2 might be represented within an XML document.

Listing 15.1 Simple RDF Statement in XML

```
<?xml version="1.0"?>
<rdf:RDF
    xmlns:rdf="http://www.w3.org/1999/02/22-rdf-syntax-ns#"
    xmlns:bs="http://www.smiggins.inc/">

  <rdf:Description
      about="http://www.smiggins.inc/Company.html">
    <bs:owner>Mr. Bill Smiggins</bs:owner>
  </rdf:Description>
```

```
</rdf:RDF>
```

The RDF documentation which is available from the W3C Web site shows various ways in which this XML document can be abbreviated. If you start to use RDF and find this form too verbose, you may find investigating the abbreviated forms worthwhile. The difficulty with abbreviating XML documents is that it makes them less readable for humans. Good software applications won't be bothered by the different forms, though human editors and authors might.

When describing more complex RDF statements, the language has a number of useful features. For a compound statement such as the one shown in Figure 15.3, `Description` elements can be nested. Listing 15.2 demonstrates how this is done.

Listing 15.2 A More Complex RDF Statement in XML

```
<?xml version="1.0"?>

<rdf:RDF
    xmlns:rdf="http://www.w3.org/1999/02/22-rdf-syntax-ns#"
    xmlns:bs="http://www.smiggins.inc/">

  <rdf:Description
      about="http://www.smiggins.inc/Company.html">
    <bs:Owner>

      <rdf:Description
          about="http://www.smiggins.com/staff/bs">
        <bs:Name>Mr. Bill Smiggins</bs:Name>
        <bs:Salary bs:unit="USD">200000</bs:Salary>
        <bs:Office>

          <rdf:Description about="Director">
            <bs:Building>Central Administration</bs:Building>
            <bs:Room>01</bs:Room>
            <bs:TelephoneExtension>372</bs:TelephoneExtension>
          </rdf:Description>

        </bs:Office>
      </rdf:Description>

    </bs:Owner>
  </rdf:Description>
```

```
</rdf:RDF>
```

RDF also includes elements that can be used to group content. Many descriptions will include elements that have to be repeated. If the entire staff of Bill Smiggins Inc. were to be represented in an RDF directory, there would be multiple values for managers, supervisors and production staff. RDF has three container types:

Bag
: holds an unordered list. The items in the list may be either literal values or references to other RDF objects. The property that contains a `Bag` has more than one value and those values may be repeated.

Sequence
: is an ordered list of values. Again each value may be either a literal or a reference to a resource. Duplicate values are allowed in a `Sequence`.

Alternative
: is used when a property has a single value which may be identified by just one of a set of literals or resources. Software that processes the RDF must know that it can choose just one of the set of values.

Listing 15.3 A Set of RDF Statements in XML

```
<?xml version="1.0"?>

<rdf:RDF
    xmlns:rdf="http://www.w3.org/1999/02/22-rdf-syntax-ns#"
    xmlns:bs="http://www.smiggins.inc/">

  <rdf:Description about="http://www.smiggins.inc/staff.html">
    <bs:production>

      <rdf:Bag>
        <rdf:li>Mary Smith</rdf:li>
        <rdf:li>Fred Kowalski</rdf:li>
        <rdf:li
          resource=
             "http://www.smiggins.com/staff/Jo%20Grainger" />
      </rdf:Bag>
```

```
    </bs:production>
  </rdf:Description>

</rdf:RDF>
```

The Resource Description Framework provides a simple yet powerful structure within which Web resources can be described. Although it can be used by many organizations to describe data which they wish to publish to subscribers, RDF is far from being the *silver bullet* for online cataloging. Examples of where it is used include the production of headlines and abstracts by online newspapers or information on stocks and share prices. These tend to be services which are pushed out to subscribers who have already decided that they wish to use this data. Pull services in which users first hunt for services then download data from those that most closely match their needs are more complex. These require a more complete approach to describing and automating their interfaces.

15.4 WEB SERVICES

The Semantic Web is little more than an idea at the time of writing. Parts of it have been developed and much of the underlying infrastructure is either already in place or could be added to the existing Web relatively easily. The major missing component, now and through the medium term, is intelligent agents. The data structuring ideas that Semantic Web requires, including taxonomies and inference rules, can be used in existing e-commerce applications. Web Services are slightly different beasts. A Web Service is a platform-neutral interface between a networked application and its users. Details of those services and interfaces which the application is making available are published using an abstract XML form. Clients wishing to use the service read the published descriptions of the interface to the Service and communicate with it using XML messages. Chapter 16 shows how message exchange and remote procedure calls can be performed using XML structures. The remainder of this chapter examines how Web Services can be described and how those descriptions can be published so that any Web-based application can discover and use them.

A Web Service has two components. Firstly, there is a server application which can be programmed in any appropriate language. This application can make use of the full set of facilities which are available both in the development language and on the platform on which it will reside. A Web Service application is really just an ordinary piece of server-side development. If it needs to be written as an Enterprise Java Bean that communicates with a transaction processing system and a relational database, then it can be. The Web Service usually resides on either a Web server such as the Open Source Apache, or within an application server such one of IBM's WebSphere products. The server will perform all of the necessary interaction with clients, taking these complexities away from the application developer. Conceptually this is similar to the way that Web servers have traditionally run CGI scripts, where the developer concentrates on the script and the server automates communication.

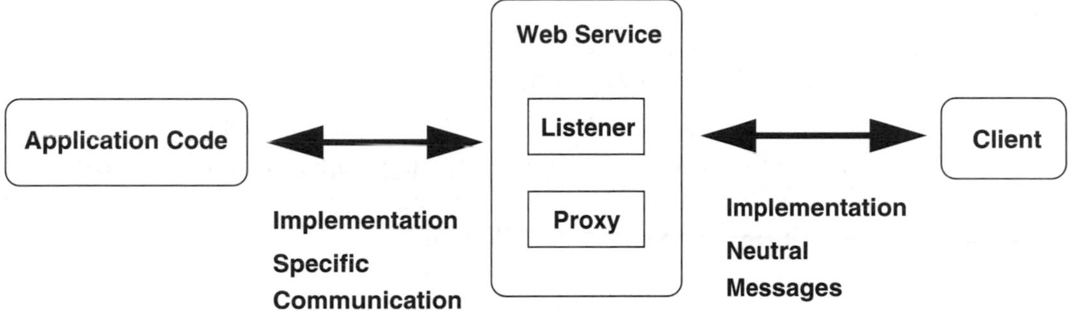

Figure 15.4 Structure of a Typical Web Service

Figure 15.4 shows how the pieces fit together. The remote client may be developed by the same team that wrote the application. In a Web Services context, though, it is more likely that the client will have been written by totally different people who have no knowledge of how the Service is implemented. The client simply needs to know that the Service exists and that it accepts and returns messages in a particular form. Messages are exchanged in a platform-neutral way, usually encapsulated within XML markup. The Web Service, more strictly the application server on which it resides, has two components: a listener and a proxy. The listener understands the transport protocol for the server which may be TCP/IP, HTTP, SOAP or some less common format. It waits for connections from clients and receives requests from them. These requests are passed to the proxy which decodes the XML, extracts the request, and converts it into a form that the application can understand. The decoded request is passed to the application which may return a response to the proxy. The response is encoded into a suitable XML message and passed to the listener which forwards it to the client.

When Web surfers are looking for information they use search engines to aid them. If they have no idea where to begin looking for a particular topic, a search engine provides a good starting point. Web Services are used by applications rather than humans, although they are implemented on top of standard Web protocols. Client applications cannot be expected to trawl through Web search engines looking for an appropriate Service. In the Web Services world, a *service provider* runs Web Services which they have either developed or bought. So that applications can find them, these services are registered with a Web Service Registry by publishing details of their interfaces. Clients search through registries until they find a Web Service that meets their needs and that they bind to and then interact with.

15.4.1 Web Services Description Language

If applications are going to operate across the Web, server programs must be able to make clients aware of what they do, what messages and instructions they can receive, and what data they will return. We've already seen that RDF goes some of the way to addressing these issues. Because RDF can be used to describe anything that can be identified with a URI, it can clearly be used to describe Web Services. Unfortunately, RDF is both too complex and yet, at the same time, too simple for the Web Services arena. RDF is too complex simply because it is intended to be a generic description language. It has a broad span of features which are not needed in Web Services.

Since Web Services are a way of allowing any server to interact with any suitable client, all of them must use the same XML structures. If the client is unable to comprehend the messages that it gets from the server, it will not be able to do business with that server. If RDF were used for describing Web Services, every service provider might invent their own grammar. Clients who wanted to interact with a Service would need to implement software to parse and manipulate each of these systems, which would mean that the main advantage of using XML would disappear instantly. The solution is to use a standard XML language which can be used to describe Web Services accurately and concisely. Working under the auspices of the W3C, Ariba, IBM and Microsoft have developed the Web Services Description Language, WSDL. WSDL won't help automate the process of discovering Web Services. That's the role of UDDI, described in Section 15.4.2, but WSDL will simplify the interaction between client applications and those services.

As you read through this discussion of WSDL you should bear one thing in mind. As a developer you should never have to read or write any WSDL code. Server applications should be able to create WSDL descriptions automatically as services are deployed on them. This is already possible using Microsoft's `.NET` platform and, using an extension developed by IBM, the facility can be added to the Apache SOAP server.

15.4.1.1 The Structure of a WSDL File WSDL is one of those XML technologies that builds upon the facilities of many of the others. As well as basic XML, WSDL uses XML Schema to define data types and, usually, SOAP as a transport. Since so many technologies are coexisting in the same document, alongside application-specific code, WSDL makes extensive use of namespaces. I'll show you an example shortly, but first some of the terminology needs explaining.

The root element of a WSDL document is the `definitions` element. This contains one or more `service` elements, each of which describes a Web Service. A `service` is a collection of ports which are the addresses of implementations of the service. A port has an abstract description called a portType and an implementation which is described with a binding. A portType contains a list of operations which define how messages are exchanged between client and server. Those messages contain parts which are typed representations of data items.

15.4.1.2 A WSDL Example Section 16.3 presents a SOAP service which can be used to search the database of recipes that has been developed throughout this book. The exact details of how that service is implemented are not important right now. The code that follows is a WSDL description of that service.

```
<?xml version="1.0" encoding="utf-8" ?>

<wsdl:definitions name="FinderDescription"
    targetNamespace="http://myrecipe.org/services/finder.wsdl"
    xmlns:soap="http://schemas.xmlsoap.org/wsdl/soap"
    xmlns:wsdl="http://schemas.xmlsoap.org/wsdl">
```

The WSDL document starts with the customary XML declaration. The root of the document is a definitions element which is used to declare all of the namespaces that are used in the document. By convention WSDL elements are part of the http://schemas.xmlsoap.org/wsdl namespace and SOAP elements within WSDL documents belong to http://schemas.xmlsoap.org/wsdl/soap. Target namespaces are used in designing XML Schema documents to conceptually separate those elements that come from the Schema Recommendation and those that are part of a particular Schema. Elements from the Schema belong to the target namespace which may, optionally, be identified by a prefix. WSDL documents may use the target namespace concept too. In this example I have declared a targetnamespace element so as to be explicit about the document but no prefix has been associated with it. In practice a Web Service is likely to be so complex that all elements should be prefixed by their namespace for clarity.

```
  <wsdl:types>
    <schema targetNamespace="http://myrecipe.org/schema/recipe.
       xsd"
           xmlns="http://www.w3.org/2000/10/XMLSchema">
      <element name="RecipeRequest">
        <complexType>
          <all>
            <element name="tgt" type="string" />
          </all>
        </complexType>
```

```
      </element>
      <element name="Recipe">
        <complexType>
          <all>
            <element name="result" type="string" />
          </all>
        </complexType>
      </element>
    </schema>
  </wsdl:types>
```

When data has to be exchanged between systems, those systems must agree upon the representations that they are using for data items. WSDL uses XML Schema to achieve this. Standard data types such as integers or strings are predefined within XML Schema and are understood by all XML Schema-compliant applications. More complex user-defined types, such as order lines or receipts, must be defined within their own XML Schemas. In this example, two data types have been declared. One is for a parameter which will be sent from the client to the Web Service as part of a remote procedure call, the other is for the result which will be returned by the service. Here both are standard strings. The XML Schema is defined within `types` elements, but could be defined in an external file and brought into the WSDL element in an `import` element. Few of the available processors support `import` so the use of `types` has, of necessity, become a *de facto* standard approach.

Notice that elements from the XML Schema namespace are not given a prefix as that namespace is declared as the default for this schema. This is done because there will be many more elements from that namespace than there will be from the target namespace within this schema. The prefix can be safely omitted if there is no possibility of a clash of names and if, by omitting the prefix, the code is more readable.

```
  <wsdl:message name="GetRecipe">
    <wsdl:part name="tgt" type="RecipeRequest" />
  </wsdl:message>

  <wsdl:message name="SetRecipe">
    <wsdl:part name="result" type="Recipe" />
  </wsdl:message>
```

The messages that will be passed between the Service and its clients are defined using `message` elements. These are abstract definitions that define but do not implement the messages. Messages can be quite complex; their content is defined using `part` elements.

For example, if several parameters are passed to a remote procedure call within a single message, each parameter is defined as a separate part.

```
<wsdl:portType name="RecipeInterface">
  <wsdl:operation name="doSearch">
    <wsdl:input message="GetRecipe" />
    <wsdl:output message="SetRecipe" />
  </wsdl:operation>
</wsdl:portType>
```

The operations and messages that a service provides are defined using portType elements. These relate the names of actual methods within the service code to the abstract messages that will be passed to them. Each portType must have a name attribute which uniquely identifies it within its WSDL document. WSDL defines four modes for interactions: one-way, request-response, solicit-response and notification. The service that this document describes is a remote procedure call in which a request is sent to the server and a result returned to the client. This is a request-response interaction with both input and output elements. Descriptions of the modes can be found in the WSDL Recommendation.

```
<wsdl:binding name="SearchBinding"
          type="RecipeInterface">
  <soap:binding style="rpc"
      transport="http://schemas.xmlsoap.org/soap/http" />
  <wsdl:operation name="doSearch">
    <soap:operation soapAction="urn:RecipeService" />
    <wsdl:input>
      <soap:body use="encoded"
          namespace="urn:RecipeService"
          encodingStyle="http://schemas.xmlsoap.org/soap/
            encoding" />
    </wsdl:input>
    <wsdl:output>
      <soap:body use="encoded"
          namespace="urn:RecipeService"
          encodingStyle="http://schemas.xmlsoap.org/soap/
            encoding" />
    </wsdl:output>
  </wsdl:operation>
</wsdl:binding>
```

Once the operations are defined, the WSDL document must describe *how* messages will be passed to individual operations. This is done using `binding` elements which must be uniquely identified within the document using their `name` attribute. Each `operation` element under the WSDL `binding` element defines the binding for a particular `portType` which was defined earlier. Here, a SOAP service is defined. The `soapAction` element identifies the name by which the SOAP server identifies this particular service.

```
  <wsdl:service name="RecipeService">
    <wsdl:documentation>A description of the service which
        searches for recipes</wsdl:documentation>
    <wsdl:port name="RecipeSearchPort"
            binding="SearchBinding">
      <soap:address
          location=
            "http://localhost:8080/soap/servlet/rpcrouter" />
    </wsdl:port>
  </wsdl:service>

</wsdl:definitions>
```

Finally the port and binding are linked and the address at which the service is located is identified. The `service` element is used for this purpose. Notice that a comment can be placed using the `documentation` element. Unlike an XML comment, this is available to clients accessing the service description. They may use it to aid the process of searching for, and using, services, or for logging purposes. They may also choose to ignore documentation if processing it is beyond their capabilities.

15.4.2 Universal Description, Discovery and Integration

Describing a Web Service is only part of the battle. If users knows the address of a Web Service they can go and use it, but often users will have no idea about how to find services. If the Web Services dream becomes a reality users may not even know that such things exist. They will simply have a need which some software somewhere can satisfy for them. In the examples at the start of this chapter, Chris making his vegetable curry did not need to know where or how to find recipes and ingredients. His desktop agent automated the process of discovering and using resources. Universal Description, Discovery and Integration, UDDI, specifies how a system of distributed registries can be used to share information about Web Services.

You might be wondering why a special system needs to be developed to share information about Web Services. After all, anyone needing information about companies or individuals could use existing X.500 directories. If Web surfers want to know about *things* they use a directory such as Yahoo! or a search engine such as Google. Infrastructure already exists which would, at first glance, seem to do exactly what UDDI does. A second look reveals how unsatisfactory existing alternatives are.

Systems for federated directories such as X.500 tend to be incomplete and inadequate. While data about Web Services could be reverse engineered into them, relatively few organizations actually use any of these systems. Traditional directory systems tend to use dedicated protocols and to share data either using proprietary networking protocols or through TCP/IP and socket communications. Such systems cannot be universal since system administrators will be unwilling to allow additional ports to be opened up on their servers and, especially, firewalls. Any directory system that is going to be widely adopted has got to use existing transport mechanisms, with HTTP being the favorite simply because of its ubiquity.

Why not use search engine technology for indexing and discovery of Web Services? Once again this is a problem of an inappropriate technology. If a client uses a search engine to find a Service, they are likely to get not only the address of the Service but information about it. For example, the search engine may return reviews of the Service, links to it, indirect mentions and pages that use similar words in otherwise unrelated content.

UDDI uses an XML document to describe a business and the Web Services that it provides. The description has three parts:

- *white pages* which list addresses and contact details,
- *yellow pages* which categorize businesses based upon standard taxonomies,
- *green pages* which contain technical details of the services the business provides, including Web Services.

Using UDDI, resources and services can be discovered relatively easily. Because the public interface to each service is described within the UDDI registry, developers of client applications know exactly what messages they can expect to exchange with it. Within UDDI registry entries, services can be described using WSDL which means that the entire process of discovery and usage can be made almost automatic.

Once a UDDI document has been created, it must be placed somewhere so that clients can access it. There is no point keeping it on the Web server run by the business since that will not aid discovery and, as I've already explained, it cannot usefully be placed on existing Web systems. If a single machine could be configured as a universal UDDI server then all registry entries could be placed there, and all client requests could be processed there. That looks like a recipe for disaster, though. It makes the server into a single

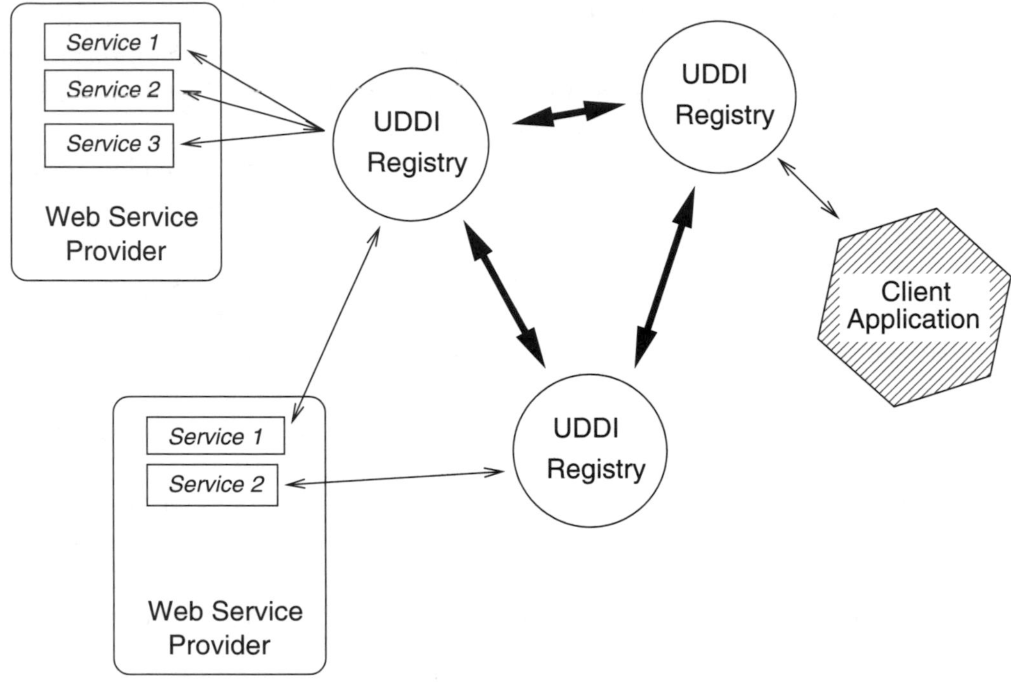

Figure 15.5 A Federation of UDDI Servers

point of failure which would have the potential to bring the entire Internet Web Services business to a crashing halt. Everything about the Internet is distributed, deliberately so. When one part of the Internet fails, however large or small it may be, the rest continues to function. Data that is universally required is replicated and distributed across many different machines in a wide variety of locations.

Computers that use the Internet to share data identify each other using numbers called IP addresses. These can be translated into strings which humans find more comfortable such as `http://www.shu.ac.uk`. Since there are millions of machines connected to the Internet, no single machine can know the names and addresses of all of the others. A system of servers, called domain name servers or DNS, is used to reconcile names and numerical addresses. When a client such as your Web browser needs to talk to a remote machine it asks its local DNS server for the address. Each DNS server knows a limited number of other names and addresses, and if it is unable to answer the query it passes a request on to other DNS servers. They, in turn, either provide the answer or forward the request. This is exactly the system that is needed for UDDI, and it's the one that has been adopted. Figure 15.5 is a simple representation of how the system might look in practice.

UDDI is not the only way of indexing servers and services. It has a lot of industry backing and is likely to be the system that survives. It is, though, a pretty complex schema and I'm not going to look at the actual XML. By the time that organizations start to deploy UDDI in large volumes, software that automates or simplifies the process should be available and no one will ever have to look at the raw XML documents. Certainly while there is even a remote possibility that the only way to use UDDI is to write the XML by hand, few will be willing to use it.

Exercises

1. What are the key differences between Web Services and the e-commerce applications which became prevalent in the late 1990s?
2. Outline a scenario in which you feel Web services would be beneficial. Consider the viewpoints of both potential users and service providers.
3. Give three reasons why the idea of a semantic Web might never be more than an academic curiosity.
4. What is meant by the term ontology?
5. Guestbooks can be found on many Websites. Typically they take a name, email address and comment from visitors. Write an RDF description of an application which could process a guestbook.

Chapter 16

Distributed Applications with SOAP

Computer software can be crudely classified by the number of processors that an application uses. Most of the software that we use every day, such as word processors or spreadsheets, is designed to run on a machine with a single processor. Most computer users operate only a single program at a time. If they are writing a document, they will minimize their word processor before attending to email. Very few people, whether at home or at work, leave long-running tasks executing in the background while they do something else.

Complex applications such as scientific simulations or weather forecasting are often run on extremely powerful computers that contain many processors. The application code is often distributed across the processors so that parts of it can be performed concurrently. These applications need so much processing power that they could never be completed in reasonable time on a single processor machine.

A third class of application distributes its code between a client PC and a more powerful server. Data and instructions are passed across a local network. This approach, called client servercomputing, is widely used in business software. A typical client server system consists of a relational database running on the server, and a smaller interface which executes on the desktop PC. As the user amends or searches the database, changes to the data are made on the server. The server may not even be in the same building as its clients and most of its users will never know that it even exists.

Increasing use of the Internet, the early promise of Web Services as described in Chapter 15, and the ever-changing needs of users are starting to break down the distinctions between these different classes of application. For example, a computer game may run happily in single player mode on a console. Equally, modern consoles can connect to the Internet so that players can match their skills against remote opponents from anywhere in the world. A word processor may store some document data locally, yet other parts of the same document can be held on remote servers. Even scientific software can benefit from new approaches. The SETI project, the Search For Extra-Terrestrial Intelligence, uses a small application which hundreds of thousands of people have downloaded to their PCs. This application downloads data from a central server, processes it and returns its results back to the same server.

Application developers can see almost limitless possibilities once they start to share data and processing. Unfortunately, developing this type of software often seems to bring limitless problems as well. The libraries, tools and design techniques required to create distributed software are often dauntingly complex. Specialized skills and knowledge are required to use them effectively. In a domain such as Web service development, a simple set of protocols and libraries that hide much of the complexity is needed. This is the point at which the Simple Object Access Protocol, SOAP, enters the picture.

16.1 AN OVERVIEW OF SOAP

By now you will be aware of the many benefits that XML delivers to developers. Factors such as the clarity, simplicity and platform independence of XML-based data structures are, perhaps, even more important in networked applications than in data storage. Consider the relatively trivial system shown in Figure 16.1. Two client machines are communicating with a single server. One client, a fixed desktop machine, has a direct network connection to the server. The other client, a laptop, is currently placed behind a firewall. The network may be a typical corporate network using Windows 2000 or Novell Netware, an intranet using the IP suite of protocols, or the Internet. In all cases the same problem pertains. How can structured data be moved around easily and quickly?

Let's consider a number of common scenarios.

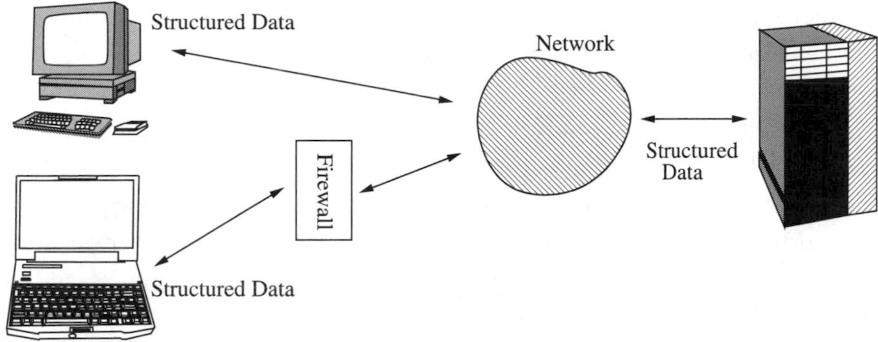

Figure 16.1 A Simple Networked Application

- Traditionally,[1] large organizations have used systems developed by single suppliers. In the days when mainframes ruled supreme, a single company, often IBM, would provide most of the software and hardware to clients. The increased use of client server systems has changed little, although software is as likely to come from Oracle or Microsoft these days.

  When everything comes from a single supplier, interoperability is not a problem. When one company dominates the marketplace everyone adheres to their standards. Third-party software houses must write programs that work near-perfectly with the operating systems, databases and applications of the market leaders if they want to survive.

  Interoperability is simplified since message structures, transport protocols and the structure of the *conversations* between applications are standardized. It doesn't even matter whether the software is used totally in-house or by external customers and suppliers. Everything is fixed and controlled.

- Modern software uses the Internet. This is a basic fact of life for developers, users and system administrators alike. The Internet not only brings many benefits, it also brings myriad difficulties. Most of the problems are related to the security of data and systems. The Internet is commonly perceived to be a jungle with the first line of defense being the installation of a firewall. Even many home users on dial-up lines are installing firewall software. Firewalls restrict the traffic that can be sent to, or from, networks or computers. If your new application uses a port that has been disabled on your firewall, that application is rendered useless. Company IT

[1] If anything as modern as computing can be said to have tradition.

managers and system administrators are often reluctant to open up new ports since doing so also opens up whole new security headaches.

- In a networked world, applications need to share data automatically, without human control. Users need to access data and services from servers that they know little about. Software is developed by thousands of small and large businesses using a wide variety of techniques on many different platforms. If these applications are going to talk to each other, they need to use simple, common message structures based around openly available standards.

Throughout this book I've stressed the benefits of XML for data structuring. If you didn't already know, you've probably guessed by now that XML can be used to solve some of the problems outlined above. SOAP provides standard message structures and common formats for data interchange. Using it means that SOAP-compatible applications can exchange requests, results and error messages. It does not guarantee that those applications will understand the content of a message once they've extracted it, but at least they can extract the content and return a reasonable error. If the two programs involved in the communication were using different protocols, they wouldn't even be able to extract the message.

As an aside, it's worth just mentioning some of the alternative technologies. The biggest players in the market are non-XML middleware technologies. Primarily these are CORBA and DCOM. CORBA, the Common Object Request Broker Architecture, is an open standard for the development of large-scale heterogeneous systems. CORBA is fearsomely complex and tends to be used in industries such as banking, aerospace and defense. DCOM is a Microsoft protocol which is used to link Windows applications together across networks. Like CORBA, DCOM is large and complex.

16.1.1 The Structure of a SOAP Packet

SOAP messages consist of packets of control information structured using XML, and a payload. The payload may be an XML document or a simple piece of data. Both client and server must include, or be able to access, code that can extract the payload from SOAP messages and code to place payloads into SOAP messages. Writing fast, accurate code that can manipulate complex XML structures is not easy. Application developers need to concentrate on the logic of their programs rather than on issues of interconnectivity. Consequently, toolkits have been developed in languages as diverse as Perl, Java, C++ and Lisp which contain all the code necessary to create and deploy SOAP-based applications. In Section 16.2, I will introduce one such toolkit, developed by IBM and Apache, for Java development.

When such toolkits are used, developers are shielded from the low-level details of how SOAP messages are structured and transmitted. That, after all, is one very good reason for using such a toolkit. Even if your application only uses XML within the SOAP packet, having some familiarity with the internal details of SOAP is useful.

16.1.1.1 A Simple Message A SOAP message is contained within an *envelope*. The envelope may contain two elements: an optional *header* and a compulsory *body*. The payload, the message being transmitted, becomes the child element of the SOAP body. Complex interactions may mean that the body has more than one child element but there can only ever be *one* body element inside a single SOAP envelope. The header element may have many children which are called *header blocks*. The header is optional; the Recommendation does not specify how it should be used, although it suggests that the header be used for control information such as may be required by intermediary nodes.[2] Figure 16.2 shows the nesting of elements within a SOAP envelope.

In building real applications, it's unlikely that you'll ever need to work with the raw XML of a SOAP packet. Usually you will handle SOAP in a high-level programming language. Many good texts follow the example of the SOAP Recommendation and give their examples in XML only. Since this book takes a more practical approach, most of the code in the remainder of this chapter is in Java. We can't examine the structure of SOAP packets without looking at some XML.

Listing 16.1 shows a relatively simple SOAP packet. The payload here is the message `Hello Chris`. The SOAP-specific content of the packet is actually very limited. If you read through the code, you should be able to pick out those parts pretty easily.

Listing 16.1 A Simple SOAP Greeting

```
<?xml version="1.0"?>
<env:Envelope
      xmlns:env="http://www.w3.org/2001/12/soap-envelope">
  <env:Header>
    <tr:transaction xmlns:tr="urn:soap-transaction"
                env:mustUnderstand="true">
      <tr:sent>2002-08-06T:11:05:00</tr:sent>
    </tr:transaction>
  </env:Header>
  <env:Body>
    <msg:greeting xmlns:msg="urn:MessageService">
      <msg:text>Hello</msg:text>
```

[2]Node types are described in Section 16.1.2.

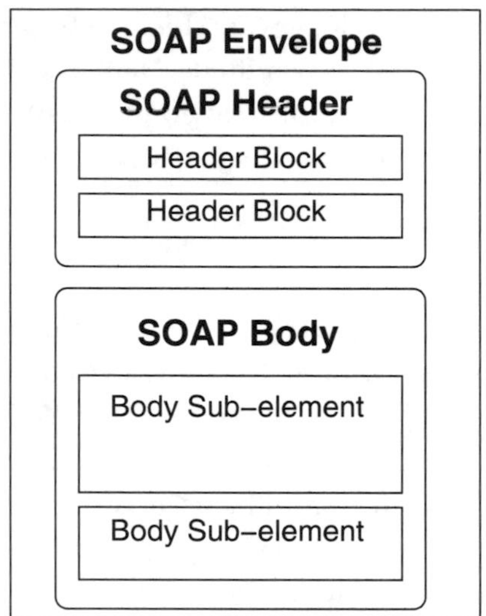

Figure 16.2 The Structure of a SOAP Packet

```
      <msg:recipient>Chris</msg:recipient>
    </msg:greeting>
  </env:Body>
</env:Envelope>
```

All elements in the message defined by the SOAP Recommendation are prefixed with `env`, following the convention used in the Recommendation itself. Of course, any prefix may be used but those used by W3C in their examples seem to become *de facto* standards which is why I've used this one. SOAP elements exist in the namespace `http://www.w3.org/2001/12/soap-envelope`. This message uses three SOAP elements, `Envelope`, `Header` and `Body`, and one attribute, `mustUnderstand`. Notice the capitalization of the names of those elements. Both the `Header` and `Body` elements may contain any valid XML structure. Each child of the `Header` forms a header block of control information. The `mustUnderstand` attribute is described in Section 16.1.3.

16.1.2 Using SOAP

SOAP messages are unidirectional communications between *SOAP nodes*. It is, perhaps, unfortunate that the word *node* is used here to mean an application when it is used in DOM, SAX and XSL to mean elements within an XML document. When discussing the transmission of SOAP packets, referring to *SOAP nodes* is much clearer than abbreviating it to *node*. A SOAP node is any application, or device, that is able to handle a SOAP message. Three types of SOAP node exist. Those that create SOAP messages are called SOAP *senders*, and SOAP nodes to which messages are sent are called *receivers*. The third SOAP node type is called an *intermediary*. SOAP intermediaries receive and handle SOAP messages but are not the intended final recipient. They are used to route messages onwards, either to the receiver or to another intermediary. Intermediary nodes may be used to add *value* to an exchange of SOAP messages, possibly by logging the messages, providing audit trails or by adding data to the message.

Individual SOAP messages are one-way communications, as are emails, letters or telegrams, but SOAP messages are meant to be used on two-way interactions. Although the SOAP Recommendation does not mandate it, the receiver is usually expected to return some form of acknowledgment. The acknowledgment may be an XML document, the result of an operation or an error code. Errors can be returned for many reasons including, for example:

- the SOAP packet has an invalid structure,
- the receiver is unable to process the request in the SOAP body,
- the receiver is unable to process the header block,
- processing the request generated a runtime error.

There is no mandatory requirement that if a sender gets an error message back from the receiver, it must handle that error. Senders can simply choose to ignore errors, although it is difficult to imagine the logic of an application that did that. Generally, error messages should be assessed by the sender and either logged or acted upon. Some errors, such as those arising from a corrupted message, can be handled programmatically. Others arising from incorrect program logic will need to passed on to a user or system administrator for handling.

16.1.2.1 Transporting SOAP SOAP defines message structures but since it is simply an XML application, it does not directly address the issue of transportation. Networked software applications rely upon complex mixtures of software and hardware to move data for them. These mixtures are assembled into *protocol stacks* which define the low-level details of message building and transmission. The great thing about protocols is that we don't need to know anything about networking to write networked software. The gory details are hidden in software libraries and applications that developers can simply use.

Many different networking protocols exist, some developed as proprietary applications, others made freely available by research and academic communities. The dominant player today is the Internet Protocol, IP, suite which, as you might guess from its name, underpins the way that the Internet works. Common applications such as email servers and Web servers use IP to transmit their data. Rather than develop a new way of transmitting data, the developers of SOAP decided that they would use two existing protocols. These protocols are hypertext transmission protocol, HTTP, which is used by Web servers, and the simple mail transmission protocol, SMTP, which is used to send email messages. The reasons for using existing protocols are obvious. Firstly, many existing applications can send and receive data in those formats. Secondly, most firewalls allow SMTP and HTTP data through without a problem.

This all means that transmitting SOAP data is easy. Messages and responses are sent either as emails or via Web servers. Since email is a slow process and most modern applications demand near-instantaneous results, HTTP is the commonest protocol used with SOAP. HTTP is also the only transport defined within the SOAP Recommendation and so in a sense it is the standard approach.

When using HTTP, the SOAP server will be a script or program that runs on the Web server. It will typically be CGI script or a Java servlet which receives its data as part of a normal Web interaction. The SOAP server will create either a result or a runtime error which the Web server will return to the client application as a normal part of the HTTP interaction. The SOAP client is another dedicated application. Although it's talking to a Web server, the client will *not* be a Web browser. The client must be a custom-built program because it is both sending and receiving XML within SOAP envelopes. The current generation of Web browsers do not understand SOAP, although future browsers may well do so.

16.1.2.2 SOAP Messaging The easiest way of using SOAP is probably in messaging applications. SOAP envelopes containing XML payloads are transmitted from one SOAP node to another. Message senders do not, normally, require a response from the recipient. The logic of particular applications may mean that a response is sent. Indeed, conversational interactions in which many messages are exchanged can be built using a series of simple unidirectional messages.

16.1.2.3 Remote Procedure Calls Messaging is used in many different types of distributed application, but the real heart of distributed computing is the remote procedure call, RPC. An RPC is an invocation, by a client application, of a procedure held on a remote server. The server returns the result of executing the procedure to the client. The procedure is invoked with a message which the client sends to the server. Most procedures require some parameter data which is sent as part of the invocation. Figure 16.3 shows a simplistic RPC interaction.

Before a remote procedure can be invoked, the client needs to know:

- the location of the server,

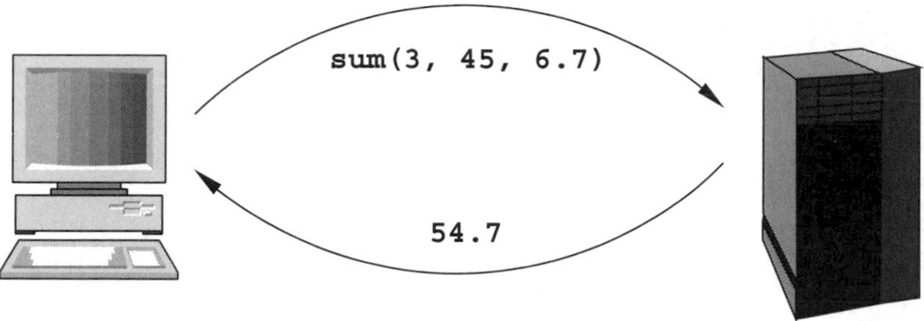

Figure 16.3 A Remote Procedure Call

- the name of the procedure,
- the data types and values of the parameters that the procedure requires,
- the data types that the procedure will return.

All but the first of the items in that list would be needed to call a procedure in a conventional program. The important difference with RPC is that no compiler is going to perform type checking for us or make sure that we are using all of the necessary parameters. More complex RPC-based systems use middleware to handle these, and other, problems. Often the procedure is defined using an interface definition language, IDL, which can be used either statically by a compiler, or dynamically at runtime to provide type checking. This is a very simplistic look at RPCs, and systems such as CORBA which rely on IDL are not really RPC-based.

Locating SOAP servers is done through URIs with requests sent using the HTTP `GET` or `POST` methods. Ensuring that the correct procedure name, parameter names and types, and return types are used could be difficult. Although the SOAP Recommendation does not specify this, using XML Schema[3] to define procedure calls is a good idea. Having a schema means that any of the available tools can be used to validate your calls.

It's worth noting that all of the code samples throughout the remainder of this chapter use RPC-style interactions.

16.1.3 SOAP Faults

Errors are always possible when server or intermediary nodes process SOAP messages. Faults may arise because the server is unable to execute the procedure, the procedure executes incorrectly or the procedure is unable to process the data sent to it. However the

[3] Or any other suitable schema language.

error arose, a SOAP fault is created which the server will send back to the client. Listing 16.2 shows a SOAP fault envelope.

Listing 16.2 A SOAP Fault

```
<?xml version="1.0"?>
<env:Envelope
      xmlns:env="http://www.w3.org/2001/12/soap-envelope">
  <env:Body>
    <env:Fault>
      <env:Code>
        <env:Value>env:Sender</env:Value>
      </env:Code>

      <env:Reason>Processing fault</env:Reason>

      <env:Detail>
        <detail>
          <message>Invalid Recipe Number</message>
          <code>37</code>
        </detail>
      </env:Detail>
    </env:Fault>
  <env:/Body>
</env:Envelope>
```

The `Fault` element must contain `Code` and `Reason` subelements. Three optional elements, `Detail`, `Node` and `Role`, may also be provided. The `Code` contains a mandatory `Value` element and an optional `Subcode`. The content of the `Value` is specified in the SOAP Recommendation, while the `Subcode` gives a more precise definition of the problem. The `Reason` element contains plain text which is intended for the user of the system rather than for automated processing. `Detail` elements provide a space for application-specific code.

SOAP provides four standard values for the `Code` element.

`VersionMismatch`
: The SOAP envelope is using an invalid namespace.

`MustUnderstand`
: The message contains a `Header` block in which the `mustUnderstand` attribute is set to `true` but the recipient did not understand the message.

`Server`

An error that was not linked to the processing of the SOAP envelope occurred on the server.

`Client`

There is a problem with the message as sent by the client.

mustUnderstand The idea that recipients can understand the messages they get is implicit in the whole SOAP concept. If the message cannot be understood an error message must be sent back. This is fine when processing the body of a message once it has been extracted from the SOAP envelope. Understanding and processing data are normal functions of applications. For example, if Bill Smiggins tries to download schematics for his household boiler from my fictitious recipe service, he'll get an error since his request doesn't make sense in that context.

The `Header` element of the SOAP envelope is different. A recipient may be able to process the body of the message but not some, or all, of the header blocks. If a particular header block contains information that *must* be processed when the message is handled, the attribute `mustUnderstand="true"` can be added to the `Header` element. If the recipient is unable to process the header block, for whatever reason, it will return a `MustUnderstand` fault. It should also send details of which header block it was unable to handle.

16.1.4 Data Types in SOAP

Different systems use different structures for data types. Even the representation of simple data types such as integers varies widely between systems. An integer may be 16, 32 or 64 bits long, may have the most significant bit accessed and stored first or last, may be signed or unsigned. Representation of characters is even more complex with encoding schemes as varied as ASCII, EBCDIC and Unicode. When data types become more complex, for example strings of characters, images or runtime objects, there may not even be agreed standards on what the data means, never mind how it should be represented.

If you are developing a networked application in which you have complete control over all components, these differences are awkward but do not form an insurmountable problem. What happens if you are building an application that anyone might access? For example, if your program is part of a large Web Service it will need to be able to talk to any potential client.

Fortunately, Section 5 of the SOAP Recommendation defines a standard set of encodings for common data types. The rules which the Recommendation defines create a straightforward type system which it says is:

> a generalization of the common features in [other] type systems...

Broadly speaking, anyone who has used high-level programming languages, database systems or schema languages should be able to work with the SOAP encodings. It's worth noting, though, that if your SOAP packages are carrying an XML payload, you can ignore SOAP encodings completely and just work with standard XML types.

Since this isn't an in-depth SOAP reference work, I'm not going to say anything more about data types. When you need more information it will be time to read the Recommendation documents.

16.2 PROGRAMMING SOAP IN JAVA

Writing your own code to create or extract SOAP packets is very rare. Libraries are available for most programming languages that you are likely to need to use. Generally accepted wisdom among software developers is that where a good quality library exists, it should be used. The developers of the library will have taken care over their code and done all that they can to minimize bugs and optimize its performance. Handling XML structures is a time-consuming process and you really want to use the smallest, fastest code that you can get your hands on. It's unlikely that you'll have time in your own projects to build that code, although trying to do so is an interesting and informative intellectual challenge.

Throughout this book I've used Java as my programming language of choice and I'm going to continue to do so in this section. The SOAP library I'm using is freely available from the Apache project. This particular SOAP implementation runs as a Java servlet within the Web server so as well as installing the library a servlet engine is needed too. Again I turned to the Apache project and downloaded their excellent Tomcat Web server. Tomcat is developed under the auspices of Apache's Jakarta project. Jakarta's mission is to develop Open Source software which is based on the Java programming language. Its projects are not all Web-based. They include Ant which is a replacement for the popular `make` utility, Regexp, a regular expression engine and a templating engine called Velocity. Further details can be found on the project Web site at:

```
http://jakarta.apache.org
```

16.2.1 Installing Apache SOAP and Tomcat

Installing Apache SOAP and Tomcat is neither simple nor intuitive. Although each has limited instructions as part of the download they are only helpful in retrospect. Looking for help from books or Web sites doesn't help either since version changes render older instructions obsolete. What I'm going to show you here is a recipe that eventually worked for me on both a Windows 2000 system and a GNU/Linux system. In fact it worked so well that I was able to transfer Java files between the two and get faultless systems-independent performance.

16.2.1.1 Downloading the Software The Apache project is a Free Software initiative with much of the work on its project done by volunteers. There isn't a great requirement on them to maintain backwards compatability or to ensure that they adhere to the highest standards of software development. But they do. As a general rule the more mature Apache projects, those that have passed out of beta and into the production phase, are well-built and well-managed applications. They are also often near the leading edge of technology. Especially in the XML arena there is a tendency to haphazard evolution of standards and implementations as developers learn more about what is possible. This does mean that there are sometimes significant changes between versions of Apache products. The instructions I give here can only be guaranteed to work with the versions of the software I'm using.

I'm going to assume that you have a working installation of a Java Development Kit. You'll need at least version 1.2, and ideally 1.4 of Java.

You'll need to download two archives from the Apache Web site. Get version 2.3.1 of SOAP from:

`http://xml.apache.org/dist/soap/version-2.3.1/`

You will want a binary version of the application; these have `bin` in their name, and come in `.zip`, for Windows, and `.tar.gz`, for Unix, formats. Version 4.0.4 of the Apache Jakarta Tomcat Web server can be downloaded from:

`http://jakarta.apache.org/builds/jakarta-tomcat-4.0/release/v4.0.4/`

If you are using an operating system such as Linux, Tomcat is available packaged as RPMs. For other systems, or if you are unsure that you can use RPMs, go to the `bin` directory. Tomcat binaries are available as `.zip`, `.tar.gz` and `.exe` formats. The `.exe` files are self-installing executables for Windows operating systems. Tomcat uses software from a number of other Apache projects. If you don't want the hassle of downloading and installing lots of Jar files, get the default distribution. If you've already got the Mail and Activation Jars then you can grab the LE version of Tomcat. This version does, though, require Java 1.4. The complete download is just four megabytes, about 33% larger than the LE version. Getting it provides peace of mind and is what I would recommend.

Create a directory on your hard drive to hold both archives when they are extracted. During the time when you are learning these technologies, I would recommend putting them on your own hard drive in your own space, if you are attached to a network. That way you don't need to worry about configuring the system for multiple users and setting environment variables will be much easier.

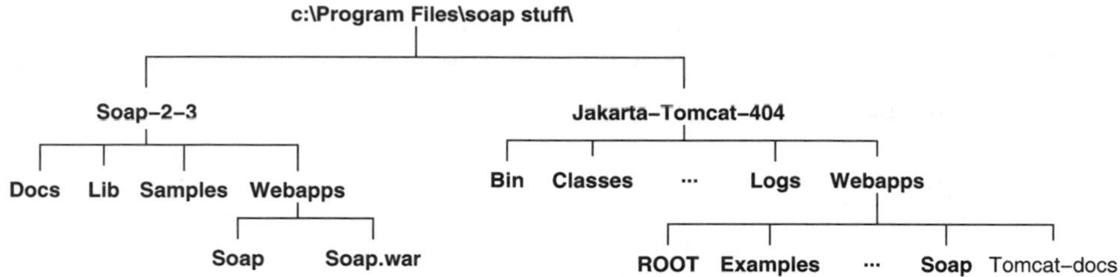

Figure 16.4 Possible Directory Structure For Tomcat And SOAP

Unzip the files into the directory, or run the self-installing archive if that's what you downloaded. You should get a structure similar to the one shown in Figure 16.4. Don't worry if the names vary; I've changed the names of the top-level directories so that they work better with my personal standards for these things. The structure that is created is important. Although you can change where you extract the archive to, you cannot move directories and files around within it.

16.2.1.2 Setting the Classpath The Java virtual machine won't automatically know where to find the Jar files which were installed from the archives. Even if you used a self-installing archive that updated the Windows registry, you still have to edit certain environment variables. In addition you will need to tell the Java environment how to find the directory that contains the source code for the SOAP services that you write.

To configure your system, edit the `CLASSPATH` environment variable. Over the years I have found surprisingly few people who know how to make even simple changes to the configuration of their PCs. Even relatively technically aware students seem to be afraid of altering the configuration of their system. In fact, many don't even know that you *can* do so. None of this is difficult to do and, provided you keep careful notes, you will be able to undo any changes that you have made quickly and easily. The only warning is that you should be careful to keep track of what you've *actually* done, not what you *think* you've done.

First, I'll show how to alter the variable in Windows 2000. I'm going to use the directory structure from Figure 16.4. My source code is going to go into a directory called `c:\soap\samples`.

Double click the `My Computer` icon on the desktop and choose `Control Panel` from the list that appears. Next choose `System`, then the `Advanced` tab. Finally choose the `Environment Variables` button. You will see a box like the one shown in Figure 16.5.

You need to have user variables, the top box, set for `PATH`, `CLASSPATH` and `JAVA_HOME`. To add new variables choose the `New...` button, to change existing settings choose `Edit...`. The `JAVA_HOME` variable should point to the top level of your

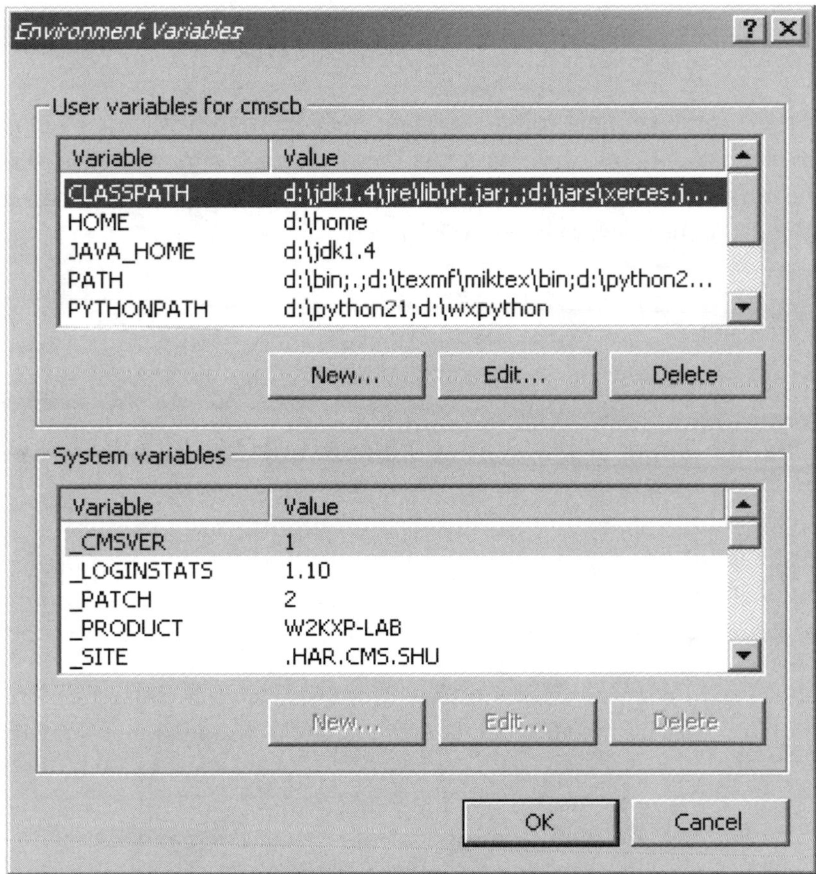

Figure 16.5 Windows 2000 Environmental Variables

Java Developer's Kit which may be inside another directory if you are using an environment such as Borland JBuilder. The `PATH` should include the directory that holds your Java interpreter, which will be `$JAVA_HOME\bin\`, and the current working directory which is identified by a dot. For example, at its simplest you might have:
`c:\jdk1.4\bin;.`

Notice the use of a semicolon to separate values within the variable. The `CLASSPATH` has to point to Java archives for Xerces, mail, activation, SOAP, the Java runtime library, the current working directory and the directory under which you are going to place your SOAP code. Here's mine (all of the code should be a single line, but this is wrapped and indented for presentation on the printed page):

```
c:\jdk1.4\jre\lib\rt.jar;.;c:\jars\xerces.jar;
        c:\jars\soap-2_3_1\lib\soap.jar;c:\code\soapapps;
```

```
c:\jars\jakarta-tomcat-4.0.4\common\lib\mail.jar;
c:\jars\jakarta-tomcat-4.0.4\common\lib\activation.jar
```

Changing the same variables on a Unix box is easier than in Windows. I edit system variables in a file called `.bashrc` which is the resource file for the bash shell. Simply open the file in your favorite text editor and make the changes to the same variables as for Windows. Here are the relevant portions of mine:

```
export JDK_HOME=/opt/jbuilder5/jdk1.3
export JAVA_HOME=/opt/jbuilder5/jdk1.3
export CATALINA_HOME=/home/fred/jars/jakarta-tomcat-404

export CLASSPATH=/opt/jbuilder5/jdk1.3/jre/lib/rt.jar:.:
   /home/fred/jars/xerces-2_0_1/xercesImpl.jar:
   /home/fred/jars/xerces-2_0_1/xmlParserAPIs.jar:
   /home/fred/jars/soap-2_3/lib/soap.jar:
   /home/fred/jars/javamail-1.2/mail.jar:
   /home/fred/jars/jaf-1.0.1/activation.jar:/home/fred/code/
```

Notice that in Linux I use slightly different paths. That's because I downloaded the LE version of Tomcat and installed the latest versions of the mail and activation APIs it requires.

16.2.1.3 Configuring Tomcat Tomcat is configured, started and stopped with scripts which are held in the `bin` directory of the installation. The startup scripts are called `startup.bat` and `startup.sh`, the scripts that stop it are called `shutdown.bat` and `shutdown.sh`. These are run from the command line and generally you will never need to change their contents. A third script is called by the startup script to change the `CLASSPATH` of the running Tomcat installation. This script overrides any value set for the current environment which means that it must be edited to match the `CLASSPATH` you set when installing the software.

To make the relevant changes, open `setclasspath.bat` or `setclasspath.sh` in your favorite editor. The `.bat` version is for Windows systems, `.sh` is for all others. The contents of the two scripts are broadly the same, allowing for differences between operating system naming conventions and scripting languages. Find the line:

```
# Set standard CLASSPATH
```

and comment out the line below it which sets a default `CLASSPATH`. In Windows this is done by preceding the line with the instruction `rem`, on Unix systems it's done with a hash character, #. Now add a new line that gives *your* `CLASSPATH` value. I add an instruction to echo this to the shell so that I know what my system is doing:

```
echo "The CLASSPATH is $CLASSPATH"
```

You should now be able to start and stop Tomcat. Check your installation by running your startup script. Point a Web browser to `http://localhost:8080` where you ought to see the Tomcat welcome screen which is shown in Figure 16.6.

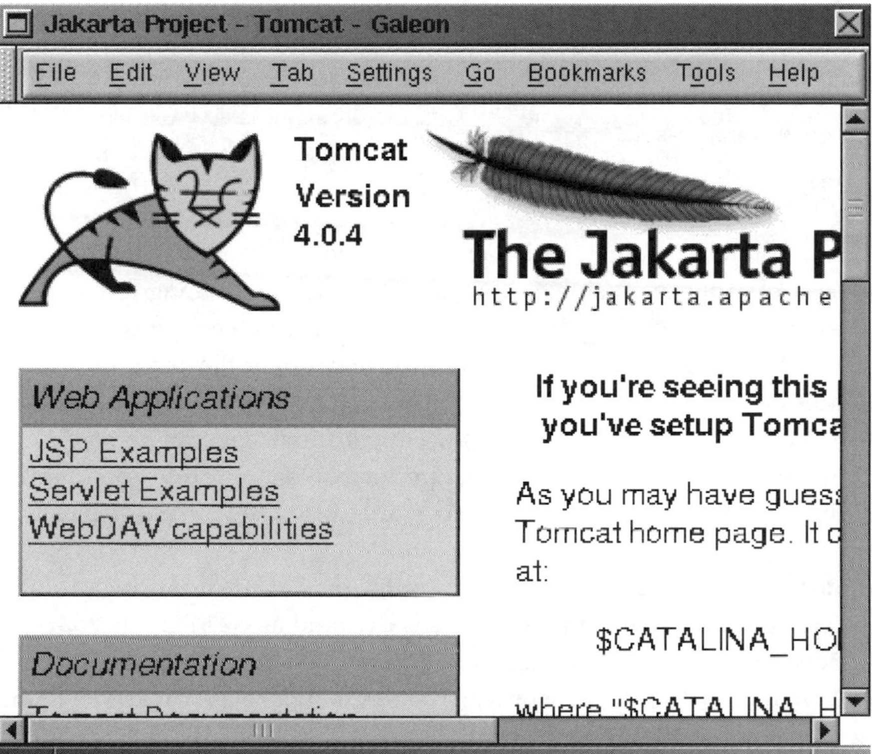

Figure 16.6 Tomcat Welcome Screen

16.2.2 Hello World

I'm going to demonstrate an RPC interaction in which the server returns a message string to the client. In the great tradition of computing examples, this is, of course, a *Hello World* example.

To run an Apache SOAP service you will need three basic components. There must be the Java code which will run on the server, a client which can access that code across a network and a descriptor file. The descriptor will be used to deploy the service, as we'll see shortly.

First, take a look at the code for the service.

Listing 16.3 Hello World Service

```
package samples.helloworld;

public class HelloWorld {
   private String name;
   public String getMessage() {
     name = "Chris";
     return "Hello " + name + " from A Soap Service";
   }
}
```

There is absolutely nothing special about that code. It's a Java class which contains just one class variable and a single method. The code is not going to be executed as a standalone program; it will only be run within Tomcat which executes SOAP requests as Java servlets. There are two important things to notice about the code.

I've placed it within a Java package structure. If you've never used packages, they provide an excellent way of structuring Java applications and can be readily converted into Java archives. Assuming that I have a directory called `c:\code\soapapps`, I create another directory below that called `samples` and, below *that*, `helloworld`. The Java code is saved in the file `HelloWorld.java` in:
`c:\code\soapapps\samples\helloworld`.

The second thing of note is that the class is declared as `public`. If your class is not `public`, Tomcat will be able to find it but will *not* be able to execute it. You'll get an error message returned to your client which states that the class cannot be found. If you take that message literally, you will waste hours, and potentially days, configuring and reconfiguring your system.

The client is somewhat more complicated, as Listing 16.4 shows.

Listing 16.4 Client For Hello World Service

```
package samples.helloworld;

import org.apache.soap.Constants;
import java.net.URL;
import org.apache.soap.Fault;
import org.apache.soap.rpc.Call;
import org.apache.soap.rpc.Response;
import org.apache.soap.rpc.Parameter;

public class HelloClient {
```

```
  public static void main (String args[]) throws Exception {
    // Build the SOAP RPC request message using the Call object
    Call call = new Call ();
    call.setTargetObjectURI ("urn:HelloWorldService");
    call.setMethodName ("getMessage");
    call.setEncodingStyleURI(Constants.NS_URI_SOAP_ENC);

    // Create a URL object, which represents the endpoint
    URL url = new URL("http://localhost:8080/soap/servlet/
        rpcrouter");

    // Send the SOAP RPC request message using invoke() method
    Response resp = call.invoke(url, "");

    // Check the response.
    if (!resp.generatedFault ()) {
      Parameter result = resp.getReturnValue ();
      System.out.println ("The result was " + result.getValue ());
    } else {
     Fault fault = resp.getFault ();
     System.out.println ("The Following Error Occurred: " + fault
         );
    }
  }
}
```

I've put the client code in the same package as the server. This does mean that they will coexist in the same directory, which is a totally artificial situation. In a real SOAP application the client and server would be held on different machines. Having them together for the purposes of experimentation doesn't actually matter since the client can only ever access the service through the Tomcat Web server.

The client application must contain all of the code necessary to build SOAP messages, communicate with remote servers and decode the responses they return. The SOAP service uses the capabilities of the Web server for its side of the communication, but the client must do everything itself. The classes that contain the necessary code are found in the `org.apache.soap` package. Rather than import the whole package, I'm only importing those classes that my program actually uses: `Constants`, `Fault`, `Call`, `Response` and `Parameter`.

The program starts by creating a `Call` object which will hold all the information necessary to perform a remote procedure call. Actually, the `Call` object encapsulates the entire RPC interaction. To access a SOAP service the program needs the service's URI, the name of the method that will be called, and any parameters that will be passed to it. The `Call` object must also define the data encoding that the call will use. In this example we're going to use the default.

The RPC is executed using the `invoke` method of the `Call` object with the result used to create a new object of the `Response` type. If a SOAP error object is returned from the service its details are extracted into a `Fault` object and displayed. If the RPC executes successfully the result is displayed.

When configuring Tomcat we made sure that the directory that contains our Java services was on the system `CLASSPATH`. This isn't sufficient information to allow the server to find and run services. Each class that defines a service may include numerous methods that can be executed as RPCs. A class may also be used in more than one service. Services must be deployed on the server so that it can accurately find and retrieve them. The server must be told the URN of the service, the class that contains it and those methods the service will use.

Apache Tomcat uses two different systems for deploying services. The easiest is to point a Web browser at:

`http://localhost:8080/soap/admin/index.html`.

The instructions for using this interface are given in the SOAP documentation. Choose the *Managing Services* button from the list on the left side of the page.

If you prefer to take a command-line approach to managing your servers, you can do this with Tomcat. The first thing that you will need is a Deployment Descriptor. This is a simple XML file which describes the service, its URN and the methods that it exposes. Listing 16.5 is just such a file for the Hello World Service.

Listing 16.5 Descriptor File

```
<?xml version="1.0"?>
<isd:service xmlns:isd="http://xml.apache.org/xml-soap/deployment
   "
          id="urn:HelloWorldService">
  <isd:provider type="java"
             scope="Application"
             methods="getMessage">
  <isd:java class="samples.helloworld.HelloWorld" static="false
     "/>
  </isd:provider>
```

```
  <isd:faultListener>org.apache.soap.server.DOMFaultListener</isd
      :faultListener>
</isd:service>
```

The content of deployment descriptors is well described in the Apache SOAP documentation. Fortunately you can get by without reading the documentation while your services are relatively simple. All that you really need to do is change the values for the `id` and `methods` attributes and the content of the `isd:java` element. Services are deployed using the `org.apache.soap.server.ServiceManagerClient` class. This takes a URL as its first parameter, then an instruction, and finally the name of a service. The following shows it in action:[4]

```
(19:33:48)chris: java org.apache.soap.server.ServiceManagerClient \
                   http://localhost:8080/soap/servlet/rpcrouter


Usage: java org.apache.soap.server.ServiceManagerClient \
                   [-auth username:password] url operation arguments
where
   username and password is the HTTP Basic authentication info
   url is the Apache SOAP router's URL whose services are managed
   operation and arguments are:
      deploy deployment-descriptor-file.xml
      list
      query service-name
      undeploy service-name
```

Although the URI for the SOAP server administration tool is `http://localhost:8080/soap/admin`, the SOAP server is really running as a servlet with the URI `http://localhost:8080/soap/servlet/rpcrouter`. If no parameters are supplied, or if the parameters are incorrect, a usage message is shown. Listing all of the deployed services is done with:

```
java org.apache.soap.server.ServiceManagerClient \
            http://localhost:8080/soap/servlet/rpcrouter list
```

If you have a deployment descriptor saved in a file called `HelloDD.xml`, its service can be deployed using:

[4] I assume that you are running the server on your local machine. Change the host name as appropriate.

```
java org.apache.soap.server.ServiceManagerClient \
      http://localhost:8080/soap/servlet/rpcrouter deploy HelloDD.xml
```

To test all of this, compile the Java code for the classes `samples.helloworld.HelloClient` and `samples.helloworld.HelloWorld` and deploy the service on a running Tomcat/SOAP system. If you run the client you should get something like the following interaction at your terminal:

```
(20:09:58)chris: java samples.helloworld.HelloClient
The result was Hello Chris from A Soap Service
```

As you work through the process of installing, configuring and testing the Apache SOAP and Tomcat applications, care and attention to detail are required at every stage. If you are lucky, everything will work straight out of the box. The sample applications which are provided with the SOAP download are a good test of your system, but there is no substitute for writing your own code. Only when you try to deploy your own applications will you start to really understand the way that the systems work together to provide a complete SOAP environment.

16.3 ACCESSING RECIPES

The *Hello World* application is deliberately trivial. Applications that are not significantly more complex can demonstrate the use of SOAP in a realistic environment. The remainder of this chapter is taken up with just such an application. I'm going to demonstrate a SOAP service that searches the database of recipes that has been used throughout the book. The service takes a string parameter which is intended to be the name of a recipe. It searches through the database looking for a recipe of the same name. If the search is successful, the content of the recipe is returned as a string. If the search is unsuccessful, an empty string will be returned to the client. Adapting the service to return the recipe in its native XML format is left as a simple exercise for readers.

In Section 12.3 I showed code which uses the Document Object Model to count the nodes in an XML tree. I'm going to modify some of that code to search for nodes within the tree. Read through the code, trying to understand it, before reading the explanations that follow each section.

```
package samples.recipefinder;

import org.w3c.dom.*;
import org.apache.xerces.parsers.DOMParser;
import org.xml.sax.*;
```

The program starts with the same imports and structure as the earlier DOM application. Notice that the class does not have a `main` method. Like `Hello World`, this code will only ever be executed through the Tomcat servlet engine.

```
public class Searcher {
   private StringBuffer recipe = new StringBuffer("");
   private String meal;

   public String doSearch(String tgt) throws Exception {
     meal = tgt;
     DOMParser domp = new DOMParser();
     domp.parse(
           "/home/fred/code/samples/recipefinder/recipe.xml");
     Document doco = domp.getDocument();
     NodeList nd = doco.getElementsByTagName("name");

     for(int i = 0; i < nd.getLength(); i++) {
       if( (nd.item(i)).getNodeType() == Node.ELEMENT_NODE ){
         String ndName = ( (nd.item(i)).getFirstChild() ).
                                       getNodeValue();

         if(ndName.compareTo(meal) == 0) {
           getRecipeContent( (nd.item(i)).getParentNode() );
           break;
         }
       }
     }
     String result = recipe.toString();
     recipe = new StringBuffer("");
     return result;

   } // doSearch
```

The `DOMParser` is used to parse the XML source document and build a DOM tree. This takes the absolute name of the XML file as a parameter. If you give just the filename or a shortened path, the parser will search relative to *its* working directory. For these SOAP applications that search will start somewhere in the directory structure of Tomcat. That's probably not where your XML file can be found so you will need to give the complete path and filename.

Once the program has created a `Document` object which represents the XML as a DOM tree, all of the recipe names are extracted into a `NodeList`:

```
NodeList nd = doco.getElementsByTagName("name");
```

In fact, this will extract everything named `name`. The program needs to iterate across these elements looking for those nodes that are elements. It then extracts the content of the element. Those element nodes that contain the name of a recipe have a text node as their first child. The program finds this and returns its value to a variable:

```
String ndName = ( (nd.item(i)).getFirstChild() ).getNodeValue();
```

If the recipe name matches the target, the parent element, the one in the `NodeList`, is passed to the `getRecipeContent` method for further processing.

```
private void getRecipeContent(Node nd) {
  NodeList offspring;

  if(nd == null)
     return;
  int type = nd.getNodeType();

  switch(type) {
    case Node.ELEMENT_NODE:
      NamedNodeMap atts = nd.getAttributes();
      if(atts.getLength() > 0) {
        for(int j = 0; j < atts.getLength(); j++)
           recipe.append( (atts.item(j)).getNodeValue() );
      }

      offspring = nd.getChildNodes();
      for(int k = 0; k < offspring.getLength(); k++)
         getRecipeContent(offspring.item(k));

      break;

    case Node.TEXT_NODE:
      recipe.append( strip(nd.getNodeValue()) );
      break;

  } // switch

} // getRecipeContent
```

Although `getRecipeContent` receives a single node from the `doSearch` method, that is sufficient to allow it to access the whole recipe. That one node is the root of a subtree which can be walked recursively. We've already seen, in Chapter 12, how to recursively manipulate a DOM tree. In this example, attributes and text nodes are appended onto a Java `StringBuffer` object. Once the entire tree has been walked and the whole recipe has been extracted, the result is passed back to the `doSearch` method. There, the `StringBuffer` is converted to a Java `String` and returned to the client.

If you are familiar with Java, you will notice that after the conversion to a `String` object, a new `StringBuffer` object is created. Since this has the same name as the existing object, the extra workload involved seems misplaced. Since we're also at the end of the program, creating an empty object appears to be, frankly, pointless. Remember, though, that the Apache SOAP server runs as a servlet. Once it has been initialized by Tomcat it remains available until the server is shut down. Loaded objects also remain available. They are not garbage collected after execution and reloaded when they are needed again. The `StringBuffer` object, `recipe`, therefore remains in memory. If the service was used again, the next recipe would simply be appended to the first one and *both* returned to the client. To avoid this, I create a new object. The one that has just been used is removed by the Java garbage collector.

> **Note:**
> After each run of a SOAP service, all dynamic data structures must be reinitialized or deleted.

The final method is used to strip unwanted whitespace out of the result string. In this particular application, using the data file that I created for it, the only whitespace characters that are a problem are `\n` and `\t`. The `strip` method removes them. In other applications whitespace handling is, of course, a more complex problem.

```
  private String strip(String src) {
    StringBuffer res = new StringBuffer();
    for(int i = 0; i < src.length(); i++) {
      if( (src.charAt(i) != '\n') && (src.charAt(i) != '\t') )
         res.append(src.charAt(i));
    }
    return res.toString();

  } // strip

} // Searcher
```

Like the *Hello World* example, the bulk of the work involved in building the recipe searching system takes place in the client. Notice that, for convenience, this client is again placed in the same package as its server.

```
package samples.recipefinder;

import org.apache.soap.Constants;
import java.net.URL;
import org.apache.soap.Fault;
import org.apache.soap.rpc.Call;
import org.apache.soap.rpc.Response;
import org.apache.soap.rpc.Parameter;
import java.util.*;

public class RecipeClient {

   public static void main (String args[]) throws Exception {
     Call call = new Call ();
     call.setTargetObjectURI ("urn:RecipeService");
     call.setMethodName ("doSearch");
     call.setEncodingStyleURI(Constants.NS_URI_SOAP_ENC);
```

The program starts almost identically to the earlier example. This is another simple RPC client; the biggest difference is that it will send a text string to the server as a parameter to its request.

```
     Vector params = new Vector();
     params.addElement(new Parameter("tgt", String.class, args
         [0], null));
     call.setParams(params);
```

Parameters must be added to the request, the `Call` object, using its `setParams` method. This method takes a `Vector` of `Parameter` objects as its argument.

The constructor for the `Parameter` object is defined as:

```
parameter(java.lang.String name, java.lang.Class type,
java.lang.Object value, java.lang.String encodingStyleURI)
```

The first argument to the constructor is the name that the argument takes in the method signature of the service code. In `Searcher.java`, the `doSearch` method is defined as:

```
public String doSearch(String tgt) throws Exception
```

Using the same name, `tgt`, for the argument to the call makes sense since it minimizes complexity. The `type` argument indicates the data type which is being passed across. When passing complex types which you may have defined yourself, you will need to make sure that the type can be accessed and understood by the compiler when it builds this code. Built-in Java types do not present any special difficulties.

The third parameter is an object, not a primitive Java type, which contains the value to be passed to the remote procedure. In this example, the value comes from the command line. If you need to enter more than one word, the phrase should be surrounded by single quotes. For example, my sample data set contains a recipe for *Sussex Gypsy Bread*. The `Searcher` class is so primitive that it will fail if asked to find that recipe from the single word *Gypsy*. The full name has, therefore, to be supplied.

The final argument to the constructor is an encoding style. If you are working with standard Java types you can simply give `null` as a value here.

Building the call now has some new steps:

- Create the `Vector`.
- Iteratively, repeating for every argument that has to be passed with the call:
  - create a new `Parameter` object which represents the data type and value of a parameter,
  - add the `Parameter` object to the `Vector`.
- Add the `Vector` to the `Call` object.

```
URL url = new URL("http://localhost:8080/soap/servlet/
    rpcrouter");
Response resp = call.invoke(url, "");

if (!resp.generatedFault ()) {
  System.err.println(resp);
  Parameter result = resp.getReturnValue ();
  System.out.println (result.getValue ());
} else {
  Fault fault = resp.getFault ();
  System.out.println ("The Following Error Occurred: ");
  System.out.println (fault);
}
```

```
    } // main

} // class RecipeClient
```

Once the code has been written and compiled, the service needs to be deployed. Using a Deployment Descriptor file and the command-line tool is easier than using Tomcat's Web interface. Listing 16.6 shows the descriptor for this example.

Listing 16.6 Descriptor File

```
<?xml version="1.0"?>
<isd:service xmlns:isd="http://xml.apache.org/xml-soap/deployment
    "
          id="urn:RecipeService">
  <isd:provider type="java"
             scope="Application"
             methods="doSearch">
  <isd:java class="samples.recipefinder.Searcher" static="false
     "/>
  </isd:provider>
  <isd:faultListener>org.apache.soap.server.DOMFaultListener</isd
     :faultListener>
</isd:service>
```

You've seen a fairly large amount of code in this chapter. Typical RPC interactions can be built, tested and deployed far more easily with SOAP than with other programming techniques. If you haven't already done so, download Apache SOAP and Jakarta/Tomcat and try these samples. Once you start programming your own RPC interactions you will find that there isn't much more to them than you've seen here – even if you are sending multiple parameters to the service and returning more than one result value.

Exercises

1. Outline the benefits of using SOAP instead of building a conventional Web system based around HTML pages and CGI scripts.
2. Describe the structure of a SOAP packet.
3. Why must SOAP servers return all errors which they create to their clients?
4. What is the `mustUnderstand` attribute used for?

5. Install and configure Tomcat. Try building an application based around the simple code from Listing 16.1.

Chapter 17

Structured Documentation Using DocBook

The origins of XML lie in SGML and HTML. Both are used to create structured documents but do so to different effect. HTML documents have a simple structure in which the parts of a document have little or no meaning. A piece of text may be marked up using an `<h1>` element, but that does not mean it has the role of a heading or a title in the document. An `<h1>` element is an instruction to a Web browser which tells it how to format content for display. SGML takes the alternative approach in which documents are structured by their meaning, not their intended appearance.

SGML is, as its name makes clear, a general-purpose form of markup. SGML documents are structured according to rules defined in DTDs. Every application of SGML requires its own DTD. Since many people will want to perform the same tasks and structure documents in similar ways, some DTDs are widely used and become *de facto* standards. One such DTD is DocBook.

17.1 INTRODUCING DOCBOOK

The DocBook DTD defines a structure and element set for the creation of technical documentation, in particular documentation in the field of computing. It has evolved over a number of years to the point where the latest version, V4.1.2, has well over 300 separate elements which can be used to describe just about anything that might need to be included in computer documentation.

DocBook can be, and indeed *is*, used to mark up source code for Unix `man` pages, Windows Help files, user manuals, design and development documents, internal documentation inside companies and even textbooks. Much of the documentation for Free Software projects such as the Linux kernel and the Gnome desktop system, as well as countless HOWTOs, user guides and FAQs are written using DocBook. The DTD is attracting new users all the time, to the point where it may be one of the best-known and most widely used structured document types around. You may wonder why DocBook is defined using a DTD rather than a schema. The DTD has been around for a long time and works well with all generations of XML and SGML tools. Schemas are relatively new, several grammars exist for them and tool support is poor. A schema for DocBook is bound to appear at some point, probably once one schema language becomes a dominant force in the market-place.

DocBook originated in a collaboration between a company called HaL Computer Systems and the publishers O'Reilly and Associates back in 1991. They developed an SGML system which could be used to exchange Unix documentation written using `nroff`. Early releases incorporated changes suggested by companies such as Digital and Novell which meant that the DTD grew in both purpose and scope. It was supported by SGML-aware editing tools such as FrameMaker and was widely used in both Novell and Sun. Following the release of version 3.0 in 1997, one of the most significant changes in the history of DocBook occurred. Until this point it had been a pure SGML system, but now efforts began to introduce an XML version. In July 1998 the Organization for the Advancement of Structured Information Standards, OASIS, formed a technical committee to guide the development of DocBook. OASIS continues to extend and improve DocBook while retaining backward compatability wherever possible, and now develops parallel SGML and XML versions.

The creation of an XML version of DocBook is important for a number of reasons. Although XML originated in the SGML community and SGML has been in use for far longer, many more people know about XML than know about SGML. Developers, authors and users are not going to use an SGML technology today if there is an XML alternative. SGML is overly-complicated, is not supported by modern Web-friendly tools and is perceived, rightly or wrongly, as yesterday's technology. XML is young, trendy and eye-catching which is why you're reading this book, isn't it? The XML version of DocBook can be used with the next generation of editing and transformation tools. XSL stylesheets are available for transformation into Web pages, XSLT, and print, XSL-FO, as described in Section 17.4.

When I started writing this book, I was going to use DocBook to structure it. After an abortive early effort I threw that idea away and instead went back to using LaTeX. I tend to think that anyone writing about a technology should use it wherever possible. A textbook is a structured document, DocBook supports them so why not use it? The problem lies not with DocBook, but with the transformation to a printable version. The stylesheets provided with DocBook produce end-results which are either ugly, certainly compared to the output from LaTeX, or can't be used. They can't be used because current transformation tools such as FOP 0.20.3, which transforms XSL to PDF, or PassiveTeX which transforms to TeX, are beta quality at their best. The problem of ugly output could have been solved by customizing the DocBook stylesheets, which would have been time consuming and difficult since I'm not a book designer. The lack of support for tools can only be solved by getting involved in projects to develop better ones.

If the author of a book about XML can't use DocBook, what use is it? DocBook is readily transformed into HTML, manual pages and help documents. It can be used with some professional editing tools, and is used successfully by publishers such as O'Reilly and Associates. Even I use it in my work as an academic. Producing design documents or system specifications with DocBook is relatively simple and the printed results look OK. It's just that, at the moment, the quality of output required for professional publishing isn't generally available.

17.2 CREATING DOCBOOK DOCUMENTS

As I mentioned earlier, the DocBook DTD contains well over 300 elements. There's no way that I can cover more than a tiny fraction of those in an overview chapter such as this one. Instead, I'm going to show how to write a small simple document using the DTD, then transform it into both HTML and PDF formats.

DocBook can be used to create three different classes of document. The most complex of these is the *book* which contains front and back matter, chapters, parts, sections, indexes and tables of contents and figures. The example which I describe later is of a book so I won't say any more at the moment. For documents that are smaller than books and that don't require the organizational complexity provided by chapters and so on, DocBook has the *article* type. Any small document, be it a memo, a piece of college work or technical documentation, can be structured using the `article` class. The final document type in DocBook is a *reference page*. Based on the Unix `manpage`, reference pages can be used for all types of reference information. They can be formatted for use with a variety of different help systems, or easily converted to HTML for use on Web sites.

17.2.1 A Simple Article

I would guess that most documents that you are likely to create with DocBook will be relatively small articles. Even if you eventually need to create document sets that span a number of books, learning to use the `article` class is the simplest way of getting to grips with the DTD. Read through the code in Listing 17.1 and compare it with the markup shown in Listing 2.9. The latter shows a letter which is described using an XML structure that I developed especially for the purpose.[1] The dedicated XML structure is more expressive than the DocBook version. It lets authors define addresses for the sender and recipient as well as the content of the letter. DocBook is a general-purpose DTD for technical, specifically computing, documentation and as such it has fewer immediately useful elements when writing a letter. I'm using the content from the earlier example simply so that the article isn't empty. The following code has been split into pieces within which I have interleaved descriptions.

Listing 17.1 A DocBook Article

```
<?xml version="1.0" standalone="no" ?>
<!DOCTYPE article SYSTEM "/usr/share/sgml/db41xml/docbookx.dtd">
```

DocBook DTDs are available for both XML and SGML documents. The Doctype declaration defines the type of document that is being created and points to the location of a suitable DTD on the local system. The DTD for XML structured DocBook documents is always called `docbookx.dtd`, while that for SGML documents is called `docbook.dtd`. Using the correct DTD is vitally important. If the wrong one is selected, tools such as `OpenJade` or `onsgmls`, which validate documents while they process them, will produce lots of errors.

The commonly used document types are: `article`, `book` and `refentry`. The latter is used to define reference pages, manual pages and help documents. The next section of the listing gives information about the author of the document:

```
<article>
  <articleinfo>
    <author>
      <honorific>Mr.</honorific>
      <firstname>William</firstname>
```

[1] A DTD for the letter is given in Section 3.8.

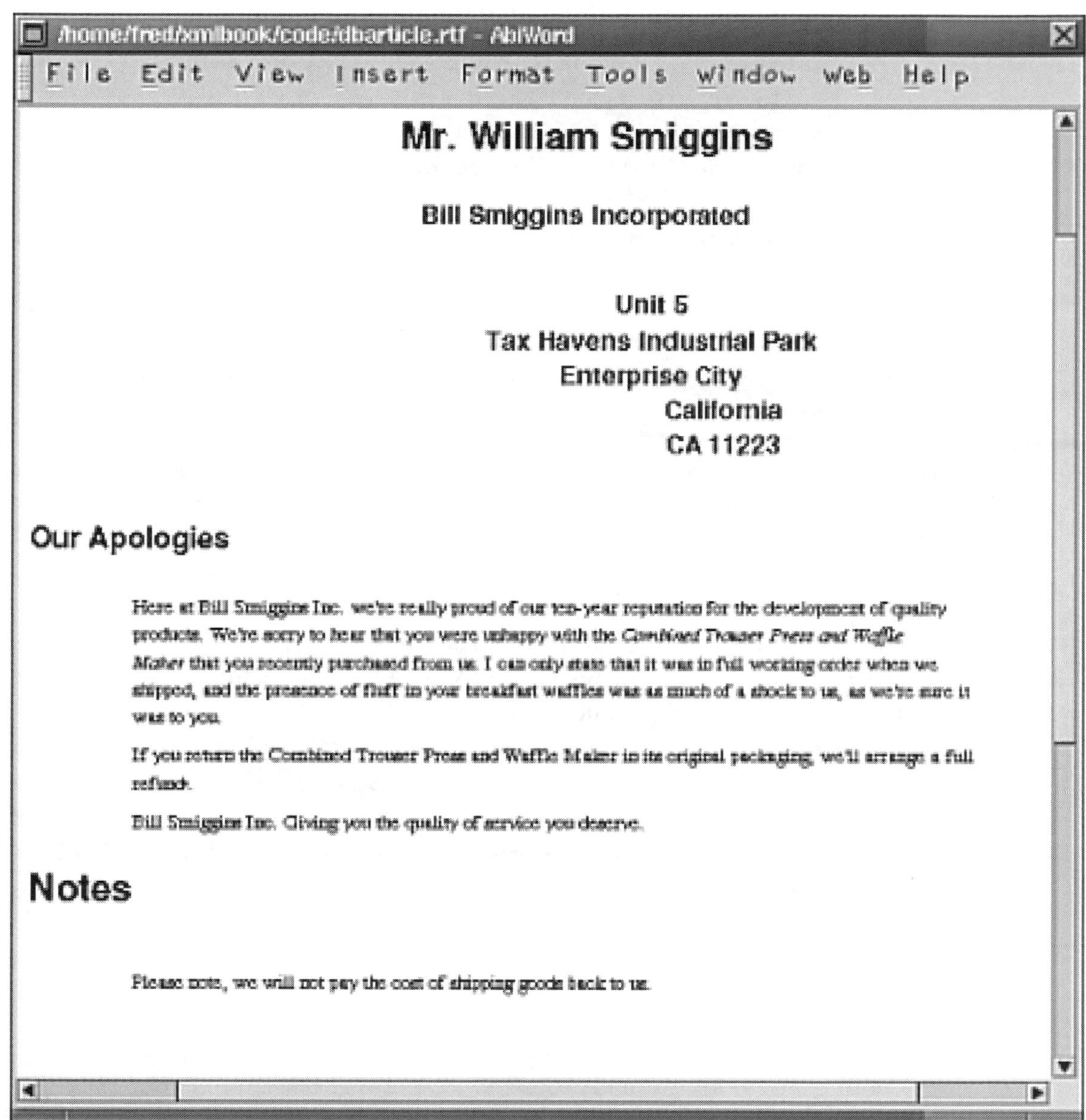

Mr. William Smiggins

Bill Smiggins Incorporated

Unit 5
Tax Havens Industrial Park
Enterprise City
California
CA 11223

Our Apologies

Here at Bill Smiggins Inc. we're really proud of our ten-year reputation for the development of quality products. We're sorry to hear that you were unhappy with the *Combined Trouser Press and Waffle Maker* that you recently purchased from us. I can only state that it was in full working order when we shipped, and the presence of fluff in your breakfast waffles was as much of a shock to us, as we're sure it was to you.

If you return the Combined Trouser Press and Waffle Maker in its original packaging, we'll arrange a full refund.

Bill Smiggins Inc. Giving you the quality of service you deserve.

Notes

Please note, we will not pay the cost of shipping goods back to us.

Figure 17.1 Simple Article Styled Using DSSSL

```
<surname>Smiggins</surname>
<affiliation>
  <orgname>Bill Smiggins Incorporated</orgname>
  <address>
```

```
        <otheraddr>Unit 5</otheraddr>
        <street>Tax Havens Industrial Park</street>
        <city>Enterprise City</city>
        <state>California</state>
        <postcode>CA 11223</postcode>
      </address>
    </affiliation>
  </author>
  <copyright>
    <year>2002</year>
  </copyright>
</articleinfo>
```

An `article` starts with some optional metadata. The `articleinfo` element contains information about the document.[2] This includes details of the authors, information about the publisher and publication date, copyright dates, version control information and cataloging details. When many documents are being stored on the same system, for instance departmental memos or software design documents, being able to index them automatically or search them using tools such as `egrep` is a useful facility. Metadata such as that contained in the `articleinfo` element becomes exceptionally useful.

An `article` may be divided into a series of sections. These provide a structured hierarchy starting at the top level with `sect1` and continuing down through `sect6`. In writing an HTML page different levels of heading, `<h1>` and so on, denote styles which should be applied to the text. The differences between `<h1>` and `<h4>` are differences of font style, decoration and family. Those elements carry no *semantic* meaning. In DocBook documents, on the other hand, the differences between `<sect1>` and `<sect4>` elements are totally about meaning, not presentation.

```
<sect1>
  <title>Our Apologies</title>
  <simpara>Here at Bill Smiggins Inc. we're really proud of
     our ten-year reputation for the development of quality
     products. We're sorry to hear that you were unhappy with
     the <emphasis>Combined Trouser Press and Waffle Maker</
     emphasis> that you recently purchased from us. I can only
      state that it was in full working order when we shipped
     , and the presence of fluff in your breakfast waffles was
```

[2]The `articleinfo` element replaces the `artheader` element which was used in version 3 of DocBook.

```
        as much of a shock to us, as we're sure it was to you.</
       simpara>

    <simpara>If you return the Combined Trouser Press and Waffle
        Maker in its original packaging, we'll arrange a full
       refund<footnote><simpara>Please note, we will not pay the
        cost of shipping goods back to us.</simpara></footnote
       >.</simpara>

    <simpara>Bill Smiggins Inc. Giving you the quality of
       service you deserve.</simpara>
  </sect1>
</article>
```

Each section has an optional `title` element which is used in indexing and numbering sections. DocBook has two elements which can be used to describe paragraphs of text. The first of these is a paragraph which holds only plain text and inline elements such as `footnote` or `emphasis`. The second type, paragraphs that contain block-level elements such as tables, lists or images, must be marked using the `para` tag. Figure 17.1 shows the result of transforming this document into RTF using the default DocBook DSSSL stylesheets. DSSSL is briefly described in Section 17.3. The formatted document is being displayed using the AbiWord editor, which is an excellent example of Free Software.

Notice that paragraphs must be expressly defined even inside elements such as `footnote`. This might seem peculiar since a footnote is only going to contain text, isn't it? Well, actually no. In DocBook, footnotes may hold block-level elements such as images, lists and tables, as well as ordinary text. This is an important point about DocBook. The DTD is large and complex and, in places, appears counter-intuitive. Difficulties encountered when using the DTD are generally caused because it is a general-purpose structure. The only way to make DocBook really usable is to have the documentation close at hand and to use a good XML editor.

DocBook is primarily described in the book *DocBook: The Definitive Guide* which is written by Norman Walsh and Leonard Muellner, and published by O'Reilly And Associates. Norman Walsh is currently the lead developer of DocBook, in particular the XML version and its associated XSL stylesheets. The fact that he probably knows more about it than anyone else means that *The Definitive Guide* is a very thorough reference work. Unusually, the guide is available free of charge for users who prefer their documentation in electronic format. Drafts of the latest edition can be downloaded from the DocBook Web site in HTML form. While I prefer nicely printed and bound books, I use the electronic documentation to supplement and update the information I get from my printed copy of the first edition which was published in 1999.

Editing large XML documents can be an awkward business. The problem is that not only do authors need to know what elements are available in the DTD, they must use them in the correct order and hierarchy. Several editors for SGML are available commercially. The more popular of these such as FrameMaker have support for XML, and may go so far as to understand DocBook straight out of the box. The XML version of DocBook can be used with commercial tools such as XML Spy, although these will not automatically apply the appropriate stylesheets, and may not support the editing of stylesheets. Such tools are intended for use in large organizations and are priced accordingly. My own preference is to use Free Software wherever possible, and if it happens to be also free of cost and high quality then so much the better. My editor of choice is Emacs which is available for most operating systems. Emacs can be used for all programming tasks, and can be extended through user-created libraries, called *modes*, which are written in a dialect of Lisp. For editing XML, I use PSGML mode. This includes code that parses the DTD so that context-sensitive menus become available. At any point in a document the editor can provide a list of valid elements and another that contains oft-used entities. It also provides syntax highlighting, context-sensitive editing and support for catalog files. The only downside is that Emacs is a very complicated piece of software which has a steep learning curve.

17.2.2 A More Complex Book

The `article` document is relatively straightforward. Using the `book` DTD gives the opportunity to show more aspects of DocBook. Some of the code from Listing 17.2.2, specifically the parts dealing with the inclusion of programming code and images, could be used in an `article` without changes.

```
<?xml version="1.0" standalone="no" ?>
<!DOCTYPE book SYSTEM "/usr/share/sgml/db41xml/docbookx.dtd">
```

Although the DTD is the same for all DocBook documents, the document type changes when making a book. The root element becomes `book` and `articleinfo` becomes `bookinfo`. The set of valid elements under `bookinfo` is the same as that allowed under `articleinfo`. The same metadata is placed inside different elements because it has different meanings. Remember, with DTDs such as DocBook, context is everything.

```
<book>
  <bookinfo>
    <title>XSL Transformation Language</title>
    <author>
      <firstname>Chris</firstname>
```

```
    <surname>Bates</surname>
  </author>
  <address><email>c.d.bates@shu.ac.uk</email></address>
  <copyright><year>2002</year></copyright>
    <publisher>
      <publishername>John Wiley And Sons</publishername>
    </publisher>
    <pubdate>
      <remark>Provisional Date</remark>
      2003
    </pubdate>
</bookinfo>
```

A book can be divided into parts or chapters. A part is a collection of chapters and cannot directly hold paragraphs. Chapters can contains sections, in the same way that articles do, or paragraphs. The hierarchy of elements is intended to provided maximum flexibility in the way that authors structure their documents. Those elements that supply conventional document structure, such as parts, chapters and sections, may each have a title which will be used in building an index for the book. Content is placed into paragraphs, tables or lists. I'm not going to examine tables. DocBook tables are based on the CALS model which is one of the standard ways of representing tables in SGML. The HTML table structure has many similarities to CALS, but is far simpler. If you read the DocBook documentation and look at some examples, building tables should be quite possible. However, it's probably a good idea to treat tables as an advanced topic. Become familiar with the basics of DocBook first, get a few transformations working and *then* try to write a table or two.

```
<part>
  <title>Formatting XML</title>

  <chapter>
    <title>Introduction</title>

    <para>The process of changing the structure of an XML document
        is called <emphasis>transformation</emphasis> and is done
        using the Extensible Stylesheet Language, XSL. Originally
        XSL was envisaged as a single language which could perform
        all possible transformations. This was impractical as the
        language would have been exceptionally complex. In software
        development complexity is often the enemy of usefulness &
```

```
mdash; once languages reach a certain level of complexity
developers will prefer to find other, simpler solutions. The
 solution to the complexity of XSL was to split it into two
 smaller, though still pretty complex, languages. XSLT, the
 XSL Transformation language was developed for the purposes
 of transforming between XML structures. The XSL Formatting
 Objects, XSL-FO, language was developed for transformations
 into printed or aural forms. I examine XSL-FO in Chapter 6, <
emphasis>this</emphasis> chapter will concentrate on XSLT.</
para>

<note>
  <title>Note</title>
  <para>Since XHTML is an XML application, transformations
     into Web pages are usually done through XSLT rather
     than XSL-FO. Because Web browsers can display XHTML,
     and in common with most XML book, the examples here
     will transform from XML to XHTML.</para>
</note>
```

Some block elements have special meanings which may be used to format them in special ways. Inline text can be stressed using the `emphasis` tag which is usually formatted in an italic font. Blocks of text can be stressed using the `note` or `warning` elements. Most stylesheets will isolate these blocks, indent them and, possibly, draw a line around them. Computer reference material often includes fragments of code. DocBook has a number of elements that can be used to identify inline code within the flow of text. These include the following partial list:

equation

Used when a mathematical equation is being included. If the equation markup is in MathML, it can be included using the `mml:math` element. Processing this requires an additional MathML module. Here is an example based on one in *The DocBook Guide.*

```
<!DOCTYPE equation
   PUBLIC "-//OASIS//DTD DocBook MathML Module V1.0//EN"
        "http://www.oasis-open.org/docbook/xml/mathml/1.0/
            dbmathml.dtd">
  <equation>
    <mml:math>
```

```
      <mml:apply>
        <mml:divide/>
      </mml:apply>
    </mml:math>
  </equation>
```

errorname
Include an error message from a program or compiler.

filename
Include the name of a file.

funcdef
The name of a function and its return type.

function
The name of a function.

informalequation
A mathematical equation without a title. This is a simplified version of the `equation` element.

markup
A piece of markup which is placed *as is* in the document.

programlisting
Source code for an entire program, or function.

Including XML in a document isn't easy. Using the `markup` element is one solution but this won't prevent tools processing the included XML sections. A better solution is to place a `CDATA` section inside the `programlisting` element. The XML is placed inside the `CDATA` so that tools know they are not expected to process it. The following code shows how this is done:

```
      <programlisting>
<![CDATA[
<?xml version="1.0"?>

<xsl:stylesheet
  xmlns:xsl="http://www.w3.org/1999/XSL/Transform"
  version="1.0">
```

```
  <xsl:template match="/message">
    <html>
      <head><title>Test</title></head>
      <body>
        <h1><xsl:value-of select="."/></h1>
      </body>
    </html>
  </xsl:template>

</xsl:stylesheet>
]]>
            </programlisting>
```

Non-text data, whether it is a still image, a video clip or a piece of audio, has to be placed in a `mediaobject` element. The code that follows shows how to include an image in a DocBook document. The image itself is placed in an `imageobject` element. This is associated with a `textobject` element and a `caption` element. The `caption` will normally be used as the caption to the image. It might seem peculiar that the `mediaobject` can be used to include moving images or audio since DocBook is often formatted into printed documents. DocBook documents may also be formatted into Web sites which obviously support more complex data types. In the future as new platform-independent data formats are inevitably developed, DocBook stylesheets that can be used for them are bound to appear. Remember, this is one of the great things about XML in general. Once data has been marked up, it can be used almost at will in a wide variety of ways. All that's needed are new stylesheets and tools that can process them.

```
<mediaobject>
  <imageobject>
    <imagedata fileref="../images/XSLTProc.eps" format="
       EPS"/>
  </imageobject>
  <textobject>
    <para>XML Plus XSLT In Opera 6</para>
  </textobject>
  <caption>
    <para>Opera 6 does a poor job of rendering XML styled
       using XSLT. In fact, it doesn't understand how to
       process XSLT.</para>
  </caption>
</mediaobject>
```

```
    </chapter>
  </part>
</book>
```

17.2.3 Parsing and Validation

I've talked, briefly, about tools that can be used to edit DocBook. Creating a document is only one aspect of using markup languages. The source file needs to be validated so that its adherence to the DTD can be guaranteed, and transformed into formats that are more reader-friendly. In Section 17.3 I will examine an old SGML-era stylesheet language, while in Section 17.4 I'll look at how XML DocBook documents can be transformed using XSL stylesheets.

When working with a complex DTD such as DocBook, guaranteeing that a document adheres to its rules is imperative. Making mistakes is easy, even when using a good editor. Performing validation of any XML document is surprisingly easy – once you get the right tools installed and configured. The favorite tool for validating XML, and SGML, documents described using a DTD is `SP`, written by James Clark. Other tools such as Xerces work well, but SP has the advantage of being written in C++, and of being developed over a number of years to the point at which it really is that rarest of software beasts, the finished article.[3] SP is a package of tools which includes a command-line parser called `nsgmls` and a library which can be embedded directly into applications on a wide variety of platforms, including Unix and Windows.

Using `nsgmls`[4] requires one or two changes to the way that a system is configured. The first thing to understand is the concept of a *catalog* file. Manipulating complex SGML documents such as DocBook documents may involve using more than one DTD. Systems that have evolved over time are likely to have different versions of the same DTD in use. For example, if you have documentation written in the SGML DocBook 3, and later start to author using the XML version of DocBook 4, your tools need to be able to find *both* DTDs and use the appropriate one. This is where the catalog comes into play. It is a plain text file which takes the public identifiers for DTD files and maps them onto real files on the local filesystem or network. A Doctype Declaration such as

```
<!DOCTYPE book PUBLIC "-//OASIS//DTD DocBook XML V4.1.2//EN"
               "file:///usr/share/sgml/db41xml/docbookx.dtd">
```

[3] A Free Software effort called OpenSP has been gently under way for some time to continue development of SP.

[4] In this section I'm using `nsgmls` and `onsgmls` interchangeably. The OpenSP version is more current and should be used in preference.

works fine on one machine. What happens if the document is moved to a different machine with its own directory structure or, more likely in this example, a different operating system? Any tool that has to process the document will begin to report errors. What we'd like to do is to automatically map the root element of the document to a Doctype Declaration, which in turn maps straight to a DTD file. Here's the catalog file on the Unix box I normally use. I have a similar file on a Windows 2000 workstation which is rarely used for XML work.

```
OVERRIDE YES

SGMLDECL "/usr/share/sgml/openjade/xml.dcl"
DOCTYPE book "/usr/share/sgml/db41xml/docbookx.dtd"

PUBLIC "-//OASIS//DTD DocBook XML V4.1.2//EN" "/usr/share/sgml/
    db41xml/docbookx.dtd"
PUBLIC "-//James Clark//DTD DSSSL Style Sheet//EN" "/usr/share/
    sgml/openjade/style-sheet.dtd"
PUBLIC "-//Norman Walsh//DOCUMENT DocBook Print Stylesheet//EN
    " "/home/fred/docbook/docbook-dsssl-1.76/print/docbook.dsl"
SYSTEM "builtins.dsl" "/usr/share/sgml/openjade/builtins.dsl"

CATALOG "/usr/share/sgml/CATALOG.db41xml"
CATALOG "/home/fred/docbook/docbook-dsssl-1.76/catalog"
CATALOG "/usr/share/sgml/openjade/catalog"
```

The `SGMLDECL` points to a special file, called a catalog, which defines the standard XML entities. Many XML tools are also capable of processing SGML, but older tools such as SP default to SGML. This declaration tells the tool to use the XML entities in preference to the default SGML ones, and points it to a file that contains them. Notice that since I use OpenSP, the XML entity file is the one distributed with it. The file then has a series of mappings of public identifiers onto local files for both the DocBook DTD and those that define the DSSSL stylesheets. The `SYSTEM` declaration of `builtins.dsl` is necessary if the OpenJade DSSSL processor is going to work properly. Catalog files can include other catalogs. If a system has lots of catalogs, nesting them in this way hides a lot of complexity. If you have DocBook installed on your system, glance at a few of its catalogs and you'll see why this is so useful.

Tools such as `onsgmls`, Emacs[5] and OpenJade will automatically look for a catalog file in the current directory when they are invoked. If there isn't a catalog in that directory,

[5]With PSGML mode.

they may still work properly provided they are pointed to a suitable file. The simplest way to do this is to set an environment variable called `SGML_CATALOG_FILES`. There's no guarantee that setting this variable will work, but it should help. Here's mine:

```
SGML_CATALOG_FILES=/usr/share/sgml/CATALOG.db41xml:/usr/share/
    sgml/CATALOG.docbook-dsssl-stylesheets:/usr/share/sgml/
    openjade/catalog:./catalog
```

When setting this variable, you need to be alert to one thing: it points to actual catalog files. Most environment variables point to a directory but this one is different. You won't see an error message if you forget to add the filenames to their directories.

Once you've installed and configured DocBook, the stylesheets, SP and Jade, and created a catalog, you'll want to test everything. One way is to create a small DocBook document like the ones shown earlier, and validate it with `nsgmls`. The parser has many different options which you can read about in its documentation. Here's a simple invocation to get you started:

```
onsgmls -w xml -sv docbook.xml
```

Because the rules of XML are stricter than for SGML, the parser needs to be told that it has to enforce them. The `-w` flag tells the parser to print warnings about anything in the document that is valid SGML but not valid in XML. Generally, `onsgmls` prints a lot of information about a document, but most users will only want to see its error messages. The `-s` flag makes it operate in silent mode in which only warnings and errors are shown. Unfortunately, when used like that, the parser simply exits if the document validates successfully. Using `-v` makes it print its version information out if nothing else. This gives confirmation and reassurance that it really was run.

17.3 STYLING DOCBOOK DOCUMENTS USING DSSSL

Two sets of stylesheets are available for DocBook. Each is capable of producing output in a variety of formats, and both can be used on any system that has an appropriate set of tools installed. The XSL stylesheets are examined in Section 17.4 and before that a more mature technology is examined. The Document Style Semantics and Specification Language, DSSSL, was developed to style, transform, manipulate and query SGML documents. In many ways it occupies the same *ecological* niche as XSL, XQuery and XPath do in the XML world. I'm only interested in those parts of DSSSL that are used for styling documents. You might notice as you look at the examples in this section, or read some of the code in the DocBook stylesheets, that the underlying concepts and meanings in DSSSL are very similar to those that underpin both XSLT and CSS.

17.3.1 Using Jade

A document marked up in DocBook and styled using appropriate DSSSL stylesheets doesn't make an instantly usable document. Throughout this book, I've shown how modern Web browsers such as Mozilla can be used to format and preview XML documents when suitable CSS or XSLT stylesheets are available. DocBook plus DSSSL doesn't work in the same way. No applications that can style and display on the fly using DSSSL have been developed. Instead, stylesheets and documents are processed to give static documents for storage, viewing and further manipulation. The most widely used DSSSL processor is Jade, written by James Clark, also the man behind SP and `nsgmls`. Jade, just like SP, continues to be developed as an Open Source project, this time called OpenJade.[6] The program is written in C++ but is available for many different platforms, including Microsoft Windows.

One big advantage of Jade, certainly compared to many XSL processors, is that it can produce several widely used types of document. I use it to produce documentation in Microsoft's Rich Text Format, RTF, which all versions of Word can edit. Since Word is probably the most widely used application for handling text documents, RTF is a much more useful output type than, for example, PDF. It certainly lacks the richness and refinement of PDF, but if you want people to read your words, you need to use a data type that they can handle without thinking. I realize that PDF readers such as Adobe Acrobat are widely, and often freely, available,[7] but the lowest common denominator is often a better choice than the best technology.

Jade doesn't stop at RTF. It can also output XML, HTML and SGML, a non-standard Flow Object Tree, FOT, a format called MIF and TeX. The TeX documents that Jade makes cannot be processed using a vanilla install of LaTeX. An additional macro package, JadeTeX, is required. This contains an application, not surprisingly called JadeTeX, which processes the TeX file to produce PDF or PostScript output. It's worth noting that both the RTF and TeX mediated output from Jade are of very high quality. One difficulty that many people, myself included, have with the current generation of XSL-FO processors is that the documents they produce are simply ugly. In fact, their quality is often so poor as to render them useless. Using TeX, in particular, as an intermediate format removes this problem since its output is of exceptionally high quality.

Using Jade requires a couple of changes to your setup. The catalog which you may have created for use with `onsgmls` won't work with Jade. The problem is in the `SGMLDECL` instruction. In the catalog I showed earlier, it points to a declaration of XML entities.

[6] I'm going to use the names Jade and OpenJade interchangeably. The two provide almost identical functionality, although the latter has more refinements and bug fixes.

[7] In my experience, though, many apparently IT-literate people don't know what to do when presented with a PDF document.

DSSSL is an SGML application and Jade needs to be able to find SGML entities as well as XML ones. A catalog cannot contain more than one `SGMLDECL`. The directory could contain more than one catalog, but Jade is unable to resolve different `SGMLDECL`s. The solution is to create a new directory to hold a DSSSL-specific catalog. Here's mine:

```
SGMLDECL "/home/fred/docbook/docbook-dsssl-1.76/dtds/decls/
    docbook.dcl"

PUBLIC "-//Norman Walsh//DOCUMENT DocBook Print Stylesheet//EN
    " "/home/fred/docbook/docbook-dsssl-1.76/print/docbook.dsl"
PUBLIC "-//James Clark//DTD DSSSL Style Sheet//EN" "/usr/share/
    sgml/openjade/style-sheet.dtd"

CATALOG "/home/fred/docbook/docbook-dsssl-1.76/catalog"
CATALOG "/usr/share/sgml/openjade/catalog"
```

The DocBook stylesheets can be modified using *driver* files. These hold pieces of DSSSL code which override that found in the main DocBook stylesheets. I'm not going to describe how to write your own modifications, although the discussion of DSSSL that follows should give you some clues. A useful starting point is provided by a file called `plain.dsl` which is part of the DocBook DSSSL distribution. To simplify the use of Jade, even if I'm not going to customize anything, I copy this into the same directory as my DSSSL-specific stylesheet. I can then invoke Jade as follows:

```
openjade -t rtf -c dsssl/catalog -d dsssl/plain.dsl /usr/share/
    sgml/openjade/xml.dcl letter.xml
```

The `-t` flag sets the output type, `-c` points to the DSSSL catalog and `-d` to the driver file I'm using. The XML declaration must be placed in the invocation ahead of the XML file which is being transformed. This is needed even though the same file is specified in the catalog file for XML documents. I have yet to find any documentation that describes this way of invoking Jade. I have found a number of alternatives both on the Web and in the DocBook and DSSSL documentation. None of those works for me on either Linux or Windows. This invocation does but you may get different results. My experience suggests that installing and configuring the DocBook DSSSL stylesheets and Jade is exceptionally frustrating. Whenever I've done so, the whole process has taken at least *six* hours simply because the error messages that Jade produces are almost completely unhelpful. Interestingly, once everything is working, those error messages start to make a lot more sense.

17.3.2 DSSSL Stylesheets

The DSSSL language is based upon the functional programming language Scheme. This is a variant of Lisp which means that the syntax of the language is incredibly simple. It also means that almost everything about the language is different to what you might expect if you have only ever programmed in languages such as Visual Basic or Java. Many Computer Science courses include at least an introduction to functional programming, although these may be going the same way as COBOL, FORTRAN and assembler programming. Fortunately the syntax of DSSSL is so clean that writing or modifying stylesheets can be done without understanding anything about Scheme programming.

The code in Listing 17.2 demonstrates a simple driver file. Any modifications that are placed in this file will override the instructions in the standard DocBook stylesheets provided the driver file is identified to Jade using the `-t` flag. The only place in the listing in which changes are required is within the `style-specification-body` element. The rest of the driver file will be identical on every system.[8]

Listing 17.2 A DSSSL Driver File

```
<!DOCTYPE style-sheet PUBLIC
          "-//James Clark//DTD DSSSL Style Sheet//EN" [
  <!ENTITY dbdsl PUBLIC "-//Norman Walsh//DOCUMENT DocBook Print
  Stylesheet//EN" CDATA DSSSL>

]>

<style-sheet>
<style-specification use="docbook">
<style-specification-body>

(element simpara
  (make paragraph
    font-size: 12pt
    line-spacing: 16pt
    font-posture: 'italic
    (process-children)))

</style-specification-body>
</style-specification>

<external-specification id="docbook" document="dbdsl">
```

[8]Expert users will, of course, alter driver files to suit their knowledge, experience and needs.

```
</style-sheet>
```

This driver contains just one modification. The font used for text in `simpara` elements, and the spacing of lines in those elements, is altered. Although there are obvious syntactic differences, the use of parentheses rather than angle brackets for example, DSSSL is a relatively easy language for readers who have used XSLT or CSS. Some terminology changes, so that what word processors call *justification* of text is called *quadding* in DSSSL.

I have struggled to find much documentation on DSSSL. It appears to be a *hacker's* technology, by which I mean that the usual answer to any question is that one should *read the source*. If you want to customize the DocBook DSSSL stylesheets, you must first find the element that you want to change in the original stylesheets, discover how it is implemented and then rewrite the code in your driver file. This is time consuming, especially for beginners, but it does lead to an in-depth understanding of how the stylesheets work.

17.4 STYLING DOCBOOK DOCUMENTS USING XSL

DSSSL is, by the standards of the modern world, a rather old technology. Although the DocBook stylesheets are under active development, and Jade produces output of the highest quality, many users would prefer a pure XML styling solution. XSL stylesheets are available as part of the standard DocBook XML distribution. These can be used to produce output in HTML, XHTML, Java Help, HTML Help and Formatting Object forms. Extension classes are supplied for use with versions 5 and 6 of the Saxon transformation engine. Unlike the DSSSL stylesheets, the XSL ones are comprehensively documented.

The stylesheets for each output format are placed in their own directory with a driver file which is used to initiate and control processing. Whichever output you are using, this file is called `docbook.xsl`, so your transformation engine may be pointed to `fo/docbook.xsl` or `html/docbook.xsl`, for example.[9] If the output from the stylesheets needs to be modified in any way, this can be done by adding a new template and listing it in the driver file. This has the unfortunate side-effect that all your applications suddenly get the new styling. That's unlikely to be either intended or desirable. The solution is to use parameters to set variables within the standard stylesheets.

Just about anything that could possibly be altered within a DocBook stylesheet is accessible through parameters. Most of the documentation that accompanies the stylesheets is taken up with more or less detailed descriptions of these parameters and how they are used. The user-customizable variables are listed in a file called `param.xsl` which is im-

[9]These are Unix paths; the slash changes to \ on a Windows machine.

ported at the end of docbook.xsl. These are global variables which means that any changes made to them elsewhere, for instance in a new driver file, apply throughout the stylesheets.

The code in Listing 17.3 shows an XSL driver file which will modify the font used in the body of a document created using XSL-FO. This defaults to Times Roman. Here it is changed to Helvetica.

Listing 17.3 XSL Driver File

```
<?xml version='1.0'?>
<xsl:stylesheet xmlns:xsl="http://www.w3.org/1999/XSL/Transform"
            version='1.0'
            xmlns="http://www.w3.org/TR/xhtml1/transitional"
            exclude-result-prefixes="#default">

<xsl:import href="/home/fred/docbook/XSL/fo/docbook.xsl"/>

<xsl:variable name="body.font.family">Helvetica</xsl:variable>
<!-- Add other variable definitions here -->

</xsl:stylesheet>
```

The variables which are listed in param.xsl provide access to only a small part of the stylesheets. When more complicated changes are required, new templates have to be written. These can be based on the standard ones and placed in a driver file like the one in Listing 17.3. These new templates are imported *after* the standard ones, thus overriding the standard definitions.

In this chapter I've only given a flavor of the possibilities of DocBook. It is a very large and very complicated DTD. For structured documentation, especially in the computing field, it is an excellent choice. Creating print documents based upon DocBook is currently best done using DSSSL, but as XSL-FO processors mature, the XSL stylesheets are sure to provide a better solution.

Exercises

1. Install the DocBook DTD and stylesheets.
2. Install software which can be used to format documents using DSSSL.
3. What advantages does DocBook give, when writing technical documentation, compared to creating your own document structure?

4. List the output formats which can be produced using the standard DocBook distribution.
5. Why might DSSSL be used instead of XSLT for a DocBook project?
6. Describe two situations in which the *article* document type might be used.
7. Describe two situations in which the *book* document type could be used.
8. Create a DocBook document which contains the data needed for a typical student essay. Include the following information:
   - title,
   - author's name,
   - creation date,
   - several paragraphs of text, formatted within a two distinct sections,
   - some footnotes,
   - an annotated bibliography.
9. Transform your essay into PDF using the DSSSL stylesheets.
10. Transform your essay into PDF using the XSLT stylesheets which come with DocBook.

Chapter 18

Defining Application Interfaces Using XUL

Most people who have heard of XML think of it as a language for creating data structures. XML has always been sold as a flexible, capable and relatively straightforward way of creating user-defined data structures. Many different types of data can be structured using XML, formatted using XSL, exchanged as SOAP messages and queried with combinations of XQuery and RDF. XML is never going to replace more powerful, and better known, technologies such as relational databases in corporate data centers. At the time that I am writing this book XML *is* replacing binary data structures in applications such as word processors and spreadsheets.

XML has potential in many different areas of life. It simplifies decision making for system developers. Rather than expending time and effort inventing data structures, developers can use XML to build a structure that is both easy to read and easy to maintain. Once a programmer or designer understands XML, it seems like an obvious candidate for data-interchange. That's why SOAP and several similar but competing messaging formats have been developed. It seems that everywhere that XML *could* be used by developers, someone *is* using it. But one area that seems an unlikely candidate for XML structures is the graphical interface to applications.

Graphical interfaces are developed using *toolkits*. A toolkit is a set of components which are drawn on the screen in combinations that create the interface to the application. Many different toolkits exist; some for specific platforms, others for use with specific programming languages. All share a number of common features,[1] among which is the ability to build standalone applications. Even the Java toolkits, AWT and Swing, which can be used inside a browser, are primarily used to build conventional standalone applications. All of which is a long-winded way of introducing a toolkit called XUL. If you like what you read here, further details on XUL and the Mozilla browser can be found at `http://www.mozilla.org`, the homepage of the Mozilla project.

18.1 INTRODUCING XUL

The Mozilla project is an open-source development project which is creating a fully featured, standards-compliant Web browser. It was created in 1997 by Netscape to continue development of their browser beyond version 4. The hope was that a thriving community of developers would join the project, much as they have with development of the Linux kernel. To kick-start the whole project, Netscape donated the code-base for their browser and the time and expense of many of their developers. Unfortunately, that code was unsuitable and little progress was made in developing it into Netscape 5. The whole project effectively started over to create a new browser. As I write this, the Mozilla project is about to release version 1.0 of their browser which runs on many operating systems, and across a wide variety of hardware devices. Netscape is now part of the giant Time-Warner-AOL media conglomerate which continues to fund most of the development work on the project.

The Mozilla project has released many beta versions of their software which have been tested by tens of thousands of users worldwide. One beta was even spun off and developed into the Netscape 6 browser. The project has always been keen to build a browser that complies with standards wherever those standards exist. This was not true of Netscape, and some Web sites worked when viewed with Netscape 4 will no longer

[1] At least all the ones I've ever used do so.

work in Mozilla. Most of those problems are caused by Mozilla's compliance with the ECMA standard for JavaScript and the W3C Document Object Model. Mozilla also complies with standards and W3C Recommendations in areas as diverse as MathML, SVG, RDF and XML.

XUL, the name is apparently pronounced *zule*, is one of a set of technologies that together make Mozilla into an extremely configurable browser. Some users, especially those used to systems such as Linux, like to change the appearance of applications so that their system better fits their needs. These changes usually take the form of *skins*, different icons and fonts which replace the default ones provided with the application. Skins do not change the functionality of the application, and they usually don't even change where menus and toolbars are drawn. Instead they change just the appearance of the software. Not all software is skinnable, although many large Open Source projects, including the popular KDE and Gnome Unix desktops, are. Mozilla has a skinning technology of its own, called *chrome*. Mozilla skins, sometimes called chromes, can be used alongside XUL to build applications that look unique. I'm not going to mention them again since there is plenty of information on the Mozilla Web site. Mozilla includes a default skin which looks like the traditional Netscape browser, and a sleeker, more modern skin. Figure 18.1 shows the differences between the two.

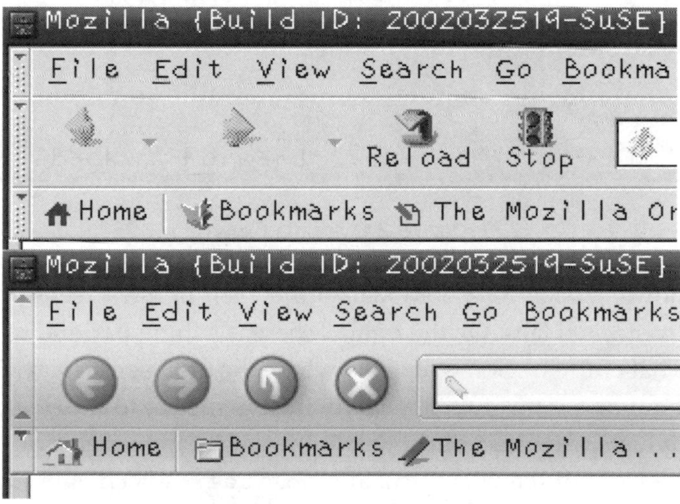

Figure 18.1 Skinned Mozilla Browsers

XUL is a GUI toolkit. Using it, applications can be easily developed in a simple text editor. The main limitation of XUL is that those applications must run inside Mozilla. This means that the language occupies the same sort of user-space as Java applets and

HTML forms. Indeed, one thing to note about XUL is that many of its *widgets*,[2] are the same as those provided in HTML for forms development. The significant difference is that a XUL application does not have to exist inside a Web page.

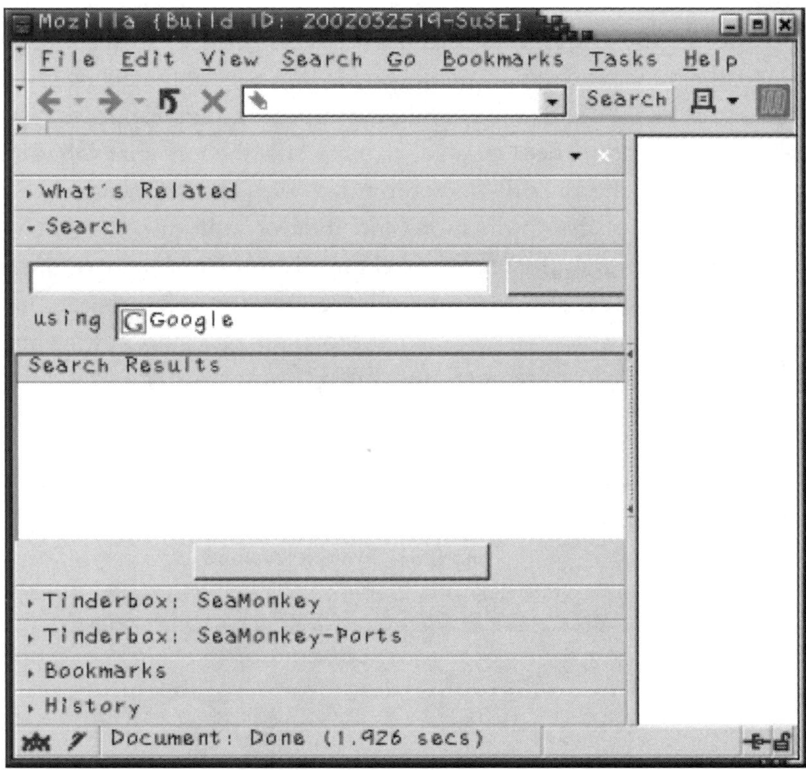

Figure 18.2 Mozilla Browser

Figure 18.2 shows version 0.9.8 of Mozilla. To the left of the screenshot you'll notice a series of vertically stacked tabs. On the right of these is a thing bar, and to the right of that an empty area. That empty region is actually where the browser displays Web pages. The tabs on the left hold additional functionality which is special to Mozilla. I've opened up the `search` tab which provides a direct link to the Web search engine of your choice. The vertical bar at the right of the tabs is called a `splitter`, which is used to interactively assign screen space between the page display area and the tabs. By clicking once in its center using the mouse, the splitter can also be used to hide the tabs.

The tabs, their content, and the splitter are all supplied with Mozilla, yet all are written in XUL. Adding functionality to the browser, so that it works on all systems, in this way

[2]The graphical components which get drawn on the screen.

cannot be done using any other technology.[3] Building unique interfaces within a browser is an appealing prospect if you are working within an intranet or building public information terminals based around Web technologies. Imagine being able to build a library catalog system, for example, which uses standard protocols such as HTTP but has the rich interface of a desktop application. This is possible with XUL. You don't even need to supply the interface components and chromes to each terminal. They can be packaged as `jar` files[4] and downloaded transparently from a Web server when needed.

XUL provides the interface, chromes provide the look, but what about the functionality? An interface component doesn't really *do* much on its own. When the user selects, for instance, a button, it creates an *event*. The interface tells application code about the event which the application can then process. In Mozilla, that application code is written using JavaScript. JavaScript is often used to provide dynamic behavior and event handling. For example, when a button is selected, the browser creates an event which is passed to a JavaScript method. That code can do many things, including modifying the properties of the window and widgets, or pass data on to other applications. Although JavaScript is a fully featured language, it is best suited to relatively simple tasks. When you need lots of complex processing, it's better to build client server style applications. The display and input are then processed by the desktop PC while the complex work is carried out on the server. This is, of course, the model used for normal Web form processing. The JavaScript on the client is then used to validate the input which the user is providing.

18.2 THE XUL WIDGETS

If you've ever used a GUI widget set, XUL will feel pretty familiar quite quickly. The contents of graphical toolkits are structured hierarchically and XUL is no exception. The root of the structure is a `window` which contains a set of boxes. Each box contains the actual widgets which get drawn on the screen.

I'm going to describe a few of the XUL widgets, how they are used and what attributes they take. The chapter finishes with a small example of how XUL can be used to build a simple application.

18.2.1 Creating Windows

The first thing that you need to understand is the basic structure of a XUL file. Because XUL is also valid XML, a XUL file starts with the XML Declaration. The next thing that

[3] So far as I am aware, anyway.

[4] Similar to the familiar zip file.

it needs is a processing instruction which tells Mozilla where to find a stylesheet that defines the appearance. The root of the XUL document is the `window` element. In the following code excerpt two namespaces are associated with the document. The first sets the default namespace for elements in the document. This is the standard namespace for XUL elements which in this example is not associated with a prefix. The second namespace associates XHTML elements with the prefix `html`. XUL files can contain both XUL and HTML elements, some of which have the same names. The prefix will be used to distinguish between the two element sets.

```
<?xml version="1.0"?>
<?xml-stylesheet href="chrome://global/skin/" type="text/css"?>

<window id="String" title="String"
  xmlns="http://www.mozilla.org/keymaster/gatekeeper/there.is.
     only.xul"
  xmlns:html="http://www.w3.org/1999/xhtml">

  <!-- Application code goes here -->

</window>
```

XUL elements have both attributes and methods. The attributes are typically set in the XML file that defines the application. The methods are accessed from the JavaScript that provides the behaviors for the application. If you've ever written any JavaScript, you'll be aware that the properties of browser windows and HTML elements can also be set from within scripts. XUL elements are the same: having defined their initial properties in XUL, those properties can be altered dynamically from the script.

In these descriptions of elements, I'm only listing a few attributes and methods. If you are writing XUL and are familiar with the HTML elements, trying to use the HTML attributes is always going to be an interesting exercise. Often they'll work in exactly the same way in both languages.

<window title="string" id="string" xmlns="string" onload="method" onunload="method" width="length" height="length">

The meanings of most of the attributes of the `window` element ought to be obvious. The `title` provides a string which will be displayed in the frame of the browser window, and the `id` attribute gives a unique identifier for the window. The `id` is needed if the window is going to be manipulated by a script. The `width` and `length` attributes take numerical values which define the size of the window in pixels. These may not work if the window is being opened within the current browser window or in a new tab inside the current browser. The `onload` and `onunload` attributes identify the names of JavaScript methods that will handle those particular events. Actually, a series of JavaScript statements *could* be used as the value of the attribute if you didn't want to place your script in a separate file.

`window.open(URI[, name[, arguments]])`

This method is used from within JavaScript to open a new XUL window. The `URI` identifies the file that contains the *content* of the window. An optional `name` may be provided, as may a comma-separated set of arguments. These include:

- `titlebar` If this flag is set, the new window will have a titlebar. Otherwise it won't.
- `close` If set, the window will have a widget that can be used to close it.
- `chrome` If this flag is set, the URI which is given as the first argument to the method is assumed to be a chrome file that defines the appearance of the window. If the flag is not set, that file is assumed to contain content which will be displayed in the window.
- `dialog` The new window will act as a dialog if this is set.
- `modal` If set, the new window is modal. The application will not return until the user has dismissed the new window. Dialog boxes are usually assumed to be modal and should have this flag set.

`window.sizeToContent()`

This method will change the size of the new window so that it is optimally fitted to its content.

The following code shows two different uses of the `open()` method. The first one points to a chrome file, the second to some content for the window.

```
window.open("chrome://features/structure/choice.xul",
            "Choose An Option", "chrome", "modal")

window.open("http://www.smiggins.com/content/main.xml",
            "Introduction", "close")
```

18.2.2 Text and Images

When writing an HTML page, authors can't simply place text anywhere and expect it to display properly in the browser. XUL has similar restrictions. Text placed inside a XUL file will be ignored by Mozilla unless it is structured correctly. That means, simply, that any text strings which are to appear in the XUL document must be either values given to element attributes, or content of elements. Two elements are used to place text directly onto the window. Other elements such as buttons can contain text but they need not concern us at the moment.

<description value="string" crop="start|end|center|none">
Text which appears in the XUL document is usually going to be contained in a `description` element. The text may be given as an argument to the `value` parameter where it's just a short string. When longer blocks of text need to be displayed they are placed as the content of the element. If the text is too long for the container it may be cropped, with missing text replaced with ellipses. The `crop` attribute described how this cropping is to be performed. Note that if this is set to the value `none`, the text may still be cropped but the ellipses will not be used as a replacement.

<label value="string" control="id" crop="start|end|center|none">
A `label` is a piece of text that is associated with, but not part of, another element such as a button or a text input field. The `control` attribute is used to identify the associated element. If the label is selected using the mouse, the focus is passed directly to that element.

<caption label="string">
A `caption` element is used in either a `groupbox` or `radiogroup` where it provides a heading for the element. If a heading has to be more complex than a simple piece of string, the `caption` element can contain a tree of other elements.

<image src="URI" width="length" height="length" onerror="method" onload="method">
Although images are not text, this element description seems to fit nicely here. The `image` element is used if you want to place a graphic onto your XUL window. The image file is identified using a URI. Its size may be set with the `height` and `width` attributes, although this is not always required. Finally, `onerror` and `onload` are used to identify JavaScript methods that will handle processing if either the image fails to load, or loads successfully.

Here's some code which shows how `description` elements can be used.

```
<?xml version="1.0"?>
<?xml-stylesheet href="chrome://global/skin/" type="text/css"?>

<window id="String" title="String"
  xmlns="http://www.mozilla.org/keymaster/gatekeeper/there.is.
      only.xul">
```

```
    <description value="A short string" style="color:blue; font-
        size:24pt"/>
    <description>This is a rather longer string which is not styled
        .</description>

</window>
```

18.2.3 Buttons

Buttons are used to select between program states. A button has two states; when it is selected it may create an event which is passed to a JavaScript method. The state of buttons may be queried by scripts so that they trigger actions after a delay rather than instantaneously. XUL includes three button types. The basic button is used to create the familiar rectangular button which includes a piece of text or an image as a prompt. Checkboxes are used to create a list from which one or more items can be selected. Radio buttons are grouped into lists from which only one item can be chosen. Generally a simple button triggers a script as soon as it is selected, whereas radio buttons and checkboxes have their state queried by scripts sometime after it is set.

<button label="string" type="checkbox|menu|menu-button|radio" tabindex="number" value="string" id="string" disabled="true|false" onclick="method" command="id">

This element is an on-screen button which the user can select with mouse or keyboard. Once selected the `button` will trigger some processing. The `label` attribute defines the string which will be displayed in the button. This can be cropped using the `crop` attribute which works here exactly as it does for `label` elements. The `button` does not have to be a typical button when it is created. It can be altered using the `type` attribute. When many items are displayed on screen, users can have the option of navigating through them using the tab key. The order in which tabbing selects elements is controlled with the `tabindex` attribute. If `disabled` is set to `true`, the button will initially be pale gray and unusable. Its state can, of course, be changed programmatically.

A button can pass its state to the script in two ways. Most commonly, a JavaScript method is associated with the `onclick` attribute. This is exactly the same approach as using the `onClick()` JavaScript method in a conventional HTML page. A more interesting approach uses the `command` attribute. In XUL a `command` element associates a JavaScript method with an identifying name. This method can be used from throughout an interface if its identifier is given as the value of a `command` attribute. The `value` attribute is given a string which can be accessed from JavaScript whenever it is required. For example, the content of the attribute might be set by one method and accessed later by a different method that needs to know the state of the button.

<checkbox label="string" command="id" checked="true|false" accesskey="letter" value="string">

A checkbox is a small box which is empty if unchecked and contains a cross if it has been selected. The `label` is a string which is drawn next to the box, usually to indicate the meaning of the box. The `checked` attribute indicates the initial state of the checkbox. The `accesskey` attribute indicates a single key which can be used to set the checkbox, generally in combination with the `ALT` key.

<radio label="string" command="id" checked="true|false" accesskey="letter" value="string" focused="true|false" image="URI" selected="true|false">

A radio button is one that can be turned on or off. They are usually placed into groups, with just one being selected. When one button is selected, the rest of the group will automatically be deselected. Radio buttons can have an image as a prompt rather than a piece of text. If an image is used, its location is given as the value of the `image` attribute.

The `focused` attribute is set to `true` when the button has the focus, which is different to being selected. The user can move through the buttons in a group by tabbing with the keyboard. As the user presses the tab key, each button, in turn, is focused and can be selected with the enter key. The `selected` attribute is a read-only property which can be queried from scripts.

<radiogroup value="string" disabled="true|false">

A `radiogroup` draws a frame around a set of `radio` elements. The frame may contain a `caption` element as an identifying label. The `radiogroup` is usually drawn as a vertical list. The element has a number of important methods:

- `appendItem(label[, value])` Adds a new `radio` element at the end of the group with the supplied label and, optionally, value.
- `focusedItem` Contains the item which currently has the focus. The focused item can be changed using this property.
- `insertItemAt(index, label[, value])` A new button can be inserted into the middle of the group using this method.
- `removeItemAt(index)` This method removes a button from the `radiogroup`.
- `selectedItem` This property holds the index of the currently selected button.

The following code shows how a button can be created and associated with a piece of code:

```
<?xml version="1.0"?>
<?xml-stylesheet href="chrome://global/skin/" type="text/css"?>

<window id="String" title="String"
  xmlns="http://www.mozilla.org/keymaster/gatekeeper/there.is.
     only.xul">

  <button style="font-family:helvetica"
    label="Process the selection"
    id="selection"
    default="true"
    onclick="alert('Processing selection)"/>

</window>
```

18.2.4 Text Widgets

Text isn't only displayed directly as labels or captions. Sometimes applications need to get text input from the user, or display complex text-based structures such as lists.

```
<textbox id="string" value="text" disabled="true|false"
maxlength="number" size="number" type="password|autocomplete|text"
multiline="true|false" oninput="method" readonly="true|false"
```

Some of the attributes here should be self-explanatory. I'll only examine those that aren't.

The `type` attribute is used to change the type of `textbox`. If it is set to `password`, the `textbox` will not display anything that the user types. When it is set to `autocomplete` a special type of `textbox` is created. This has a pop-up which contains a list of completions for the string that the user has started to enter. Further information on auto-completion can be found in the XUL documentation. If the `type` attribute is set to `text`, an ordinary input box is created. This is the default state and can be safely assumed.

If `multiline` is set to `true`, the input from the user can span more than one line. When the user presses `Enter`, a new line of text begins.

The `oninput` attribute is used to associate a piece of JavaScript with the `textbox`. When the user changes the text in the box the method will be called. This could be a useful way of validating input, although it would mean that a method call would happen each time that a character was typed.

The `textbox` element has a number of properties. These include:

- `readonly` Can be used to change the `textbox` so that further input is impossible but the element has not been disabled.
- `textLength` This property is read-only and contains the length of the string that has been entered.
- `value` This holds the text that has been entered into the `textbox`. The text can also be changed by altering the value of this property.

<menubar accesskey="letter" command="id" image="URI" disabled="true|false" label="string" value="string">

This element defines a container for `menu` elements. The attributes have the meanings defined above for earlier elements.

<menu accesskey="letter" image="URI" disabled="true|false" label="string"allowevents="true|false">

This element defines a menu item which appears inside a `menubar` and which works like a button. If `allowevents` is set to `true`, any events are passed through to the children of the element.

<menulist editable="true|false">

This element is used to create drop-down lists from which the user can select one item. The element must contain a `menupopup` element which, in turn, contains `menuitem` elements which hold the choices. The selected item is displayed in the `menulist`. If the `editable` attribute is set to `true`, the user can select items by typing directly into the `menulist` rather than selecting from a list. The element has a number of useful methods and properties. Those not defined below have the same meaning as for the `radiogroup` element which is defined above.

- `appenditem(label[, value])`
- `insertItemAt(index, label[, value])`
- `removeItemAt(index)`
- `selectedItem`
- `selectedIndex` Holds the index of the chosen element. If no item has been chosen this will be set to `-1`.

<menupopup>

This element is a container for the content of menu elements. Although it can contain any element, it usually holds `menuitem` elements. It has a great number of properties, attributes and methods. Since these have changed, with many being added for recent versions of Mozilla, you are advised to consult the XUL documentation.

`<menuitem accesskey="letter" checked="true|false" command="id" disabled="true|false" image="URI" label="string" name="string" selected="true|false" type="checkbox|radio" value="string">`

Individual items within a menu or popup list are defined using the `menuitem` element. The `menuitem` may be part of a `radiogroup` or be a `checkbox` if the `type` attribute is set.

18.2.5 Layout

XUL is a fully featured toolkit. In addition to the elements I've outlined so far, it can be used to create lists, toolbars, trees, columns and status bars. As with the `menupopup` element, these are all complex elements. Since this chapter is an introduction rather than a XUL reference, you should consult the documentation for more details.

One final set of XUL elements do need to be covered: those concerned with the layout of elements on the screen. You can't add arbitrary elements to your applications and expect them to appear in the order and at the positions you expect. All toolkits contain widgets or layout managers which can be used to control the behavior and location of elements. In XUL layout is done through a box model. The layout of the screen is divided into a network of boxes. Elements are placed inside boxes which arrange them either vertically or horizontally. Alignment and justification of elements can be controlled by adding space as padding at the ends of boxes.

`<groupbox>`

This element draws a thin box around the elements it contains. It may contain a `caption` element which will be used as the header for the box.

`<box orient="horizontal|vertical">`

This element contains any number of other elements. The elements it contains will not overlap each other. By default children are laid out along the horizontal axis, although this can be changed using the `orient` attribute.

`<hbox>`

A box element whose content is laid out horizontally.

`<vbox>`

A box element whose content is laid out vertically.

<spacer flex="number">

This element occupies space but contains nothing. Its `flex` attribute is used to control how far it will expand. Flexible elements can grow or shrink as required to fill the space that has been allocated to them. Elements with larger `flex` values will adjust more than those with smaller values. It's worth noting that the `flex` attribute can be applied to many other XUL elements. This is another attribute with which you should experiment to see how it works.

<splitter collapse="none|before|after" resizeafter="closest|farthest|grow" resizebefore="closest|farthest">

This element is a bar that appears inside a container, effectively splitting it in two. The `splitter` can be dragged across the screen so the relative sizes of the two parts of the container are altered. It can also be collapsed so that one part of the container is hidden.

If the `collapse` attribute is set to `none`, the container is not collapsed when the `grippy` on the `spitter` is clicked. When set to `before`, those elements that are in the container before the `splitter` are hidden. The value `after`, obviously, hides elements that occur after the `splitter`.

When the `splitter` is dragged, not all elements resize equally. The `resizebefore` and `resizeafter` elements control this behavior. The value `closest` indicates that the element nearest to the `splitter` will be resized. Given `farthest`, the element that is the most distant will be resized. When `resizeafter` is given the value `grow`, the container itself rather than its elements is resized.

grippy

This element appears on a `splitter` and acts as a handle with which the `splitter` can be moved.

18.2.6 Adding Behavior

I've already mentioned that callbacks which process user events are written in JavaScript. One XUL element, `command`, is used to associate a single callback with a set of events.

<command disabled="true|false" label="string" oncommand="method">

If the `disabled` attribute is `true` all elements that use the `command` element for their event processing are disabled. The `label` attribute defines a string which can be inherited by all elements that use the command. The elements can use the string as a default label. The `oncommand` attribute defines a JavaScript method which will be used to process events associated with the `command` element.

18.3 USING XUL

Knowing what the XUL elements are and having some understanding of how they work are two very different things. The only way to understand how a XUL application is really built is to build one. Figure 18.3 shows a simple application which lets users choose a recipe and then displays its source code. Actually, I ought to be honest about this. The code that builds the GUI works as shown. The code that handles buttons, text and events, and that extracts the recipe into the GUI, doesn't exist. The screenshot is a bit of a fake, but I think that's justified since this isn't a book about JavaScript. The XUL interface code works properly. The interface I've created runs, but the script that creates the data is missing. JavaScript is a relatively simple language which includes most of the functionality that you would expect to find in a programming language. Developing the code to create the data and populate the interface is left as an exercise.

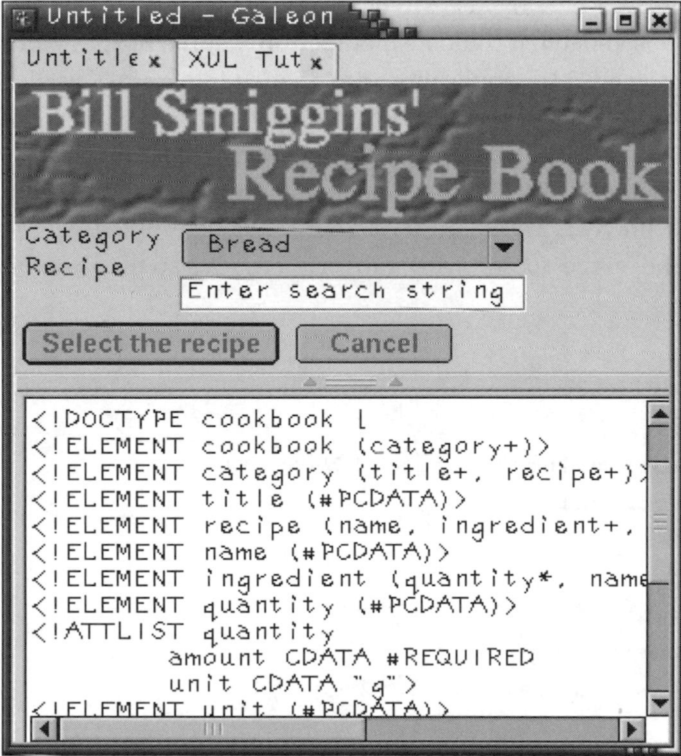

Figure 18.3 A Simple XUL Interface

I've broken the GUI code into fragments. If you extract and reassemble them in the same order as they appear here, the application will work properly.

Listing 18.1 Interface to Select and Display Recipes

```
<?xml version="1.0"?>
<?xml-stylesheet href="chrome://global/skin/" type="text/css"?>

<window id="displayRecipe" title="Recipe Book"
  xmlns:html="http://www.w3.org/1999/xhtml"
  xmlns="http://www.mozilla.org/keymaster/gatekeeper/there.is.
     only.xul">

  <box><image src="recipeLogo.png" /></box>
```

The code starts off in conventional XUL form with an XML declaration and a processing instruction which includes a standard Mozilla chrome stylesheet. The application begins with a `window` element as the root. I'm declaring two namespaces for this: one for XUL elements and one for XHTML elements. Although the application doesn't use any XHTML in this version, it could be modified so that the recipe is formatted as HTML before being displayed. XUL applications are divided into a set of vertical and horizontal boxes. Here, I start with a `box`, which defaults to a horizontal layout. Into this I place an image. The size of the image doesn't need to be specified either in the `image` tag or in the containing `box` element. Instead, the correct amount of space is allocated automatically. My experience with XUL in Mozilla 0.9.8 and 0.9.9 suggests that specifying height and width sizes for the image doesn't work properly, anyway, so this is an important point to note.

```
  <vbox>
    <hbox>
      <vbox>
        <label value="Category" />
        <label value="Recipe" />
      </vbox>
      <vbox>
        <menulist>
          <menupopup>
            <menuitem label="Bread"/>
            <menuitem label="Chicken"/>
            <menuitem label="Curry"/>
            <menuitem label="Thai Vegetarian"/>
          </menupopup>
        </menulist>
        <textbox value="Enter search string"
```

```
            id="recipe_search" />
    </vbox>
  </hbox>
```

The top half of the application contains the controls which are placed in a vertically oriented box as a pair of horizontal rows. The controls consist of the input elements and their associated labels in one row, and the buttons in the lower row. Languages such as Java and TCL are associated with graphical toolkits which use layout managers to arrange elements on the screen.[5] In such systems, GUIs are defined with elements positioned *relative* to each other. Usually their positions are worked out within some form of grid which the layout manager tweaks to get an exact end-result.

That's the approach being used here. The interface is split into nested grids of columns and rows. Associating a label with a control can be done in two ways. The label and control can be placed into a single horizontal row. This will place them neatly together, but if two or more rows are used, there is no guarantee that they will line up in a pleasing manner. In this case I want the labels aligned vertically, and the controls arranged similarly. If label and control were in a single hbox, the gaps between them would be identical on every row. This would mean that the controls would not be vertically aligned at their left edge.

```
  <hbox>
    <button style="font-family:helvetica;
             color:green; font-weight:bold"
         label="Select the recipe"
         id="process"
         default="true"
         onclick="alert('Loading Data')"/>

    <button style="font-family:helvetica;
             color:red; font-weight:bold"
         label="Cancel"
         id="cancel"/>

    <spacer flex="1" />
  </hbox>
</vbox>
```

[5]AWT and Swing for Java and Tk for TCL.

Arranging the buttons is more straightforward. They are placed into a horizontal box. Below the box, a `spacer` element is placed so that if the window is resized, the pleasing arrangement of the controls is not disturbed. Notice that CSS-type styling can be applied to the text on the buttons to alter the appearance of their text.

```
  <splitter collapse="before">
    <grippy />
  </splitter>
```

The two halves of the window are separated using a `splitter`. When this is clicked to collapse the window, the controls will be hidden because the `collapse` attribute is set to the value `before`.

```
  <box>
    <textbox id="recipe_output" multiline="true"
          width="350" height="200"/>
  </box>
</window>
```

Finally, the recipe is displayed in a `textbox`. This holds many lines of text and so has its `multiline` attribute set to `true`. The `height` and `width` of the `textbox` are defined in pixels.

That's a very simple interface but it does demonstrate how to put a XUL application together. In the finest textbook tradition, adding JavaScript functionality is left as an exercise for the reader.

Exercises

1. Give three reasons why basing applications around a Web browser might be a good idea.
2. Why would developers want to use XUL widgets rather than HTML forms?
3. List and describe as many applications written in XUL as you can find.
4. Using XUL, create the interface to a simple Web guestbook. Users must be able to enter their name, email address and a comment, and to view existing messages held on the system.

References

1. *The World Wide Web Consortium.* `http://www.w3.org`, 1994-2002.

   The W3C is a consortium of academics, businesses and other interested parties who develop the technologies which make the Web work. Almost all of the important Web standards, which they call Recommendations, are developed by the W3C. Their Web site includes links to all of their public documents alongside introductory, background and reference material. Historical versions of documents are sometimes if you need to see how Recommendations have evolved.

2. *Sun's Java Portal.* `http://java.sun.com`, 1995-2002.

   Sun Microsystems developed Java, their engineers know more about the language than anyone else. If you want bang up-to-date information and in-depth articles, you won't do better than looking at this Web site. You can also download the very latest Java technologies from here – free of charge, of course.

3. *IBM Developerworks.* `http://www-106.ibm.com/developerworks`, 2000-2002.

   IBM has embraced the concept of open source more firmly than any other major computer company. They produce vast amounts of Open Source and Free software and contribute to community projects such as Apache. IBM engineers sit on many technical committees which agree the standards for protocols and applciations. Alongside those contributions, IBM employees write large quantities of technical and training material. This Web site provides a central portal through which that material, plus columns written by developers from all over the World can be shared. Effectively, Developerworks is a set of free online magazines covering technologies as diverse as XML, Java, Linux and networking.

4. *Cetus Links*. `http://www.cetus-links.org`, 2002.

Ordered, edited and collated collections of links on particular topics are exceptionally useful ways of finding information on the Web. Cetus originally collated links relating to object-oriented technologies. That remit seems to have grown sufficiently that programming languages and XML are now included. This site includes links to over 18,000 others. Not all those links work since Web sites disappear over time – but plenty do.

5. *The Cover Pages*. `http://www.oasis-open.org/cover/`, 2002.

This site is hosted by Oasis. For a number of years now Robin Cover has been providing authoritative commentary and reference material on all things XML and SGML. Much of the material here is links to other content creators but it's well chosen. Although the site doesn't present a comprehehnsive guide to everything in the markup World, it does present some of the best.

6. *The Internet FAQ Archive*. `http://www.faqs.org`, 2002.

This Web site contains two types of document which you might find useful. Firstly, as the name suggests, there are the Frequently Asked Questions lists, the FAQs, of many Usenet newsgroups. These can be a wonderful source of informaion since they often present the distilled knowledge of relatively large Internet communities. A warning, though. Not everything which you read in a FAQ will necessarily be accurate or complete. The second type of document is the Request For Comment. True Internet standards, such as those for protocols like HTTP or TCP, are developed through an open process. A proposal document, the Request For Comment or RFC, are produced and put before Internet users for their comments. Software implementations are based on final versions of the RFC. As with W3C Recommendations, RFCs are not standards, although many become standardized by the ISO, IEEE or ECMA.

7. Bert Bos, Håkon Wium Lie, Chris Lilley, and Ian Jacobs. *Cascading Stylesheets, level 2*. `http://www.w3.org/TR/REC-CSS2`, 1998.

8. David C. Fallside. *XML Schema Part 0: Primer*. `http://www.w3.org/TR/xmlschema-0/`, 2001.

The XML Schema specification is spread across three documents. Part One looks at data structures, part two looks at datatypes. If you want to use XML Schema in your own applications, these provide far more complexity and far less information than you really need. The place for users to start is with Part 0. This is a good introduction to XML Schema, although it does assume a lot of knowledge about XML in the reader. You'll probably want to have a few simple Schema documents to hand as you read through the Primer to help you make sense of it.

9. Eric Miller. *Semantic Web*. `http://www.w3.org/2001/sw/`, 1998-2001.

This Web address is the front page for links to all of the Semantic Web activity at W3C. Eric Miller is the technical lead on the project. Links from here go off to draft Recommendations and introductory material.

10. Håkon Wium Lie and Bert Bos. *Cascading Stylesheets, level 1*. `http://www.w3.org/TR/REC-CSS1`, 2 edition, 1999.

11. James Clark. *XSL Transformations*. `http://www.w3.org/TR/xslt`, 1999.

    A new version of XSLT is being developed as I write. Software which is capable of processing XSLT will mostly still be using version 1.0 for some time to come.

12. James Clark and Steve DeRose. *XML Path Language*. `http://www.w3.org/TR/xpath`, 1999.

13. Michael Kay. *XSLT Programmer's Reference*. Wrox Press, 2 edition, 2001.

    Comprehensive and efinitive, this is *the* guide to XSLT. It's not for beginners though, since it's nearly 1,000 pages of useful information.

14. Norman Walsh and Leonard Muellner. *DocBook The Definitive Guide*. O'Reilly and Associates, 1999.

    DocBook is a large and complex DTD. Using it from the provided documentation is almost impossible since it contains so many different elements. This printed guide is somewhat out of date now – XML receives only a cursory mention. A new edition is being written at the moment and can be downloaded from the DocBook Web site at `http://www.docbook.org`

15. Sharon Adler, Anders Berglund, Jeff Caruso, Stephen Deach, Tony Graham, Paul Grosso, Eduardo Gutentag, Alex Milowski, Scott Parnell, Jeremy Richman, and Steve Ziles. *Extensible Stylesheet Language*. `http://www.w3.org/TR/xsl/`, 2001.

16. Tim Bray, Jean Pauli, C.M. Sperberg McQueen, and Eve Maler. *Extensible Markup Language 1.0*. `http://www.w3.org/TR/2000/REC-xml-20001006`, 2 edition, 2000.

Appendix A
Business Letter in XML

```
<?xml version="1.0"?>

<!DOCTYPE letter[
  <!ELEMENT letter (header, content)>
    <!ATTLIST letter title CDATA #IMPLIED>
  <!ELEMENT sender (name, address?)>
  <!ELEMENT recipient (name, address?)>
  <!ELEMENT name (title?, firstname*, surname)>
  <!ELEMENT address (line1, line2?, line3*, city, (county|state)
     ?, country?, code?)>
  <!ELEMENT date (dayname?, day?, month?, year?)>
  <!ELEMENT signature (greeting, (name | firstname))>
  <!ELEMENT header (metadata*, sender, recipient, date, signature
     )>
  <!ELEMENT content (para+, footnote*)>
  <!ELEMENT para (#PCDATA | emphasis)*>
  <!ELEMENT footnote (para+)>
  <!ELEMENT title (#PCDATA)>
```

```
  <!ELEMENT firstname (#PCDATA)>
  <!ELEMENT surname (#PCDATA)>
  <!ELEMENT line1 (#PCDATA)>
  <!ELEMENT line2 (#PCDATA)>
  <!ELEMENT line3 (#PCDATA)>
  <!ELEMENT city (#PCDATA)>
  <!ELEMENT county (#PCDATA)>
  <!ELEMENT state (#PCDATA)>
  <!ELEMENT country (#PCDATA)>
  <!ELEMENT code (#PCDATA)>
  <!ELEMENT dayname (#PCDATA)>
  <!ELEMENT day (#PCDATA)>
  <!ELEMENT month (#PCDATA)>
  <!ELEMENT year (#PCDATA)>
  <!ELEMENT emphasis (#PCDATA)>
  <!ELEMENT greeting (#PCDATA)>
  <!ATTLIST greeting
    type (formal | informal | other) "formal">
  <!ELEMENT metadata (keyword+)>
  <!ELEMENT keyword (#PCDATA)>
    <!ATTLIST keyword value CDATA #REQUIRED>
]>

<letter title="Complaint of 03/03/00">
  <header>
    <metadata>
      <keyword value="complaint" />
      <keyword value="trouser press" />
      <keyword value="waffle maker" />
    </metadata>
    <sender>
      <name>
        <title>Mr.</title>
        <firstname>William</firstname>
        <firstname>James</firstname>
        <surname>Smiggins</surname>
      </name>
      <address>
```

```
      <line1>Bill Smiggins Incorporated</line1>
      <line2>Unit 5</line2>
      <line3>Tax Havens Industrial Park</line3>
      <city>Enterprise City</city>
      <state>California</state>
      <code>CA 11223</code>
    </address>
  </sender>
  <recipient>
    <name>
      <firstname>Bill</firstname>
      <surname>Gates</surname>
    </name>
    <address>
      <line1>Microsoft Inc.</line1>
      <city>Seattle</city>
      <country>United States</country>
    </address>
  </recipient>
  <date>
    <dayname>Thursday</dayname>
    <day>27</day>
    <month>December</month>
    <year>2001</year>
  </date>
  <signature>
    <greeting type="formal"></greeting>
    <firstname>Bill</firstname>
  </signature>
</header>

<content>
  <para>Here at Bill Smiggins Inc. we're really proud of our
     ten-year reputation for the development of quality
     products. We're sorry to hear that you were unhappy with
     the <emphasis>Combined Trouser Press and Waffle Maker</
     emphasis> that you recently purchased from us. I can only
      state that it was in full working order when we shipped
```

```
        , and the presence of fluff in your breakfast waffles was
         as much of a shock to us, as we're sure it was to you.</
        para>
    <para>If you return the Combined Trouser Press and Waffle
        Maker in its original packaging, we'll arrange a full
        refund<footnote><para>Please note, we will not pay the
        cost of shipping goods back to us.</para></footnote>.</
        para>
    <para>Bill Smiggins Inc. Giving you the quality of service
        you deserve.</para>
  </content>

</letter>
```

Appendix B
Recipe Book in XML

```
<?xml version="1.0"?>

<!DOCTYPE cookbook [
<!ELEMENT cookbook (category+)>
<!ELEMENT category (title+, recipe+)>
<!ELEMENT title (#PCDATA)>
<!ELEMENT recipe (name, ingredient+, cooking*, serves?, method)>
<!ELEMENT name (#PCDATA)>
<!ELEMENT ingredient (quantity*, name)>
<!ELEMENT quantity (#PCDATA)>
<!ATTLIST quantity
  amount CDATA #REQUIRED
  unit CDATA "g">
<!ELEMENT unit (#PCDATA)>
<!ELEMENT amount (#PCDATA)>
<!ELEMENT name (#PCDATA)>
<!ELEMENT cooking (note+)>
```

```
<!ELEMENT note (#PCDATA)>
<!ELEMENT serves (#PCDATA)>
<!ELEMENT method (instruction+)>
<!ELEMENT instruction (#PCDATA)>
]>

<cookbook>
  <category>
    <title>bread</title>
    <recipe>
      <name>The Basic Loaf</name>
      <ingredient>
        <quantity amount="825" unit="ml" />
        <name>Warm water</name>
      </ingredient>
      <ingredient>
        <quantity amount="20" unit="g" />
        <name>Granulated Dried Yeast</name>
      </ingredient>
      <ingredient>
        <quantity amount="20" />
        <name>Sugar</name>
      </ingredient>
      <ingredient>
        <quantity amount="450" />
        <name>Stoneground wholemeal flour</name>
      </ingredient>
      <ingredient>
        <quantity amount="900" />
        <name>Strong white bread flour</name>
      </ingredient>
      <ingredient>
        <quantity amount="20" />
        <name>Salt</name>
      </ingredient>
      <ingredient>
        <quantity amount="55" />
        <name>Fresh Lard</name>
```

```
    </ingredient>
    <cooking>
      <note>Bake at gas number 8 for 15 minutes</note>
      <note>Bake at 230c for 15 minutes</note>
    </cooking>
    <method>
    <instruction>Add the yeast and sugar to the warm water and
        leave to activate</instruction>
    <instruction>Sieve the flour and salt into a large bowl</
       instruction>
    <instruction>Crumble the lard into the flour until it has
       a &quot;breadcrumb&quot; texture</instruction>
    <instruction>Mix the liquid into the flour</instruction>
    <instruction>Turn onto floured surface and knead for 300
       strokes</instruction>
    <instruction>Form into a ball, place in a warm place until
        doubled in size</instruction>
<instruction>Knead for another 100 strokes</instruction>
    <instruction>Form into a ball, place in a warm place until
        doubled in size</instruction>
    <instruction>Form into five loaves and leave to rise for
        30 minutes</instruction>
    <instruction>Bake!</instruction>
    </method>
  </recipe>

  <recipe>
    <name>Sussex Gypsy Bread</name>
    <ingredient>
      <quantity amount="250" unit="g" />
      <quantity amount="10" unit="oz" />
      <name>Self Raising Flour</name>
    </ingredient>
    <ingredient>
      <name>Pinch Of Salt</name>
    </ingredient>
    <ingredient>
      <name>Pinch Of Mixed Spice</name>
```

```
</ingredient>
<ingredient>
  <quantity amount="0.5" unit="teaspoon"/>
  <quantity amount="2.5" unit="ml"/>
  <name>Ground Ginger</name>
</ingredient>
<ingredient>
  <quantity amount="100" unit="g"/>
  <quantity amount="4" unit="oz" />
  <name>Soft Brown Sugar</name>
</ingredient>
<ingredient>
  <quantity amount="150" unit="g" />
  <quantity amount="6" unit="oz" />
  <name>Sultanas</name>
</ingredient>
<ingredient>
  <quantity amount="2" unit="oz" />
  <quantity amount="50" />
  <name>Chopped Peel</name>
</ingredient>
<ingredient>
  <quantity amount="150" />
  <quantity amount="6" unit="oz" />
  <name>Treacle</name>
</ingredient>
<ingredient>
  <quantity amount="1" unit="table spoon" />
  <quantity amount="15" unit="ml" />
  <name>Milk</name>
</ingredient>
<ingredient>
  <quantity amount="1" />
  <name>Egg</name>
</ingredient>
<ingredient>
  <quantity amount="0.5" unit="teaspoon" />
  <quantity amount="2.5" unit="ml" />
```

```
    <name>Bicarbonate Of Soda</name>
  </ingredient>
  <cooking>
    <note>Preheat oven to 180C/350F/Gas 4.</note>
  </cooking>
  <method>
    <instruction>Mix together flour, salt, spice, sugar and
       fruit in bowl.</instruction>
    <instruction>Warm treacle and milk in a pan, do not boil
       , remove from heat, add egg and whisk well.</
       instruction>
    <instruction>Dissolve the bicarbonate of soda in a
       little water and add with the treacle to the dry
       ingredients in the bowl.</instruction>
    <instruction>Mix well and pour into a greased 1 kilo/2lb
        loaf tin.</instruction>
    <instruction>Bake for 45 minutes, then reduce heat to
        160C/325F/Gas 3 and cook for a further 30 minutes.</
       instruction>
  </method>
</recipe>

<recipe>
  <name>Buns For Fun</name>
  <ingredient>
    <quantity amount="3" unit="oz" />
    <quantity amount="80" />
    <name>Butter</name>
  </ingredient>
  <ingredient>
    <quantity amount="300" unit="ml" />
    <quantity amount="10" unit="fl oz" />
    <name>Milk</name>
  </ingredient>
  <ingredient>
    <quantity amount="55" />
    <quantity amount="2" unit="oz" />
    <name>Fresh Yeast</name>
```

```
</ingredient>
<ingredient>
  <quantity amount="25" />
  <quantity amount="1" unit="oz" />
  <name>Dried Yeast</name>
</ingredient>
<ingredient>
  <quantity amount="80" />
  <quantity amount="3" unit="oz" />
  <name>Caster Sugar</name>
</ingredient>
<ingredient>
  <quantity amount="7.5" unit="ml" />
  <quantity amount="1.5" unit="teaspoon" />
  <name>Ground Cardamom</name>
</ingredient>
<ingredient>
  <quantity amount="2.5" unit="ml" />
  <quantity amount="0.5" unit="teaspoon" />
  <name>Salt</name>
</ingredient>
<ingredient>
  <quantity amount="800" />
  <quantity amount="1.25" unit="lb" />
  <name>Strong White Flour</name>
</ingredient>
<ingredient>
  <quantity amount="25" />
  <quantity amount="1" unit="oz" />
  <name>Raisins</name>
</ingredient>
<ingredient>
  <quantity amount="1" />
  <name>Egg</name>
</ingredient>
<cooking>
  <note>Preheat the oven to 225C/425F/Gas 7.</note>
</cooking>
```

```
      <method>
        <instruction>Melt the butter in a small saucepan. Add
           the milk and heat until the liquid is lukewarm (at
           body temperature).</instruction>
        <instruction>Mix together the sugar, ground cardamom,
           salt, yeast and flour in a bowl.</instruction>
        <instruction>If you are using fresh yeast, stir it into
           the milk until it dissolves. If using dried yeast,
           mix it with the flour mixture.</instruction>
        <instruction>Pour the milk mixture into the flour
           mixture, mix well or use your hands to knead the
           dough until it is smooth and firm.</instruction>
        <instruction>Sprinkle a little flour over the top and
           cover the bowl with plastic wrap. Put the bowl in a
           warm place for approximately 1 hour. The dough should
            rise to about twice the size.</instruction>
        <instruction>Put a few raisins into each lump of dough
           and roll it into a ball. Make different shaped buns,
           decorating with more raisins. Put the finished shapes
            onto a greased baking sheet. Let the buns rise for
           about 20 minutes.</instruction>
        <instruction>Brush the buns with egg or a little milk
           and place them in the centre of the oven for about
            10-15 minutes, until they are golden brown. Cool on
           a rack and serve.</instruction>
      </method>
    </recipe>
  </category>

  <category>
    <title>meat</title>
    <recipe>
      <name>The Meat Loaf</name>
    </recipe>
  </category>
</cookbook>
```

Appendix C
Business Letter Schema

```
<?xml version="1.0"?>
<xsd:schema xmlns:xsd="http://www.w3.org/2001/XMLSchema">

  <!-- Define the actual document -->
  <xsd:complexType name="letter">
    <xsd:sequence>
      <xsd:element ref="header" />
      <xsd:element ref="content" />
    </xsd:sequence>
    <xsd:attribute name="title" type="xsd:string" />
  </xsd:complexType>

  <!-- Define elements which are referred to -->
  <xsd:element name="content">
    <xsd:complexType mixed="true" >
      <xsd:sequence>
        <xsd:element name="emphasis" type="xsd:string" />
      </xsd:sequence>
```

```
    </xsd:complexType>
  </xsd:element>

  <xsd:element name="header">
    <xsd:complexType>
      <xsd:sequence>
        <xsd:element ref="metadata" />
        <xsd:element name="sender" type="personType" />
        <xsd:element name="recipient" type="personType" />
        <xsd:element name="date" type="dateType" />
        <xsd:element name="signature" type="signatureType" />
      </xsd:sequence>
    </xsd:complexType>
  </xsd:element>

  <xsd:element name="metadata">
    <xsd:complexType>
      <xsd:sequence>
        <xsd:element name="keyword" type="xsd:string" />
      </xsd:sequence>
      <xsd:attribute name="value" type="xsd:string" />
    </xsd:complexType>
  </xsd:element>

  <!-- define complex types -->
  <xsd:complexType name="dateType">
    <xsd:sequence>
      <xsd:element name="dayname" type="daynameType" />
      <xsd:element name="day" type="xsd:gDay" />
      <xsd:element name="month" type="xsd:gMonth" />
      <xsd:element name="year" type="xsd:gYear" />
    </xsd:sequence>
  </xsd:complexType>

  <xsd:complexType name="personType">
    <xsd:sequence>
      <xsd:element name="name" type="fullNameType" minOccurs="1"
              maxOccurs="1"/>
```

```
    <xsd:element name="address" type="addressType"
             maxOccurs="1" />
  </xsd:sequence>
</xsd:complexType>

<xsd:complexType name="fullNameType">
  <xsd:sequence>
    <xsd:element name="title" type="titleType" minOccurs="1"
             maxOccurs="1"/>
    <xsd:element name="firstname" type="nameType" minOccurs
       ="0"
             maxOccurs="unbounded" />
    <xsd:element name="surname" type="nameType" maxOccurs
       ="1" />
  </xsd:sequence>
</xsd:complexType>

<xsd:complexType name="addressType">
  <xsd:sequence>
    <xsd:element name="line1" type="addressLineType"
             maxOccurs="1" />
    <xsd:element name="line2" type="addressLineType"
             maxOccurs="1" />
    <xsd:element name="line3" type="addressLineType"
             maxOccurs="1" />
    <xsd:element name="city" type="addressLineType"
             maxOccurs="1" />
    <xsd:choice>
      <xsd:element name="county" type="addressLineType"
             maxOccurs="1" />
      <xsd:element name="state" type="addressLineType"
             maxOccurs="1" />
    </xsd:choice>
    <xsd:element name="code" type="xsd:string" minOccurs="1"
             maxOccurs="1"/>
    <xsd:element name="country" type="countryType"
             maxOccurs="1" />
  </xsd:sequence>
```

```
</xsd:complexType>

<xsd:complexType name="signatureType">
  <xsd:sequence>
    <xsd:element name="greeting" type="greetingType"
              maxOccurs="1"/>
    <xsd:choice>
      <xsd:element name="firstname" type="nameType" />
      <xsd:element name="name" type="fullNameType" />
    </xsd:choice>
  </xsd:sequence>
</xsd:complexType>

<xsd:complexType name="greetingType">
  <xsd:sequence>
    <xsd:element name="greeting" type="xsd:string" />
  </xsd:sequence>
  <xsd:attribute name="type">
    <xsd:simpleType>
      <xsd:restriction base="xsd:NMTOKEN">
        <xsd:enumeration value="formal" />
        <xsd:enumeration value="informal" />
        <xsd:enumeration value="other" />
      </xsd:restriction>
    </xsd:simpleType>
  </xsd:attribute>
</xsd:complexType>

<!-- define simple types -->
<xsd:simpleType name="nameType">
  <xsd:restriction base="xsd:string">
    <xsd:maxLength value="32" />
  </xsd:restriction>
</xsd:simpleType>

<xsd:simpleType name="daynameType">
  <xsd:restriction base="xsd:string">
    <xsd:maxLength value="9" />
```

```
      </xsd:restriction>
    </xsd:simpleType>

    <xsd:simpleType name="titleType">
      <xsd:restriction base="xsd:string">
        <xsd:maxLength value="4" />
      </xsd:restriction>
    </xsd:simpleType>

    <xsd:simpleType name="addressLineType">
      <xsd:restriction base="xsd:string">
        <xsd:maxLength value="48" />
      </xsd:restriction>
    </xsd:simpleType>

    <xsd:simpleType name="countryCodes">
      <xsd:restriction base="xsd:NMTOKEN">
        <xsd:enumeration value="FR" />
        <xsd:enumeration value="UK" />
        <xsd:enumeration value="USA" />
        <xsd:enumeration value="OTHER" />
      </xsd:restriction>
    </xsd:simpleType>

    <xsd:simpleType name="countryType">
      <xsd:union memberTypes="xsd:string countryCodes" />
    </xsd:simpleType>

</xsd:schema>
```

Appendix D
Recipe Book Schema

```
<?xml version="1.0"?>
<xsd:schema xmlns:xsd="http://www.w3.org/2001/XMLSchema">

<xsd:element name="cookbook">
<xsd:complexType>
  <xsd:sequence>

    <xsd:element name="category" minOccurs="1"
            maxOccurs="unbounded">
    <xsd:complexType>
      <xsd:sequence>
        <xsd:element name="title" type="xsd:string" minOccurs
           ="1"
              maxOccurs="1"/>

        <xsd:element name="recipe" minOccurs="1"
              maxOccurs="unbounded">
```

```
<xsd:complexType>
  <xsd:sequence>

    <xsd:element name="name" minOccurs="1" maxOccurs
       ="1"
            type="xsd:string" />

    <xsd:element name="ingredient">
    <xsd:complexType>
      <xsd:sequence>
        <xsd:element name="quantity"
                type="quantityType" />
        <xsd:element name="name" type="xsd:string" />
      </xsd:sequence>
    </xsd:complexType>
    </xsd:element><!-- ingredient -->

    <xsd:element name="cooking">
    <xsd:complexType>
      <xsd:sequence>
        <xsd:element name="note" maxOccurs="unbounded"
                type="xsd:string" />
      </xsd:sequence>
    </xsd:complexType>
    </xsd:element><!-- cooking -->

    <xsd:element name="serves" type="xsd:string"
            maxOccurs="unbounded" />

    <xsd:element name="method">
    <xsd:complexType>
      <xsd:sequence>
        <xsd:element name="instruction"
                maxOccurs="unbounded"
                type="xsd:string" />
      </xsd:sequence>
    </xsd:complexType>
    </xsd:element><!-- method -->
```

```
          </xsd:sequence>
        </xsd:complexType>
        </xsd:element><!-- recipe -->

      </xsd:sequence>
    </xsd:complexType>
    </xsd:element><!-- category -->

  </xsd:sequence>
</xsd:complexType>
</xsd:element><!-- cookbook -->

<xsd:complexType name="quantityType">
  <xsd:sequence>
    <xsd:element name="quantity"/>
  </xsd:sequence>
  <xsd:attribute name="amount" type="xsd:string" />
  <xsd:attribute name="unit" type="xsd:string" />
</xsd:complexType>

</xsd:schema>
```

Appendix E
Business Letter Formatting Object Stylesheet

```
<?xml version="1.0"?>
<!DOCTYPE book SYSTEM "/usr/share/sgml/db41xml/docbookx.dtd">

<xsl:stylesheet version="1.1"
           xmlns:xsl="http://www.w3.org/1999/XSL/Transform"
           xmlns:fo="http://www.w3.org/1999/XSL/Format">

  <xsl:output method="xml"
          version="1.0"
          indent="yes"
          encoding="iso-8859-1"/>

  <xsl:variable name="footnotes" select="//content/para/footnote
     "/>
```

```
<xsl:template match="/letter">
  <fo:root>
    <fo:layout-master-set>
      <fo:simple-page-master
          master-name="basic"
          page-height="297mm"
          page-width="210mm"
          margin-left="25mm"
          margin-right="25mm"
          margin-top="25mm"
          margin-bottom="25mm">
        <fo:region-body margin="10mm" />
        <fo:region-before extent="10mm" />
        <fo:region-after extent="25mm" />
      </fo:simple-page-master>
    </fo:layout-master-set>

    <fo:page-sequence master-name="basic">
      <fo:flow flow-name="xsl-region-body">

        <xsl:variable name="rside" select="'end'" />
        <xsl:variable name="lside" select="'start'" />

        <xsl:call-template name="address_table">
          <xsl:with-param name="side" select="$rside" />
          <xsl:with-param name="add" select="header/sender/
             address" />
          <xsl:with-param name="nom" select="header/sender/
             name" />
        </xsl:call-template>

        <xsl:call-template name="address_table">
          <xsl:with-param name="side" select="$lside" />
          <xsl:with-param name="add" select="header/recipient
             /address" />
          <xsl:with-param name="nom" select="header/recipient
             /name" />
        </xsl:call-template>
```

```
        <xsl:call-template name="dater"/>
        <xsl:apply-templates select="//content"/>
        <xsl:call-template name="salut"/>

      </fo:flow>
    </fo:page-sequence>

  </fo:root>
</xsl:template>


<xsl:template name="address_table">
  <xsl:param name="side" />
  <xsl:param name="add" />
  <xsl:param name="nom" />

  <fo:list-block
      font-size="10pt"
      font-family="serif"
      text-align="{$side}">
    <fo:list-item>
      <fo:list-item-label><fo:block/></fo:list-item-label>
      <fo:list-item-body>
        <fo:block>

          <xsl:if test="$nom/title">
            <xsl:value-of select="$nom/title" /> 
          </xsl:if>

          <xsl:for-each select="$nom/firstname">
            <xsl:value-of select="." /> 
          </xsl:for-each>

          <xsl:value-of select="$nom/surname" />
        </fo:block>
      </fo:list-item-body>
    </fo:list-item>
```

```
    <xsl:for-each select="$add/child::*">
      <fo:list-item>
        <fo:list-item-label><fo:block/></fo:list-item-label>
        <fo:list-item-body>
          <fo:block>
            <xsl:value-of select="."/>
          </fo:block>
        </fo:list-item-body>
      </fo:list-item>

    </xsl:for-each>
  </fo:list-block>
</xsl:template>


<xsl:template name="greet">
  <xsl:variable name="nom" select="//header/recipient/name" />
  <fo:block
      text-align="start"
      font-size="10pt"
      space-after="10pt"
      font-family="serif">

    Dear 
    <xsl:if test="$nom/title">
      <xsl:value-of select="$nom/title" /> 
      <xsl:value-of select="$nom/surname" />
    </xsl:if>
    <xsl:if test="not($nom/title)">
      <xsl:for-each select="$nom/firstname">
        <xsl:value-of select="." /> 
      </xsl:for-each>
      <xsl:value-of select="$nom/surname" />,
    </xsl:if>
  </fo:block>
</xsl:template>
```

```
<xsl:template name="salut">
  <fo:block
      text-align="start"
      font-size="10pt"
      font-family="serif"
      space-before="10pt"
      space-after="32pt"
      keep-with-previous="always"
      keep-with-next="always">

    <xsl:variable name="msg" select="//header/signature/
       greeting" />

    <xsl:if test="$msg">
      <xsl:if test="$msg/@type">
        <xsl:variable name="tmp" select="$msg/@type"/>
        <xsl:if test="$tmp='formal'">
          <xsl:if test="$msg=''">
            Yours Faithfully,
          </xsl:if>
        </xsl:if>
        <xsl:if test="$tmp='informal'">
          <xsl:if test="$msg=''">
            Yours Sincerely,
          </xsl:if>
        </xsl:if>
        <xsl:if test="not($msg='')">
          <xsl:value-of select="$msg"/>,
        </xsl:if>
      </xsl:if>
    </xsl:if>
  </fo:block>

  <xsl:variable name="nom" select="//header/signature" />
  <fo:block
      text-align="start"
      font-size="10pt"
```

```
        font-family="serif"
        keep-with-previous="always">

      <xsl:if test="$nom/firstname">
        <xsl:value-of select="$nom//firstname"/>
      </xsl:if>

      <xsl:if test="not($nom/firstname)">
        <xsl:if test="$nom/name/title">
          <xsl:value-of select="$nom/name/title" /> 
          <xsl:value-of select="$nom/name/surname" />
        </xsl:if>
        <xsl:if test="not($nom/name/title)">
          <xsl:for-each select="$nom/name/firstname">
            <xsl:value-of select="." /> 
          </xsl:for-each>
          <xsl:value-of select="$nom/name/surname" />
        </xsl:if>
      </xsl:if>
    </fo:block>
  </xsl:template>


  <xsl:template name="dater">
    <fo:block
        text-align="end"
        font-size="10pt"
        font-family="serif"
        space-after="10pt">

      <xsl:variable name="dy" select="//header/date"/>

      <xsl:if test="$dy/dayname">
        <xsl:value-of select="$dy/dayname"/>, 
      </xsl:if>
      <xsl:if test="$dy/day">
        <xsl:value-of select="$dy/day"/> 
      </xsl:if>
```

```
    <xsl:if test="$dy/month">
      <xsl:value-of select="$dy/month"/>, 
    </xsl:if>
    <xsl:if test="$dy/year">
      <xsl:value-of select="$dy/year"/>.
    </xsl:if>
  </fo:block>

  <xsl:call-template name="greet"/>

</xsl:template>


<xsl:template match="para">
  <fo:block
      font-size="10pt"
      font-family="serif"
      line-height="13pt"
      text-align="justify"
      space-after="10pt">
    <xsl:apply-templates />
  </fo:block>
</xsl:template>


<xsl:template match="emphasis">
  <fo:inline font-style="italic">
    <xsl:value-of select="."/>
  </fo:inline>
</xsl:template>


<xsl:template match="footnote">
  <fo:footnote>
    <xsl:variable name="tmp" select="para"/>
    <xsl:for-each select="$footnotes/para">
      <xsl:if test="$tmp=.">
        <xsl:variable name="var" select="position()"/>
```

```
        <fo:inline font-size="8pt" vertical-align="super"
           color="red">
          <xsl:value-of select="$var" />
        </fo:inline>
      </xsl:if>
    </xsl:for-each>

    <fo:footnote-body>
      <fo:block font-size="10pt">
        <fo:inline font-size="8pt" vertical-align="super"
           color="red">
          <xsl:value-of select="position() div 2" />
        </fo:inline> 
        <xsl:value-of select="para" />
      </fo:block>
    </fo:footnote-body>

  </fo:footnote>
</xsl:template>


</xsl:stylesheet>
```

Appendix F
Recipe Formatting Object Stylesheet

```
<?xml version="1.0"?>
<!DOCTYPE book SYSTEM "/usr/share/sgml/db41xml/docbookx.dtd">

<xsl:stylesheet version="1.1"
            xmlns:xsl="http://www.w3.org/1999/XSL/Transform"
            xmlns:fo="http://www.w3.org/1999/XSL/Format">

<xsl:output method="xml"
         version="1.0"
         indent="yes"
         encoding="iso-8859-1"/>

<xsl:variable name="recipe" select="//category[1]/recipe[3]"/>
```

```
<xsl:template match="/cookbook">
  <fo:root>
    <fo:layout-master-set>
      <!-- the margins on the page go outside the page body
      which includes all regions -->
      <fo:simple-page-master
            master-name="recipeContent"
            page-height="297mm"
            page-width="210mm"
            margin-left="25mm"
            margin-right="25mm"
            margin-top="10mm"
            margin-bottom="25mm">
        <!-- the region-body must have margins which are at
           least the
        size of the extents for the other regions if you want to
            put
        content into those regions-->
        <fo:region-body margin-top="10mm" margin-bottom="25mm"/>
        <fo:region-before extent="10mm" />
        <fo:region-after extent="25mm" />
      </fo:simple-page-master>
    </fo:layout-master-set>

    <fo:page-sequence master-reference="recipeContent">
      <fo:static-content flow-name="xsl-region-after">
        <fo:block text-align="center" font-style="italic"
           font-size="9pt" color="navy">
          Page <fo:page-number/>
        </fo:block>
      </fo:static-content>

      <fo:static-content flow-name="xsl-region-before">
        <fo:block text-align="end" font-style="italic" font-size
           ="9pt" color="navy">
          <xsl:call-template name="showTitleSmall"/>
        </fo:block>
      </fo:static-content>
```

```
        <fo:flow flow-name="xsl-region-body">
          <xsl:call-template name="showTitle"/>
          <xsl:call-template name="showIngredients" />
          <xsl:call-template name="showNotes"/>
          <xsl:call-template name="showMethod" />
        </fo:flow>
      </fo:page-sequence>

    </fo:root>
</xsl:template>


<xsl:template name="showTitle">
    <fo:block text-align="center" font-size="24pt" space-after="16
       pt" font-family="sans-serif" color="purple" border-color="
       purple" border-style="groove" border-width="thin" padding
       ="5pt" background-color="wheat">
      <xsl:value-of select="$recipe/name"/>
    </fo:block>
</xsl:template>


<xsl:template name="showTitleSmall">
    <fo:block>
      <xsl:value-of select="$recipe/name"/>
    </fo:block>
</xsl:template>


<xsl:template name="showIngredients">
    <fo:table border-width="1pt" border-color="purple" border-style
       ="groove" table-layout="fixed" space-after="16pt">

      <fo:table-column column-width="60mm"/>
      <fo:table-column column-width="15mm" number-columns-repeated
         ="2"/>
```

```
<fo:table-body>
  <fo:table-row text-align="center" color="darkgreen"
     background-color="wheat" font-weight="bold"
     border-width="1pt" border-color="purple" border-style="
     solid">
    <fo:table-cell padding="4pt" border-bottom="solid">
      <fo:block>Ingredient</fo:block>
    </fo:table-cell>
    <fo:table-cell padding="4pt" border-bottom="solid">
      <fo:block>Amount</fo:block>
    </fo:table-cell>
    <fo:table-cell padding="4pt" border-bottom="solid">
      <fo:block>Unit</fo:block>
    </fo:table-cell>
  </fo:table-row>

  <xsl:for-each select="$recipe/ingredient">
    <fo:table-row border-width="1pt" border-color="purple"
       border-style="solid">
      <fo:table-cell padding="4pt" padding-left="8pt"
         text-align="start" border-bottom="solid"
         border-right="solid" border-color="purple">
        <fo:block>
          <xsl:value-of select="name"/>
        </fo:block>
      </fo:table-cell>
      <fo:table-cell padding="4pt" text-align="end"
         border-bottom="solid" border-color="purple">
        <fo:block>
          <xsl:value-of select="quantity/@amount"/>
        </fo:block>
      </fo:table-cell>
      <fo:table-cell padding="4pt" text-align="center"
         border-bottom="solid" border-color="purple">
        <fo:block>
          <xsl:value-of select="quantity/@unit"/>
        </fo:block>
      </fo:table-cell>
```

```
        </fo:table-row>
      </xsl:for-each>
    </fo:table-body>
  </fo:table>

</xsl:template>


<xsl:template name="showNotes">
  <xsl:variable name="tmp" select="$recipe/cooking/note"/>
  <xsl:for-each select="$tmp">
    <fo:block space-after="4pt">
      <fo:inline font-style="italic"
            color="purple"
            font-size="10pt">
        Note <xsl:value-of select="position()"/>:
      </fo:inline>
      <xsl:value-of select="."/>
    </fo:block>
  </xsl:for-each>
</xsl:template>


<xsl:template name="showMethod">
  <fo:block space-after="10pt" font-size="16pt" font-weight="bold
     " font-family="sans-serif" color="navy" space-before="16pt
     ">
    The Method
  </fo:block>
  <fo:list-block provisional-distance-between-starts="15mm"
     provisional-label-separation="5mm">
    <xsl:for-each select="$recipe/method/instruction">
      <fo:list-item>
        <fo:list-item-label start-indent="7mm" end-indent="
           label-end()">
          <fo:block><xsl:value-of select="position()"/>.</fo:
             block>
        </fo:list-item-label>
```

```
        <fo:list-item-body start-indent="body-start()">
          <fo:block><xsl:value-of select="." /></fo:block>
        </fo:list-item-body>
      </fo:list-item>
    </xsl:for-each>
  </fo:list-block>
</xsl:template>


</xsl:stylesheet>
```

Index

D

Y

The P.
Handbo

The Configuration and Systems Guide

By David Dick

Dumbreck Publishing

The P.C. Support Handbook

ISBN 0-9541711-1-X